Discursive Psychology

Discursive Psychology is the first collection to systematically and critically appraise the influence and development of its foundational studies, exploring central concepts in social psychology such as attitudes, gender, cognition, memory, prejudice and ideology. The book explores how discursive psychology has accommodated and responded to assumptions contained in classic studies, discussing what can still be gained from a dialogue with these inquiries, and which epistemological and methodological debates are still running, or are worth reviving.

International contributors look back at the original ideas in the classic papers, and consider the impact on and trajectory of subsequent work. Each chapter locates a foundational paper in its academic context, identifying the concerns that motivated the author and the particular perspective that informed their thinking. The contributors go on to identify the main empirical, theoretical or methodological contribution of the paper and its impact on consequent work in discursive psychology, including the contributors' own work. Each chapter concludes with a critical consideration of how discursive psychology can continue to develop.

This book is a timely contribution to the advance of discursive psychology by fostering critical perspectives upon its intellectual and empirical agenda. It will appeal to those working in the area of discursive psychology, discourse analysis and social interaction, including researchers, social psychologists and students.

Cristian Tileagă is Senior Lecturer in Social Psychology in the Department of Social Sciences at Loughborough University, UK.

Elizabeth Stokoe is Professor of Social Interaction in the Department of Social Sciences at Loughborough University, UK.

Explorations in Social Psychology series

Books in this series:

Rhetoric, Ideology and Social Psychology
Essays in honour of Michael Billig
Edited by Charles Antaki and Susan Condor

Terrorism, Trauma & Psychology
A multilevel victim perspective of the Bali bombings
Gwendoline Patricia Brookes, Julie Ann Pooley and Jaya Earnest

Psychological War Trauma and Society
Like a hidden wound
Irit Keynan

The Nature of Prejudice
Society, discrimination and moral exclusion
Cristian Tileagă

Discursive Psychology
Classic and contemporary issues
Edited by Cristian Tileagă and Elizabeth Stokoe

Discursive Psychology
Classic and contemporary issues

Edited by
Cristian Tileagă and
Elizabeth Stokoe

LONDON AND NEW YORK

First published 2016
by Routledge

2 Park Square, Milton Park, Abingdon, Oxfordshire OX14 4RN
711 Third Avenue, New York, NY 10017

Routledge is an imprint of the Taylor & Francis Group, an informa business

First issued in paperback 2017

Copyright © 2016 C. Tileagă & E. Stokoe

The right of the editors to be identified as the author of the editorial material, and of the authors for their individual chapters, has been asserted in accordance with sections 77 and 78 of the Copyright, Designs and Patents Act 1988.

All rights reserved. No part of this book may be reprinted or reproduced or utilised in any form or by any electronic, mechanical, or other means, now known or hereafter invented, including photocopying and recording, or in any information storage or retrieval system, without permission in writing from the publishers.

Notice:
Product or corporate names may be trademarks or registered trademarks, and are used only for identification and explanation without intent to infringe.

British Library Cataloguing in Publication Data
A catalogue record for this book is available from the British Library

Library of Congress Cataloging in Publication Data
Discursive psychology: classic and contemporary issues/edited by Cristian Tileaga and Elizabeth Stokoe.
    pages cm
    Includes bibliographical references and index.
    1. Discursive psychology. I. Tileaga, Cristian, 1975–.
II. Stokoe, Elizabeth.
BF201.3.D566 2016
150.19′8 – dc23
2015002453

ISBN: 978-0-415-72160-8 (hbk)
ISBN: 978-0-8153-5765-0 (pbk)

Typeset in Galliard
by Florence Production Ltd, Stoodleigh, Devon, UK

Contents

List of illustrations viii
List of contributors ix
Acknowledgments xiv

Introduction: the evolution of discursive psychology:
From classic to contemporary themes 1
CRISTIAN TILEAGĂ AND ELIZABETH STOKOE

PART I
Epistemology and method 13

1 Interpretative repertoires, conversation analysis and
  being critical 15
  ANN WEATHERALL

2 Hitting ontological rock bottom: Discursive psychology's
  respecification of the realism/relativism debate 29
  CLARA IVERSEN

3 Conversation analysis and discursive psychology:
  Taking up the challenge of Sacks' legacy 43
  ALEXANDRA KENT

4 Natural and contrived data 57
  SIMON GOODMAN AND SUSAN A. SPEER

5 Questions of context: Qualitative interviews as a source
  of knowledge 70
  TIM RAPLEY

PART II
Cognition, emotion and the psychological thesaurus — 85

6 What happened to post-cognitive psychology? — 87
HEDWIG TE MOLDER

7 From Loughborough with love: How discursive psychology rocked the heart of social psychology's love affair with attitudes — 101
SALLY WIGGINS

8 Discursive psychology and emotion — 114
CARRIE CHILDS AND ALEXA HEPBURN

9 Recasting the psychologist's question: Children's talk as social action — 129
CARLY W. BUTLER

10 Seeing the inside from the outside of children's minds: Displayed understanding and interactional competence — 147
KARIN OSVALDSSON

11 From script theory to script formulation: Derek Edwards' shift from perceptual-realism to the interactional-rhetorical — 162
NEILL KOROBOV

PART III
Social categories, identity and memory — 179

12 Reorienting categories as a members' phenomena — 181
RICHARD FITZGERALD AND SEAN RINTEL

13 Some relevant things about gender and other categories in discursive psychology — 194
SUE WIDDICOMBE

14 Dilemmas of memory: The mind is not a tape recorder — 210
STEVEN D. BROWN AND PAULA REAVEY

15 A forgotten legacy? Towards a discursive psychology of the media — 224
FREDERICK THOMAS ATTENBOROUGH

PART IV
Prejudice, racism and nationalism   241

16 Re-theorizing prejudice in social psychology:
   From cognition to discourse   243
   MARTHA AUGOUSTINOS

17 'Race stereotypes' as 'racist' discourse   257
   KEVIN DURRHEIM

18 Fact and evaluation in racist discourse revisited   271
   JOHN DIXON AND STEPHANIE TAYLOR

19 Banal nationalism, postmodernism and capitalism:
   Revisiting Billig's critique of Rorty   289
   STEPHEN GIBSON

Index   303

Illustrations

Figures

7.1	Family meal interaction	109
18.1	Whites' opposition to the principle and implementation of racial equality in post-apartheid South Africa	281

Tables

18.1	Traditional vs. discursive approaches to attitudes	273
18.2	Measuring racial attitudes	275

Contributors

Frederick Thomas Attenborough is Academic Co-ordinator for Sociology in the School of Humanities, Bishop Grosseteste University, Lincoln, UK. Frederick is interested in how people utilise the inherently interactive properties of texts (for example, books, Facebook posts, tweets) to attempt various social actions (for example, describing, claiming, accusing). He is currently developing 'mediated stylistics', an approach to textual analysis that brings the analytic toolkit of stylistics to bear on specifically mediated texts.

Martha Augoustinos is Professor of Psychology and Co-Director of the Fay Gale Centre of Research on Gender at the University of Adelaide. Martha has published widely in the field of social psychology and discourse, in particular on the nature of racial discourse in Australia. This has involved mapping the trajectory of the 'race debate' in Australian public discourse since 1995 and has included an analysis of how Indigenous Australians are constructed in everyday conversation and political rhetoric. More recently this work has been extended to analysing public discourse on asylum seekers and refugees. She is co-author of *Social Cognition: An Integrated Introduction* (second edition, 2006, Sage) with Iain Walker and Ngaire Donaghue, and co-editor with Kate Reynolds of *Understanding Prejudice, Racism and Social Conflict* (2001, Sage).

Steven D. Brown is Professor of Social and Organizational Psychology at the University of Leicester. His research interests are around social remembering in vulnerable groups, affect and embodiment and process philosophy. He is author of *Vital Memories: Agency, Affect and Ethics* (2013, Routledge, with Paula Reavey), *Psychology Without Foundations: History, Philosophy and Psychosocial Theory* (2009, Sage, with Paul Stenner) and the *Social Psychology of Experience: Studies in Remembering and Forgetting* (2005, Sage, with David Middleton).

Carly W. Butler is Senior Lecturer in Social Psychology and member of the Discourse and Rhetoric Group at Loughborough University. She has written extensively on children's interactions and membership categorisation analysis. She is the author of *Talk and Social Interaction in the Playground* (2008, Ashgate).

Carrie Childs is Lecturer in Psychology at the University of Derby. She completed her PhD at Loughborough University where she was a member of the Discourse and Rhetoric Group. Her research interests are in discursive psychology and conversation analysis. Her recent work focuses on the interactional deployment of mental state terms in family interaction.

John Dixon is Professor of Social Psychology at the Open University, UK. His research interests span across the areas of intergroup contact and social change, the micro-ecology of segregation, intergroup relations and human geography. He has written extensively on these topics. He has acted as editor of the *British Journal of Social Psychology*, and has recently co-authored *Beyond Prejudice: Extending the Social Psychology of Conflict, Inequality and Social Change* (with Mark Levine, Cambridge University Press).

Kevin Durrheim is Professor of Psychology at the University of KwaZulu-Natal, where he teaches social psychology and research methods. He writes on topics related to racism, segregation and social change. He has co-authored *Race Trouble* (Durrheim, Mtose and Brown, 2011, Lexington Press) and *Racial Encounter* (Durrheim and Dixon, 2005, Routledge); and is co-editor of *Research in Practice* (1999, 2006, UCT Press) and *Numbers, Hypotheses and Conclusions* (2002, UCT Press).

Richard Fitzgerald is Senior Lecturer in the School of Journalism and Communication, University of Queensland, Australia. He has published extensively in the areas of MCA and Discourse Analysis with particular interests in the organisation of cultural knowledge and identity in interaction and broadcast news. He is currently preparing an edited collection with William Housley titled *Advances in Membership Categorisation Analysis* due in 2015 (Sage).

Stephen Gibson is a Social Psychologist based at York St John University, UK. He holds BSc, MSc and PhD degrees from Lancaster University. He has research interests in areas such as national identity and citizenship, the representation of peace and conflict, and dis/obedience. The common thread linking these areas of interest is the influence of discursive and rhetorical psychologies, and as such he also has an interest in the development of discursively-informed qualitative research methods in psychology. He is co-editor of *Doing Your Qualitative Psychology Project* (with Sullivan and Riley, 2012, Sage) and *Representations of Peace and Conflict* (with Mollan, 2012, Palgrave).

Simon Goodman is a Senior Lecturer in Psychology at Coventry University. His research explores the discursive construction of asylum seekers and refugees, and his interests include discourse analysis, the social construction of categories, boundaries and prejudice, particularly in relation to asylum seeking, social inequality, the far right and rioting behaviour.

Alexa Hepburn is Reader in Conversation Analysis in the Social Sciences Department at Loughborough University. Broad interests include theoretical and analytical innovations in psychology and understanding the rights and competencies of young people. Recent studies focus on the notation and analysis of laughing and crying, advice delivery and how resistance is managed in helpline interaction, aspects of self-repair, and threats in family mealtimes. She is author of *An Introduction to Critical Social Psychology* and co-editor (with Sally Wiggins) of *Discursive Research in Practice: New Approaches to Psychology and Interaction*, which began to explore possibilities for the application of discursive psychological research. She is currently co-authoring (with Galina Bolden) *Transcribing for Social Research*.

Clara Iversen is a Postdoctoral Researcher in the Department of Sociology at Uppsala University. Her research interests concern how artifacts are used in interaction and how participants manage issues of agency and knowledge.

Alexandra Kent is a Lecturer in Psychology at the School of Psychology at Keele University. Her research combines a theoretical reworking of the way language and psychology are understood with detailed technical analyses of empirical data using conversation analysis. Her research interests include family mealtime interaction, the negotiation of power and authority in interaction, children's talk and socialisation, and parenting practices.

Neill Korobov is an Associate Professor and co-Director of the PhD programme in the Department of Psychology at the University of West Georgia, USA. He is interested in the architecture of people's conversations and stories for the study of identity. His research is situated in Discursive Psychology, straddling critical discursive and conversation analytic methods. For the last several years he has been studying the stories that young adults tell about their romantic and sexual experiences. He is interested in the ways couples pursue intimacy during moments of initial romantic attraction – that is, how potential romantic partners ostensibly 'connect' or create affiliation while bantering, telling stories, or formulating desires.

Karin Osvaldsson is Senior Lecturer in Social and Cultural Analysis at the Department of Child Studies, Linköping University, Sweden. She received her PhD in Child Studies from Linköping University in 2002. Working within the main framework of ethnomethodology and discursive psychology, Osvaldsson is currently engaged in research on identity and social interaction in various settings, including detention homes for troubled youth, emergency rescue services and internet counselling organisations.

Tim Rapley is Lecturer at the Institute of Health and Society, Newcastle University, UK. He is interested in conducting empirical studies of medical work, knowledge and practice and social studies of research. He has written an introductory textbook, *Doing Conversation, Discourse and Document Analysis* (2007, Sage), and contributed the chapter 'Some Pragmatics of Data Analysis', for the third edition of David Silverman's (2010) edited collection *Qualitative Research: Theory, Method and Practice*.

Paula Reavey is Professor of Psychology at London South Bank University, as well as leading and consulting on projects at the Maudsley and Royal Bethlem hospitals. She has co-edited several volumes and has also published two monographs, *Psychology, Mental Health and Distress* (with John Cromby and Dave Harper, 2013, Palgrave) and *Vital Memory: Ethics, Affect and Agency* (with Steven D. Brown, 2015, Routledge).

Sean Rintel is a Postdoctoral Researcher at Microsoft Research Cambridge (UK) in the Human Experience and Design group and a Lecturer in Strategic Communication at the University of Queensland. He received his PhD in 2010 from the University at Albany, State University of New York, chaired by Professor Emerita Anita Pomerantz. His research focuses on how the affordances of communication technologies interact with language, social action and culture. He has published on video-mediated communication, Internet Relay Chat, social media, online television websites, phatic technologies, memes and internet culture, and tele-rehabilitation.

Susan A. Speer is a Senior Lecturer in Psychology at the University of Manchester. She has published discursive and conversation analytic research on gender and language (gender identity, transsexualism, sexism and heterosexism), methodological issues (ethics, realism and relativism, natural and contrived data), and a range of conversational phenomena (self-praise, hypothetical questions). She is the author of *Gender Talk: Feminism, Discourse and Conversation Analysis* (2005, Routledge) and co-editor (with Elizabeth Stokoe) of *Conversation and Gender* (2011, Cambridge University Press).

Elizabeth Stokoe is Professor of Social Interaction in the Department of Social Sciences at Loughborough University, UK. Her current research interests are in conversation analysis, membership categorisation, and social interaction in various ordinary and institutional settings, including neighbour mediation, police interrogation, role-play and simulated interaction. She is the co-author of *Discourse and Identity* (with Bethan Benwell, 2006, Edinburgh University Press) and co-editor of *Conversation and Gender* (with Susan Speer, 2011, Cambridge University Press).

Stephanie Taylor is a Senior Lecturer in Psychology, Social Sciences at the Open University. Her narrative-discursive research investigates gendered identities and subjectification in specific social sites (creative work, places of residence, the nation) in the contexts of late modernity and neoliberalism. She is the author of *Narratives of Identity and Place* (2010, Routledge), co-author of *Contemporary Identities of Creativity and Creative Work* (with Karen Littleton, 2012, Ashgate) and co-editor of *Gender and Creative Labour* (with Bridget Conor and Rosalind Gill, 2015, Sociological Review Monographs).

Hedwig te Molder is Associate Professor of Communication Science and Full Professor of Science and Technology Communication at the University of

Twente. She studies social interaction, with a special interest in how people handle issues of science and technology in their everyday lives. Her main resources for analysis are discursive psychology and conversation analysis. She has co-authored (with Jonathan Potter) *Conversation and Cognition* (2005, Cambridge University Press), which received, in 2007, the Distinguished Book Award from the American Sociological Association.

Cristian Tileagă is Senior Lecturer in Social Psychology in the Department of Social Sciences at Loughborough University. His interests include discursive psychology, prejudice, collective memory, political discourse and interdisciplinarity. He is the author of *Political Psychology: Critical Perspectives* (2013, Cambridge University Press) and co-author of *Psychology and History: Interdisciplinary Explorations* (with Jovan Byford, 2014, Cambridge University Press).

Ann Weatherall is a Reader in Psychology at Victoria University, New Zealand. Her interests include conversation analysis, discursive psychology, feminist psychology, gender and language, and language and social psychology. She is author of *Gender, Language and Discourse* (2002) and is currently holding lead editorial roles for *Gender and Language* and *Women's Studies Journal* (NZ).

Susan Widdicombe is Senior Lecturer in Social Psychology at Edinburgh University. Her theoretical and empirical interests are in self and identities, with a focus on personal and social identity and cultural variations in self-conception and individuality. She has written extensively on identity as a social accomplishment. She is the author of *The Language of Youth Subcultures: Social Identity in Action* (with Robin Woffitt) and co-author of *Identities in Talk* (with Charles Antaki).

Sally Wiggins is a Senior Lecturer in Psychology at the University of Strathclyde, Glasgow. Her research focuses on understanding the dynamics and interactional management of eating practices in everyday family mealtimes. Recent work has examined concepts such as appetite, satiety and food preferences in terms of their discursive constitution and social relevance.

Acknowledgments

This book is the result of a collective effort. We would like to thank all colleagues involved in this project who have responded so positively to our call for papers. We are very grateful for their enthusiastic response. We feel that the end product of their involvement – this book – is a timely testament to the richness and diversity of discursive psychology, all around the world. And, obviously, many thanks to Charles Antaki, Michael Billig, Susan Condor, Derek Edwards, Jonathan Potter and Margaret Wetherell for writing such wonderful papers. We would like to thank Jane Madeley, Clare Ashworth and Emily Bedford at Routledge for believing in this project and for their patience during the editorial process.

Introduction: the evolution of discursive psychology
From classic to contemporary themes

Cristian Tileagă and Elizabeth Stokoe

This is a book about the evolution, contribution and impact of the body of work known as Discursive Psychology (DP). Beginning in psychology, over the past twenty-five years DP has developed into a massively influential field with trajectories throughout the range of academic disciplines and substantial national and international impact on how we understand and study psychology, and particularly how we conceptualise language and social action.

From its 'undisciplined beginnings' (Billig, 2012) DP developed into an original and innovative programme of research into the 'normative order of everyday life' (Edwards, 2012: 434). DP's early eclecticism has sprung into a systematic approach to all things social – from everyday interactional encounters to institutional settings and the analysis of wider social issues and social problems.

To define DP, we borrow one from one of its founders and main proponents, Derek Edwards. To do DP,

> is to do something that psychology has not already done in any systematic, empirical, and principled way, which is to examine how psychological concepts (memory, thought, emotion, etc.) are shaped for the functions they serve, in and for the nexus of social practices in which we use language.
> (Edwards, 2012: 427)

This volume takes DP's *respecification* of these concepts as its subject matter and is designed to give the reader an enriched understanding of the particular background of discursive psychology. The main aim of this volume is to invite a clearer recognition of, and engagement with, the early intellectual debates, origin stories, that have driven the discursive psychological project forward. It also aims to give the first systematic representation of its contemporary intellectual image.

We have collected in this volume commentaries and reflections on key ideas of the discursive project in social psychology found in 'classic studies' written by current and former members of the Discourse and Rhetoric Group at Loughborough University: Charles Antaki, Michael Billig, Susan Condor, Derek Edwards, Jonathan Potter and Margaret Wetherell. The commentators are a mixture of both younger and established, internationally renowned, scholars, whose own work has been inspired and driven by ideas in these foundational texts. These classic studies have played a key role in the emergence of DP; that is, they are not only highly cited, but have defined the shape that discursive psychology takes today. Most of the studies were conducted in the 1980s and 1990s but we have also included some more recent papers written after 2000. The various ways in which DP has developed its concepts, methodological apparatus, and so on, can be traced back to a number of such studies. DP's main theoretical and methodological tenets have been explained and illustrated in various edited collections and special issues (Hepburn and Wiggins, 2005; Hepburn and Wiggins, 2007; te Molder and Potter, 2005; Wiggins and Potter, 2008; Augoustinos and Tileagă, 2012). However, there is no collection of systematic and critical appraisal of its foundational, 'key' or classic studies.

What makes a DP 'classic'?

The papers we included here are highly cited, but, paradoxically, have not been the concern of direct exegesis. Although they are discussed in some introductory textbooks (e.g., McKinlay and McVittie, 2008), with very few exceptions they have not been, routinely, subjected to critical scrutiny. We selected the papers as part of what we are defining as DP's received canon. In asking our contributors to engage critically and reflectively with them, we wanted to recuperate their value for discursive psychology's project, and also make their argument more accessible to a larger audience. Our aim is to remind both colleagues and critics of the value of critical engagement with discursive psychology's received canon. The studies are not classics because of their age. Although some of the earlier papers have aged well, retaining their relevance, it is their significance to a new discursive psychology public that guided our selection. They are papers that, in some cases, contain guidelines for doing DP but, more often, DP's commitment to following analytic recipes is downplayed. They are consciously not concerned with guidelines, but with providing a grounding for a certain philosophy, orientation, to researching social life. The studies explored in this book are challenging psychology's received ideas about epistemology, theory, method, etc. They are concerned with human accountability, human affairs in a general sense, in and as part of everyday and institutional practices.

In our selection we wanted to capture what we think is particular and original about discursive psychology: its diversity. Contrary to superficial impressions, DP is a diverse field of enquiry. This is a book that emphasises the diversity of topics, issues, variety and breadth of assumptions, and their place in the discursive psychology project. It is the first anthology to address DP as an established field of study, which is developing an original and critical understanding of the role of discourse and social practices for the study of social and psychological phenomena and social issues. Although some caricature DP as ignoring issues of power, politics, social problems, etc., DP engages directly with such issues as both resource and topic. The example of numerous applied interventions designed around researching and unpacking interactional practices (Stokoe et al., 2012), as well as the example of research studies using interviews or public texts to explore the reproduction of inequality and unequal power relations (Tileagă, 2005; Hanson-Easey and Augoustinos, 2011), are all examples of DP in the service of some particular critical agenda.

This book is therefore intended both as an introduction to discursive psychology for scholars new to the field, as well as more advanced intellectual tool for those who wish to understand discursive psychology in more depth. The chapters are retrospective, looking back at the innovations made in the papers under discussion, but also prospective, tracking the impact on, trajectory of, and contribution to subsequent work. The book asks what can still be gained from a dialogue with these classic studies, and which epistemological and methodological debates are still running, or are worth resurrecting. What remains of the challenges set out by seminal texts and debates they have engendered? How can DP inspire a new generation of (social) psychologists to conduct innovative and groundbreaking studies looking at practical problems in the real world? What are some of the intellectual threads that can push DP into the future? The upshot is to promote new ways of thinking about the epistemological and methodological *grounds* of what discursive psychologists do, the ideas they explore, the critiques they develop, the research avenues they take, the impact that some of their ideas have (or might have in the future). We are extremely grateful to colleagues that have responded so positively to this project.

Understanding the particular background of discursive psychology

The term 'discursive psychology' was first coined by Edwards and Potter (1992) in their book of the same title. DP's roots lie in a variety of theoretical-philosophical and empirical traditions. In addition to ethnomethodology and conversation analysis, these include the language philosophy of Wittgenstein (1958) and Austin (1962), constructivist approaches to human development (e.g., Vygotsky, 1978), and social studies of science (e.g., Gilbert and Mulkay, 1984).

DP's original goal was to unpack, critique and 'respecify' (Button, 1991) the topics of social, developmental and cognitive psychology, and their methods of investigation (Edwards and Potter, 2001). It therefore aimed to challenge mainstream psychology in much the same way that ethnomethodology and conversation analysis challenged mainstream sociology (see Benwell and Stokoe, 2006). DP comprises a fundamental shift from treating psychological states (e.g., anger, intention, identity) as operating behind talk, causing people to say the things they do. In this way, DP challenges the traditional psychological treatment of language as a channel to underlying mental processes, and the experimental study of those processes. Instead, it studies how common sense psychological concepts are deployed in, oriented to and handled in the talk and texts that comprise social life. Thus language is not treated as an externalisation of underlying thoughts, motivations, memories or attitudes, but as *performative* of them. Note that these are not *ontological* claims about the status of 'inner minds' or 'external realities'. The external world, or people's traits and dispositions, are treated by speakers as common sense evidential resources for making inferences, building descriptions, resisting accusations of interest, and so on.

DP understands discourse as *action oriented*, whereby actions are to be analysed in their situated context rather than as discrete units of activity (Potter, 2003). Discourse is both *constructed*: people talk by deploying the resources (words, categories, common sense ideas) available to them, and *constructive*: people build social worlds through descriptions and accounts thereof (Wetherell, 2001). DP therefore examines members' *situated* descriptions of persons, categories, events and objects, drawing heavily on conversation analysis for its analytic method. It investigates, for example, how 'factual' descriptions are produced in order to undermine alternative versions, to appear objective and reasonable or weak and biased, and deal with the speaker's and others' motives, desires, intentions and interests (Billig, 1987; Edwards and Potter, 1992).

Since its inception in the late 1980s and early 1990s, DP has developed along two main trajectories. DP's original engagement with ethnomethodology and conversation analysis substantially influenced the evolution of its methods and analytic focus and, in recent years, has in turn influenced many in conversation analysis, particularly with regards to debates about action description (e.g., Edwards, 2005) and cognition (see the special issue of *Discourse Studies*, 2006). A second, 'critical' DP strand is more closely aligned to post-structuralism, with approaches to analysis combining attention to conversational detail with wider macro-structures and cultural-historical contexts (Wetherell, 1998). The two trajectories, and the classic 'debate' between Wetherell and one of the founders of conversation analysis, Emanuel Schegloff, is revisited in Chapter 1 of this book.

The two traditions have resulted in quite distinct bodies of empirical work. On one hand, CA-aligned DP focused studies on understanding the way psychological matters, understood as oriented-to issues in interaction, impact on the design and organisation of everyday and institutional encounters, from child protection helplines (e.g., Hepburn and Potter, 2012) to police interviews with suspects (e.g., Stokoe and Edwards, 2007), and from interaction in care homes for disabled persons (e.g., Antaki, 2013) to investigating psychiatric assessments of different patient groups (e.g., Speer and McPhillips, 2013). On the other hand, DP studies of how interaction, conversation and texts operate within wider social, cultural and political contexts (Tileagă, 2011; Augoustinos et al., 2011).

It is perhaps appropriate to note that most of the misunderstandings of the discursive psychology project are, arguably, misunderstandings of its particular background and subsequent trajectory. Novices sometimes find the landscape of DP bewildering. There are at least three important characteristics that should find their way in any description of DP. These deal with what DP is not.

First, as Potter argues, 'DA/DP is neither a self-contained paradigm nor a stand-alone method that can be easily mix-and-matched with others' (2003: 787). Edwards notes that DP,

> rests upon a very different, and non-causal conception of what makes social actions orderly and intelligible. Rather than conceiving of people's thoughts and actions as resulting from the interplay of a range of causal variables, DP approaches them as things done and understood with regard to an empirically and conceptually tractable normative order.
>
> (Edwards, 2012: 432)

Second, DP is not a universal approach to discourse, talk-in-interaction, or ideology, but is concerned with particular claims in particular settings that have particular consequences. DP offers particularistic answers to general questions and reframes debates around psychology's central quandaries (experience, mind-body, the nature of self and identity, categorisation, prejudice, and so on). We argue that it is DP's particularism that constitutes DP's original contribution to psychology and the social sciences. Those who equate DP's particularism with reductionism routinely miss its central epistemological thrust and theoretical, and empirical, diversity.

Third, there is a tendency to pigeonhole DP among qualitative approaches. Although it can be broadly situated within 'qualitative psychology', it does not share its overall ontological and epistemological orientation. Neither does it share its methods; the main proponents of DP study the world using what Stokoe (2012) describes as 'designedly large-scale' qualitative data; that is, databases of hundreds of instances of recorded encounters, rather than small-scale interview studies of talk generated through a researcher. This does not mean, however, that DP cannot and does not enter into a constructive dialogue with the different/various branches of qualitative inquiry such as action research, narrative research, ethnography, and other styles of doing discourse analysis.

Outline of chapters

Each chapter offers a critical reflection of a foundational text using a similar structure which includes: a) summarising the paper, and locating it in its academic context – identifying the concerns that motivated the author/s, and the particular perspective that informed their thinking; b) identifying the main empirical, theoretical or methodological contribution of the paper and its impact on subsequent work in DP, including the author's own work; and c) concluding with a critical consideration of how DP can continue to develop. Chapters can be read in the order suggested in the outline. However, most chapters can be read (and used) on their own by researchers with specific interests. The book is divided into four sections: Epistemology and method;

Cognition, emotion and the psychological thesaurus; Social categories, identity and memory; and Prejudice, racism and nationalism. These sections unite several threads that run through this volume.

The first section, 'Epistemology and method', focuses on discursive psychology's concern with, and debate over, the context of discursive analyses of talk and text, the realism/relativism controversy, and the production and analysis of 'naturalistic' data. The chapter by Ann Weatherall discusses the legacy of Margaret Wetherell's work and revisits the (Wetherell-Schegloff) debate between post-structuralism and conversation analysis (Schegloff, 1997; Wetherell, 1998). In her rereading of this seminal debate, Weatherall argues that what is key is to keep 'live, political matters in systematic and grounded analyses of texts and talk'. She argues that advancing critical agendas is not the sole prerogative of critical discursive approaches (in the Wetherell lineage). Weatherall uses the example of feminist conversation analysis to illustrate how this too can advance various critical agendas. In the next chapter, Clara Iversen offers a cogent rereading of the realism/relativism debate in Edwards et al. (1995). Iversen urges discursive psychologists not to abandon or paper over 'old' debates and consider carefully some of the new epistemological assumptions that have replaced them. Like Weatherall, Iversen points to the value of taking relativism seriously without compromising critical agendas and/or cumulative research programmes.

Next, Alexandra Kent revisits an early account of the relevance of conversation analysis for discursive psychology. She identifies the key epistemological and methodological features of conversation analysis that have contributed to the development of discursive psychology. She argues that the contemporary reliance on the apparatus of conversation analysis for the study of socialisation practices, social categories, intersubjectivity, and so on, is grounded in a series of principles derived from conversation analysis's cumulative research programme. The cumulative findings of CA are a good basis for any discursive analysis, especially when what is at stake is demonstrating the pervasiveness of social order 'at all points' (as Sacks would argue). Given the continuous relevance of conversation analysis in discursive psychology researchers ought to discuss more directly not only the advantages, but also some of the challenges brought about by using conversation analysis in their work.

In the next chapter, Simon Goodman and Susan Speer address the distinction between naturally occurring and contrived data drawing on the work of Jonathan Potter. They argue against viewing naturally occurring and so-called 'contrived' data as discrete 'types'. They contend that research using contrived data (data from interviews or focus groups) can also yield productive findings. By considering carefully the relationship between method, context and source of data discursive psychologists can offer more insightful analyses into situated discursive and social practices. Overestimating the primacy of the naturalistic record risks losing sight of other ways of producing data, which can still be considered 'natural'. Chapter 5, by Tim Rapley, also engages with questions and arguments around context, method and nature of data, when assessing what can be gained from treating interviews as both topic and resource.

The second section, 'Cognition, emotion and the psychological thesaurus', deals with papers that are core in DP's challenge to psychology's conventional way of dealing with notions such as cognition, thought, understanding, attitudes and emotion, as products of individual mental states. Chapters in this section discuss and illustrate DP's concerted attempt at the respecifcation of psychology's traditional thesaurus as situated discursive practices. Hedwig te Molder revisits discursive psychology's post-cognitive aspiration and offers a commentary on the status assigned to cognition in the analysis of interaction. te Molder argues that the flourishing, and promise, of post-cognitive interaction research lies in careful analysis of participants' situated practices rather than 'real' thinking and underlying, putative, cognitions.

The chapter by Sally Wiggins offers critical reading of how discursive psychology is challenging social psychologists' understandings of the concept of 'attitudes'. Wiggins charts the move from attitudes to evaluations by focusing on two substantive aspects raised in the work of Jonathan Potter: the subtle and contingent variation of evaluative practices in social interaction, and the need for attending to subject-object relations. Discursive psychologists should not abandon the concept of 'attitudes' but instead provide a more refined description of actual evaluative practices people use in their everyday lives.

Carrie Childs and Alexa Hepburn explore the legacy of DP's respecifcation of emotion taking as their starting point Derek Edwards's work on 'emotion discourse'. The discursive psychology of emotion is presented as an enterprise that treats emotions as something that can be 'invoked, described and made accountable for the purposes of actions in talk'. Childs and Hepburn give numerous examples of interactive uses of emotion terms, and discuss the various interactional consequences of avowing or ascribing emotions in everyday and institutional settings. Childs and Hepburn identify new avenues for a discursive psychology of emotion: the study of empathy, emotion and experience, etc. Carly Butler offers a contemporary exegesis of Derek Edwards's work on DP and developmental issues. She considers thought and understanding in children's talk as situated discursive practice, and argues that developmental psychology and discursive psychology could benefit from a more systematic dialogue and interdisciplinary ethos.

In a similar vein, Karin Osvaldsson addresses the critique of 'theory of mind' found in a seminal paper written by Charles Antaki. She uses the example of child development and the measurement of children's competence to make the case that psychological models based on putative inner mental states and capabilities cannot account satisfactorily for the relationship between social interaction, development and issues of cognitive competence. In her view discursive psychology plays a crucial role in illuminating the contextually bound ways in which thinking and understanding is displayed in social interaction, 'the steps and actions that people take to make themselves understandable to each other'. A shift from perceptual-realism to rhetoric and situated interaction is also to be found in discursive work on script formulations.

Neill Korobov argues that this shift is paramount in understanding how one can analyze in non-cognitive terms psychological notions (like scripts) that are traditionally described in cognitive terms.

The third section examines DP's core writing in the areas of 'Social categories, identity and memory'. This is, of course, not removed from DP's respecifcation project, and attends to the nature and uses of social categories and identities, interactional dimensions of memory and remembering, script formulations, as well as DP's engagement with studying mediated discourses of various kinds. In their respective chapters, Richard Fitzgerald and Sean Rintel and Sue Widdicombe take up the issue of categorisation as something 'we do things with', and expand it to a series of fresh insights for researching social categories and identities in talk and text. Fitzgerald and Rintel use the example of affinities between discursive psychology and membership categorisation analysis to call for a re-orientation towards researching categories as members' phenomena. Widdicombe's exegesis brings the question of why, how and when categories become relevant to bear upon traditional social psychological work in social identity and self-categorisation theories. She argues that researcher-generated questions can be profitably replaced or complemented with questions that arise from the careful appraisal of 'identity categories in everyday contexts, as used and oriented to by participants'. Both chapters argue against an *a priori* notion of social categories and identities. Both argue that starting with participants' orientations is crucial to 'an understanding of society and its categories through interactions of members'. Whereas traditional social psychological approaches propose a perceptual-realist take on categories and identities, discursive approaches emphasise the situated – rhetorical and interactional – nature of categories and identities.

The topic of early work on interactional remembering and contemporary reverberations is discussed by Steven D. Brown and Paula Reavey. Although they are in broad agreement with the basic assumptions of a discursive psychology of remembering they argue that the full potential of a discursive psychology of memory is not fulfilled without the acknowledgment and inclusion of what authors call 'extra-discursive matters', issues of embodied action, mediated communication, temporality, biography, morality, and so on.

Frederick T. Attenborough is showing how DP can be used to recontextualise and redescribe mediated communication in the public sphere. DP is not antinomical to a project of charting the rhetorical, interactive, situated communications of the media; quite the contrary – with an analytic apparatus attuned to the various uses and functions of common sense psychological thesaurus, and sensitivity to analysing descriptions/accounts, DP is perfectly positioned to contribute to a systematic project of analysing media in action.

The final section, 'Prejudice, racism and nationalism', deals with DP's longstanding concern with ideology, and questions of context(s) that move the analysis beyond the mechanics and pragmatics of moment-by-moment turn-taking. DP has a long tradition of what Jonathan Potter has recently called 'more ideological streams of discourse work' (2012: 437). The papers chosen for this section are only a few, illustrious, early examples of this trend in researching prejudice, racism and nationalism. The commentators are the exponents of an established strand of discourse work that engages more closely with the findings and insights of mainstream (social) psychology, and urges discursive psychology to include in their analyses issues such rhetoric, embodied verbal and non-verbal practices, material and extra-discursive environments, mediated communication and wider power dynamics at societal level.

Martha Augoustinos revisits the story of the significance of the rhetorical turn in social psychology for the study of prejudice, and how this opened a new and original way to examine the language of prejudice in text and talk. The quandaries of everyday and institutional prejudice can be more confidently approached and analysed by using discursive and rhetorical methods.

Kevin Durrheim offers a commentary on Condor's classic critique of race stereotypes in social psychology. Durrheim credits Condor's work as the first systematic attempt at highlighting that stereotyping and prejudice originate in the interactional context between people. Yet, as Durrheim argues, race stereotypes are not only constructed linguistically but also, in contradictory and ambivalent ways, in discourses and social practices (including those of researchers) that support or critique inequality and dominance. In developing an argument around stereotyping and prejudice, Durrheim also points to some of the limits of discursive analysis of stereotyping and prejudice.

In their rereading of the Potter and Wetherell 1988 classic John Dixon and Stephanie Taylor make a case for researching racist evaluations by establishing (necessary) links between the physical environments in which evaluations are constructed and wider power struggles within a society. They show how a critique of the traditional concept of 'attitude' does not have to be limited to the primacy of linguistic constructions. Treating racial evaluations as more than linguistic evaluations and understanding the relationship between discursive practices and what they call 'embodied practices of social evaluation' is as important.

Stephen Gibson engages with Billig's 'banal nationalism' thesis as an illustration of ideological analysis of broader ideological themes. He shows how Billig's critique of Rorty proceeds by uncovering unstated assumptions and hidden ideological themes. Gibson argues that ideological analysis should retain its place in discursive psychology as a driver for critical agendas – not only in identifying and analyzing broader societal ideological themes but also as a tool against the increasingly conventional and conventionalised academic capitalism.

*

Over the course of more than twenty-five years, DP has developed, and transformed, into an original and innovative programme of research with far-reaching impact for psychology and for many other disciplines. Researchers have been drawn to its radically reversed understanding of language as an action-oriented, world-building resource, rather than a tool of transmission and straightforward communication from one mind to another. They have also been drawn to its methods for understanding social life and its rejection of more traditional, researcher-driven (whether qualitative or quantitative) ways to understand human sociality. As Loughborough DARG members ourselves, we are very proud to work in the traditions built by our colleagues and are passionate about its contribution to psychology and beyond, as well as to its comprehensibility. We hope that this book contributes to make DP's transformation, and DP's particularism, understandable, and hope that it works to dismiss what are often caricatured misunderstandings of its broader aims and vision, as well as local practices for empirical working. We also hope it will help foster more critical perspectives upon DP's intellectual and empirical agenda. Discursive psychology is, and can continue to be, an intellectual home for any researcher that takes seriously the study of situated social practices.

References

Antaki, C. (2013) 'Two conversational practices for encouraging adults with intellectual disabilities to reflect on their activities', *Journal of Intellectual Disability Research*, 57: 580–8.

Augoustinos, M. and Tileagă, C. (2012) 'Twenty five years of discursive psychology', *British Journal of Social Psychology*, 51: 405–12.

Augoustinos, M., Hastie, B. and Wright, M. (2011) 'Apologizing for historical injustice: Emotion, truth and identity in political discourse', *Discourse & Society*, 22: 507–31.

Austin, J.L. (1962) *How to do things with words*. Oxford: Clarendon Press.

Benwell, B. and Stokoe, E. (2006) *Discourse and identity*. Edinburgh: Edinburgh University Press.

Billig, M. (1987) *Arguing and thinking: A rhetorical approach to social psychology*. Cambridge: Cambridge University Press.

Billig, M. (2012) 'Undisciplined beginnings, academic success and discursive psychology', *British Journal of Social Psychology*, 51: 413–24.

Button, G. (1991) 'Introduction: Ethnomethodology and the foundational respecification of the human sciences', in G. Button (ed.) *Ethnomethodology and the Human Sciences* (pp. 1–9). Cambridge: Cambridge University Press.

Discourse Studies (2006) 'Discourse, interaction, and cognition' (special issue), 8(1).

Edwards, D. (2005) 'Moaning, whinging and laughing: The subjective side of complaints', *Discourse Studies*, 7: 5–29.

Edwards, D. (2012) 'Discursive and scientific psychology', *British Journal of Social Psychology*, 51: 425–35.

Edwards, D. and Potter, J. (1992) *Discursive psychology*. London: Sage.

Edwards, D. and Potter, J. (2001) 'Discursive psychology', in McHoul and M. Rapley (eds) *How to analyse talk in institutional settings: A casebook of methods* (pp. 12–24). London and New York: Continuum International.

Edwards, D., Ashmore, M. and Potter, J. (1995) 'Death and furniture: The rhetoric, politics and theology of bottom line arguments against relativism', *History of the Human Sciences*, 8: 25–49.

Gilbert, G.N. and Mulkay, M. (1984) *Opening Pandora's box: A sociological analysis of scientists' discourse.* Cambridge: Cambridge University Press.

Hanson-Easey, S. and Augoustinos, M. (2011) 'Complaining about humanitarian refugees: The role of sympathy talk in the design of complaints on talkback radio', *Discourse & Communication*, 5: 247–71.

Hepburn, A. and Potter, J. (2012) 'Crying and crying responses', in A. Peräkylä and M-L. Sorjonen (eds) *Emotion in interaction* (pp. 194–210). Oxford: Oxford University Press.

Hepburn, A. and Wiggins, S. (eds) (2005) 'Developments in discursive psychology', *Discourse & Society* (special issue) 16(5).

Hepburn, A. and Wiggins, S. (eds) (2007) *Discursive research in practice: New approaches to psychology and interaction.* Cambridge: Cambridge University Press.

McKinlay, A. and McVittie, C. (2008) *Social psychology and discourse.* Oxford: Wiley-Blackwell.

Potter, J. (2003) 'Discursive psychology: Between method and paradigm', *Discourse & Society*, 14: 783–94.

Potter, J. (2012) 'Re-reading discourse and social psychology: Transforming social psychology', *British Journal of Social Psychology*, 51: 436–55.

Potter, J. and Wetherell, M. (1988) 'Accomplishing attitudes: Fact and evaluation in racist discourse', *Text*, 8: 51–68.

Schegloff, E. (1997) 'Whose text? Whose context?', *Discourse & Society*, 8: 165–87.

Speer, S. and McPhillips, R. (2013) 'Patients' perspectives on psychiatric consultations in the Gender Identity Clinic: Implications for patient-centered communication', *Patient Education and Counseling*, 91: 385–91.

Stokoe, E. (2012) 'Moving forward with membership categorization analysis: Methods for systematic analysis', *Discourse Studies*, 14: 277–303.

Stokoe, E. and Edwards, D. (2007) ' "Black this, black that": Racial insults and reported speech in neighbour complaints and police interrogations', *Discourse & Society*, 18: 337–72.

Stokoe, E., Hepburn, A. and Antaki, C. (2012) 'Beware the "Loughborough School" of social psychology: Interaction and the politics of intervention', *British Journal of Social Psychology*, 51: 486–96.

te Molder, H. and Potter, J. (2005) *Conversation and cognition.* Cambridge: Cambridge University Press.

Tileagă, C. (2005) 'Accounting for extreme prejudice and legitimating blame in talk about the Romanies', *Discourse & Society*, 16: 603–24.

Tileagă, C. (2011) '(Re)writing biography: Memory, identity, and textually mediated reality in coming to terms with the past', *Culture & Psychology*, 17: 197–215.

Vygotsky, L.S. (1978) *Mind in society: The development of higher psychological processes.* Cambridge, MA: Harvard University Press.

Wetherell, M. (1998) 'Positioning and interpretative repertoires: Conversation analysis and post-structuralism in dialogue', *Discourse & Society*, 9: 387–412.

Wetherell, M. (2001) 'Debates in discourse research', in M. Wetherell, S. Taylor and S. J. Yates (eds) *Discourse theory and practice: A reader.* London: Sage and Open University.

Wiggins, S. and Potter, J. (2008) 'Discursive psychology', in C. Willig and W. Stainton Rogers (eds) *The Sage handbook of qualitative research in psychology* (pp. 72–89). London: Sage.

Wittgenstein, L. (1958) *Philosophical investigations.* Oxford: Blackwell.

Part I
Epistemology and method

1 Interpretative repertoires, conversation analysis and being critical

Ann Weatherall

Target article: Wetherell, M. (1998) 'Positioning and interpretative repertoires: conversation analysis and post-structuralism in dialogue', *Discourse & Society*, 9: 387–412.

Introduction

The target article of this chapter – Wetherell's (1998) 'Positioning and interpretative repertoires: Conversation analyses and poststructuralism' – was written in response to Schegloff's (1997) *Whose text? Whose context?* His rebuttal to her response furthered the debate (Schegloff, 1998). Those three publications generated additional discussion threads also published in *Discourse & Society*. One was Weatherall (2000), which focused on the implications of Wetherell's and Schegloff's views for feminist gender and language studies, where the implications of the debate for critical research have generated ongoing discussion (Kitzinger, 2007; Weatherall et al., 2010; Speer, 2001; Stokoe and Smithson, 2001; Speer and Stokoe, 2011; Weatherall and Gallois, 2003). Another discussion thread of the debate was Billig (1999), who contributed to the debate by critiquing the rhetoric of conversation analysis. However, space limitations do not permit that to be part of the present discussion.

The Wetherell–Schegloff debate aired fundamental theoretical, analytic and applied issues for discourse analytic work within the social sciences. Indications of the considerable import of what was discussed and the widespread scholarly impact of the two papers are citations to them. As this chapter was being written, the *Web of Science Core Collection* records nearly 500 citations to Wetherell (1998) and over 300 to Schegloff (1997) – *Google Scholar* has well over double those counts for Wetherell and more than triple for Schegloff. One of the general matters at stake in this debate was how best to motivate and conduct principled, insightful and scholarly social scientific analyses of talk (and, to a lesser extent, written texts). Producing rigorous analyses of psychological topics and concerns grounded in language-in-use is central to discursive psychology (Edwards, 2012; Potter, 2012).

A particular aspect of Wetherell's (1998) contribution was that she directly raised an emerging schism between 'non-critical' and 'critical' lines of discourse analytic inquiry within psychology. That is, between researchers who were drawing on conversation analytic work and those following post-structuralist or Foucauldian lines of inquiry. Both traditions importantly informed Potter and Wetherell's (1987) discursive reformulation of social psychology and Wetherell advocated for a continuation of that earlier kind of synthetic approach, albeit further strengthening a post-structuralist perspective on discourse and subjectivity in the interests of radical, democratic political projects. Citations to Wetherell (1998) largely legitimate and motivate politically inspired styles of discourse analysis without serious recourse to Schegloff's (1997) critique. In contrast, the political and applied relevance of conversation analytic studies within discursive psychology has become accountable (Antaki, 2011; Stokoe, Hepburn and Antaki, 2012).

A further feature of the Wetherell–Schegloff debate that resonated with discourse analytic approaches within psychology concerned the legitimacy of invoking social categories such as gender, race or sexuality – when those categorisations are not observably relevant for the participants who are engaged in the interaction being analysed. Schegloff (1997) made a compelling case for a conversation analytic mentality that makes no *a priori* assumptions on what categorisations of the data are analytically relevant in a stretch of talk. He argued that analyses should be grounded in the observable or endogenous concerns of the participants in an interaction. Discourse analytic studies of identity within psychology were already embracing the kind of approach Schegloff was advocating (Antaki and Widdicombe, 1998). For example, Edwards (1998) examined how different person category terms, such as *girl* and *woman*, were mobilised in a couple's counselling session to formulate a referent in ways that served the interests of the speaker.

Margaret Wetherell has been a key figure in the emergence of what has become known as 'critical discursive psychology' and her work continues to merge very different social science traditions to topics important in psychology, such as emotion (Wetherell, 2012). With Potter, she was among the first to import constructionst theories of language as discourse in social psychology. They also established the 'interpretative repertoire' as a conceptual unit for discourse analytic studies of psychological topics and concerns (Wetherell, Stiven and Potter, 1987). She was a co-author of *Discourse and Social Psychology* (Potter and Wetherell, 1987), which was a foundational text in the development of discursive psychology. Wetherell and Potter's (1992) *Mapping the language of racism* illuminated the relationships between racialised social identities, language practices and ideology in ways that had never been done before within social psychology.

This chapter will proceed by discussing three aforementioned representative texts – Wetherell, Stiven and Potter (1987), Potter and Wetherell (1987) and Wetherell and Potter (1992) – in order to locate the target article within its theoretical, empirical and historical context. The views expressed in 'Positioning and interpretative repertoires: Conversation analysis and post-structuralism in dialogue' (Wetherell, 1998) stemmed from ongoing concerns – critique in the service of producing grounded and politically relevant analyses of social life, productive synthesis of social scientific theories and discourse methods to produce new insights, and methodological development in the analysis of actual language practices. It also clearly marked a point of departure from the shared work with Jonathan Potter who, along with Derek Edwards (Edwards and Potter, 1992), continued to advocate and progress the relevance of conversation analysis for discursive psychology (Edwards, 1995; Te Molder and Potter, 2005). After considering the academic context informing Wetherell (1998), it will be considered more closely as a response to Schegloff's (1997) paper. The chapter will conclude with a discussion of the ramifications of the debate on gender and language research and on criticality in discursive psychology.

Academic context and concerns

Wetherell's early discursive work (Wetherell, Stiven and Potter, 1987; Potter and Wetherell, 1987) was done at a time when the scientific canon of psychology was the target of sustained critique. Social psychology was challenged for being pervasively experimental, excessively quantitative, and overly reliant on university students as research subjects (e.g., Gergen, 1978; also see Weatherall, Gavey and Potts, 1992). The complexity of socially mediated behaviours within culture, history and politics, for example, was not being given serious consideration (Israel and Tajfel, 1972). Furthermore, feminists were contesting the claims of objectivity and neutrality in psychology where sexist assumptions permeated research designs and gender inequality was being naturalised by claims of innate female inferiority (Grady, 1981; Shields, 1975; Weisstein, 1968). Poststructuralist and postmodern ideas were being applied to psychology – a 'discursive turn' was underway, offering new ways of understanding the relationships between the self or subjectivity, language and power (Henrique, et al., 1984).

Wetherell et al.'s (1987) discursive study of gender inequality in the workplace was part of the critical milieu of its time. They challenged psychological research on prejudice and discrimination for being over reliant on the concepts of attitudes and personality traits. For example, negative attitudes towards women and fear of success were being used to explain gender segregation in the labour market. Attitudes and personality theoretically transcend social context, but Wetherell et al. noted the recruitment, retention and promotion of women are mediated by situational variables. Linking attitudes and personality variables directly to behaviours in complex social environments has been difficult to do. Wetherell et al. suggested that some of the problems associated with traditional psychological analyses could be resolved with a shift in research emphasis away from stable internal traits towards the systems of sense-making that people deploy in their understanding of employment opportunities.

The shift Wetherell et al. (1987) were making necessitated the development of new methods of analysis, which could deal with multiple and complex ways social objects were talked about. They proposed 'practical ideologies' as a unit of analysis. Practical ideologies refer to 'the often contradictory and fragmentary complexes of notions, norms and models, which guide conduct and allow for its justification and rationalisation' (Wetherell, et al., 1987: 60). In developing the notion of practical ideologies, Wetherell et al. drew on a broad range on theoretical influences. Speech act theory was used to highlight language as quintessentially a form of social action. The idea for notions, norms and models guiding everyday conduct was taken from ethnomethodology. The influence of poststructuralism was important for understanding that what people say is not just a reflection of their thoughts and attitudes, for example, but is inseparable from power and politics that produce possible meanings.

Wetherell et al. (1987) proposed the proper site for the investigation of practical ideologies was language-in-use. They recorded university students taking part in group discussions on attitudes towards their careers. At the time, interviews and focus groups were rarely used in social psychology. Since then, such methods have been critiqued and largely usurped in discursive psychology by studying language use in natural ecological settings, that is *in situ* (Edwards and Stokoe, 2004; Potter and Hepburn, 2005; 2012). Methodological limitations of researcher-generated talk aside, Wetherell et al's analysis identified two practical ideologies – *individualism* and *practical considerations* – used by the students to discuss their careers. Those themes were mobilised flexibly in discussions about gender and employment patterns to both endorse the concept of gender equality and to deny sexism in practice. On the one hand, participants suggested it was up to individuals regardless of gender to show that they had the knowledge, experience and skills worthy of employment. On the other, there were practical considerations (e.g., lack of adequate childcare) making the employment of women a problem.

The analytic concept of practical ideologies illuminated a new aspect of discrimination – the subtle rhetorical management of talk about inequality. Gender inequality was not just a matter of sexist attitudes or flawed personality but could be studied as part and parcel of language-in-use. The notion of practical ideologies was replaced by 'interpretative repertoires' in Potter and Wetherell (1987). However, the notions are similar – basic conceptual analytic units for identifying the ways social objects can be variously constructed in texts and talk for different interactional ends. Interpretative repertoires are *practical* resources, like building blocks, for fashioning meaning fitted to interactional concerns such as accountability and personal stake and interest. Interpretative repertoires are *ideological* in the sense they are part of a social and moral order that is tied to historical and cultural contexts. Interpretative repertoires are conceptual units that usefully operationalise the constructive and ideological nature of descriptions – over 150 studies to date are recorded in *Web of Science* as using the notion of interpretative repertoires, which shows its usefulness in discourse analytic work.

The critique of social psychology presented in Wetherell et al. (1987) was more fully developed in Potter and Wetherell (1987). That book further progressed a discourse analytic perspective across a broad range of psychological topics including attitudes, identity, categorisation and social representations. It importantly established a constructionist approach to the study of language for investigating psychological matters (Potter, 2012). Action became the analytic focus rather than cognition. Potter and Wetherell described the range of methodological influences shaping their distinctive form of discourse analysis, which included conversation analysis, ethnomethodology and linguistic philosophy (e.g., Coulter, 1979). These sources were influential because they underscored the importance of studying language-in-use, that language was a form of action in its own right and that the everyday and mundane aspects of life have an identifiable order. The notion of interpretative repertoire, taken from studies in the sociology of scientific knowledge (Gilbert and Mulkay, 1984), was proposed as a way of identifying and describing the order that scaffolds ordinary, everyday life as it is made available in talk and texts.

Wetherell and Potter (1992) further discussed the theoretical underpinnings of interpretative repertoires. Poststructuralist theories of meaning featured more prominently in Wetherell and Potter (1992) than in Potter and Wetherell (1987), perhaps because the subject matter of that work – racism – is inherently political. Wetherell and Potter also illustrated the way the interpretative repertoire as a conceptual analytic unit could be used in an empirical study. They demonstrated the ways the social status of Māori (the indigenous people of New Zealand) was rationalised and legitimated in research interviews and written texts. One finding was that race, culture and nation could be constructed in different ways, including as heritage, as therapy and as ideology. The various constructions were used in diverse ways to account for important societal matters, such as ethnic-based social conflict and its resolution. Evident from the analysis and the findings was the influence of Marxist studies of ideology and poststructuralist theories of discourse. Interpretative repertoires were understood to be implicated in the instantiation and reproduction of social and economic relations. Thus, Wetherell and Potter further highlighted the deeply and pervasively political aspects of the practical sense-making resources people draw upon to describe the world and justify their views.

The three key works discussed so far show the historical context from which the target article emerged and the academic concerns informing its production. Common interests that run through the work discussed include producing critical analyses of social life grounded in actual talk, the synthesis of a range of theoretical and methodological approaches to develop new insights into social behaviour, and conducting systematic rigorous empirical analyses of talk and texts. These aspects of Wetherell's work are also clearly part of the target article – which will be discussed after Schegloff's (1997) paper that prompted it.

Conversation analysis and politics

The title of Schegloff's (1997) paper, 'Whose text? Whose context?', captures its central concern – the issue of the researcher's perspective in an analysis of talk and texts. A key matter for him was whether researchers' concerns with broader socio-political matters should guide scholarly analyses in the first instance. He challenged the legitimacy of critical analysis, such as those offered by feminist language researchers, on the grounds they imposed a gendered analysis of the talk even when participants gave no indication it was a relevant aspect of the context for them. The question 'whose context?' recognises there are multiple ways of characterising an occasion of talk that may shape its form and progression. Speakers have a range of social identities that might be consequential for their conduct in talk – a speaker's gender, age or occupation may influence what they say and how they say it. Schegloff's question asks how best to warrant the use of one formulation about the relevant features of context, over another, in an analysis of talk.

Schegloff (1997) entertained some candidate criteria for legitimising relevant aspects of context. One of his proposals was truthfulness. However, truth is not necessarily helpful for resolving questions of relevant context. For example, his own paper was an invited talk, produced in the absence of his wife and presented at a professional conference, which are all true. Furthermore, ideas associated with postmodernism and poststructuralism challenge the notion of truth, which makes it a problematic basis for those claiming access to it. A second possible criterion he suggested was explanatory adequacy. That benchmark is typically used in experimental social psychology where important features of context are the independent factors that have a measurable and statistically significant impact on the dependent variables. For example, gender, age or some other categorisation of participants in a study is legitimatised because those factors can account for a statistically significant amount of the variation found in responses.

A different solution to that of truthfulness and explanatory adequacy is the one offered by conversation analysis. From a conversation analytic viewpoint the formulation or formulations of context that should be privileged are those characterisations of it that are used by the participants. In Schegloff's (1997) own words:

> we are dealing with sentient beings who themselves orient to their context under some formulation of formulations; who grasp their own conduct and that of others under the jurisdictions of some relevancies and not others; who orient to some of the identities they separately and collectively embody and, at any given moment, not others ... and because it is *those* characterisations which are privileged in the *constitution of socio-interactional reality* ... (they) therefore have a prima facie claim to being privileged in efforts to *understand* it.
>
> (Schegloff, 1997: 166–7; emphasis in the original)

To illustrate his argument, Schegloff (1997) presented some data and an analysis of it. One case was taken from a conversation between an estranged couple, Marcia and Tony, who were talking about Joey – their son. Joey had been visiting his mother and was returning to his father by plane because his

Dad's car, which he had at his Mum's had been vandalised, outside her house. The conversation proceeds with considerable overlapping talk and interruption. Schegloff suggested the overlapping talk and interruptions could be understood, from a critical discursive perspective, in terms of gender and power. However, Schegloff contested the legitimacy of that kind of analysis. Instead he considered the courses of action that the parties themselves – Marcia and Tony – were pursuing. For Marcia it was some kind of affiliation from Tony with her stance on the car being vandalised. For Tony it was his concern with getting his car back. The overlaps and interruptions are evidence of the participants' non-aligned concerns and not about their gendered identities, at least in terms of what is directly observable in the talk.

Schegloff (1997) suggested it is a kind of theoretical imperialism, albeit often well-intentioned, to stipulate the terms upon which texts or talk will be analysed – a gendered analysis in the case of Marcia and Tony. From the perspective of conversation analysis, it is imperialistic because that kind of critical gendered analysis leaves no place to consider what is relevant from the point of view of the participants whose talk is being analysed. A gender analysis can be relevant but its significance should be bound, according to Schegloff, to participants' already constructed and interpreted world. Schegloff also provided an example in which gender was observably a participants' matter. It was an extract from a mealtime where one of the participants helps himself to butter ignoring requests from two women to pass it to them, which he accounts for by saying 'ladies last'. Schegloff suggested that such moments may provide occasions for discovering how gender categories can be inferentially linked to ongoing courses of action.

Conversation analysis and interpretative repertoires

If critical analyses seek to link power and domination to particular features of talk-in-interaction, then Schegloff's (1997) position was that predetermined terms of reference have no legitimate place in a technical analysis. That position fundamentally challenges critical discourse analytic work where political commentary is part and parcel of the analysis of actual instances of talk. In Wetherell's (1998) response to Schegloff, she appreciated the integrity and rigour of conversation analysis but took issue with his position of the (ir)relevance of political matters to an understanding of particular stretches of talk. In contrast to Schegloff, she suggested a 'complete' analysis of participants' displayed concerns should also include a consideration of what she called 'the argumentative texture of social life' (Wetherell, 1998: 294). That 'argumentative texture' refers to the broader, cultural and historical context that, according poststructuralism, constitutes knowledge and systems of meaning; produces 'subject positions', and instantiates power relations.

For Wetherell (1998), then, a 'complete' analysis *should* include the kind of grounded understanding of talk that conversation analysis provides. However, following poststructuralist thinking and consistent with the 'synthetic' discourse analytic approach she was developing at the time, she argued it should also consider the broader systems of meaning that produce the subjectivities available for participants to take up in talk. To demonstrate her position, Wetherell analysed a stretch of talk from both conversation analytic and poststructuralist viewpoints. She then presented her evaluation of the adequacy of what each approach offered.

The data she presented was taken from a series of focus group discussions with young men that were designed to explore middle class masculine identities. The talk was generated in response to the researcher asking for a description of events that led one of the men in the group – Aaron – to being with four different women in one night. Wetherell used a conversation analytic perspective to attempt to translate empirically highly theoretical and conceptual concepts such as intelligibility, subjectivity and power. For example, the notion of 'subject positions' was operationalised in the various ways Aaron was actually described in the interviews. For example, Aaron being drunk and getting lucky are ways of understanding and making sense of his actions. Wetherell (1997) suggested that simply examining the descriptions of Aaron as a form of local action within the interview produced a limited analysis. She proposed interpretative repertoires provided a conceptual link between the broader historical, political context and what is actually said in talk. Relevant cultural repertoires included 'male sexuality as performance' and an 'ethics of sexuality' legitimised by relationships and reciprocity. Wetherell suggested those cultural repertoires provided a discursive context that gave meaning to the boasts or shamefulness of promiscuous sexual behaviour. Wetherell's critical discourse analysis of gender and sexuality considers locally occasioned and the broader discursive context in which it occurs. Wetherell argued that the kinds of insights conversation analysis can provide on its own are too narrow and restrictive to allow critical commentary.

Wetherell's earlier work drew upon a broad range of influences, including poststructuralist theory and conversation analysis, to establish interpretative repertoires as a viable unit for discursive analyses of psychological projects and topics. Wetherell (1998) was clearly linked to her earlier intellectual projects. She advocated integrating the grounded rigour of conversation analysis with a consideration of poststructuralist ideas about sense making, which was methodologically innovative. For Wetherell, that synthesis was a way of providing innovative and politically relevant social psychological understandings of social life that were broadly relevant. In her view, grounding poststructuralist ideas about meaning making and identities into micro-analyses talk was just good scholarship and not intellectual hegemony.

In Schegloff's (1998) reply to Wetherell he concedes little of his original position. He maintained the legitimacy of a conversation analytic mentality that asks 'why that now' as a way of grounding claims in participants' locally displayed understandings of what is happening. Instead of turning to critical theory for political insights, he suggested what is needed is more systematic conversation analytic observations about people's conduct and the ways they are produced and understood. He was also somewhat critical of Wetherell's analysis because it failed to consider how her participants may have been responding to the questions as being *research prompted*, which would add further analytic insights into the ways the interactions proceeded in the way they did. The kinds of limitations signalled by Schegloff of qualitative interviews have also been identified as a general problem of critical discursive work in psychology (Potter and Hepburn, 2005).

Schegloff (1998) concluded his reply by acknowledging that the questions asked by conversation analysis may not be the same as those that critical researchers may want to pose. He acknowledged that a synthetic approach may offer insights that a conversation analytic approach cannot – but those insights risk being subjective and ideological. Finally, he asked critical researchers not to underestimate the reach of conversation analysis but to understand that its potential for critical commentary may not yet be fully realised by virtue of a lack of research taking its perspective. Some of that potential has now been realised in more recent conversation analytic work on gender.

Gender, language and conversation analysis

Schegloff's (1997) vehemently bottom-up, participant-centred and -oriented approach is confronting and challenging to all critical discourse analysis, but it singled out, in particular, feminist work on gender and language. Conversation analysis requires that gender not be invoked, in the first instance, in a feminist analysis of talk. In contrast Wetherell's (1997) position is more palatable – a credible analysis considers the broader meaning systems upon which everyday sense-making practices depend, as well as attending to participants' own orientations to what is relevant. Of course gender can be understood as one of those broader meaning systems. The identification of a person as belonging to one of two gender groups is a fundamental guide to how a person is perceived, how their behaviour is interpreted and how they are responded to in everyday interaction and throughout the course of their life. Arguably it is a relevant backdrop to any social scientific analysis of social life (Weatherall, 2000).

Feminist language researchers have engaged with and responded to the issues raised in the Wetherell–Schegloff debate in various ways (Weatherall et al., 2010). At one end of the spectrum is an insistence that all critical work is about power relations in society and that invoking that interest is grounds enough for invoking the politics of social categories in an analysis (e.g., Weatherall, 1996). However, that position is untenable for both Schegloff and Wetherell who agree that a systematic and grounded analysis of talk and context is fundamental to credible empirical analyses of talk. More aligned with Wetherell's position than with Schegloff's are feminist discourse analytic approaches that endorse synthetic approaches that draw upon speaker's displayed understandings of their worlds *in situ* as well the broader knowledge frameworks those understandings rest upon (e.g., Baxter, 2003; Riley, 2002).

Other gender researchers have taken up Schegloff's challenge entirely on conversation analytic terms. Speer and Stokoe (2011) summarised two key issues that need to be resolved for an analysis of social categories, such as gender, to pass the evaluative of conversation analysis. One is the problem of relevance. The legitimacy of invoking a social categorisation as relevant to a stretch of interaction rests on the analysis demonstrating that it is one that participants themselves are oriented to. The other issue is what Speer and Stokoe referred to as procedural consequentiality. That is, once an identity category has been established as relevant, its consequentiality for the progression of action in interaction must be demonstrated.

Establishing gender relevance and procedural consequentiality can, in some cases, be quite straightforward. For example, Butler and Weatherall (2011) examined a case of a young boy, William, who for a time in the school playground assumed an identity of a girl, Charlotte. Butler and Weatherall used conversation analysis to identity how that cross-gender identity was accomplished during one interaction. Three key practices were identified as resources that the children used – the management of epistemic status (William knowing things that only Charlotte would have epistemic access to), the use of person reference forms and the accountability of gender categorisations and activities bound to those categorisations. Accomplishing a cross-gender identity is a breach in normative practices. Studying breaches brings into sharp relief everyday practices. It is one way systematic practices for accomplishing gender can be understood without recourse to broader meaning systems.

Breaches are quintessentially unusual occurrences. So studying them is only a partial solution to identifying gender relevance and procedural consequentiality in everyday settings. The study of repair – or when participants interrupt the normative progression of talk to address troubles in hearing speaking or understanding – is another potentially fruitful area for research on gender relevance. Cases of gender repair show the kinds of gender troubles that participants are orienting to as important and in need of addressing. Repair segments also show what kind of resolutions adequately address the oriented to trouble (Stokoe, 2011; Weatherall, 2002, 2015).

Aside from breaches and conversational repair, an obvious candidate for investigation into possible practices that demonstrate gender relevance is the use of gendered reference terms. However, Kitzinger (2007) showed that the use of terms such as 'woman' was not necessarily evidence that gender was relevant and procedurally consequential. On the flipside of Kitzinger's point, Jackson (2011) made a case that a speaker's self-referential 'I', far from being neutral can be oriented to as gendered. The work of Kitzinger and Jackson show that gender relevance cannot simply be reduced to using terms that are marked for gender. However, the use of gendered category terms and the activities bound to them, in their sequential environment of turns in talk, has been established as a fruitful site for demonstrating gender relevance and procedural consequentiality (Stokoe, 2006). An important direction for future research is to further examine the ways gender categories, and the activities that are inferentially bound to them, are part of a social order that has a gendered structure.

Critical conversation analysis

A foundational contribution of conversation analysis to social science was its recognition that everyday life was actually something that was achieved, orderly and amenable to scientific analysis. An early goal of conversation analysis was to document the structures of talk that accomplished the mundane (Sacks, 1984). Kitzinger (2005) further developed that foundation by adding to it a queer gaze. She documented the ways heterosexuality was routinely used as a resource for accomplishing mundane actions in ordinary interactions. The practices that she identified were heterosexual topic talk including heterosexual jokes and references to rites of passage such as marriage, and person reference terms such as husband and wife. Kitzinger argued that it was those kinds of practices that are a resource for constituting a taken-for-granted world that is normatively heterosexual.

Conversation analysis has been embraced as a productive rather than a restrictive methodology for feminist research (Stokoe, 2000; Weatherall, 2002; Wowk, 1984). Kitzinger and Frith (1995) used insights from conversation analysis around refusals to develop a critique of communication campaigns that advocated '*just saying no*' as a way to refuse unwanted sexual advances. Kitzinger and Frith pointed out that refusals in ordinary talk are typically mitigated and elaborate. Bald rejections are counter to the ways refusals are done mundanely. Recommending bald rejections as a practice for turning down unwanted sexual advances risks legitimises men's claims of misunderstanding when women's refusals take an everyday form. Another example of conversation analysis being used with a critical lens was Kitzinger's (2005) analysis of coming out as lesbian or gay in university tutorial classes. She found that coming out was regularly done in the middle of a turn constructional unit, which exploited turn-taking structures to ward off responses to that revelation.

'Feminist conversation analysis' was the name used to refer to an approach advocated that used conversation analysis to advance a critical agenda (Kitzinger 2000, 2005, 2007; Speer 1999). Speer (1999) noted that the combination of 'feminist' with conversation analysis can be construed as oxymoronic because it is seemingly contradictory to combine a political perspective with a supposedly objective scientific one. Another critique has been that the pairing of *feminist* with *conversation analysis* actually sullies the integrity of conversation analysis (Wowk, 2007). Controversy about the name aside, feminist conversation analysis has shown some of the promise of conversation analysis for developing critical commentary (see Speer, 2001; Speer and Stokoe, 2011; Weatherall, 2012). It can be done as Schegloff (1998) indicated, without having to import matters external to participants' concerns into the analytic approach.

Discursive psychology and the politics of being critical

Wetherell (1998) advocated one way of keeping live, political matters in systematic and grounded analyses of texts and talk. She suggested a synthesis of conversation analysis with poststructural ideas about language, power and knowledge provided as a scholarly way forward. Her goal has been to develop a rigorous discourse analytic approach capable of producing intelligent and politically informed commentary on social psychological topics and concerns. Her synthetic approach has been influential. Her critical discourse analytic approach has broad uses and can be deployed for data not amendable to conversation analysis, including written texts (e.g., Kirkwood, Liu and Weatherall, 2005) and monologic, political speech (e.g., Augoustinos, LeCouteur and Soyland, 2002). Critical and feminist conversation analytic studies have demonstrated that conversation analytic work can cast interesting light on political matters. Being critical does not necessarily have to draw upon broader contextual information as part of the analytic approach. Thus to a certain extent Wetherell's (1998) critique of conversation analysis is no longer as applicable as it was at the time of its writing. Nevertheless, the merit of Wetherell's approach on its own terms is evidenced by its significant impact on psychology (Augoustinos, 2013). Wetherell's reluctance to be tied to disciplinary boundaries, even when pursuing social psychological topics and questions, may account for the broad reach of the discourse analytic approach she championed. Furthermore it points to her own vision of the future (Wetherell, 2011), where for social psychology to survive and thrive it needs to engage more thoroughly and intelligently with work outside its traditional boundaries.

References

Antaki, C. (ed.) (2011) *Applied conversation analysis*. Basingstoke: Palgrave-Macmillan.
Antaki, C. and Widdicombe, S. (1998) (eds) *Identities in talk*. London: Sage.
Augoustinos, M. (2013) 'Discourse analysis in psychology: What's in a name?', *Qualitative Research in Psychology, 10*: 244–8.
Augoustinos, M., LeCouteur, A. and Soyland, J. (2002) 'Self-sufficient arguments in political rhetoric: Constructing reconciliation and apologizing to the Stolen Generations', *Discourse & Society, 13*: 105–42.
Baxter, J. (2003) *Positioning gender in discourse: A feminist methodology*. Basingstoke: Palgrave.
Billig, M. (1999) 'Whose terms? Whose ordinariness? Rhetoric and ideology in conversation analysis', *Discourse & Society, 10*: 543–58.
Butler, C. and Weatherall, A. (2011) ' "This is Charlotte" A case of passing in children's talk-in-interaction', in S. Speer and E.H. Stokoe (eds), *Gender and conversation* (pp. 231–49). Cambridge: Cambridge University Press.
Coulter, J. (1979) *The social construction of mind. Studies in ethnomethodology and linguistic philosophy*. London: MacMillan.
Edwards, D. (1995) 'Sacks and psychology', *Theory and Psychology, 5*: 579–96.
Edwards, D. (1998) 'The relevant thing about her: Social identity categories in use', in C. Antaki and S. Widdicombe (eds), *Idenitites in talk* (pp. 15–33), London: Sage.
Edwards, D. (2012) 'Discursive and scientific psychology', *British Journal of Social Psychology, 51*: 425–35.
Edwards, D. and Potter, J. (1992) *Discursive psychology*. London: Sage.

Gergen, K.J. (1978) 'Experimentation in social psychology: A reappraisal', *European Journal of Social Psychology*, 8: 507–27.

Gilbert, G.N. and Mulkay, M. (1984) *Opening Pandora's box: A sociological analysis of scientists' discourse*. Cambridge: Cambridge University Press.

Grady, K.E. (1981) 'Sex bias in research design', *Psychology of Women Quarterly*, 4: 628–35.

Henriques, J., Hollway, W., Urwin, C., Venn, C. and Walkerdine, V. (1984) *Changing the subject: Psychology, social regulation and subjectivity*. London: Methuen.

Israel, J. and Tajfel, H. (eds) (1972) *The context of social psychology: A critical assessment*. London: Academic Press.

Jackson, C. (2011) 'The gendered I', in S. Speer and E.H.Stokoe (eds) *Gender and conversation* (pp. 31–47). Cambridge: Cambridge University Press.

Kirkwood, S., Liu, J.H. and Weatherall, A. (2005) 'Challenging the standard story of indigenous rights in Aotearoa/New Zealand', *Journal of Community & Applied Social Psychology*, 15: 1–13.

Kitzinger, C. (2000) 'Doing feminist conversation analysis', *Feminism & Psychology*, 10: 163–93.

Kitzinger, C. (2005) '"Speaking as a heterosexual": (How) does sexuality matter for talk-in-interaction?', *Research on Language and Social Interaction*, 38: 221–65.

Kitzinger, C. (2007) 'Is "woman" always relevantly gendered?' *Gender and Language*, 1: 39–49.

Kitzinger, C. and Frith, H. (1999) Just say no? The use of conversation analysis in developing a feminist perspective on sexual refusal, *Feminism & Psychology*, 10: 293–316.

Potter, J. (2012) 'Re-reading *Discourse and Social Psychology*: Transforming social psychology', *British Journal of Social Psychology*, 51: 436–55.

Potter, J. and Hepburn, A. (2005) 'Qualitative interviews in psychology', *Qualitative Research in Psychology*, 2: 281–307.

Potter, J. and Hepburn, A. (2012) 'Eight challenges for interview researchers', J.F. Gubrium and J.A. Holstein (eds) *Handbook of interview research* (second edn) (pp. 555–70). London: Sage.

Potter, J. and Wetherell, M. (1987) *Discourse and social psychology*. London: Sage.

Riley, S. (2002) 'Constructions of equality and discrimination in professional men's talk', *British Journal of Social Psychology*, 41: 443–61.

Sacks, H. (1984) 'On doing "being ordinary"', in J. Maxwell Atkinson and J. Heritage (eds) *Structures of social action: Studies in conversation analysis* (pp. 413–29). Cambridge: Cambridge University Press.

Schegloff, E.A. (1997) 'Whose text? Whose context?', *Discourse & Society*, 8: 165–87.

Schegloff, E.A. (1998) 'Reply to Wetherell', *Discourse & Society*, 9: 413–16.

Shields, S. (1975) 'Functionalism, Darwinism and the psychology of women: A study of social myth', *American Psychologist*, 3: 195–211.

Speer, S.A. (1999) 'Feminism and conversation analysis: An oxymoron?', *Feminism & Psychology*, 9: 471–8.

Speer, S.A. (2001) 'Reconsidering the concept of hegemonic masculinity: Discursive psychology, conversation analysis and participants' orientations', *Feminism & Psychology*, 11: 107–35.

Speer, S.A. and Stokoe, E. (2011) *Conversation and Gender*. Cambridge, UK: Cambridge University Press.

Stokoe, E.H. (2000) 'Towards a conversation analytic approach to gender and discourse', *Feminism & Psychology*, 10: 552–63.

Stokoe, E. (2006) 'On ethnomethodology, feminism, and the analysis of categorical reference to gender in talk-in-interaction', *The Sociological Review*, 54: 467–94.

Stokoe, E. (2011) '"Girl – woman – sorry!": On the repair and non-repair of consecutive gender categories', in S.A Speer E. and Stokoe (eds) *Conversation and Gender* (pp. 85–111). Cambridge University Press.

Stokoe, E. and Edwards, D. (2004) 'Discursive psychology, focus group interviews and participants' categories'. *British Journal of Developmental Psychology*, 22: 499–507.

Stokoe, E. and Smithson, J. (2001) 'Making gender relevant: Conversation analysis and gender categories in interaction', *Discourse & Society*, 12: 243–69.

Stokoe, E., Hepburn, A. and Antaki, C. (2012) 'Beware the "Loughborough School"? Interaction and the politics of intervention'. *British Journal of Social Psychology*, 51: 486–96.

Te Molder, H. and Potter, J. (eds) (2005) *Conversation and Cognition*. Cambridge: Cambridge University Press.

Weatherall, A. (1996) 'Language about men and women: An example from popular culture'. *Journal of Language & Social Psychology*, 15: 59–75.

Weatherall, A. (2000) 'Gender relevance in talk-in-interaction and discourse', *Discourse & Society*, 11: 286–8.

Weatherall, A. (2002) 'Towards understanding gender and talk-in-interaction', *Discourse & Society*, 13: 767–81.

Weatherall, A. (2012) 'Conversation analysis as feminist research: A response to Whelan'. *Qualitative Research in Psychology*, 9: 1–6. DOI: 10.1080/14780887.2011.635468.

Weatherall, A. (2015) Sexism in language and talk-in-interaction, *Journal of Language and Social Psychology*, 33: 1–17.

Weatherall, A. and Gallois, C. (2003) 'Gendered identity: Complexities/intersections. A social psychology perspective' (pp. 487–508), in J. Holmes and M. Meyerhoff (eds), *Handbook of gender and language*. Malden, MA: Blackwell Publishing.

Weatherall, A., Gavey, N. and Potts, A. (2002) 'So whose words are they anyway?' *Feminism & Psychology*, 12(4): 533–41.

Weatherall, A., Stubbe, M., Sutherland, J. and Baxter, J. (2010) 'Conversation analysis and critical discourse analysis in language and gender research: Approaches in dialogue', in J. Holmes and M. Marra (eds) *Femininity, Feminism and Gendered Discourse* (pp. 217–47). Newcastle upon Tyne, UK: Cambridge Scholars.

Weisstein, N. (1968/1993) 'Psychology constructs the female; or the fantasy life of the male psychologist (with some attention to the fantasies of his friends, the male biologist and the male anthropologist', *Feminism & Psychology*, 3: 195–210.

Wetherell, M. (1998) 'Positioning and interpretative repertoires: Conversation analysis and post-structuralism in dialogue', *Discourse & Society*, 9: 387–412.

Wetherell, M. (2011) 'The winds of change: Some challenges in reconfiguring social psychology for the future', *British Journal of Social Psychology*, 50: 399–404.

Wetherell, M. (2012) *Affect and emotion: A new social science understanding*. London: Sage.

Wetherell, M. and Potter, J. (1992) *Mapping the language of racism. Discourse and the legitimation of exploitation*. New York: Columbia University Press.

Wetherell, M., Stiven, H. and Potter, J. (1987) 'Unequal egalitarianism: A preliminary study of discourse and employment opportunities', *British Journal of Social Psychology*, 26: 59–71.

Wowk, M.T. (1984) 'Blame allocation, sex and gender in a murder interrogation', *Women's Studies International Forum*, 7: 75–82.

Wowk, M.T. (2007) 'Kitzinger's feminist conversation analysis: Critical observations', *Human Studies*, 30: 131–55.

2 Hitting ontological rock bottom

Discursive psychology's respecification of the realism/relativism debate

Clara Iversen

Target article: Edwards, D., Ashmore, M. and Potter, J. (1995) 'Death and furniture: The rhetoric, politics and theology of bottom line arguments against relativism', *History of the Human Sciences*, 8: 25–49.

If your work has ever been dismissed for being relativist in an intellectual argument, 'Death and furniture' is the text you would have wanted to hold in your hand at the time. Not only does the paper provide you with solid counter-arguments; it also guides you into the philosophy of discursive psychology (henceforth DP). Instead of taking a position in the realism/relativism debate, Edwards, Ashmore, and Potter respecify the entire issue. They show that the debate is built on a realist notion of reality. Any responses from relativists will come off as arguing for an 'unreality'—a positive counter version of the realist reality. Therefore, the authors suggest that relativism should dismiss the occupation with ontology in favor of a purely epistemological analysis. This means that questions about the relation between knowledge and reality are disavowed; knowledge is investigated and understood in its own right, as practice that builds versions of reality. The paper is a shining example of how DP studies reveal rhetoric that constructs factual descriptions. Deploying a systematic reflexive orientation to realist rhetoric in various texts and contexts, Edwards et al. (1995) demonstrate the work of such rhetoric and offer a radically new understanding of taken-for-granted standpoints in scientific discussions. As such, 'Death and furniture' contributes to a general discussion of ontology and epistemology and lays the ground for a DP philosophy of respecification and reflexivity.

In this chapter, I start out by summarizing the 'Death and furniture' paper's argument in relation to some of the main issues that motivated its writing. I then describe how it has contributed to developing debate and empirical work in social science. I exemplify its continuous relevance with analysis of data concerning child abuse. Finally, I argue that the paper is still central to understanding the commitment to relativism for discursive researchers exploring social issues.

But surely not this? Bottom line in social science debate

Discursive psychology developed in an environment where scientific practice was becoming an object of study alongside other social phenomena. The social aspects of knowledge had of course been discussed and analyzed before. Idealist philosophers of science (e.g., Plato and Kant) had argued that people's experience of the world is seriously limited by their ability to observe it. In sociology of knowledge such proposals were met with calls for universal rules of craftsmanship and integrity that would enable scientists to stand above the interests of different groups in society (e.g., Merton 1938, 1972). What the new sociology of scientific knowledge (SSK) suggested was a shift, from trying to control and delimit the influence of social factors, to studying what members of scientific communities consider knowledge to be and how they produce and defend their respective versions (Gilbert and Mulkay 1984, Latour 1987, Latour and Woolgar 1986).

As opposed to the treatment of science as generating increasingly accurate facts about the world, SSK uses constructionist perspectives (Mulkay 1991). According to a constructionist view, there is no epistemological difference between scientific knowledge and everyday knowledge or between good science and bad (Barnes 1992). Instead, science is understood as a form of knowledge that operates in different scientific communities (cf. Latour and Woolgar 1986). The engagement with the social aspects of scientific practice in SSK carries two implications: first, it challenges the distinction between 'practice' and 'world' by showing that knowledge is relative to procedures and norms within social communities. Scientists are understood as forming their objects of study rather than merely representing them. Second, the constructionist view suggests that this reflexive nature of scientific practice should be embraced—scientists may actually gain something from turning skepticism against their own work (Ashmore 1989: 92).

In response to the relativist description of factual discourse, researchers with a realist view started to voice their concerns. Early discursive psychologists were criticized for being uninvolved, applying constructionism as a value-free technology, and for simply reifying problematic discourses (Parker and Burman 1993). DP researchers had to defend their positions against arguments such as "Are you seriously trying to suggest that trees and houses, the stars in the sky, my great uncle Roger are not real?" (see Edley 2001: 435). Either rejecting the constructionist perspective completely or appreciating constructionist views on some phenomena, realist researchers argued for the need of a bottom line—a limit for what may reasonably be called constructed and deconstructable.

It is such bottom line arguments that the paper 'Death and furniture' investigate. The authors identify two kinds of rhetorical moves used to question a relativist stance: one is Furniture—the statement that some reality cannot be denied—and the other is Death—the statement that some reality should not be denied. In the following, I will summarize how Edwards et al. (1995) deconstruct different aspects of these claims and how they argue for the impossibility of the whole realism/relativism debate.

The Furniture argument: Are you crazy?

Realists use the Furniture argument to suggest that, independent of any description, there is an objective world. What exactly this objective world consists of varies between different realist descriptions, but often referred objects are tables, chairs, roses, rocks, sticks, and stones. According to the Furniture argument, such objects instruct people in the same way (see e.g., Collins 1990: 50). Therefore, they are not subjected to any semantically based interpretation. Rather, they are said to represent "the naked truth"—a fact beyond argument.

Edwards et al. (1995) discuss how different Furniture objects are used in the realism/relativism debate. The first object that they present is the table. The example of the table usually occurs some time into a heated discussion when the realist starts hitting the table with their hand while (not seldom red-faced and agitated) shouting: "But this table, then, does it not exist? How can this banging be unreal?" Edwards et al. (1995) tell us that this argument is efficient, not because of its aggressive and sometimes frightening delivery, but because (1) academic arguments occur in rooms where these objects are easily accessible, (2) furniture seem to be external to those arguments, and (3) hitting furniture works as a non-verbal act. Accessing no equivalent asset, relativists find themselves in a difficult situation, having to refute the obvious.

But looking closely, Edwards et al. (1995) expose this argument for what it is: a meaningful, situated action with pragmatic motives. Hitting furniture is saying to the relativist: "I dare you to show me that this table is unreal." Thereby, hitting the table becomes meaningful as an example of objective reality. In a different context, hitting the table might mean "put the food here." The action is thus understandable as an example of unrepresented reality only in the context of the situated discussion. Edwards et al. (1995) term this *the Realist Dilemma*: pointing to a table as an example of unconstructed reality is precisely doing the action of constructing it as a piece of unconstructed reality. Thereby, hitting the table is constructing what it suggests is only doing representing.

In a less sophisticated response, the relativist can also suggest that tables are constructed by man and therefore dependent on meaning making for their existence. To ward off such arguments, realists may use the rock as an example of an indisputably unconstructed part of reality. This argument goes something like "what happens when we stumble against a rock is similar for all." Like the example of the table, the rock example asks us to accept it as obvious. However, neither the rock nor the people stumbling against it are available as actual events in a discussion between realists and relativists. Thus, the rock is not a presentation of a piece of reality; it is a story. Edwards et al. (1995) identify this story as a prototypical account; that is, it is not a story about someone specific who stumbles on a rock in a particular situation. Rather, it tells us about an idealized event, supposedly known to all. Edwards et al. (1995) persuasively demonstrate that the reality-producing trick with this story is a change of footing between the narrator and the person stumbling (see Goffman 1981). The rock example is simultaneously telling us about a situation and asking us to experience the situation as if it was not introduced by this telling.

A third example related to the Furniture argument is the text. According to this argument, there is a bottom line to the ways a text can be interpreted. Therefore, the text can be said to be more real than the rest of the world. Edwards et al. (1995) dismiss this argument by suggesting that it is impossible to know in advance of any discussion between people who have read a text what their interpretations will be. Furthermore, what readers understand as a wrong interpretation is based on social judgment.

Edwards et al. (1995) strip the Furniture argument from its 'naked-truthness' by comparing it to other rhetorical strategies identified in previous research. The table example is compared to rhetorical devices that construct objects and events as obvious, for example drawing on common knowledge by quoting idioms (Drew and Holt 1988). Just like the Furniture argument, such devices assume that the only reasonable thing is to agree with them. The rhetorical device of footing set to work in the rock example is compared to the empiricist repertoire used by scientists when they claim that "data showed X," thereby removing themselves and their actions in the scientific process. By not just going along with the table, rock, and text as examples of reality, Edwards et al. (1995) show them for what they are: parts of an argument.

The reality that cannot be denied is introduced in argument in the form of specific descriptions of it, but realists do not treat them as descriptions, stories, or accounts but rather as unconstructed reality. Edwards et al. (1995: 27) highlight that realist arguments that purport to be "above rhetoric" are in fact "arguments of no argument." They show that realists unreflexively deploy reality in argument without attending to the idea that descriptions, stories, accounts—language—provide the building blocks of reality construction.

The Death argument: Inducing guilt

The Death argument has an ontological side that links directly to the Furniture argument: it suggests that only a fool could deny the occurrence of death, disaster, misery, tragedy, and the like. Similar to the rock story, this ontological aspect of the Death argument suggests that knowledge about death is forced upon us. But there is also what Edwards et al. (1995) call the "Siren Version" of the Death argument. This version takes its fuel from a politico-moral domain and suggests that relativism actually produces bad things (Death) by not taking them seriously. These versions work causally: if the reality of abuse, inequality, and war are understood as relative to knowledge in different communities, on what grounds can they be condemned? By questioning the firm status of reality, well-meaning relativists are said to lack the incentive to slow down and stop a fatal development.

If the Furniture argument works by questioning its opponents' sanity, the Death argument does the trick by inducing guilt. Whereas the realist position is described as responsible and ethical—as recognizing the good things that should not be undermined and the bad things that should not be made possible—the relativist position is described as "anything goes"; a position short of a basis for commitment and therefore inactive, indifferent, and, consequently, responsible for any bad thing that may happen.

Edwards et al. (1995) point out that a shortcoming of this argument is that it assumes that rejecting realism is the same thing as rejecting everything realists think is real. Just as researchers who analyze norms in interaction do not refrain from acting according to those norms in their everyday lives, seeing values as relative to arguments does not entail a lesser need for holding beliefs. Studying the activities in people's lives, whether it may be when scientists conduct experiments or when people walk their dogs, does in no way drive relativists to live in a parallel, value-free universe. Edwards et al. (1995) suggest that, on the contrary, it is precisely the fact that relativists have to argue for their values that make them prone to a more ethical stance. Relativists are forced to examine their own convictions; to explain and justify why bad things are bad and good things are good. Thus, relativism does not preclude commitment. The kind of "pragmatic pragmatism" that Edwards et al. (1995) advocate presupposes a commitment to the value of social/discursive deconstruction and social accomplishments, rather than adhering to a truth beyond (de)construction.

Furthermore, Edwards et al. (1995) note that realism has no exclusive claim upon making the world a better place. Rhetorical constructions, such as "it's just the way things are," use reality as a motive for inaction. And reality is a problematic foundation for claims of good and bad, right and wrong, as it ends up with something being good only because it is true.[1] To the racist argument "Black people smell bad," which was used to justify Jim Crow practices, the antiracist realist would have to prove that people cannot tell the difference between how different "racial" categories smell. The ethics as well of productiveness of this line of research can be questioned. Relativists, on the other hand, can criticize the opponents' assumptions, methods, and rhetoric (such as the assumption that people who smell bad should be separated from those who smell good, see Becker 1998: 200f). Edwards et al. (1995) note that realists do in fact use these methods of critique and skepticism. However, they only use them against their opponents. By contrast, relativism requires its proponents to be reflexive also in relation to their own position.

The issue of reflexivity, however, means that relativists can never claim victory in the realism/relativism debate. With the Death argument, relativists are ascribed the belief that every view is equally valid. As well as the above described problem of indifference, this position also holds a *Relativist Dilemma* corresponding to the realist dilemma: how can we argue for a relativist stance when this position itself must be relative? Below, I will describe how Edwards et al. (1995) tackle this problem.

Relativism as social science *par excellence*

Although Edwards et al. (1995) convincingly dismiss Death and Furniture arguments, they still withhold that both the realist and the relativist dilemmas make for a difficult debate. Because realists cannot represent reality outside conversation and because relativists cannot claim that their perspective is more valid than realism, each side's argument gets cancelled in a discussion.

Edwards et al. (1995) argue that this problem originates from the fact that the realism/relativism debate is built on a realist notion of ontology and epistemology; any relativist argument against the realist version is heard as an ontological one, implying that there is no reality. However, Edwards et al. (1995) argue that relativism is fundamentally different from realism. Drawing on Feyerabend (1975), Latour (1987), Rorty (1985), and Smith (1988), they put forward the idea that relativism should refuse to be put as a positive statement opposed to realism. Instead, relativism is a (non)position, "offered as a meta-level (or one more step back) epistemology that can include and analyse realism and relativism alike, *viewed as rhetorical practices*" (Edwards et al. 1995: 41, emphasis in original). According to this statement, relativists can abandon questions of what exists; they can simply study text and talk as versions relating to other versions. This view holds a basic critique of approaches that adopt a referential theory of meaning by using text and talk as pathways to objects in the world or an inner subjective world. Abandoning ontological issues separates DP from cognitivist constructionist theories as well as from efforts in critical discourse analysis to formulate an extra-discursive foundation of social practices.

Edwards et al. (1995) claim that the most powerful tools in conducting social science, such as arguing, deconstructing, and denying, are relativist in their nature. But unlike realists, relativists understand their own work, and not just their opponents', to rely on social conditions. Therefore, relativism is social science *par excellence*: it does the job of questioning the assumptions that permeate different social practices, including its own. Realism, by contrast, should be understood as an efficient rhetorical device rather than a serious intellectual position:

> Hitting tables and invoking death are, at best, shorthand; at worst, ignorance; at least, rhetoric. *Shorthand* because they subsume the rhetoric and semiosis of situated actions. *Ignorance* because the way they are deployed against relativism is to deny that subsumed process while relying directly upon it. *Rhetoric* because not only are they rhetorically constructed and deployed, but they remain useful even after deconstruction, as devices that stand emblematically for the whole range of "oh come on now" appeals to obviousness and straightforward, unvarnished truth and necessity that all rhetoricians, or so we are told, enjoy.
> (Edwards et al. 1995: 42, emphasis in original)

The 'Death and furniture' paper does two important things: it shows realism as a rhetoric that does not acknowledge its own existence and it promotes relativism from being in second position, responding to the conditions set up by relativism, to a model approach of social science. By showing how reflexive concern with realism can illuminate some of the dilemmas of relativists, it formulates the epistemological philosophy of discursive psychology.

Contribution and impact

The broad range of books and articles that uses the 'Death and furniture' paper is an indication of its tremendous and long-lasting value in renewing social science debate. It has become a given in constructionist text books (Augoustinos, Walker, and Donaghue 2014, Burr 2003, Jørgensen and Phillips 2002, to name a few). Furthermore, the paper is cited in a large number of publications in different areas (383 citations in Google Scholar at the writing of this chapter). The most influential aspect of the paper is the explication that relativism implies a move from a positive stance that suggests that there is no reality, to a negative position that questions the distinction between world and practice. In this section, I will describe the areas in which the paper has been mostly cited and exemplify its relevance with data from my own research.

The most profound impact of the paper goes beyond empirical work in DP to a broad discussion of epistemological and ontological issues. Not surprisingly, the paper yielded defensive responses from writers identifying as realists. For example, Parker (1999) argues that the 'Death and furniture' paper reduces reality to some turns in conversation. O'Neill (1995) suggests that it aims to silence its opponents as well as to downplay the fact that relativism can be used to justify anything. Such critique repeats the arguments that the 'Death and furniture' paper deals with by portraying relativism as unbalanced and extreme (the Furniture argument) and as rendering its proponents unable to act (the Death argument) (for a response, see Potter 1998). Relativists are yet again positioned as positively arguing for a different and unreal reality as well as for separating the world from politics (see also Gill 1995, Nightingale and Cromby 1999).

A more interesting take on the paper engages with the move from ontology to epistemology. Edwards (1997) develops this notion in his book *Discourse and cognition*, showing the value of a purely epistemological approach to psychological statements. Others use the shift as a base for theoretical development of constructionism in general. Edley (2001) suggests that the distinction between ontological and epistemological forms of constructionism exhausts many disputes within constructionist research and removes much of the extremism that this work has been ascribed. Furthermore, Gergen (2001a) draws on 'Death and furniture' and suggests that with an epistemological focus, constructionist discussions allow researchers to replace the search for truth with communal deliberations on future outcomes. Not having to aim for truth enables researchers to work towards more of what they think is good, and less of what they think is bad. Gergen (2001b) further argues that a relativist stance is in no way opposed to psychological science. On the contrary, it opens up for new questions. When arguments about what is real are revealed as pointless, realist discourse can be both used and analyzed rhetorically. From the many articles using the 'Death and furniture' paper as a way of describing their approach, it is also clear that 'Death and furniture' was an important step in consolidating the theory of DP (e.g., Horton-Salway 2001, Tileagă 2006).

Feminist studies employ the deconstruction of the Death argument in advocating that relativism does not imply that inequalities, manifested for example as men's violence against women, are unreal or that relativists adopt an intrinsically insensitive stance towards women's suffering (Hepburn 2000, Speer 2000). In a similar way, the 'Death and furniture' paper has been important for justifying the empirical study of different forms of abuse with relativist approaches (Iversen 2013). For instance, Hepburn (1997: 30) suggests that investigation of school bullying benefits from "the flexibility of a position in which discourses can be drawn upon strategically to achieve particular ends in particular contexts." McMartin (1999) uses the paper in arguing that sexual abuse is no less real for being viewed as a construction. This is precisely because relativism is not a positive statement opposed to ontological realism. Describing abuse and inequality as constructed, researchers simply mean that victims, perpetrators, institutional agents, etc., use common knowledge when they deal with the aftermath of abuse. To understand and change victim and perpetrator positions, and to develop institutional responses towards abuse, it is fruitful to analyze how such knowledge is deployed. Epistemological relativism offers moral and political strengths because nothing has to be taken as "just there".

My own research on child abuse has benefited from arguments in the 'Death and furniture' paper in a related sense. Below I will illustrate the value of understanding talk about child sexual abuse as rhetorical work rather than as a representation of reality. The excerpt comes from a police interview with a man who is being interviewed about sexually assaulting two girls in the woods nearby a cycling path. The excerpt is transcribed by the police; I did not have access to the audio file.

U2:Mt1-2008

```
01    P:    Du måste ju få en sexuell njutning av det här,
            You must get some kind of sexual pleasure from this,
02                eftersom att du har fått utlösning i skogen
            since you had a release in the woods
03                tillsammans med dom här två flickorna, få
            together with those two girls, get
04                nåt tillbaka sexuellt av det här?
            something back sexually from this?
05    S:    Jag vet inte det, då jag inte kommer ihåg det där.
            I don't know that, as I don't remember that.
06                Men med nånting har det väl blivit då liksom.
            But something has like probably happened.
07                Men det finns inte uppe i min skalle då liksom.
            But it's nowhere in my head y'know.
```

We can assume that the institutional agenda in a police interview is to get more information from suspects on what has happened and their intentions regarding the offence (cf. Edwards 2008). Now a realist analysis would be concerned with the reality behind the suspect's response (that he does not remember how his sperm ended up at the crime scene). It would likely not take the suspect's words for truth but with different methods, such as asking the same question in varied ways, try to assess what is actually inside the suspect's head. The problem with this approach is that there is no way to actually know. The realist will still only have the suspect's words to go on. A relativist analysis, by contrast, focuses on what the suspect's "no knowledge" claim is doing in its sequential, rhetorical, and institutional context.

Employing this kind of analysis, we can first note that the police interrogator's (P) first pair part in lines 1–4 offers as little agency as possible to the suspect (S). The fact that the issue of sexual pleasure is in S's epistemic domain (primarily known by him) is undermined as P can produce evidence (the sexual release) of his claim. The yes/no declarative is therefore better understood as doing accusing than asking for information. In response, S offers something that may be the closest you can come to admitting guilt without actually doing it. He does co-operate by offering an answer. However, prefacing the turn with "I don't know that" (line 5) produces what comes next as a best guess rather than a certain fact (Keevallik 2011). The account for not knowing, "as I don't remember that" (line 5), is not disputing what P is saying (which may be futile in the case of "hard evidence"), but not confirming it either. Drew (1992) suggests this to be the usefulness of claiming "not remembering": it avoids directly challenging a version but still manages to neutralize it. In line 6, S agrees that "something has like probably happened." By using "probably," S still relays the responsibility for the correctness of this version to P. Finally, "But it is nowhere in my head y'know" makes explicit that the event is not in S's epistemic domain. Thus, S is doing what looks like a partial admission, while making use of the epistemic stance that P displayed in lines 1–4. By relaying the epistemic responsibility to P, S does not contribute any new information, neither does he admit to any kind of intentionality.

Analyzing the speaker's responses as rhetorical tells us nothing about their intentions or about the actual state of their minds. Instead, it tells us about (1) how speakers might avoid being attributed intentionality, (2) how "no knowledge" responses work to such end, and (3) about the practicality of this work in particular institutional environments. By making use of, revealing, and contesting the assumptions that the preceding turn communicates, the suspect's response gives the analyst information about how such assumptions may work for, or against, the institutional agenda. A dismissal of the direct line between what people say and their psychological state is neither robbing people of intentionality nor crediting it to them, but demonstrating how it is oriented to in institutional settings. Such analysis is directly relevant for institutional development. Furthermore, it can be an integral part of "changing the world": revealing and criticizing the work that psychological discourse (such as "it's nowhere in my head") do will, in extension, change discourse.

By recognizing the reflexive nature of the discourse of suspects and police interrogators, as well as of researchers analyzing their talk, relativists put their versions of the world on trial. Therefore, reflexivity makes ethical discussion and practice necessary.

'Death and furniture' is, at heart, a piece of deconstructive writing, unrivalled in the early DP canon. Its reflexive engagement with realist discourse has been an important step in showing the shortcomings of realist rhetoric, as well as producing an environment from where constructionists can develop their analyses. As shown in this section, 'Death and furniture' engender constructionist research that is relevant as academic critique as well as for developing institutional practice. In the last section of the chapter I will suggest that this double function of critique and contribution in DP is one of its most significant features. Revisiting 'Death and furniture' can allow DP researchers to pursue this work in a reflexive, cumulative program.

May the realist-relativist debate rest in peace? The future of death and furniture

In today's scientific discussions, researchers in DP are rarely seen as fools denying reality or as indifferent to the lives of other people.[2] The value of analyses of social practices in institutional and everyday settings is beginning to sink in. No doubt, work that carries on the legacy of the 'Death and furniture' paper by showing the applicability of DP (Hepburn and Wiggins 2007, cf. Antaki 2011, Stokoe, Hepburn and Antaki 2012) has a key role in this change. DP has moved from the early years of being "the new kid in town" to a more mature status where epistemological and ontological discussions no longer need to occupy the main part of academic presentations.

Does this mean that DP has advanced from the status of revolutionary science to normal science in the sense that Kuhn (1970) suggested is typical of scientific development? And is such consensus a desirable state? Should discursive psychologists focus on developing analytic techniques and solving puzzles internal to its own academic practices instead of social problems (cf. Kuhn 1970)? I think that DP researchers would say no. Social science, according to the epistemological philosophy that Edwards et al. (1995) outlined, is characterized by the co-existence of a number of incommensurable theories rather than by an all-inclusive paradigm (cf. Feyerabend 1970). Simply solving puzzles is not an option in an environment where there are multiple claims to what social science should do.

So is DP, on the other extreme, "just" a program of respecification? A recent discussion is whether DP is (and should be) limited to being a nail in the eye of approaches that adopt a referential theory of meaning. Kitzinger (2006: 68) suggests that DP fails to develop a "rigorous cumulative research programme of empirical findings on its own terms" because it is tied up generating "always only another demonstration that cognitions are produced and made relevant in talk." According to such critique, the aim of showing that psychological issues are best understood as social actions severely constrains DP's appeal to broader projects. Kitzinger's point is thus that DP does not, albeit being important to renew the discipline of psychology, offer an accumulative understanding of social organization.

Drawing on Edwards et al. (1995), such critique can be responded to with two remarks. One is that DP's demonstrating that psychology rests on problematic assumptions does not exclude a cumulative research program (just like a relativist stance does not imply inaction). The other is that DP's critique against cognitive psychology is not limited to psychology as an academic discipline; realist psychology is at the heart of our understanding of what it means to be a person both in everyday life and in a number of other academic disciplines, such as literature, history, economy, and sometimes sociology.

That the first point is valid can be seen in how classic DP papers are referred to and developed in more recent work. For instance, Edward's (1999) seminal work on how people describe and invoke emotion in everyday discourse has been advanced in studies of emotional displays, such as crying (Hepburn 2004). Such research does not merely carry on the project of respecifying psychology; it builds on and develops prior studies while showing the rhetorical work done by psychological claims. The renewed interest for affiliation with subjective stance within the kindred approach of conversation analysis (CA) is an indication of the second point. Studying how people manage subjective stance in interaction, whether affective or epistemic, has been an essential part of DP from the beginning (e.g. Edwards 1995, 2005, 2007). In this sense, DP has developed the suggestion in CA that it is as knowing and feeling subjects people are invited to participate in interaction (Pomerantz 1984). A focus on respecification and reflexivity, on the one hand, and on how psychological matters are used to accomplish things, on the other, is thus not a limiting feature but something that all studies of social practice can benefit from. By explicitly embracing the linkage of these two projects, DP researchers may fuel the discussion that Edward's et al. (1995) started and increase DP's value for the development of social science.

The 'Death and furniture' paper continues to provide a philosophical base for criticizing realist accounts, and perhaps also more than that. It shows that subjective and objective reality can never be accepted as constituting bottom line arguments. Treating them as absolute, independently existing entities is proof of realists hitting ontological rock bottom, desperately thumping on tables, throwing rocks, and raving about theirs and others' mortality. But the DP project of showing the shortage of such arguments is not rhetoric swagger. Far from just being dismissed as "another case of realism", referential claims about meaning are criticized because they often justify problematic practices. The recuperation of 'Death and furniture' is both an impetus for engaging in empirical cumulative research of social practice and a reminder that scientific activity is always itself a social activity.

Notes

1 Furthermore, referring to truth as a means for justifying terror is a well-known rhetoric; for instance, the web journal of the Swedish Nazi Party (Svenskarnas parti) is entitled "The Realist" (realisten.se).
2 Death and Furniture arguments still occur (see Corcoran 2009) but are efficiently rebutted (Potter 2010).

References

Antaki, C. (ed.) (2011) *Applied conversation analysis. Intervention and change in institutional talk*. New York: Palgrave Macmillan.
Ashmore, M. (1989) *The reflexive thesis*. Chicago: The University of Chicago Press.
Augoustinos, M., Walker, I., and Donaghue, N. (2014) *Social cognition: An integrated introduction* (third edn). London: Sage.
Barnes, B. (1992) "Realism, relativism and finitism," in D. Raven, L. van Vucht Tiessen, and J. de Wolf (eds) *Cognitive realism and social science* (pp. 131–47). New Brunswick, NJ: Transaction Publishers.
Becker, H.S. (1998) *Tricks of the trade: How to think about your research while you're doing it*. Chicago: University of Chicago Press.
Burr, V. (2003) *Social constructionism* (second edn). New York: Routledge.
Collins, H.M. (1990) *Artificial experts: Social knowledge and intelligent machines*. Cambridge: MIT Press.
Corcoran, T. (2009) "Second nature", *British Journal of Social Psychology*, 48: 375–88.
Drew, P. (1992) "Contested evidence in courtroom cross-examination: The case of a trial for rape," in P. Drew and J. Heritage (eds) *Talk at work: Interaction in institutional settings* (pp. 470–520). Cambridge: Cambridge University Press.
Drew, P. and Holt, E. (1988) "Complainable matters: The use of idiomatic expressions in making complaints," *Social Problems*, 35: 398–417.
Edley, N. (2001) "Unravelling social constructionism," *Theory and Psychology*, 11: 433–41.
Edwards, D. (1995) "Two to tango: Script formulations, dispositions and rhetorical symmetry in relationship troubles talk," *Research on Language and Social Interaction*, 28: 319–50.
Edwards, D. (1997) *Discourse and cognition*. London: Sage.
Edwards, D. (1999) "Emotion discourse," *Psychology and Culture*, 5: 271–91.
Edwards, D. (2005) "Moaning, whinging and laughing: The subjective side of complaints," *Discourse Studies*, 7: 5–29.
Edwards, D. (2007) "Managing subjectivity in talk," in A. Hepburn and S. Wiggins (eds), *Discursive research in practice: New approaches to psychology and interaction* (pp. 31–49). Cambridge: Cambridge University Press.
Edwards, D. (2008) "Intentionality and mens rea in police interrogations: The production of actions as crimes," *Intercultural Pragmatics*, 5: 177–99.
Edwards, D., Ashmore, M., and Potter, J. (1995) "Death and furniture: The rhetoric, politics and theology of bottom line arguments against relativism," *History of the Human Sciences*, 8: 25–49.
Feyerabend, P. (1970) "Consolations for the specialist," in I. Lakatos and A. Musgrave (eds) *Criticism and the growth of knowledge* (pp. 196–230). Cambridge: Cambridge University Press.

Feyerabend, P. (1975) *Against method*. London: New Left Books.
Gergen, K.J. (2001a) "Construction in contention: Toward consequential resolutions," *Theory and Psychology*, *11*: 419–32.
Gergen, K.J. (2001b) "Psychological science in a postmodern context," *American Psychologist*, *56*: 803–13.
Gilbert, G.N. and Mulkay, M. (1984) *Opening Pandora's box: A sociological analysis of scientists' discourse*. Cambridge: Cambridge University Press.
Gill, R. (1995) "Relativism, reflexivity and politics: Interrogating discourse analysis from a feminist perspective," in S. Wilkinson and C. Kitzinger (eds) *Feminism and discourse: Psychological perspectives* (pp. 165–86). London: Sage.
Goffman, E. (1981) *Forms of talk*. Oxford: Basil Blackwell.
Hepburn, A. (1997) "Teachers and secondary school bullying: A postmodern discourse analysis," *Discourse and Society*, *8*(1): 27–48.
Hepburn, A. (2000) "On the alleged incompatibility between relativism and feminist psychology," *Feminism and Psychology*, *10*: 91–106.
Hepburn, A. (2004) "Crying: Notes on description, transcription, and interaction," *Research on Language and Social Interaction*, *37*: 251–90.
Hepburn, A. and Wiggins, S. (eds) (2007) *Discursive research in practice: New approaches to psychology and interaction*. Cambridge: Cambridge University Press.
Horton-Salway, M. (2001) "Narrative identities and the management of personal accountability in talk about ME: A DP approach to illness narrative," *Journal of Health Psychology*, *6*: 247–59.
Iversen, C. (2013) *Making questions and answers work: Negotiating participation in interview interaction*. Uppsala: Acta Universitatis Upsaliensis.
Jørgensen, M.W. and Phillips, L. (2002) *Discourse analysis as theory and method*. London: Sage.
Keevallik, L. (2011) "The terms of not knowing," in T. Stivers, L. Mondada, and J. Steensig (eds) *The morality of knowledge in conversation* (pp. 184–206). Cambridge: Cambridge University Press.
Kitzinger, C. (2006) "After post-cognitivism," *Discourse Studies*, *8*: 67–83.
Kuhn, T.S. (1970) "Logic of discovery or psychology of research?," in I. Lakatos and A. Musgrave (eds) *Criticism and the growth of knowledge* (pp. 1–23). Cambridge: Cambridge University Press.
Latour, B. (1987) *Science in action: How to follow scientists and engineers through society*. Cambridge: Harvard University Press.
Latour, B. and Woolgar, S. (1986) *Laboratory life: The construction of scientific facts*. Princeton: Princeton University Press.
McMartin, C. (1999) "Disclosure as discourse: Theorizing children's reports of sexual abuse," *Theory and Psychology*, *9*: 503–32.
Merton, R.K. (1938) "Science and the social order," *Philosophy of Science*, *5*: 321–37.
Merton, R.K. (1972) "Insiders and outsiders: A chapter in the sociology of knowledge," *The American Journal of Sociology*, *78*: 9–47.
Mulkay, M. (1991) *Sociology of science: A sociological pilgrimage*. Milton Keynes: Open University Press.
Nightingale, D.J. and Cromby, J. (1999) *Social constructionist psychology: A critical analysis of theory and practice*. Buckingham: Open University Press.
O'Neill, J. (1995) "'I gotta use words when I talk to you': A response to Death and Furniture," *History of the Human Sciences*, *8*: 99–106.

Parker, I. (1999) "Against relativism in psychology, on balance," *History of the Human Sciences*, *12*: 61–78.

Parker, I. and Burman, E. (1993) "Against discursive imperialism, empiricism and constructionism: Thirty-two problems with discourse analysis," in E. Burman and I. Parker (eds) *Discourse analytic readings: Repertoires and readings of texts in action* (pp. 155–72). London: Routledge.

Pomerantz, A. (1984) "Agreeing and disagreeing with assessments: Some features of preferred/dispreferred turn shapes," in J.M. Atkinson and J. Heritage (eds) *Structures of social action: Studies in conversation analysis* (pp. 57–101). Cambridge: Cambridge University Press.

Potter, J. (1998) "Fragments in the realization of relativism," in I. Parker (ed.) *Inquiries in social construction: Social construction, discourse and realism* (pp. 27–47). London: Sage.

Potter, J. (2010) "Contemporary DP: Issues, prospects, and Corcoran's awkward ontology," *British Journal of Social Psychology*, *49*: 657–78.

Rorty, R. (1985) "Solidarity or objectivity?," in J. Rajchman and C. West (eds) *Post-analytic philosophy* (pp. 3–19). New York: Columbia University Press.

Smith, B.H. (1988) *Contingencies of value: Alternative perspectives for critical theory*. Cambridge: Harvard University Press.

Speer, S.A. (2000) "Let's get real? Feminism, constructionism and the realism/relativism debate," *Feminism and Psychology*, *10*: 519–30.

Stokoe, E., Hepburn, A., and Antaki, C. (2012) "Beware of the 'Loughborough School' of social psychology? Interaction and the politics of intervention," *British Journal of Social Psychology*, *51*: 486–96.

Tileagă, C. (2006) "Discourse, dominance, and power relations: Inequality as a social and interactional object," *Ethnicities*, *6*: 476–97.

3 Conversation analysis and discursive psychology
Taking up the challenge of Sacks' legacy

Alexandra Kent

Target article: Edwards, D. (1995) 'Sacks and psychology', *Theory & Psychology*, 5: 579–96.

The Edwards (1995) review essay 'Sacks and Psychology' discussed the implications for psychology that he saw as arising from the definitive two-volume 1992 set of Harvey Sacks' *Lectures on Conversation*. Edwards (1995) highlighted how Sacks' approach to the study of social life (and language in particular) addressed key topics for psychology. In this chapter I examine how discursive psychologists have taken up Edwards' challenge to apply Sacks' foundational work in conversation analysis to topics of traditional psychological enquiry. I will revisit some of the topics addressed by Edwards and consider how the epistemological and methodological approach of conversation analysis has contributed to the development of discursive psychology as a discipline. I will conclude by considering what challenges discursive psychologists face when using conversation analysis for their research and how the two fields might engage with and inform each other moving forwards.

Between 1964 and 1972 Harvey Sacks routinely recorded the lectures he gave at the UCLA and Irvine campuses of the University of California. Some have subsequently appeared in publications (e.g., Sacks, 1975, 1978, 1979, 1980, 1984, 1985, 1987). However, in 1992, his *Lectures on Conversation* were made publicly available for the first time in a two-volume set edited by Gail Jefferson and introduced by Emmanuel Schegloff.

Edwards (1995) published an essay in *Theory and Psychology* reviewing Sacks' *Lectures on Conversation*. A review essay might seem like an unusual choice of paper to include in this collection of classic discursive psychology (DP) papers, but Edwards did far more than just review the lectures. Although Sacks addressed the bulk of his work to the social sciences, and sociology in particular, many of the core topics covered in his lectures speak to some of psychology's central interests. Edwards (1995) aimed to make explicit the implications of Sacks' work for psychology and demonstrate how work in discursive psychology could profitably build on Sacks' foundation. He states 'any analysis of how conversational interaction works has an immediate relevance for *social* psychology, and might be considered, without further comment, *as* social psychology' (Edwards, 1995: 580, emphasis in original). This provocative claim is one that discursive psychologists have been consistently arguing and presenting evidence for in the twenty years since Edwards (1995) published his review of Sacks' (1992) two-volume set of *Lectures on Conversation*.

Since Edwards wrote his review, both conversation analysis and discursive psychology have flourished and developed as scholarly fields of inquiry. Perhaps it is now worth pausing to take stock and reflect on the role conversation analysis has played in the development of DP as a discipline, and how the two fields might continue to influence each other moving forwards. How have discursive psychologists responded to the legacy left by Harvey Sacks?

CA's influences on DP

There can be no doubt that methodologically DP has been 'profoundly influenced by conversation analysis' (Potter, 2006: 132). Contemporary discursive psychology is 'keen to borrow CA methods where it can' (Antaki, 2004: 670). DP publications are increasingly drawing on conversation analytic literature to support their claims and provide methodological rigour to their analyses. Here I wish to highlight three key features of conversation analysis originating in Sacks' lectures that make it particularly useful (and consequentially influential) for discursive psychologists.

Formulating research questions

Sacks' Lecture 30 (Spring 1966) is mostly comprised of a Q&A session with his students. In answer to one student's question about whether an analyst can go looking for something in a conversation such as 'how attitudes to authority develop', Sacks (1992: 471) delivered a now-familiar rule that analysts should 'pose those problems that the data bears' rather than approaching the data with pre-conceived ideas about what one might find. This was a radical suggestion that ran contrary to the prevailing practices in Sacks' home discipline of sociology. Sacks encouraged his students to reframe traditional research questions in interactional terms. In fact he abandoned the concept of a predefined research question on the grounds that it brought analytic concepts and frameworks into the analysis that were not grounded in the participants' concerns.

True to Sacks' vision, both conversation analysis and discursive psychology are data-driven approaches to research. That is to say a researcher ideally begins with (naturally-occurring) data and generates the analysis in a 'bottom-up' approach in which the data determines the direction of the analysis rather than beginning with theory and testing the data from the top-down to see how well it fits theory-driven expectations.

Naturally occurring data

Sacks' use of naturally occurring data has become a defining characteristic for both CA and DP. Rather than assuming in advance what would be important and designing his research to generate that data,

> Sacks' move ... was to focus empirically on the specifics of his data; the data being whatever conversations and texts that he found in everyday and institutional settings, anywhere except his own interventions to make them happen.
>
> (Edwards, 1995: 593)

The specifics of the data for Sacks included an appreciation of pervasiveness of social order 'at all points' (Lecture 33: 484). The task then became to discover and describe how normal everyday interaction operates.

Out of Sacks' early insights grew the principle of studying naturally occurring data, or at least treating the interaction as a social event unavoidably shaped by and for the context in which it occurs. Contemporary conversation analysis almost exclusively focuses (as the name suggests) on conversational interaction. However, as Edwards (1995: 583) comments, much of Sacks' early work dealt with 'textual materials drawn from a variety of sources, including some brilliant analyses of extracts from the Old Testament'. For discursive psychologists what matters is that the situated nature of the text or talk is preserved and recognised in the analysis. For example, Potter and Hepburn (2008: 276) state when DP does work with open-ended interviews, they 'will be treated as interactional events rather than as places where participants' views can be excavated'. On the situated nature of interviews see Puchta and Potter (2002), Widdicombe and Wooffitt (1995), Potter and Hepburn (2012), Alby and Fatigante, (2014); see also Chapter 5 in this volume.

DP's interactionally grounded critique of the use of open-ended interviews as a research method marks an important milestone in the development of the discipline. Whereas conversation analysis used naturalistic data from the outset, discursive psychology emerged out of, and distinguished itself from, its earlier incarnation of discourse analysis by almost completely abandoning open-ended interviews as a research method (Hepburn and Wiggins, 2007).

Participants' orientations

In addition to advocating the use of naturally occurring data and refraining from imposing analyst-driven questions, Sacks (1992, Lecture 8, Spring 1966) sets out the importance of considering participants' orientations within any analysis. For Schegloff (2007a: 476) this is a vital component of a robust analysis: 'there must be analysis to show the claim is grounded in the conduct of the parties, not in the beliefs of the writer'. Otherwise interpretive glosses and common-sense assumptions originating with the analyst rather than the participants can creep unexamined into the analysis and get reproduced in the conclusions.

For any interactionally grounded analysis, including DP, 'the key issue is not abstract descriptive adequacy, but practical relevance to the interactional business at hand' (Hepburn and Wiggins, 2007: 4).

Contemporary DP has embraced the importance of demonstrating the interactional relevance of a given object of analysis and grounding it in the moment-by-moment orientations of the participants. In preserving the primacy of the participants' understandings of the interaction rather than imposing or importing preconceived theoretical constructs and subjective interpretations by the analyst, both CA and DP have succeeded in minimising the 'interpretive gap' between the research conclusions and the raw data on which they are based. Edwards (2012: 428) defines the interpretive gap as 'the distance between the object under scrutiny and, via method, data processing, and inferences, what you eventually want to say about it'. In the case of Hepburn and Potter's (2011) conversation analytically informed DP analysis of threats they were able to outline the basic structure of threats (and distinguish them from warnings and admonishments). They considered the response options made available by a threat (and how participants might evade standard response options). Finally, they discussed the implications of their analysis for social psychological discussion of power, resistance and asymmetry. This is an important example of how CA's methodological rigour pays dividends for discursive psychologists, particularly when critiquing and re-specifying traditional psychology.

Despite working with the same types of data (naturally occurring interactions) and having a data-driven approach to analysis that is grounded in the participants' orientations, CA and DP researchers have generated distinct bodies of work. Within CA the most sustained attention lies in its consideration of the structural organisation of talk-in-interaction. This has generated an impressive volume of empirical findings resulting in our current understanding of turn taking (Sacks, Schegloff and Jefferson, 1974); sequence organisation (Schegloff, 1968, 1972, 2007b); repair (Schegloff, Jefferson and Sacks, 1977) and so on. The programme of work advanced by conversation analysts over the past fifty years can now be characterised as 'composing a body of theorizing about the organization of interaction' (Schegloff, 2005: 456).

In contrast, 'DP has tended to focus on participants' formulations and categories, and had picked up on issues of turn organisation and sequential placements in a less thoroughgoing way' (Hepburn and Wiggins, 2007). In part this interest was certainly inspired by Sacks, for whom a key focus lay in the situated selection of categorical person references. Although Sacks' work on membership categorisation has not remained a central concern for CA, it has important implications for discursive psychology (these are addressed in detail in Part 3 of this volume). Edwards (1995: 583) highlights several works, now considered to be forerunners of modern discursive psychology that resonate with and have been influenced by Sacks' work on the construction and deployment of membership categories (e.g., Billig, 1987; Edwards, 1991; Edwards and Potter, 1992a, 1993; Potter and Wetherell, 1987; Widdicombe and Wooffitt, 1990).

Discursive psychologists have maintained a clear interest in the interactional relevance of descriptions, evaluations and categories in interaction. Such work continues to demonstrate the importance of situating descriptions and evaluations in their local context as social actions rather than assuming a priori that they unproblematically reflect an internal mental state. Importantly, contemporary DP work has built on CA findings to develop the sequential underpinning of the analyses of the situated and rhetorical purposes for which descriptions are designed and produced. A good example of the outcome of the increasing methodological synergy between CA and DP is Sally Wiggins' work on assessments and evaluations of food during mealtime conversations (Wiggins, 2001, 2002, 2004; Wiggins and Potter, 2003). In this way discursive psychologists have capitalised on the weight of empirical findings obtained using conversation analytic methods to advance their own research interests.

Both CA and DP commit to using naturalistic data, begining the analysis with data rather than theory, and prioritising participants' orientations. Despite this, their respective literatures published over the past twenty-five years demonstrate that shared methodological principles are insufficient to capture and determine the unique interests and contributions to knowledge from the two approaches. For discursive psychologists, Edwards (1995: 594) proposes that 'the solution is to ask a different question, but still recognisably a psychological one, and, moreover, one that the data bears'. That is to say, to borrow the methodological approach from CA without abandoning a core interest in psychological matters.

DP and psychology

Initially 'the political impulse of . . . discursive work was to question psychology' (Parker, 2012: 472) and was primarily addressed as a critique of traditional research within psychology on topics such as attitudes, memory and cognition. The general goal was to reframe the terms of the debate within psychology and shift the research emphasis from what talk refers to (for instance, a mental state, emotion, belief, memory), to what talk does (the discursive practices through which such referents are invoked). However, contemporary DP has gone far beyond this original aspiration and 'is a programme of work that can, and these days largely does, go on with little or no reference to, nor critical engagement with, other kinds of psychology' (Edwards, 2012: 427).

Contemporary DP remains well positioned to engage with psychology, providing a distinct theoretical voice with a strong empirical base in which to substantiate its claims. A key insight from Sacks' lectures is that 'social life is organised so that people can take part in it, and learn to take part in it, via its publicly displayed nature'(Edwards, 1995: 589). As such DP is well placed to contribute to our understanding of socialisation processes and (drawing once again on insights from CA) is beginning to generate a growing body of empirical work. A developmental discursive psychology would entail, the study of how children come to be competent users of public forms of accountability – how they learn to talk and act in recognizable and accountable ways, which is to say, in ways describable and explicable as persons within some social order

(Edwards and Stokoe, 2004: 500)

Work by Wootton (1997) and Forrester (2002, Forrester and Reason, 2006; Forrester and Cherington, 2009) has demonstrated the importance of considering the issue of competent membership as a contingent and negotiable affair dependent on the moment-by-moment organization of talk. Increasingly, discursive psychologists are able to contribute to developmental psychology and offer descriptions of concrete practices through which we might observe the situated performance of abstract processes such as socialisation. For example, Sterponi (2009) examined socialisation practices and moral accountability during family conversations. She identified a practice used by parents for vicarious accounting 'namely accounts, or explanations, provided by parents *for* a child's misbehavior' (2009: 441). Vicarious accounts could be used to support children in learning social acceptable practices for providing accounts. Recurrently the parent's vicarious accounts 'set up constraints on children's autonomy of action, neutralizing more subversive and blameworthy interpretations of their problematic conduct' (Sterponi, 2009: 441).

Certainly, since Edwards' (1995) review of Sacks' lecture was published, discursive psychology has undeniably moved methodologically closer to CA. (e.g., Edwards, 1995, 1997, 2000; Potter, 1997; Potter and Hepburn, 2003; Wiggins and Potter, 2003). Yet, at the same time (as this very volume shows), it has sought and developed a dialogue with approaches seeped in rhetorical, textual and ideological approaches (e.g., Augoustinos and de Garis, 2012; Tileagă, 2011) that advocate a more cautious relationship with conversation analysis (Wetherell, 1998; Billig, 1999a, b). For a contemporary exegesis of debates around DP and CA see Chapter 1 in this book.

DP's particularism

While DP researchers may increasingly be choosing to capitalise on the empirical rigour of conversation analysis, they have by no means relinquished DP's own particular theoretical and epistemological background.

Constructionism

DP's interest in categories reflects its constructivist epistemology in that 'category description of persons, things or events are always ones that could have been otherwise, such that actually occurring descriptions are always contingent, particular and occasioned phenomena' (Edwards, 1995: 580–1). As a consequence it highlights the situated nature of talk; a core analytic interest for discursive psychologists (Potter, 2005).

Almost all introductions to DP will emphasise its interest in the 'constructed and constructive' character of discourse (Kent and Potter, 2014: 295). DP's approach to constructionism emerged through its engagement with the sociology of scientific knowledge (e.g., Gilbert and Mulkay, 1984) and within the broader discourse analytic tradition within social psychology (e.g., Potter and Wetherell, 1987). The particular variant of constructionism advocated by discursive psychologists (outlined by Potter and Hepburn, 2008) is significant for is emphasis on performance rather than perception. This can be contrasted, for example, with the sense of linguistic constructionism associated with Benjamin Whorf (1956) in which 'linguistic categories constructed the *perceptual* world for language users in a speech community' (Potter and Hepburn, 2008: 278).

The 'foregrounding of construction as an issue' is one of the ways in which DP can be distinguished from CA as a separate intellectual endeavour (Potter and Hepburn, 2008: 276). DP researchers place a greater emphasis than CA researchers on understanding how participants produce, sustain and contest their social realities through discourse. This is particularly evident in the strands of discursive psychology that explore the ways in which interaction constructs broader cultural tropes (such as morality, ideology and prejudice). Part 4 of this book offers several examples of this kind of work.

The constructionist agenda of discursive psychology dictates its interest in how psychological and societal concepts such as ideology, morality, memory and emotion are produced through language. Engagement with Sacks' work and conversation analysis in particular has focused discursive psychologists' ability to make empirical claims about the actual practices through which accounts, evaluations and descriptions are produced in interaction and the purposes to which they are employed in situ (e.g., Tileagă's 2005, 2010 work on moral accounting and prejudice). Although CA's primary focus does not concern constructionist epistemological issues in the way that DP's particular agenda does, it can nonetheless be used methodologically in the service of some constructionist projects.

Anti-cognitivism

When discussing the influence of Sacks work on contemporary DP it is without doubt necessary to consider that 'probably the most salient characteristic of DP, at least at we practice it, [is] that it rejects the cognitivist assumption that minds are revealed or expressed in what people say' (Edwards and Potter, 2005: 245). This position motivated early DP work such as Edwards' (1994, 1995, 1999) work on script formulations, dispositions and emotion talk and Edwards and Potter's (1992b) work on discursive remembering. It continues to exert a profound influence over contemporary DP studies.

DP focuses on the practical ways in which people deal with each others in terms of their 'desires, motives, institutional allegiances, and so on' (Potter, Edwards and Wetherell, 1993: 392). Instead of viewing bits of mental apparatus (e.g., motives) as ways of explaining social action, DP advocates an entirely different starting position for research; one in which the invocation of a purported mental states is treated as a topic for analysis in its own right to help explicate the social practice in which it is embedded. For example, Antaki and Horowitz (2000: 170) demonstrate that by invoking someone's motives by describing someone as having 'a personal stake in the matter, an interested party' you can undermine their position and effectively disqualify them from commentary on the topic under discussion.

Sacks' comments during his lectures indicate his view that the analysis of interaction could (in fact should) begin with performance rather than cognition. In Lecture 1 (1992: 11) he suggested that analysts need not be concerned with how fast people think or whether they are thinking at all, 'just try to come to terms with how it is that the thing comes off'. This leads to the position that it is possible, indeed desirable, to study social action through people's talk without requiring reference to their internal mental states.

Edwards (1995) was keen to highlight the potential for a radically different understanding of the relationship between cognition and behaviour based on Sacks' insights. Sacks' work offered a profoundly new basis of assumption, that 'the orderliness of social life and its intelligibility stem not from a set of updated knowledge structures in a sense-making cognitive being, but from how social actions flexibly unfold as situated performances' (Edwards, 1995: 590).

DP's early work on cognitive phenomena have been profitably developed and enhanced through insights from conversation analysis. For example, Barnes and Moss (2007) analysed reports of 'private thoughts' (RPTs) across a range of interactional environments. They describe RPTs as 'objects people use in doing social life to communicate a thought or a feeling, specifically when speaker-feelers want to characterize "how it appeared to me then" for an overhearing audience or in appeals to shared experience' (Barnes and Moss, 2007: 141). They demonstrated that RPTs cannot be dismissed as a straightforward representation of what was actually thought or felt. They illustrated that through precisely co-ordinated moves in interaction, participants could use reports of their private thoughts or feeling as a tool for doing intersubjectivity work (Drew, 2003).

Similarly, in her analysis of 'I don't know' Weatherall (2011: 317) drew on CA's technical understanding of turn-construction units, pre-sequences and progressivity to demonstrate that instead of just reporting a cognitive absence of knowledge, '*I don't know*s function as a prepositioned hedge – a forward-looking stance marker displaying that the speaker is not fully committed to what follows in their turn of talk.' In this respect it is clear to see the analytic advantage for discursive psychologists to be gained by harnessing the empirical apparatus of conversation analysis in their research. It enables them to go beyond the now well-documented observations that talk is action and cannot be treated as a neutral reflection of the speaker's internal world. CA provides a technical language to describe the nature of the action being performed by referring to cognitive phenomena such as thoughts, feelings and memories.

Although less explicitly concerned with cognitive matters, CA's methodological apparatus (specifically its requirement to ground analytic claims in the interactional relevance of the action for the participants) means that it has also tended to produce non-cognitive accounts of social action. Its focus on matters of sequential organisation has traditionally meant it has not focused extensively on what Potter (2005: 743) calls 'issues of mind'. However, recently that has begun to change.

An emerging strand of conversation analytic work investigates 'the social organization of cognitive displays and embodiments' (Kitzinger, 2006: 67). This line of work has begun to suggest that an analysis of the sequential organisation of talk can reveal whether cognitive shifts have actually occurred in the mind of the speaker or whether they were being employed for rhetorical purposes (Golato, 2010; Heritage, 2005; Maynard, 2003). For discursive psychologists, this move is seen as an attempt to link interactional phenomena to underlying cognitive states rather than investigating them on their own terms (Potter, 2005) and has generated some tension between the approaches (e.g., Drew, 2005; Potter, 2006; Kitzinger, 2006).

Sacks' (1992: 11) concluded his first lecture by telling his students 'don't worry about whether they're 'thinking'.' That is to say he suggested that an analysis of how people do what they do is sufficient in its own terms without recourse to an invisible set of abstract cognitive concepts. Much of the methodological rigour and empirical robustness of conversation analysis rests on its very tight focus on the demonstrable interactional relevance of target phenomena and the minimal interpretive gap between the data and the analytic claims being made (Edwards, 2012). Sacks' tenets to use naturalistic data, privilege participants' orientations and ask the questions that the data bears rather than imposing preconceived analyst understandings set the bar high for those attempting to analyse interaction, but they provide a deep integrity to the analysis that has stood the test of time (Schegloff, 2005). DP has taken Sacks' insights into a systematic programme of work that cautions researchers against the seductive nature of cognitive explanations for behaviour, and against inadvertently 'imposing cognitivist assumptions on conversational materials' (Potter, 2006: 131).

Summary

In his review, Edwards (1995) clearly identified strong points of contact between Sacks' work and the emerging fields of discursive psychology and conversation analysis. Here I have attempted to sketch out some of the ways in which Sacks' insights have contributed to the landscape of contemporary discursive psychology and influenced its relationship with conversation analysis. In the first section I outlined three key tenets of conversation analysis to emerge from Sacks' work. Each of these has exerted a powerful influence on the shape of contemporary discursive psychology.

Pose the questions that the data bears

Sacks advocated a radical approach to research that dispensed with the traditional research question and instead started with close description of the data. On one level this prescription requires the analysis to adopt a data-driven approach to analysis, something that both CA and DP typically do. However, DP is also motivated by epistemological and disciplinary concerns that influence the sorts of data analysts are likely to seek out. For DP the topical interest in psychological matters, a commitment to CA's methodological principles and a foregrounding of constructionist concerns combine to produce a modified version of Sacks' approach that, while still driven by data, focuses the analysis on interactional phenomena that reveal how participants orient to, produce and contest psychological resources.

Use naturalistic data

Unlike conversation analysis, discursive psychology did not originally work with naturalistic materials but adopted them as a result of engaging with conversation analytic work. The switch towards relying on naturally occurring data provided discursive psychology with a way of clearly distinguishing its work from that of other discourse analytic traditions through a sustained critique of the research interview as a data collection tool. It helps to establish DP as an independent programme of work, though closely allied to conversation analysis.

Privilege participants' orientations

CA's foregrounding of participants' concerns and the requirement to demonstrate the interactional relevance for participants of any analytic claim is the cornerstone of its methodological rigour and empirical power. It is what has enabled CA to generate an extensive and robust body of empirical evidence for the orderliness and organisation of social interaction. This body of work has been very profitably utilised by discursive psychologists to support their own analyses, but more importantly has inspired discursive psychologists to be as rigorous in their own analysis and more closely anchor their analytic claims in members' interactional concerns.

Some very notable contemporary strands of DP draw heavily on CA methods, but, as a field, DP is much more varied. Not all strands of discursive psychology embrace conversation analytic principles – they are more concerned with the relationship between discourse and broad sociocultural themes. Arguably, the limitations of a conversation analytic methodology in fact make it harder to study the discursive construction of some of the central phenomena of interest to DP (e.g., stereotypes, ideological frameworks, social identity).

I would suggest that contemporary DP studies have shown that, although CA demands a very locally situated analysis and sets high standards for empirical soundness, greater dividends are possible by grounding broader cultural themes in members' orientations within the interaction. With care, and where the data can bear such an analysis, it is possible to not only locate sociocultural concepts (e.g., sexism) in interaction but also explicate the concrete practices through which they are perpetuated (e.g., Speer, 2001, 2002). Once the practices have been identified, researchers are then uniquely able to work with participants (most notably practitioners within institutions) to apply the findings directly to the real world settings from which they were derived (e.g., Stokoe, 2014).

Despite adopting many of Sacks' principles, DP's particular stance remains staunchly constructionist and adamantly anti-cognitivist. In this respect it is at odds with conversation analysis, which has a far less explicit epistemological position *vis a vis* cognition and social constructionism. Recent moves by conversation analysts to try to find evidence for cognitions in interaction are troubling for DP and have provoked tensions (e.g., Drew, 2005; Potter, 2006; Kitzinger, 2006). Specifically, DP has criticised CA for importing cognitivist assumptions and imposing them on the data and failing to sufficiently privilege participants' orientations to the interactions relevance of their interlocutors' actions. CA researchers might adopt a more explicit epistemological position regarding cognition and might profitably borrow from DP in much the same way as DP has evolved to take advantage of the methodological power of CA.

In conclusion, the robust and compelling empirical findings generated through conversation analytic work can be used to substantiate discursive constructionist analyses of interaction. In this sense CA represents a powerful tool for discursive psychologists and has substantially influenced the development of the field. However, one can still identify epistemological tensions, as well as affinities, between the two approaches. With their shared interest in the performative role of language, CA and DP can continue their dialogue and cross-fertilisation by focusing the lens of their analytic microscopes on different interactional phenomena and by posing different questions for their data to bear.

References

Alby, F. and Fatigante, M. (2014) 'Preserving the respondent's standpoint in a research interview: Different strategies of "doing" the Interviewer', *Human Studies*, 37: 239–56.
Antaki, C. (2004) 'Reading minds or dealing with interactional implications?' *Theory & Psychology*, 14: 667–83.
Antaki, C. and Horowitz, A. (2000) 'Using identity ascription to disqualify a rival version of events as "interested"', *Research on Language & Social Interaction*, 33: 155–77.
Augoustinos, A. and de Garis, S. (2012) '"Too black or not black enough": Social identity complexity in the political rhetoric of Barack Obama', *European Journal of Social Psychology*, 42: 564–77.
Barnes, R. and Moss, D. (2007) 'Communicating a feeling: The social organization of "private thoughts"', *Discourse Studies*, 9: 123–48.
Billig, M. (1987) *Arguing and thinking*. Cambridge: Cambridge University Press.
Billig, M. (1999a) 'Whose terms? Whose ordinariness? Rhetoric and ideology in conversation analysis', *Discourse & Society*, 10: 543–58.

Billig, M. (1999b) 'Conversation analysis and the claims of naivety', *Discourse & Society*, 10: 572–76.

Drew, P. (2003) 'Precision and exaggeration in interaction', *American Sociological Review*, 68: 917–38.

Drew, P. (2005) 'Is confusion a state of mind?', in H. te Molder and J. Potter (eds) *Conversation and cognition* (pp. 161–83). Cambridge: Cambridge University Press.

Edwards, D. (1991) 'Categories are for talking: On the cognitive and discursive bases of categorization', *Theory & Psychology*, 1: 515–42.

Edwards, D. (1994) 'Script formulations: A study of event descriptions in conversation', *Journal of Language & Social Psychology*, 13: 211–47.

Edwards, D. (1995) 'Sacks and psychology', *Theory & Psychology*, 5: 579–97.

Edwards, D. (1997) *Discourse and cognition*. London: Sage.

Edwards, D. (1999) 'Emotion discourse', *Culture & Psychology*, 5: 271–91.

Edwards, D. (2000) 'Extreme case formulations: Softeners, investment, and doing nonliteral', *Research on Language and Social Interaction*, 33: 347–73.

Edwards, D. (2012) 'Discursive and scientific psychology', *British Journal of Social Psychology*, 51: 425–35.

Edwards, D. and Potter, J. (1992a) *Discursive psychology*. Sage: London.

Edwards, D. and Potter, J (1992b) 'The Chancellor's memory: Rhetoric and truth in discursive remembering', *Applied Cognitive Psychology*, 6: 187–215.

Edwards, D. and Potter, J. (1993) 'Language and causation: A discursive action model of description and attribution', *Psychological Review*, 100: 23–41.

Edwards, D. and Potter, J. (2005) 'Discursive psychology, mental states, and descriptions', in H. te Molder and J. Potter (eds) *Conversation and cognition* (pp. 241–59). Cambridge: Cambridge University Press.

Edwards, D. and Stokoe, E. (2004) 'Discursive psychology, focus group interviews and participants' categories', *British Journal of Developmental Psychology*, 22: 499–507.

Forrester, M.A. (2002) 'Appropriating cultural conceptions of childhood', *Childhood*, 9: 255–76.

Forrester, M.A. and Cherington, S.M. (2009) 'The development of other-related conversational skills: A case study of conversational repair during the early years', *First Language*, 29: 166–91.

Forrester, M.A. and Reason, D. (2006) 'Competency and participant in acquiring a mastery of language: A reconsideration of the idea of membership', *The Sociological Review*, 54: 446–66.

Gilbert, G.N. and Mulkay, M. (1984) *Opening Pandora's box: A sociological analysis of scientists' discourse*. Cambridge: Cambridge University Press.

Golato, A. (2010) 'Marking understanding versus receipting information in talk: Achso. and ach in German interaction', *Discourse Studies*, 12: 147–76.

Hepburn, A. and Potter, J. (2011) 'Threats: Power, family mealtimes and social influence', *British Journal of Social Psychology*, 50: 99–120.

Hepburn, A. and Wiggins, S. (2007) 'Discursive research: Themes and debates', in A. Hepburn and S. Wiggins (eds) *Discursive research in practice: New approaches to psychology and interaction* (pp. 1–28). Cambridge University Press.

Heritage, J. (2005) 'Cognition in discourse', in H. te Molder and J. Potter (eds) *Conversation and cognition* (pp. 184–202). Cambridge: Cambridge University Press.

Kent, A. and Potter, J. (2014) 'Discursive social psychology', in T. Holtgraves (ed.) *Handbook of language and social psychology* (pp. 295–313). Oxford University Press.

Kitzinger, C. (2006) 'After post-cognitivism', *Discourse Studies*, 8: 67–83.

Maynard, D.W. (2003) *Bad news, good news: Conversational order in everyday talk and clinical settings*. Chicago, IL: University of Chicago Press.

Parker, I. (2012) 'Discursive social psychology now', *British Journal of Social Psychology*, 51: 471–7.

Potter, J. (1997) 'Discourse analysis as a way of analysing naturally occurring talk', in D. Silverman (ed.), *Qualitative research: Theory, method and practice* (pp. 144–60). London: Sage.

Potter, J. (2005) 'Making psychology relevant', *Discourse & Society*, 16: 739–47.

Potter, J. (2006) 'Cognition and conversation', *Discourse Studies*, 8: 131–40.

Potter, J. and Hepburn, A. (2003) '"I'm a bit concerned": Early actions and psychological constructions in a child protection helpline', *Research on Language & Social Interaction*, 36: 197–240.

Potter, J. and Hepburn, A. (2008) 'Discursive constructionism', in J.A. Holstein and J.F. Gubrium (eds) *Handbook of constructionist research* (pp. 275–93). New York: Guilford.

Potter, J. and Hepburn, A. (2012) 'Eight challenges for interview researchers', J.F. Gubrium and J.A. Holstein (eds) *Handbook of interview research* (second edn) (pp. 555–70). London: Sage.

Potter, J. and Wetherell, M. (1987) *Discourse and social psychology: Beyond attitudes and behaviour*. London: Sage.

Potter, J., Edwards, D. and Wetherell, M. (1993) 'A model of discourse in action', *American Behavioral Scientist*, 36: 383–401.

Puchta, C. and Potter, J. (2002) 'Manufacturing individual opinions: Market research focus groups and the discursive psychology of attitudes', *British Journal of Social Psychology*, 41: 345–63.

Sacks, H. (1975) 'Everyone has to lie', in B. Blount and M. Sanches (eds), *Sociocultural dimensions of language use* (pp. 57–80). New York: Academic Press.

Sacks, H. (1978) 'Some technical considerations of a dirty joke', in J. Schenkein (ed.) *Studies in the organisation of conversational interaction* (pp. 249–70). New York: Academic Press.

Sacks, H. (1979) 'Hotrodder: A revolutionary category', in G. Psathas (ed.), *Everyday language: Studies in ethnomethodology* (pp. 7–14). New York: Irvington.

Sacks, H. (1980) 'Button button who's got the button?' in D. Zimmerman and C. West (eds), 'Special issue on language and social interaction', *Sociological Inquiry*, 50: 318–27.

Sacks, H. (1984) 'On doing "being ordinary"', in J.M. Atkinson and J. Heritage (eds), *Structures of social actions: Studies in conversation analysis* (pp. 413–19). Cambridge: Cambridge University Press.

Sacks, H. (1985) 'The inference-making machine: Notes on observability', in T.A. Dijk (ed.) *Handbook of discourse analysis (Volume 3: Discourse and dialogue)* (pp. 13–22). London: Academic Press.

Sacks, H. (1987) 'On the preferences for agreement and contiguity in sequences in conversations', in G. Button and J.R.E. Lee (eds) *Talk and social organisation* (pp. 54–69). Clevedon: Multilingual Matters.

Sacks, H. (1992) *Lectures on conversation* (Volumes I–II). Oxford: Wiley-Blackwell.

Sacks, H., Schegloff, E. and Jefferson, G. (1974) 'A simplest systematics for the organisation of turn-taking for conversation', *Language*, 50: 696–735.

Schegloff, E. (1968) 'Sequencing in conversational openings', *American Anthropologist*, 70: 1075–95.

Schegloff, E. (1972) 'Notes on a conversational practice: Formulating place', in D. Sudnow (ed.) *Studies in social interaction* (pp. 75–119). New York: Free Press.

Schegloff, E. (2005) 'On integrity in inquiry . . . of the investigated, not the investigator', *Discourse Studies*, 7: 455–80.

Schegloff, E. (2007a) 'A tutorial on membership categorization', *Journal of Pragmatics*, 39: 462–82.

Schegloff, E. (2007b) *Sequence organisation in interaction: A primer in conversation analysis*. Cambridge: Cambridge University Press.

Schegloff, E., Jefferson, G. and Sacks, H. (1977) 'The preference for self-correction in the organization of repair in conversation', *Language*, 53: 361–82.

Speer, S.A. (2001) 'Reconsidering the concept of hegemonic masculinity: Discursive psychology, conversation analysis and participants' orientations', *Feminism & Psychology*, 11: 107–35.

Speer, S.A. (2002) 'Sexist talk: Gender categories, participants' orientations and irony', *Journal of Sociolinguistics*, 6: 347–77.

Sterponi, L. (2009) 'Accountability in family discourse: Socialization into norms and standards and negotiation of responsibility in Italian dinner conversations', *Childhood*, 16: 441–59.

Stokoe, E. (2014) 'The Conversation Analytic Role-play Method (CARM): A method for training communication skills as an alternative to simulated role-play', *Research on Language & Social Interaction*, 47.

Tileagă, C. (2005) 'Accounting for extreme prejudice and legitimating blame in talk about the Romanies', *Discourse Society*, 16: 603–24.

Tileagă, C. (2010) 'Cautious morality: Public accountability, moral order and accounting for a conflict of interest', *Discourse Studies*, 12: 223–39.

Tileagă, C. (2011) 'Rewriting biography: Memory, identity and textually-mediated reality in coming to terms with the past', *Culture & Psychology*, 17: 197–215.

Weatherall, A. (2011) 'I don't know as a prepositioned epistemic hedge', *Research on Language & Social Interaction*, 44: 317–37.

Wetherell, M. (1998) 'Positioning and interpretative repertoires: Conversation analysis and post-structuralism in dialogue', *Discourse & Society*, 9: 387–412.

Whorf, B.L. (1956) *Language, thought and reality: Selected writings of Benjamin Lee Whorf* (J.B. Carroll, ed). Cambridge, MA: MIT Press.

Widdicombe, S. and Wooffitt, R. (1990) '"Being" versus "doing" punk: On achieving authenticity as a member', *Journal of Language & Social Psychology*, 9: 257–77.

Widdicombe, S. and Wooffitt, R. (1995) *The language of youth subcultures: Social identity in action*. Hemel Hempstead: Harvester Wheatsheaf.

Wiggins, S. (2001) 'Construction and action in food evaluation: Examples from conversation', *Journal of Language & Social Psychology*, 20: 445–63.

Wiggins, S. (2002) 'Talking with your mouth full: Gustatory "mmm"s and the embodiment of pleasure', *Research on Language & Social Interaction*, 35: 311–36.

Wiggins, S. (2004) 'Talking about taste: Using a discursive psychological approach to examine challenges to food evaluations', *Appetite*, 43: 29–38.

Wiggins, S. and Potter, J. (2003) 'Attitudes and evaluative practices: Category vs. item and subjective vs. objective constructions in everyday food assessments', *British Journal of Social Psychology*, 42: 513–31.

Wootton, A. (1997) *Interaction and the development of mind*. Cambridge: Cambridge University Press.

4 Natural and contrived data

Simon Goodman and Susan A. Speer

Target article: Potter, J. (2004) 'Discourse analysis as a way of analysing naturally occurring talk', in D. Silverman (ed.) *Qualitative research: Theory, method and practice* (pp. 200–21). London: Sage.

In this chapter we assess the impact of Jonathan Potter's (2004) classic text 'Discourse analysis as a way of analysing naturally occurring talk'. This text has had a major impact on discursive psychology and other qualitative approaches by stimulating methodological debate about the merits and limitations of different 'types' of data. It is important to note that the 2004 version of this text is actually an updated version of an earlier piece (Potter 1997), and includes a discussion of the debate the original piece stimulated (e.g., Speer 2002a). Potter's text itself builds upon his own previous work (Potter and Wetherell 1995) and develops the work of others, notably conversation analysts Sacks (1984) and Heritage (1984), who had already called for an analytical focus on non-contrived 'actual events' (Sacks 1984: 26).

This chapter begins with an outline of the main argument developed by Potter, which is that discursive psychologists should focus on data that exists independently of researchers (naturally occurring talk), rather than data that is 'got up' (Potter 2004: 205) for the purpose of analysis. Next, we consider how this argument has been developed in subsequent work in discursive psychology and conversation analysis. We argue that the analysis of naturally occurring data can generate fascinating insights into the action orientation of everyday talk. However, developing ideas from our own work, we also suggest that researcher-generated and naturally occurring data need not be viewed as discrete 'types' in the way that Potter suggests. Like us, Potter acknowledges that 'contrived' (2004: 206) data can be 'naturalised' (e.g., 2002) and treated as a topic in its own right. However, we suggest that this does not go far enough and that all data can be viewed as either natural or contrived, depending on what the researcher wants to do with it and what consequences the interactional setting has for the phenomenon being analysed. We conclude by considering the implications of this debate for the 'natural/contrived' distinction and future interaction research.

The argument for naturally occurring data

Potter defines naturally occurring data as 'spoken language produced entirely independently of the actions of the researcher' (2004: 205) and cites a range of examples of types of data that fit this definition: '(everyday conversations over the telephone, the records of a company board meeting, or the interaction between doctor and patient in a surgery' (2004: 205). Naturally occurring talk is contrasted favourably with its alternative, data that is 'got up' by the researcher (2004: 205) using traditional research methodological techniques such as interviews and focus groups. Potter, however, explicitly distinguishes naturally occurring interviews, such as broadcast news interviews, from researcher-generated interviews, applying what he later referred to as the '(conceptual) dead social scientist's test – would the data be the same, or be there at all, if the researcher got run over on the way to work?' (2002: 541).

Potter (2004) argues that naturally occurring data is preferable to data 'got up' by researchers because it is completely free of any researcher influence. Potter deems researcher influence to be problematic for three key reasons: First, researcher influence means the data is 'contrived' (2004: 206). Potter regards contrived data as artificial and as something that does not reflect the world as it would be without researcher intervention. Second 'it is subject to powerful expectations about social science research fielded by participants' (2004: 206), which suggests a problem with demand characteristics where research participants may act in a particular way because they are aware that they are taking part in social science research. Finally, Potter suggests that 'there are particular difficulties in extrapolating from interview talk to activities in other settings' (2004: 206) because 'contrived' data are 'affected by the formulations and assumptions of the researcher' (2004: 206). Potter's view reflects a broader concern that 'researcher effects' (where the mere presence of a researcher can influence research findings, for example by inducing behaviour that is deemed by the participant to be what the researcher expects), are problematic and to be avoided (e.g., Bryman 2004, Coolican 2009).

Potter illustrates his argument for naturally occurring data with examples of naturally occurring broadcast interviews between Princess Diana and the UK journalist, Martin Bashir[1], and Salman Rushdie and David Frost, an article from the British *Guardian* newspaper and a relationship counselling session. He uses this data to demonstrate features of the action orientation of talk in natural settings. Potter focuses on the phrase 'I dunno', showing how it functions as a 'stake inoculation' (2004: 212) to fend off suggestions that the speaker has a personal interest (or 'stake', see Edwards and Potter 1992) in the things they are saying (Potter 1996), which could potentially be used to undermine their claim. In sum, Potter's argument is that research is most effective when being used to address a phenomenon in its natural setting, free from any intervention by a researcher. His argument represents an implicit criticism of the large body of discourse analytic work that has generated 'contrived' data.

In later writing Potter and Hepburn (2005, see also Potter and Hepburn 2012) develop Potter's (2004) argument. Potter and Hepburn's (2005) text is discussed by Rapley (this volume), which demonstrates the wide and ongoing impact of Potter's (2004) text. Potter and Hepburn further highlight potential problems with researcher-generated interviews that can limit their usefulness. They are particularly critical of what they refer to as the 'failure to consider interviews as interaction' (2005: 290), whereby the interactional element of the interview is ignored in favour of treating participant responses in isolation from the context of the interview itself. While other researchers may treat interviews as interaction (e.g., Holstein and Gubrium 1995) Potter and Hepburn suggest that this interaction is rarely properly addressed. Potter and Hepburn consider this lack of focus on interaction problematic, and they characterise this limitation as potentially avoidable. They go further, however, by suggesting other *un*avoidable problems with interviews that have major implications for the use of interviews, including that the researchers' agendas and concepts will always be apparent (or 'flood') the interview and that issues of stake and interest – features of talk that have been shown to be central to interaction (and therefore discursive psychology, Edwards and Potter 1992) are rarely addressed fully, which can result in missing what the talk is being designed to do.

Potter and Hepburn (2005) therefore advocate the value of reflexivity as one key element of the discursive approach (Edwards and Potter 1992). From this perspective researchers need to attend actively and reflexively to their own involvement with and creation of data. Potter and Hepburn claim this is a necessary step to conducting systematic analysis of interview data. They present contrived interview data as problematic when there is not sufficient reflexive orientation to how knowledge is produced in interviews. In discursive psychology this reflexive orientation is addressed in the conversational, turn-by-turn analysis of the ways in which talk is used to perform actions that deal with speakers' interest and accountability in specific contexts. This sets discursive analysis apart from what other qualitative approaches advocate (cf. Smith, Hollway and Mishler (2005) and Rapley (this volume) for responses to the Potter and Hepburn article).

Developing Potter's argument for naturally occurring data

There are now a range of illuminating discursive findings using naturally occurring data (e.g., Auburn 2005; Benneworth 2009; Edwards and Stokoe 2011; Stokoe 2009). In previous work (Goodman and Speer 2007) we analysed a range of sources of naturally occurring data including television news and debate programmes, newspaper articles, election campaign material and a political speech. By using naturally occurring data, we were able to demonstrate how the classification of asylum seekers was not just something that we were interested in as researchers, but was something that could also be demonstrated to be a concern for the participants. Consider Extract 1, below – a statement made by Peter Hitchens, a British newspaper columnist and opponent of asylum seeking, during a televised debate programme:

(1) [Goodman and Speer 2007: 170. Asylum: Face the Nation, BBC1, July 23, 2003]

```
1 the most ... inflammatory language which is used is ... the false
2 use of ... the words 'asylum seekers' to describe people who
3 are in fact illegal immigrants
```

Through analysis of this extract we were able to claim that the categorisation of asylum seekers is something that participants in the asylum debate topicalise themselves. This, in turn, gave us the legitimacy to explore the uses of categories around asylum seeking by participants in the asylum debate without imposing our own definitions and ideas on the data. The analysis of category use showed that references to 'illegal immigrants' oriented to the practical action of undermining arguments for asylum seekers, so that this category was most commonly used in opposition to asylum seeker rights.

This example demonstrates the usefulness of focussing on naturally occurring data rather than interview data in which we seek politicians' views on asylum seeking, for example. By using naturally occurring, instead of contrived, data we were able to identify important elements of a debate without influencing that debate. However, despite the benefits of focussing on naturally occurring data in this way, Potter's (2004) clear favouring of naturally occurring data and Potter and Hepburn's (2005) critique of social scientific interviews have proved to be controversial. It is the debates around these arguments that we turn to next.

Challenging Potter's natural/contrived distinction

Speer (2002a: 516) points to a contradiction between the two positions that state (1) that bias in the form of context effects is not a problem but is a fundamental aspect of all interaction, that can be celebrated and explored; and (2) that naturally occurring data is superior to contrived data because it is free of the interviewer's bias/influence.

Speer claims that since all data must be recorded and consent must be sought from all participants to meet ethical standards, it is impossible for any research to be truly free of the researcher. In this sense '*all* data are researcher-prompted and thus contrived' (2002a: 516, emphasis in original). Speer (2002a: 518) concludes by stating that the distinction between natural and contrived data is 'inherently problematic' but that this 'need not necessarily involve abandoning the concept of naturally occurring data' (which some might argue is still rhetorically useful). Rather, we need to be clearer and more consistent about what exactly constitutes the object of our analyses' (2002a: 521). Speer's (2002a) paper led to a number of responses (Lynch 2002; Potter 2002;

Ten Have 2002) and a rejoinder. (We return to this point later when Speer's proposed solution is discussed.)

In a related challenge to Potter's argument for a natural/contrived distinction, Griffin (2007a; 2007b) suggests that the concept of natural data is problematic as 'No talk or other practice is "natural" in the sense of being unmediated by the context of the occasion in which it is generated' (2007a: 248). Griffin takes issue with Potter and Hepburn's (2005) suggestion that the research interview is too 'flooded' with the researcher's agenda and instead claims that participants are far more active than this position would suggest, stating this 'perspective gives the researcher and the research project overwhelming dominance over the research encounter, relegating other participants to relatively passive "feeder" roles' (2007a: 250). Griffin states that for her the value of researcher interviews is that they constitute a meeting of the researcher's and, importantly, the participants' agendas. For Griffin this means that analyses should address 'those points at which the agendas and perspectives of interviewers and interviewees interact' (2007a: 261), which means that 'natural' data totally separate from the researcher is not something to strive for.

We have now outlined two of the main challenges to Potter's argument for the primacy of 'naturally occurring' data. As we demonstrate above, we have used what has been termed 'naturally occurring' data in our research. However, alongside Potter (e.g., Wetherell and Potter 1992), we have also used 'contrived' data (that is, data that would fail Potter's 'dead social scientist' test) and have actively engaged with our participants. For us, depending on the ways in which the data is being used, 'naturally occurring' and 'contrived' data need not be viewed as discrete types.

Naturalising 'contrived' interview data

We will now demonstrate the ways in which the natural/contrived distinction can be viewed as problematic, with examples from our own analyses, showing how 'contrived' data can be treated as 'natural' depending on the purpose of the analysis. This means that 'contrived' data can be 'naturalised' so that the features of the research setting can become the topic of the analysis and therefore can be treated as 'natural'. Speer (2012; Speer and Stokoe 2014) has demonstrated that contrived materials, including social science interviews and focus groups can be 'naturalised', or treated as natural, in ways that contribute to our understanding of interaction (also see Maynard et al. 2002). It is worth noting that here that we and Potter (2002) are in agreement over the possibility of naturalising data.

Speer and Stokoe (2014) highlight the advantages of naturalising 'contrived data'. The data show how consent gaining (an important part of ethical data collection) can operate very differently in practice from how it is described in theory. The following extracts from the analysis occurred at the start of telephone interviews with gender identity clinic patients:

(2) [Speer and Stokoe 2014: 62–63 Pre-recorded Message 5. 2:44]

```
1   Int:   Uh::m, I'm happy to go on longer if you are but you
2          must say if you wan- need to stop or anything like
3          [that.]
4   Pt:    [Yes.]
5   Int:   .hhh Uh::m pt. t. the interview'll be ta:ped if
6          that's okay with [you:
7   Pt:                     [Yes that's [fine by me,
8   Int:                                [.hhh
9          Uh:::m, an' I'll write hand-written notes at the same
10         ti:me, [.hhh
11  Int:          [Uh huh,
```

(3) [Speer and Stokoe 2014: 63. Patient Telephone Interview 2. 00:51]

```
1   Int:  I'm just gonna tick boxes to show that I've-
2         I've taken you through this information.
4         (0.2)
5   PL:   Okay,
6   Int:  Pt. .hhh Uh:m:, pt. so the interview will be ta::ped, with
7         your con↑se:nt, if that's oka:y? .hh[h
9   Pt:                                       [Yep.
10  Int:  And I'll write hand-written notes at the same ti:me,
11        ((Rustling - 0.4))
12  Pt:   Mm hmm,
```

In their analysis Speer and Stokoe (2014: 63) use this seemingly contrived data naturalistically to show how the recording party invites the recipient to confirm that it is 'okay' to record (Extract 2, line 5–6; Extract 3, lines 6–7) before continuing delivering information about the study. The recipient subsequently gives their consent (Extract 2, line 7; Extract 3, line 9). They therefore demonstrate how the conversational practices of requesting consent constrain opting out of participation.

This next example of naturalisation can be seen in Goodman et al.'s (2014) research with asylum-seeking refugees. The aim of this project was to understand how refugees talk about their situation in the UK. While issues of asylum and refuge are particularly topical in UK debates (as Goodman and Speer's (2007) research demonstrates), asylum seekers themselves tend not to be heard and are generally absent from the discursive literature about this topic[2]. Like Griffin (2007a) advocates, Goodman et al. approached their research motivated by their interest in the topic, and specifically what they considered a social/political problem of the mistreatment of asylum seekers. In the following example the interviewer (A3) is asking a participant to elaborate on a point about not wishing to return to her country of origin.

(4) [Goodman et al., 2014: 27–8. Extract 6: P9]

```
1  A3: So you would never return to Kenya because you would be
2       worried about yourself?=
3  P9: =How can go I I face death how can I go I face death? How
4       even if yourself how you can go to a place where you face
5       death (A3: no I know) I can die there it is better I die
6       here better than I go.
7  A3: No you're right it's better to be safe
8  P9: Because here I don't have anything good here I don't have
9       any life here you understand my life what I explained to you
10      I do not have a good life here but I am safe I stay here
11      because (.) for here I have never been happy even one day
12      here (A3: no) I have never been happy one day
```

In this extract the participant can be seen to be drawing on the notion of safety as a justification for remaining in the UK. This safety is presented as more important than her happiness, so P9 states that she is willing to stay in the UK and be unhappy as this is preferable to having no safety outside of the UK. Importantly, this 'helps to position P9 as a legitimate refugee as she is placing importance on safety over anything else' (Goodman et al., 2014: 28). The interview context can be seen to be directly influencing the interaction in this extract. For example, the interviewee refers to 'you understand my life what I explained to you' (line 9), which references the interview setting where the interviewee is expected to explain her 'story' as a refugee to the interviewer. In this case the interviewee is using the interview context, and the previous telling of her circumstances as an interactional resource to bolster her claim about requiring safety above everything else.

The key finding of the analysis is that asylum seekers make complaints about their situation in ways that manage their identity as *legitimate* refugees. These asylum seekers are therefore orienting to the pervasive suggestion that asylum seekers are economic migrants rather than refugees (an argument identified in Goodman and Speer's (2007) analysis of what Potter would describe as 'naturally occurring' data). In the case of this 'contrived' data then, the presence of the interviewers/members of the host country meant that questions of legitimacy, which are relevant to the ongoing wider asylum debate, are present and especially relevant. Indeed the talk of the asylum seekers in this interview data must be understood in relation (and response) to the televised debate data (Goodman and Speer 2007) described above. This speaks to Speer's (2002a) argument that what counts as contrived (interviews gotten up to elicit the stories/accounts of asylum seekers) and natural (in this case real asylum seekers interacting with real British citizens) is not absolute.

Potter agrees that data can be 'naturalised' in the ways demonstrated above. Where we disagree with him is regarding the *implications* naturalisation has for the natural/contrived distinction, with Speer suggesting that this allows us to transcend the distinction and Potter rejecting this claim. For Potter naturalisation is not enough to challenge (or 'blunt' 2002: 541) the natural/contrived distinction he makes. Instead Potter argues that 'the possibility of studying how a particular bit of social research is contrived does not show that the contrived/natural distinction is not useful' (2002: 541) and that 'treating method as topic is not the same as using it to find something out' about the world/our participants (2002: 539). This means that for Potter naturalisation is a beneficial tool, but he rejects Speer's claim that this renders the natural/contrived distinction problematic, claiming instead that naturalisation is not the same as being able to do effective research in its own right on 'contrived data'. For Potter, naturalising 'contrived' data serves to highlight the influence of these contrived contexts on the interaction, which reflects his critique of 'contrived' methods; for him the contrived/natural distinction remains.

Procedural consequentiality

Speer further challenges the contrived/natural distinction by arguing that 'What are natural data and what are not is not decidable on the basis of their type and/or the role of the researcher within the data. *All* data can be natural or contrived depending on what one wants to *do* with them' (Speer 2008: 307, emphasis in original). Speer (e.g. 2002a; 2002b; 2008) argues that rather than the researchers deciding what counts as natural or contrived data, it may make more sense to assess how the participants in a given conversation orient (or not) to the context and to the influence of the researcher. It is argued that decisions about what data to use should be informed instead by the notion of procedural consequentiality, which refers to the impact of the interactional context on the phenomenon of interest. Schegloff says that two questions need to be asked to help us determine whether a setting is procedurally consequential for a particular phenomenon:

> How does the fact that the talk is being conducted in some setting (e.g. 'the hospital') issue in any consequence for the shape, form, trajectory, content or character of the interaction that the parties conduct? And what is the mechanism by which the context-so-understood had determinate consequences for the talk.
>
> (Schegloff 1992: 111)

To illustrate this, Schegloff (1991) refers to two studies (Levelt 1983 on self-repair and West and Zimmerman 1983 on interruptions) and shows how in the first, but not second, the setting placed limitations on who could talk. The former, as well as the latter, study took place in an experimental setting. Schegloff concluded that the experimental setting in the former study was procedurally consequential for self-repair, while in the latter (if one were to analyse the data for a study of self-repair) it was not (Speer 2002a: 520). This means that decisions about what data may be used for analysis need to be made with consideration given to what influence the context may have on the phenomenon of interest and how talk plays out. In some 'contrived' situations, therefore, the contrived nature of the interview may well impact on the phenomenon of interest, whereas in other 'contrived' situations it may not. To demonstrate the importance of procedural consequentiality, Speer (2012) conducted a comparative analysis of hypothetical questions in data from four different settings, including those that Potter would describe as contrived: ordinary conversations, research interactions, broadcast news interviews, and doctor–patient consultations. In the following extract Speer, as the interviewer, can be seen asking her interviewee a hypothetical question:

(5) [Speer 2012: 358–9. One-to-one, semi-structured interview: 19.3.97: 19 Side A]

```
1   Int: >So do you think-< marriage would change your leisure in
2        any way.
3        (0.8)
4   Mag: ↑Uhmm:: (2.4) ↑I don't know I probably wouldn't go- like I
5        probably wouldn't go: clubbing as much or (1.2) things like
6        tha:t.
7        (0.4)
8   Mag: But yeah I mean you'd- [>probably coz you'd<] have=
9   Int:                        [  W h y  n o t ? ]
10       (0.8)
11  Mag: hhh Oh just coz I'd be older an' I'd be- you know you °yo-
12       could think oh you've got to be more kind of grown up about
13       things°.
14  Int: But if [they] created like night clubs fo::r (0.8) thirty=
15  Mag:        [( )]
16  Int: =year old women. and men. to go to. Or i- would- would that
17       be good?
18       (1.2)
19  Mag: Mm::: as long as y- (well it yo-) >you can just see those
20       kind of places as being full of lecherous old men though
21       can't you.< You know men who are (.) divo:rced or looking
22       for a fling, looking for some: (.) somebody their of their
23       age whose gonna (1.0) you know (0.4) °it has that kind of
24       i(h)mage about it°. (Sarah goes to) these over twenty-fives
25       things (0.4) 'n it's
26  Int: [ Mm,
27  Mag: [ full of old people > °isn't it really° <.
28       (0.4)
29  Int: Mm[ :
30  Mag:   [ I don't know I think I'd rather just not go after a
31       certain (.) I'd rather (0.2) say 'Right when I hit (0.2)
32       thirty .hh >I'm never gonna go to a club again<'
```

Speer (2012: 359) shows how her hypothetical question (lines 14–17) is an 'attempt by the interviewer to probe and unpack the reasoning behind Maggie's views on this topic', which appears to be a generic function of hypothetical questions across the data. However, Speer also shows that the hypothetical question worked differently in this contrived setting. Here it was found to be 'more provocative and challenging in its design' than in other settings (2012: 359). Rather than taking this difference to mean that the interview data should be viewed as 'unnatural', this analysis demonstrates that apparently 'contrived' interviews are not unique in affecting the way the phenomenon functions. Instead, each setting has its own interactional affordances that are procedurally consequential for the way hypothetical questions run off in each case. This supports our call to determine the use of data based on procedural consequentiality rather than a problematic contrived/natural distinction.

What is the future of the debate about natural contrived data?

The methodological issues addressed here are not only relevant for discursive and conversation analysts, but linguists (e.g., Mann 2011) and qualitative researchers more generally (e.g., Roulston 2010) are starting to question the use of interviews for the reasons Potter has identified. It is worth noting that no parties in these debates have argued that either 'naturally occurring' or 'contrived' data cannot yield helpful findings. There is (limited) agreement that both types of data can and should be used for analysis. It also seems clear that this debate is not about to be settled, with passionate disagreement on both sides. Our view, developed here, is that a natural/contrived distinction is problematic and such data need not be viewed as discrete types. What we hope to have demonstrated is that, like conversation analysts before him, Potter (2004) developed a strong argument for the use of naturally occurring data that is supported by the (growing) body of discursive work that has used this data to better understand the way talk is oriented to practical action in natural settings. Nevertheless, discursive and conversation analytic work continues to use so-called contrived data.

We therefore argue that both 'natural' and 'contrived' data can be used for analysis because, as demonstrated throughout this chapter, analyses of both can yield useful findings. Where we disagree with Potter is that for us this contrived/natural distinction can be transcended and rather than making decisions based on what is 'natural' and what is 'contrived', we argue that decisions about what data can be used for analysis can be based instead on what the researcher is trying to do with the data and what impact the interactional context has on the phenomenon being studied, focussing on the procedural consequentiality of the research context. Potter's call for analysis of naturally occurring data, and the novel findings that it has brought to discursive psychology, can only be a good thing for the discipline and we fully expect a focus on naturally occurring data to increase over the coming years. Alongside this, interviews continue to be used and, as Potter and Hepburn (2005) have acknowledged, will most likely continue to dominate.

The debate over which kind of data is best, or as we've argued here, if it is useful to talk in terms of two distinct types of data at all, will continue. This is likely to encourage a more nuanced understanding of the ways that methods and the context of data relate (Speer 2002a: 521) and it may also encourage more social scientists to analyse interview data as an interaction. This is important as it can guide researchers to make informed methodological decisions about appropriate data for their research questions and to consider the impact of the context in which data is produced. It is likely that this debate will reignite again – if or when it does there is scope for further research to explore exactly what impact the interview context and the social science interviewer has on the ways participants manage their stake and interest in interviews. Any further debate has the possibility of developing and increasing methodological rigour.

Notes

1 A verbatim transcript of the interview can be found at www.bbc.co.uk/news/special/politics97/diana/panorama.html.
2 See Goodman et al. (2014) for discussion of the three exceptions.

References

Auburn, T. (2005) 'Narrative reflexivity as a repair device for discounting "cognitive distortions" in sex offender treatment', *Discourse & Society*, 16: 697–718.

Benneworth, K. (2009) 'Police interviews with suspected paedophiles: A discourse analysis', *Discourse & Society*, 20: 555–69.

Bryman, A. (2004) *Social research methods*. Oxford: Oxford University Press.

Coolican, H. (2009) *Research methods and statistics in psychology* (fifth edn). London: Routledge.

Edwards, D. and Potter, J. (1992) *Discursive psychology*. London: Sage.

Edwards, D. and Stokoe, E. (2011) '"You don't have to answer": Lawyers' contributions in police interrogations of suspects', *Research on Language & Social Interaction*, 44: 21–43.

Goodman, S., Burke, S., Liebling, H. and Zasada, D. (2014) '"I'm NOT happy, but I'm ok": How asylum seekers manage talk about difficulties in their host country', *Critical Discourse Studies*, 1: 19–34.

Goodman, S. and Speer, S.A. (2007) 'Category use in the construction of asylum seekers', *Critical Discourse Studies*, 4: 165–85.

Griffin, C. (2007a) 'Being dead and being there: Research interviews, sharing hand cream and the preference for analysing "naturally occurring data"', *Discourse Studies*, 9: 246–69.

Griffin, C. (2007b) 'Different visions: A rejoinder to Henwood, Potter and Hepburn', *Discourse Studies*, 9: 283–7.

Heritage, J. (1984) *Garfinkel and ethnomethodology*. Cambridge: Polity Press.

Holstein, J. and Gubrium, J. (1995) *The active interview*. London: Sage

Levelt, W.J.M. (1983) 'Monitoring and self-repair in speech', *Cognition*, 14: 41–104.

Lynch, M. (2002) 'From naturally occurring data to naturally organized ordinary activities: Comment on Speer', *Discourse Studies, 4*: 531–7.

Mann, S. (2011) 'A critical review of qualitative interviews in applied linguistics', *Applied Linguistics, 32*: 6–24.

Maynard, D.W., Houtkoop-Steenstra, H., Schaeffer, N.C. and van der Zouwen, J. (2002) *Standardization and tacit knowledge. Interaction and practice in the survey interview.* New York: John Wiley.

Potter, J. (1996) *Representing reality: Discourse, rhetoric and social construction.* London: Sage.

Potter, J. (1997) 'Discourse analysis as a way of analysing naturally occurring talk', in D. Silverman (ed.) *Qualitative research: Theory, method and practice* (pp. 144–60). London: Sage.

Potter, J. (2002) 'Two kinds of natural', *Discourse Studies, 4*: 539–42.

Potter, J. (2004) 'Discourse analysis as a way of analysing naturally occurring talk', in D. Silverman (ed.) *Qualitative research: Theory, method and practice* (second edn) (pp. 200–21). London: Sage.

Potter, J. and Hepburn, A. (2005) 'Qualitative interviews in psychology: Problems and possibilities', *Qualitative Research in Psychology, 2*: 281–307.

Potter, J. and Hepburn, A. (2012) 'Eight challenges for interview researchers', in J.F. Gubrium and J.A. Holstein (eds) *Handbook of interview research* (second edn) (pp. 555–70). London: Sage.

Potter, J. and Wetherell, M. (1995) 'Natural order: Why social psychologists should study (a constructed version of) natural language, and why they have not done so', *Journal of Language & Social Psychology, 14*: 216–22.

Roulston, K. (2010) 'Considering quality in qualitative interviewing', *Qualitative Research, 10*: 199–228.

Sacks, H. (1984) 'Notes on methodology', in J.M. Atkinson and J. Heritage (eds) *Structures of social action: Studies in conversation analysis* (pp. 21–7). Cambridge: Cambridge University Press.

Schegloff, E. (1991) 'Reflections on talk and social structure', in D. Boden and D.H. Zimmerman (eds) *Talk and social structure: Studies in ethnomethodology and conversation analysis* (pp. 44–70). Cambridge: Polity Press.

Schegloff, E. (1992) 'On talk and its institutional occasions', in P. Drew and J.C. Heritage (eds) *Talk at work* (pp. 101–34). Cambridge: Cambridge University Press.

Smith, J., Hollway, W. and Mishler, E. (2005) 'Commentaries on Potter and Hepburn, "Qualitative interviews in psychology: problems and possibilities"', *Qualitative Research in Psychology, 2*: 309–25.

Speer, S.A. (2002a) '"Natural" and "contrived" data: A sustainable distinction?', *Discourse Studies, 4*: 511–25.

Speer, S.A. (2002b) 'Transcending the "natural"/"contrived" distinction: A rejoinder to Ten Have, Lynch and Potter', *Discourse Studies, 4*: 543–8.

Speer, S.A. (2002c) 'What can conversation analysis contribute to feminist methodology? Putting reflexivity into practice', *Discourse & Society, 13*: 783–803.

Speer, S.A. (2008) 'Natural and contrived data', in P. Alasuutari, J. Brannen and L. Bickman (eds) *The Sage handbook of social research methods* (pp. 290–312). London: Sage.

Speer, S.A. (2012) 'Hypothetical questions: A comparative analysis and implications for "applied" vs. "basic" conversation analysis', *Research on Language & Social Interaction, 45*: 352–74.

Speer, S.A. and Stokoe, E. (2014) 'Ethics in action: Consent-gaining interactions and implications for research practice', *British Journal of Social Psychology*, *51*: 54–73.

Stokoe, E. (2009) '"I've got a girlfriend" Police officers doing "self-disclosure" in their interrogations of suspects', *Narrative Inquiry*, *19*: 154–82.

Ten Have, P. (2002) 'Ontology or methodology? Comments on Speer's "natural" and "contrived" data: A sustainable distinction?', *Discourse Studies*, *4*: 527–30.

West, C. and Zimmerman, D. (1983) 'Small insults: A study of interruptions in cross-sex conversations between unacquainted persons', in B. Thorne, C. Kramarae and Henley (eds) *Language, gender and society*. Rowley, MA: Newbury House.

Wetherell, M. and Potter, J. (1992) *Mapping the language of racism: Discourse and the legitimation of exploitation*. London: Harvest Wheatsheaf.

5 Questions of context
Qualitative interviews as a source of knowledge

Tim Rapley

Target article: Potter, J. and Hepburn, A. (2005) 'Qualitative interviews in psychology: Problems and possibilities', *Qualitative Research in Psychology*, 2: 281–307.

Potter and Hepburn's (2005) paper questioning the role of interviews for psychology is part of a (potentially subversive) tradition of raising questions about the status of the interview as a knowledge-producing machine. This tradition calls for a shift away from seeing the interview as resource, as an economical way to access information about the world outside of the interview context, to making sense of the interview as a deeply linguistic, moral, interactional and situational affair. The immediate reception was interesting. It created a debate, which sought to recover the interview from what their critics saw as their overly-local focus on the mundane dynamics of the interview interaction. Since then, despite the questions about questioning that the article raised, those engaged in studies *using* interviewing seem to have made relatively few concessions. Equally, those involved in studies *of* interviews have continued to focus on the local context of the interview interaction, with the broader contexts of the knowledge-producing machine, like recruitment interactions and data analysis practices, remaining relatively unquestioned.

Questioning methods

Potter and Hepburn's (2005) work is part of longer tradition, one in which researchers from various psychological, sociological and anthropological traditions focused explicitly on relatively fine-grained analysis of interactional practices in qualitative interviews. Those by Baker (1983, 1984), Baruch (1981), Briggs (1986), Mishler (1986), and Watson and Weinburg (1982) were central in beginning to document how the work of the interviewer comes off in real time. The discourse analytic tradition (e.g., Potter and Mulkay 1985; Potter and Wetherell 1987) also begun to question the naïve realism of treating interviews as giving an unmediated window on life beyond the interview and sought to unsettle the neutralism of the interviewer. Since then, we have seen a slow but steady growth in work that focuses on various aspects of interaction in qualitative interviews (see Roulston's (2006) review). This has shown that the interview is clearly not a 'naturally occurring' conversation, but does comes off in and through co-ordinating, quite unspectacular and mundane conversational resources (Hester and Frances 1994; Rapley 2004). This style of research has not been without its critics. Notably, Hammersley (2003) offers a critique of what he describes as the 'radical criticism' of interview studies that has emerged[1].

Some work has focused more explicitly on the identity in interviews, exploring how interviewees (and to a lesser extent interviewers) work to produce themselves as specific types of people in relation to the topics of talk. They can offer up analysis of how interviewees produce themselves as as 'morally adequate' (e.g., Baker 1984, 1997; Baruch 1981; Rapley 2001). In other contexts, such identity work may be more explicitly tied to issues of expertise and knowledge (e.g., Roulston 2001; Lee and Roth 2004) or rights and responsibilities (see Baruch 1981). Researchers have also begun to explore specific aspects of the phenomena that emerge in interviews, including question–answer sequences (Mazeland and Have 1996) complaints (Roulston 2000; Roulston, Baker and Liljestrom 2001) and laughter (Grønnerød 2004). Centrally, this work argues that before we make assertions about what people are saying, or how they are saying it, we can examine how both interviewers and interviewees work to locally manage their identities, talk and interaction.

Potter and Heburn's (2005) paper can, in one sense, been seen as part of the ethnomethodological tradition of 'therapeutic respecification'. They seek to demonstrate the seen but unnoticed assumptions, the practical action and reasoning, that is embedded in how qualitative psychologists think and work with interview data. A related strand of work seeks to explore and map interaction in structured, telephone and face-to-face, survey-style interviewing (e.g., Antaki and Rapley 1996; Maynard et al. 2002; Suchman and Jordon 1990). This demonstrates how the mundane work of doing surveys, over a range of contexts, intimately impacts on the collection of 'raw data'[2].

In this way, by respecifying the phenomenon of how we conduct, analyse and report interviews, such research seeks to offer up new potential practical and, in some cases, theoretical directions. Potter and Hepburn solely focus on the range of practices that can be glossed as qualitative interviews, as, irrespective of the terminology applied – open, semi-structured, etcetera – they all have family resemblances – a researcher asks someone a question, the interviewee talks on that topic and then explores, through follow-up questions, different aspects of the topic.

Questions (about and for interviewing research)

Potter and Hepburn's paper is divided into three main sections. First, they position the interview within contemporary psychological work and explore the critiques. Second, they seek to demonstrate what they define as contingent problems and necessary problems. By this they mean, problems are

> contingent in the sense that they are not necessary features of doing interview research, but could be (relatively easily) *fixed*, or at least attended to ... [S]ome problems ... are necessary (*endemic and inescapable*) to the enterprise of researching with interviews
>
> (Potter and Hepburn 2005: 205, emphasis added)

Finally, they offer an alternate vision, one where researchers forgo the interview in favor of engaging with naturally occurring data, or what they refer to as 'naturalistic records' (ibid.: 301). The potential impact of the paper was immediately evident, as people sought to refute their (radical) alternate vision. In the same issue of the journal, three prominent researchers wrote extensive commentaries on the article. Some years later, this alternate vision was again the focus of critique, and another round of (critical) commentaries ensued.

Opening questions

Initially, Potter and Hepburn situate the interview as the taken-for-granted method of choice – interviews are positioned as 'the natural way to do nonexperimental, nonquestionniare and nonsurvey work in psychology' (p. 284). And this position is not only relevant to psychology, but the contemporary disciplines that engage with qualitative approaches. As Atkinson and Silverman (1997) note, we are living in an interview society, where in both research and the broader contemporary culture the interview, is *the* method used to gain access to another. It is the contemporary technology of the self, a space in which we know at a glance the norms and rules, a space through which we gain 'authentic' access to the other.

They then outline five (inter)related 'contingent problems' that, with what they see as relative ease, can be managed. Let's take the first three as a whole, as they all relate to the same issue, representational practices when analysing and reporting interview research. They cover (1) the relative absence of the interviewer's talk, (2) the absence of the interactional dynamics and texture of interview talk, and (3) the relative inability to link analytic claims to interview text. The device they used to demonstrate this is something others, including me (e.g., Rapley 2001), often like to use. Initially, they present a conventional orthographic transcript – with textual punctuation, ordered grammatical sentences – which only presents the interviewee's talk on a topic. They then add another layer of context: the interviewer's question; the interviewee's talk prior to the question; and the interviewer's brief utterances (like 'yes' and 'oh yeah yeah'), which occurs mid-flow of the interviewee's talk. In this way, they begin to recover how the interviewee's talk emerged in and though a flow of talk. It occurred in a specific context.

Second, they then take the same stretch of talk and reproduce it using the Jeffersonian transcription system. With this, we see a transformation, from the ordered, readable-at-a-glance, stretch of talk to a (radically) new format.

The interview talk is now 'blown up' under a conversation analytic microscope, where a different order of features is brought to the forefront. We have line numbers with relatively short lines of talk, finely timed pauses scattering the talk, stress, perturbations and intonational contours appear, and above all, the relative monologue of orthographic representation is replaced by a dynamic, almost line-by-line toing-and-froing between speakers. Above all, a more complex interaction comes into focus for the reader, and with that we glimpse the context of interviewee's talk – that this emerges in and through collaboration.

As they note, the call for a more dialogical representation has been repeated by a range of people. Some advocate, notably those in early discursive psychology (Potter and Wetherell 1987), using a Jefferson-lite style where some grosser elements of interactional work are added. However, they feel this is no longer sustainable as analysts, alongside journal editors, reviewers and readers need access to the phenomenon that a full Jeffersonian transcription can offer. Given this, it is interesting to note that they offer the reader access to the audio-recording of this stretch of interview via a web address[3]. The key issue for me is that such a thought, almost ten years later, is still very rare. Clearly, this reliance on text alone is in part due to the custom and practice of researchers, and in part how researchers orient to the ethics committees they work with. These norms developed in a different age of technological possibilities. However, in some contexts, with some interviewees, it could be appropriate to discuss with them the possibility of using audio-tracks alongside articles.

The discussion of engaging with more vibrant transcription is used by Potter and Hepburn (2005: 289) to make the case that:

> The analysis of broader patterns and ideological talk should be able deal with the specifics of what is going on in the talk rather then simply a reconstructed, simplified and distorted version of it. Not only *should* it be able to deal with this, but it also will be most effective and persuasive if it *does* deal with it.
>
> (emphasis in original)

Two features are key here. First, note the way that non-Jeffersonian transcriptions are rendered as 'reconstructed, simplified and distorted' (ibid.). Now this is strong claim, with clear repercussion for the status of data that others work with[4]. And this positions a Jeffersonian transcript as representing the 'real' action, perhaps not as simply as being authentic, complex and representative, but offering something in some way 'closer' to the phenomenon.

Second, this echoes back to prior debates where the norms of CA came under critique from (discursive) psychologists. In a response to an article by Schegloff (1997), Wetherell (1998) cites an interview[5] with 'three young white middle-class men concerning an episode in one participants recent sexual history' (p. 387). She argues that if we just attend to the local context of the talk a lot of other important issues (e.g., sexuality and gender performance) are lost in the analysis. In a reply to Wetherell, Schegloff highlights that what is important, and what is missing from her account, 'is that the entire exchange appears to be researcher-prompted' (1998: 415). He notes

> Rather then begin with gender ideologies, one might propose, the analysis begins by addressing what the parties to the interaction understand themselves to be doing in it, what sort of interaction they show themselves to be collaboratively constructing. Each utterance could then be understood by reference to its place in that enterprise.
>
> (ibid.: 415)

Schegloff's solution, to the broader analytic problem, is to engage in close analysis, in part enabled and represented by Jeffersonian transcription. In this way, Potter and Hepburn's 'contingent problem' of 'the conventions of representation of interaction' (2005: 206), heralds a much more fundamental, 'necessary problem'.

They raise one final issue of representation – how the 'block-of-text' style of monologues does not enable analysts to neatly demonstrate where a specific analytic claim is supported. In this way, the short lines, with line numbers, enables those who undertake Jeffersonian transcription to tightly align their claims with discrete features of the text. Again, this refers back to the broader point, and the Schegloff–Wetherell debate, that those who undertake work on 'broad themes' (Potter and Hepburn 2005: 289) demonstrate them in action, and point to, instead of glossing, the specifics of the interview.

The next contingent problem they raise, the problem of contexts of recruitment, also echoes back to Schegloff's (1998) discussion. They note that we, as readers of papers, should have some access to two interrelated features, the category the interviewees are recruited as – e.g., as heterosexual young men, sexually active teenagers, etc. – and interviewees' understanding of the interest of the interviewer generated through the recruitment process and introductory chat – e.g., to discuss sexuality and gender orientations. Researchers can then document, in some way, the potential assumptions about the type of people, the type of talk and the type of actions that interviewees are positioned as being responsible for. This begins to echo discussions by Briggs (2007), who argues that by focusing on the work *within* the interview, we miss the broader work *of* interview research and I will briefly return to this topic in the conclusion.

Potter and Hepburn (2005) end their discussion of 'necessary problems' with a cumulative point. If we take the four issues seriously, we need to recognise that interviews come off in and through interaction. This interactional work needs to be recovered for both analysts and readers. In taking the interactional quality of interviews seriously, serious questions are raised about how we, analytically, make sense of interviews. This leads them to discuss inescapable (analytic) problems.

Follow-up questions

Their discussion of the necessary problem is centered on demonstrating that there 'is a profound complexity in interview material' (p. 297). This has consequences for how we can make sense of interview data and it is 'rarely explicitly expressed' (ibid.). As outlined above, the radical critique positions the very mundane interactional processes embedded in the conduct of interviews as introducing excessive noise in the data about the phenomenon under study. The dynamic, interactional work necessary to produce data for any form of analysis 'bleeds into' the data.

They outline four deeply related issues. These are data-led, brief demonstrations targeted at topics of potential relevance to a psychological audience.

1. Flooding the interview with social science agendas

They demonstrate how an interview question can shape the trajectory of talk in terms of topics. Interview questions are routinely embedded with social science theorizing, as they either explicitly or implicitly highlight some ways of thinking and/or speaking about a topic. Interviewers responses can mark the interviewees' talk as newsworthy, and in turn further shape the trajectory of the topic. As they note,

> these issues face us with the possibility that a piece of interview research is chasing its own tail, offering up its own agendas and categories and getting those same agendas and categories back in a refined or filtered or inverted form.
>
> (p. 293)

They contrast a teacher being asked by a researcher to discuss teachers' constraints on time and resources, with 'a sequence of staff room troubles telling talk' (p. 292). They contrast the interview as a 'knowledge producing machine' with an emergent moment of naturally-occurring troubles talk. So, for them, one constrains and enables the potential trajectories, explicitly incites general accounts, and is 'researcher-prompted'. Whereas the other offers a specific moment of the phenomenon-in-action.

2. Interviewer's and interviewee's footing

How do you make sense of the various footings that emerge and weave through interviews? We have interviewers, at times, speaking for the research project, or speaking as a neutral observer, a collaborative researcher, and speaking from personal experience. We have interviewees asked to speak as a member of category, but 'are they speaking as individuals with an institutional identity or as persons with their own unique and idiosyncratic preferences?' (p. 293).

We have layers of shifting identity work, emerging from the questions, answers and the brief response tokens ('mm hm') to news tokens ('Oh, yeah').

3. Interviewer's and interviewee's stake and interest

They note this is 'both profound and complex' (p. 295) and, again, under-researched. For example, little research has focused on interviewers' introduction in pre-interview, often off-tape talk, where the researchers' stake is introduced. In my own practice, I have seen the impact of this is in action: where an interviewee, once I re-iterated, mid-interview, I was not a member of the clinical team she was commenting on, shifted to offer a much more critical account of that team.

4. Reproduction of cognitivism

We have a contrast between interviewers' reports on social processes and observing the organization of social processes in action. As they note, in reference to the transcript, 'here the teacher is being asked as a teacher not to be a teacher but to *formulate* features of the lives of teachers and what causes them to act in particular ways' (298, emphasis in original). Interviewees can be treated as a resource, offering 'conceptual rumination' (p. 297). Early work in discourse analysis questioned this assumption and shifted the focus onto such objects as interpretative repertoires. However, this returns us to Schegloff's (1998) response to Wetherell, such activities – say heteronormativity – are deeply situated in the context of their production and cannot easily extrapolated to other contexts. They outline that this caution needs to be extended to using cognitive language as somehow giving unmediated access to psychological phenomena. Talking about how you are 'stressed' or 'emotional' does inter-actional, moral and identity work (e.g., Firth and Kitzinger 1998; Hepburn and Brown 2001). The closing section reaffirms the problematics:

> Whatever the analytic perspective, inferring things appropriately from interviews involves understanding what is going on in them interactionally, and that in turn involves the complex and demanding task of analyzing the development of an implicit research agenda, identifying footing shifts, explicating orientations to stake and so on.
> (Potter and Hepburn 2005: 300)

Alongside offering a direction in the research agenda for the social studies of interviews, they caution the (relatively) unproblematic use of interviews and ask researchers to question whether they are essential. As they note, generating knowledge about sensitive topics is often raised as a rationale. However, as has been shown (e.g., Potter and Hepburn 2004; Butler et al. 2009), it is possible, albeit takes time. They end the article with the moral tale that has underwritten the paper, and is a central tenet to the radical critique of interviews, conversation analysis and (contemporary) discursive psychology – in order to understand a phenomenon, why rely on reports and accounts, why not observe the phenomenon-in-action? In this way, the contingent and necessary problems are avoided.

Answers (and criticisms)

Immediately following the article, three prominent researchers where given space to write commentaries. Each offered a specific trajectory of support, debate and criticism. At times the problematics they raised overlapped, at other points their discussion was, in part, reflexively documenting their own research interests. For example, Jonathan A. Smith, the key thinker in the development of Interpretative Phenomenological Analysis, offered a supportive commentary in general terms, but questioned the potential monadic view of Potter and Hepburn's vision. For him, such a focus denies the plurality of qualitative psychologies, each with their own norms, practices and objectives. He sought to recover the virtue of the interview to enable knowledge on 'personal sense making' (Smith et al. 2005: 311)[6] to be explored. Wendy Hollway focused on the work of subjectivity and narrative analysis, and contrasted the overly-local focus on immediate question-answer sequences with how 'The meaning of any part of an interview (or conversation) inheres in the whole' (ibid.: 312). Finally, Elliot Mishler offered a poetic deconstruction of the theoretical backdrop to Potter and Hepburn's piece. He outlined a broader debate – one that is played out in a range of journal articles and chapters (see for example Hester and Eglin 1997; Lynch and Bogen 1994): how the development of the norms of conversation analytic work reflect a neo-positivistic turn, and so loose the ethnomethodological foundations[7]. In what follows, I outline what I see as the main criticisms and then discuss Potter and Hepburn's response. Initially, I will focus on representational practices, then focus on questions of interview practice.

Questions (of representation and practice)

Smith and Hollway highlight that decisions about the style of representational practice should be led by analytic concerns. For them, the purpose of analysis, should lead the format of transcription. For Smith, you could undertake a layered approach, where you might produce different transcripts – with different forms of notation – to focus on different aspects, and then you could 'attempt' (Smith et al. 2005: 310) a synthesis. Both position a Jeffersonian transcript as imposing a specific professional vision (cf. Goodwin 1994), in which the notation interrupts the flow and for Hollway you lose 'much more meaning' (Smith et al. 2005: 313). Smith offers a similar position: 'it is extremely difficult to parse interview features and substantive topics at the same time' (ibid.: 310). They mark the demonstration of interactional dynamics as complicating making sense of 'topics' or 'meaning'.

Alongside this, all three seek to problematise that Jeffersonian transcription can offer idealized access to the phenomenon. As Hollway notes

> ... the belief that the more detailed and rigorous the transcription, the more faithful the researcher can be to the meanings and connotations of the conversation. Implication in their claims that transcription can be total and therefore leave nothing out on which meaning depends ... The audio record is still a far richer record than a Jeffersonian transcription.
>
> (Smith et al. 2005: 313)

There is no neutral or atheoretical style of representation and that notation 'cues the reader to a particular type of reading' (ibid.: 310). This echoes Watson's (1997 a, b) comments on how the categorical identifications on transcripts, for example the category-identification like 'Teacher', 'works to select and privilege one sociological characterization of ... exchanges over other potential characterizations' (1997a: 84). Mishler offers a range of alternate formats and traditions for transcribing interaction and notes that the visual field is missing. Smith also questions which of the range of *potential* interactional features should be included, which are essential, and whether video would be the necessary next step.

Finally, Hollway takes Potter and Hepburn's call to understand the context of the recruitment very seriously and extends that vision. For her,

> The responses of the interviewee at a particular juncture do not just relate back to the last few utterances of the interviewer and not just the last question. They are built up out of the whole history of the research encounter: how they where recruited, what they were told the interview was about, what happened before the tape recorder was switched on, the continuous dynamics (not just conscious) between interviewer and interviewee.
>
> (Smith et al. 2005: 312)

She challenges the radically-local view of much of CA and DP, where the context of immediately prior talk is seen to be orientated to in what follows. For her, Potter and Hepburn's approach draws out the 'most inconsequential, least important aspects of the data' (ibid.: 313). She offers a different direction, one in which the questions of context emerges in and through the overarching encounter, potentially through episodes separated by time. This does not appear to be in the direction of the discursive work of Mehan, Hertweck and Meihls' (e.g., 1986) 'constitutive ethnography', in which the proximal and distal are engaged, or following the various strands of action, through actor-network theory.

Relatively less space is devoted to unpacking the four necessary problems. Both Smith and Hollway position some of the practical problems as needing a practical, pedagogic solution. For example, for Hollway, issues of flooding are tied to 'asking inept questions' (Smith et al. 2005: 311). Well-designed questions, such as narrative questions, have the potential to 'elicit experience-near accounts' (ibid.: 313).

Answering (the critics)

Potter and Hepburn seek to affirm their 'therapeutic' directions. They outline that they where not attempting to direct others to undertake a CA or DP analysis of interviews. Instead, they where seeking to stimulate a direction of debate and research that explores the interactional conduct of interviews. They, 'hope this will lead to a more evidence-based approach to the design, conduct and analysis of interviews' (Smith et al. 2005: 319). Echoing the debate within medicine, this positions prior work as situated in custom and practice. And since this work, 'evidence-base' producing research on interviewing has been undertaken. For example, Irvine, Drew and Sainsbury (2010) compared the interactional dynamics of face-to-face and telephone interviews on the same topic in order to discover what, if anything, was the impact of different modes of interaction. For Potter and Hepburn, any training should be based on examples of the real-time, interactional work of interviews. Roulston (2010) argues that we should be actively encouraging researchers to transcribe their own interview recordings and ask them to focus on how they interact, as opposed to solely focusing on the topical content.

In responding to the questions around representation, they note that all transcription is theoretically embedded, but for them, given that interviews are interactional affairs –which they mark as none of the commentators disputing – we need at least some basis for representing this. For them, '(c)urrent common representational practices in interview research in psychology typically wipe out evidence of the collaborative construction of "findings"'(Smith et al. 2005: 320). Current transcription norms are inadequate and irrespective of approach, what people are saying – 'topics' or 'meaning' – emerges in and through interactional work.

Finally, I want to note that relatively limited focus was given to Potter and Hepburn's alternate, their vision of the primacy of the naturalistic record. Hollway, does offer a description that an interview 'in important respects resembles a naturalistic conversation' (p. 313). In a footnote, they caution against this view. There may be resemblances to everyday conversations, but, interviews have a 'characteristic and identifiable institutional form' (ibid.: 324). As noted in the introduction, a body of interactional studies has focused exactly on highlighting the interactional asymmetries between interviewers' and interviewees' actions. Although the preference for working with naturalistic data is not taken up, in any detail by these commentators, it is engaged with in other articles that sought to further question Potter and Hepburn's (2005) arguments.

Follow-up questions (about being there)

Two years later the debate is returned to in a paper by Christine Griffin (2007a). She positions Potter and Hepburn's (2005) article as arguing that naturalistic records should replace interviews as 'the default technique' (p. 248). She sees this as part of broader attempt of colonization, where demands for working with 'naturally-occurring talk' are moving beyond the domains of conversation analysis and discursive psychology. Griffin, in part, following Ashmore and Reed's (2000) critique of the norms of conversation analysis[8], renders those involved in doing work on naturalistic records as being concerned not to 'distort or influence the material collected for analysis' (Griffin, 2007a: 249). Although not described by such as Griffin, the discourse of hygiene seems central. Those doing naturalistic work seek to gain data that has 'not been "got up" by the researcher' (ibid.: 249), avoid 'contaminating the field' (ibid.: 253) and 'have taken no active part' (ibid.: 253) in the situation. Centrally, they can seek to distance themselves 'outside the research process' (ibid.: 253).

Griffin (2007a) wants to recover the research interview (and ethnographic work), to recognize the 'creative potential of the researcher's presence as an active part of the research encounter and the value offered by a reflexive analysis of such interactions' (p. 264). She focuses on two extracts from a research interview, where she is interviewing five young women,[9] 11–13 years old, about consumption practices. Her empirical argument centers on demonstrating that

> In both of these episodes my research agenda intertwined with the young women's interests and practices. It would be a mistake to view *all* aspects of this interaction as 'got up' solely for my benefit, or as questionable value for research analysis
>
> (ibid.: 265, emphasis in original)

She seeks to show how the interview can be analysed as both topic and resource.

Henwood (2007) then offers a supportive commentary on Griffin's paper, also employing a discourse of hygiene. She positions those as embracing naturalistic records as 'fear[ing] any involvement by the researcher for threatening to distort the integrity of interactional data' (p. 274). Potter and Hepburn's (2007) commentary follows, where this position is refused. This is not about a 'positivistic wish for neutrality' (p. 278). Following the early discourse analytic work on the interview, which advocated an active, engaged, confrontational interviewer, they still felt it difficult to achieve the 'desired *activity*' (p. 278, emphasis in original). They felt drawn to naturalistic records, given the potential they offered. They repeat the arguments that made in their 2005 paper and the response to their commentators. Working with interviews offers an additional layer of analytic complexity. They repeat that their 2005 paper was a therapeutic intervention, that it would be 'fruitful to gain more understanding of the operation of qualitative interviews using the resources of contemporary interaction analysis' (p. 279) and that such work could 'support better interview research' (p. 279).

In her response, Griffin (2007b) returns to an appeal for a place for engaged, active, research. She argues that a focus on both topic and resource is possible, 'although there is undoubtedly an urgent need for more good examples' (p. 284). To treat the interview as only giving access to the immediate here-and-now context of production is to deny something vital.

> [I]n my view *both* the talk (and other activities) that are generated for the benefit (or hindrance) of the researcher *and* the talk that is produced for other audiences and in relation to wider ideological configurations can fruitfully be the focus for analysis. In practice, it may not be possible to make a sharp distinction between talk that is generated for different audiences and in relation to different discursive, relational and ideological contexts.
>
> (p. 286, emphasis in original)

So the analytic uncertainty, the inability, at times, to make a 'sharp distinction', generated in and through the contextual complexity, is something Griffin accepts, given what she feel she gains from 'being there'.

Final closing questions

Since the article and debates outlined above, despite the questions about questioning that the articles raise, little appears to have changed. Those engaged in psychological studies using research interviews seem to have made few, if any, concessions. We have not seen a growth in work that focus on both topic and resource in relation to research interviews. Those involved in working with naturalistic records have not returned, in any noticeable way, to the research interview. We have not seen a growth in work that focuses on studying the psychological research interview as an 'interactional event in all its institutional and normative particulars' (Potter and Hepburn 2007: 278). Some work has been undertaken, for example, Abell et al.'s (2006) analysis of interviewers' acts of self-disclosure.

In reading the work of those doing studies of the local contexts of the interview interaction, what is interesting for me is that the focus has remained on the immediate context of the interview talk. As Briggs (2007) has outlined elsewhere and as Potter and Hepburn (2005) and Hollway (Smith et al. 2005) both briefly hint at, the actual interview is but one moment in a much broader trajectory. The broader contexts of the knowledge-producing machine, like recruitment interactions and data analysis practices, remain relatively unquestioned. In this way, to echo Schegloff's discussion of Wetherell's data, each interview could be then be understood by reference to its place in the enterprise. Following Briggs (2007), I have suggested elsewhere (Rapley 2012) a need to shift from a focus on the mundane interactional work *in* interviews to a broader focus on the situated, pragmatic work *of* interview research.

Notes

1. See Rapley (2012) for a response.
2. See also the work on focus groups (e.g., Myers and MacNaghten 1999, Puchta and Potter 2004)
3. Although at the time of writing, the link was no longer working.
4. Which those responding to the article, in part take up (see below).
5. Which she also labels as a 'group discussion' and 'small group interview'.
6. The journal conventions meant that all three commentaries and the reply are cited as a single reference, Smith et al. (2005) – where possible, I will highlight which specific author said what.
7. In their reply, especially in footnote 2, they offer an extended critique of what they see as his 'poorly grounded stereotypes of positions and claims' (ibid.: 324). They seek to recover the legitimacy of CA for those naïve to this debate.
8. See also Ashmore, MacMillan and Brown (2004) and Reed and Ashmore (2000) for related discussion.
9. It is interesting to note that neither Wetherell (1998) or Griffin's (2007a) draw on data from one-to-one interviews.

References

Abell, J., Locke, A., Condor, S., Gibson, S. and Stevenson, C. (2006) 'Trying similarity, doing difference: The role of interviewer self-disclosure in interview talk with young people', *Qualitative Research*, 6: 221–44.

Antaki, C. and Rapley, M. (1996) '"Quality of life" talk: The liberal paradox of psychological testing', *Discourse and Society*, 7: 293–316.

Ashmore, M. and Reed, D. (2000) 'Innocence and nostalgia in conversation analysis: The dynamic relations of tape and transcript [45 paragraphs]. *Qualitative Sozialforschung/Forum: Qualitative Social Research*, 1(3), Art. 3. Available at http://nbn-resolving.de/urn:nbn:de:0114-fqs000335 (accessed on 16 December, 2013).

Ashmore, M., MacMillan, K. and Brown S.D. (2004) 'It's a scream: Professional hearing and tape fetishism', *Journal of Pragmatics*, 36: 349–74.

Atkinson, P. and Silverman, D. (1997) 'Kundera's immortality: The interview society and the invention of the self', *Qualitative Inquiry*, 3: 304–25.

Baker, C.D. (1983) 'A "second look" at interviews with adolescents', *Journal of Youth & Adolescence*, 12: 501–19.

Baker, C.D. (1984) 'The search for adultness: Membership work in adolescent-adult talk', *Human Studies*, 7: 301–23.

Baker, C.D. (1997) 'Membership categorization and interview accounts', in D. Silverman (ed.), *Qualitative research: Theory, method and practice* (pp. 162–76). London: Sage.

Baruch, G. (1981) 'Moral tales: Parents' stories of encounters with the health profession', *Sociology of Health & Illness*, 3: 275–96.

Briggs, C. (1986) *Learning how to ask: A sociolinguistic appraisal of the role of the interview in social science research*. Cambridge: Cambridge University Press.

Briggs, C. (2007) 'Anthropology, interviewing, and communicability in contemporary society', *Current Anthropology*, 48: 551–80.

Butler, C.W., Danby, S., Emmison, M. and Thorpe, K. (2009) 'Managing medical advice seeking in calls to Child Health Line', *Sociology of Health & Illness*, 31: 817–34.

Firth, H. and Kitzinger, C. (1998) '"Emotion work" as a participants resource: A feminist analysis of young women's talk in interaction', *Sociology*, 32: 299–320.

Goodwin, C. (1994) 'Professional vision', *American Anthropologist*, 96: 606–33.
Griffin, C. (2007a) 'Being dead and being there: Research interviews, sharing hand cream and the preference for analysing "naturally occurring data"', *Discourse Studies*, 9: 246–69.
Griffin, C. (2007b) 'Different visions: A rejoinder to Henwood, Potter and Hepburn', *Discourse Studies*, 9: 283–7.
Grønnerød, J.S. (2004) 'On the meanings and uses of laughter in research interviews: Relationships between interviewed men and a woman interviewer', *Young*, 12: 31–49.
Hammersley, M. (2003) 'Recent radical criticism of interview studies: Any implications for the sociology of education?' *British Journal of Sociology of Education*, 24: 119–26.
Henwood, K.L. (2007) 'Beyond hypercriticality: Taking forward methodological inquiry and debate in discursive and qualitative psychology', *Discourse Studies*, 9: 270–5.
Hepburn, A. and Brown, S.D. (2001) 'Teacher stress and the management of accountability', *Human Relations*, 54: 531–55.
Hester, S. and Eglin, P. (eds) (1997) *Culture in action: Studies in membership categorization analysis*. Lanham, MD: International Institute for Ethnomethodology and Conversation Analysis and University Press of America.
Hester, S. and Francis, D. (1994) 'Doing data: The local organization of a sociological interview', *British Journal of Sociology*, 45: 675–95.
Irvine, A., Drew, P. and Sainsbury, R. (2010) *Mode effects in qualitative interviews: A comparison of semi-structured face-to-face and telephone interviews using conversation analysis*. University of York, York : Social Policy Research Unit
Lee, Y.-J. and Roth, W.-M. (2004). 'Making a scientist: Discursive "doing" of identity and self-presentation during research interviews' [37 paragraphs]. *Forum Qualitative Sozialforschung / Forum: Qualitative Social Research*, 5(1), Art. 12. Available at http://nbn-resolving.de/urn:nbn:de:0114-fqs0401123 (accessed on 16 December, 2013).
Lynch, M. and Bogen, D. (1994) 'Harvey Sacks' primitive natural science', *Theory, Culture & Society*, 11: 65–104.
Maynard, D.W., Houtkoop, H., Schaeffer, N.C. and van der Zouwen, H. (eds) (2002) *Standardization and tacit knowledge: Interaction and practice in the survey interview*. New York: Wiley Interscience.
Mazeland, H. and Have, P. ten. (1996) 'Essential tensions in (semi-)open research interviews', in I. Maso and F. Wester (eds), *The deliberate dialogue: Qualitative perspectives on the interview* (pp. 87 113). Brussels, Belgium: VUB University Press.
Mehan, H., Hertweck, J. and Meihls J.L. (1986) *Handicapping the handicapped: Decision making in students' educational careers*. Standford: Standford University Press.
Mishler, E.G. (1986) *Research interviewing: Context and narrative*. Cambridge, MA: Harvard University Press.
Myers, G. and MacNaghten, P. (1999) 'Can focus groups be analysed as talk?', in R. Barbour and J. Kitzinger (eds) *Developing focus group research: Politics, theory, and practice*. London: Sage.
Potter, J. and Hepburn, A. (2004) 'Analysis of NSPCC call openings', in S. Becker and A. Bryman (eds) *Understanding research methods for social policy and practice* (pp. 311–13). London: The Policy Press.
Potter, J. and Hepburn, A. (2005) 'Qualitative interviews in psychology: Problems and possibilities', *Qualitative Research in Psychology*, 2: 281–307.
Potter, J. and Hepburn, A. (2007) 'Life is out there: A comment on Griffin', *Discourse Studies*, 9: 277–83.

Potter, J. and Mulkay, M. (1985) 'Scientists' interview talk: Interviews as a technique for revealing participants' interpretative practices', in M. Brenner, J. Brown and D. Canter (eds) *The research interview: Uses and approaches*. London: Academic Press.

Potter, J. and Wetherell, M. (1987) *Discourse and social psychology: Beyond attitudes and behaviour*. London: Sage.

Puchta, C. and Potter, J. (2004) *Focus group practice*. London: Sage.

Rapley, T. (2001) 'The art(fulness) of open-ended interviewing: Some considerations on analysing interviews', *Qualitative Research*, 1: 303–23.

Rapley, T. (2004) 'Interviews', in C. Seale, G. Gobo, J.F. Gubrium and D. Silverman (eds), *Qualitative research practice* (pp. 15–33). London: Sage.

Rapley, T. (2012) 'The (extra)ordinary practices of qualitative interviewing', in J. Gubrium, J. Holstein, A.B. Marvasti and K.D. McKinney (eds) *The SAGE handbook of interview research: The complexity of the craft*. London: Sage.

Reed, D. and Ashmore, M. (2000). The naturally-occurring chat machine. *M/C: A Journal of Media and Culture*, 3(4). Available at http://journal.media-culture.org.au/0008/machine.php (accessed on 16 December, 2013).

Roulston, K. (2000) 'The management of "safe" and "unsafe" complaint sequences in research interviews', *Text*, 20: 1–39.

Roulston, K. (2001) 'Data analysis and "theorizing as ideology"', *Qualitative Research*, 1: 279–302.

Roulston, K. (2006) 'Close encounters of the "CA" kind: A review of literature analyzing talk in research interviews', *Qualitative Research*, 6: 515–34.

Roulston, K. (2010) 'Considering quality in qualitative interviewing', *Qualitative Research*, 10: 199–228.

Roulston, K., Baker, C.D. and Liljestrom, A. (2001) 'Analyzing the researcher's work in generating data: The case of complaints', *Qualitative Inquiry*, 7: 745–72.

Schegloff, E. (1997) 'Whose text? Whose context?', *Discourse & Society*, 8: 165–87.

Schegloff, E. (1998) 'Reply to Wetherell', *Discourse & Society*, 9(3): 457–60.

Smith, J.A., Hollway, W. and Mishler, E.G. (2005) 'Commentaries on Potter and Hepburn, "Qualitative interviews in psychology: Problems and possibilities"', *Qualitative Research in Psychology*, 2(4): 309–25.

Suchman, L. and Jordon, B. (1990) 'Interactional troubles in face-to-face survey interviews', *Journal of the American Statistical Association*, 85: 232–41.

Watson, D.R. (1997a) 'Ethnomethodology and textual analysis', in D. Silverman, *Qualitative research: Theory, method and practice* (first edn). London: Sage.

Watson, D.R. (1997b) 'Some general reflections on "categorization" and "sequence" in the analysis of conversation', in S. Hester and P. Eglin (eds) *Culture in action: Studies in membership categorization analysis*. Lanham, MD: International Institute for Ethnomethodology and Conversation Analysis and University Press of America.

Watson, D.R. and Weinberg, T.S. (1982) 'Interviews and the interactional construction of accounts of homosexual identity', *Social Analysis*, 11: 56–78.

Wetherell, M. (1998) 'Positioning and interpretative repertoires: Conversation analysis and post-structuralism in dialogue', *Discourse & Society*, 9: 387–412.

Part II
Cognition, emotion and the psychological thesaurus

6 What happened to post-cognitive psychology?

Hedwig te Molder

Target article: Potter, J. (2000) 'Post-cognitive psychology', *Theory & Psychology*, 10: 31–7.

It is fifteen years since Jonathan Potter (2000: 31) declared that now was 'an occasion for risking big thoughts about what comes next'. He was referring to the future of a psychology outside the cognitivist paradigm. Derek Edwards' *Discourse and cognition* (1997) had been published a few years before. The time was ripe for the development of a full-blown alternative to the cognitivist perspective that had been dominating psychology since it parted from behaviourism.

As is clear from the contents of Potter's manifesto – and the fact that the article was published in *Theory & Psychology* – his appeal was predominantly directed at psychologists (and psychologists in the making). Even though that was the case, the post-cognitive project never became part of mainstream psychology. More than anything else, it sparked discussion and critical self-examination among interaction analysts. This chapter focuses on the actual and potential implications of post-cognitive thought for interaction analysis, and does so in two ways.

First, on a more abstract level, I will re-examine the discussion on cognition that is reflected by the collection of papers in *Conversation and cognition* (te Molder and Potter 2005). Despite its apparent non-cognitivist character, conversation analysis (CA) occasionally shows signs of nostalgia: it is longing for a world in which cognition represents firm ground and real evidence. Discursive psychology (DP), on the other hand, consistently treats cognition as a participant's achievement, and a practical resource in interaction. This makes it more radical from a philosophy of science point of view and for some, though unjustly, more conservative in terms of the extent to which the approach is truly interactional.

Second, I will discuss an emerging subfield in CA – epistemics-in-action – and review some of its achievements in the light of post-cognitivist criteria. While the field bears a strong resemblance with some of the long-standing key ambitions of DP, there is little or no uptake of earlier insights from DP. I want to argue that cross-fertilization between CA and DP is essential here. It can prevent epistemics from slipping into a more traditional understanding of knowledge before the benefits of a post-cognitivist approach have been reaped.

Conversation and cognition

What is post-cognitivism? The core is perhaps most elegantly formulated by Harvey Sacks, founder of CA, when he reassures analysts about the kind of concerns they need *not* have:

> Don't worry about how fast they're 'thinking'. First of all, don't worry about whether they're thinking. Just try to come to terms with how it is that the thing comes off. Because you'll find that they can do these things. [. . .] Look to see how it is that persons go about producing what they do produce.
> (Sacks 1992: 11)

Sacks's key advice is to focus is on practices – how do participants go about producing what they do produce – rather than on processes under the skull. Note how he presents this focus as methodological rather than ideological. Trust participants' skillfulness and take their abilities for granted; only then researchers will be able to decipher *how* participants do it. It is not necessary to assume that cognition does not exist, or define it as a no-go area. It should be put between brackets, by way of methodology, in order to be able to recognize and analyse participants' practices. There is no 'neat Chomskian realm of underlying processes and entities' (Potter 2000: 36) to rely on; instead the researcher must content himself with the ostensibly messy but 'rich surface of language' (Edwards, 2006a: 41).

The focus on natural conversation has major implications for how one understands human behaviour. One of the defining features of a traditional cognitive worldview is the idea that mental states *precede* people's talk and behaviour. Behaviour can be explained in terms of motives, intentions, beliefs, etc., that drive, cause and predict that behaviour. While not all cognitivist studies claim cause-and-effect relationships, they nonetheless carry the aura of causality and explanatory power, and the corresponding promises of prediction and applicability. The aim or suggestion of causal explanation is a crucial difference with the framework of normative accountability that underlies CA and DP (Edwards 2006a). Behaviour is not understood 'from the outside', as driven by mental predicates, but 'from within', by looking at how people understand *each other*. People do and define actions against a background of what is normal and proper. But norms and rules are not simply obeyed; they can be *made* relevant and thus also constitute the situation as understandable in a particular way.

The 'usefulness' of cognition versus interaction

In a way Sacks's post-cognitivist notion of human action makes things a lot easier. As an analyst you no longer have to worry about *whether* people think, let alone how *fast* they think. You can take all that for granted and leave it where it is. However, there is no sense of relief in most cases. The lack of causality is often framed as a methodological inadequacy (cf. Edwards, 2012). It is not seen as a choice for a perspective that neatly fits the requirements of the object of study. It is positioned as having no firm ground, no reality to start from ('this is how people really think'; 'this is how it really is'). As a consequence, a post-cognitive framework is more easily framed in terms of what it lacks or can*not* do than in terms of what it *can* do. It functions as a second-best alternative, waiting for real evidence to come. Interestingly, some of these sentiments can also be found among interaction analysts themselves.

Judging from Sacks's quote, one would think that (a form of) non-cognitivism would be a matter of course among conversation analysts. However, from the collection of papers in *Conversation and cognition* (te Molder and Potter, 2005) a different picture arises. Originally, the volume was meant to set up a post-cognitive project in the broadest sense of the word. Leading conversation and interaction analysts were invited to examine and theorize on the status of cognition in interaction. Its aim was to further flesh out the post-cognitive perspective that we, Jonathan Potter and I, thought that CA (already) was, and to make it more widely known, i.e., outside the relatively small circle of CA scholars. The volume ended up full of sophisticated studies but it was much less agreeing about the role of cognition in interaction than we had expected. Simplifying to some extent, three sorts of conceptualizations of cognition in relation to interaction can be found in the book:

1. According to some contributors *cognitive aspects can and must be distinguished from interactional features.* Robert Sanders, for example, proposes to ground and justify, or challenge, the observational claims that are made in discourse studies by testing the assumptions on cognition on which they rest, thereby arguing against Sacks's advice not to worry about people's capacities to think fast. Paul Drew recognizes cognitive moments in the interaction – for example: the intention to decline an invitation, or a state of confusion – which allow the analyst to establish the actual mental state of an interactant (for a thorough discussion of Drew's contribution, see Potter 2006). Anita Pomerantz argues that it is possible and useful to let participants, who were part of an interactional study, share their views of what actually happened with the researcher in the form of video-stimulated comments. She suggests that CA is already more cognitivist than it thinks it is. In this sense, her method would only make explicit what is already assumed or hinted at in CA work. The similarity between these different reasons for distinguishing between cognitive and interactional features within the analysis, is the assumption that (only) with the help of cognition it is possible to establish participants' *real* understandings (Pomerantz), *actual* intentions or confusions (Drew), or to test whether participants' competencies *actually* match the assumptions on cognition on which interaction studies rest (Sanders). In short, the complementarity

of a cognitive to an interactional framework consists of its capacity to provide proof that otherwise would not be available. However, this move reflexively marks the interactional results as not providing the necessary (extra) substantiation, as if the studies cannot stand on their own feet even when the goal of the analysis is different, namely shedding light on the normative organization of the talk.

2. A second set of scholars develops *an agnostic view of cognition* on the basis that it is hard to establish whether or when we deal with 'real' motives, intentions, attitudes, etc. We should therefore not jump to conclusions when it comes to analyzing cognitions. John Heritage's chapter is an example of this. It focuses on how the particle 'Oh' is used to display remembering, or not having expected a particular answer to a question, and how it is bound up with knowledge entitlement issues. Heritage's proposal is to prioritize and prefer an interactional approach to the change of state token 'Oh', over a cognitive view of it. There *may* be a relationship between the cognition and the display of that mental state in interaction but we cannot be certain, for example because cognitive states may be withheld. We must refrain from making statements about cognition when we lack the evidence, and that is usually the case. Robert Hopper's analysis of a corpus of calls made from and to President Johnson's office soon after he became president of the US, is a thorough examination of possible evidence for the existence of so-called pre-strategies in talk. He concludes, very similar to Heritage, that mental states of this kind are very hard to pin down, which should make analysts reluctant to draw conclusions of a cognitive nature. Contributions from this perspective suggest that a cognitive 'check' or embedding of what can be discerned interactionally, could be important but unfortunately there is no(t enough) evidence on which to base these claims. What they do not make clear, however, is *why* a cognitive element would be necessary and/or what it adds to the existing interaction analysis.

3. Third, there is the discursive psychological view of cognition, as represented by the chapter from Derek Edwards and Jonathan Potter. While it propagates an agnostic stance regarding cognition, it does not do so out of a lack of possible evidence. Here, *cognition is put between brackets*, not because it is declared non-existent or it cannot be proven, but because it is most fruitfully seen as a participants' resource *pur sang*. Interaction is an area on its own that warrants investigation, and for this area to become researchable, one has to 'methodically' ignore the cognitive realm. Edwards (1997: 99) points out that 'conversational exchange is the area in which motives and intentional states are at stake for participants, and is therefore analytically prior to the mental states that supposedly precede it.' In this respect, the DP view on cognition remains closest to the perspective that Harvey Sacks originally seems to have developed: do not worry about cognition, but let it sit where it sits.

DP as the radical version of post-cognitivism

Without it ever having been its objective – on the contrary – the volume on *Conversation and cognition* shows the unease of conversation analysts when confronted with the role of cognition in and for interaction analysis. The argument for a (partly) cognitive approach is predominantly based on 'negative' reasons: what do we miss when we leave out cognition? This question anticipates that we would miss a lot, most likely real proof for what we conclude on the basis of our interactional analyses. My argument is not that the question about what we would miss is an unjustified one. Its focus is, however, too narrow. We must also wonder and ponder a bit more about what exactly we *gain* by focusing on (what seem to be) surface matters, at the expense of diving into the (again seemingly) deep waters of cognition. Though perhaps cognition can be 'done', we do not need it to show the robustness of our studies that focus on a different terrain – a terrain for which the chosen methods seem highly appropriate. This is difficult for a perspective that, despite its achievements, has always remained somewhat marginal. But its unique focus and systematic nature of inquiry is also the main and the best reason for its attractiveness.

In line with its post-cognitivist nature and aim, DP has always resisted the inclination to draw a line and define a place that is beyond interactional scrutiny (cf. Edwards, Ashmore and Potter 1995). This is best expressed in its interest in the mind/world, or subject/object, distinction (Edwards and Potter 1992; Edwards 1997) as a participants' rather than an analysts' topic. Precisely where we seem to bump into a domain that should be reserved for the researcher, namely the distinction between reality and subjectivity or cognition itself, discursive psychologists become truly interested and turn it into a participants' matter. Cognition is consistently dealt with *practically*, that is, as something managed in talk, up to the point that the distinction between cognition and reality itself is at stake for participants. Rather than this being a unique situation, it is common practice in everyday talk. The DP interest is there because it concerns an essential part of what people do in their talk, if not unavoidable and omnipresent. Rather than presupposing a particular boundary between the objective world and the subjective mind, talk is studied for how participants draw the line themselves, and the kind of interactional business that it performs.

In the early days of DP, the interest was particularly in how things and events come to be established as factual and objective. Bound up with this interest, there was a focus on how stake and interest are managed by speakers – confessed, countered, or treated as irrelevant – so as to protect the factuality of their descriptions, or, conversely, how speakers attribute them to others in order to undermine an account's objectivity (Potter 1996). Displays of ignorance ('I don't know') can be drawn upon as to play down the speaker's stake in a particular description, in this case speaker Jimmy's proneness to see his wife's 'sociability' as revealing 'sexual availability':

```
7    Jimmy:    Connie had a short skirt on I don' t know
```
(Potter, 1996: 131, DE-JF:C2:S1:10 – emphasis added)

Precisely at the point where Jimmy could be accused of jealously inspecting the length of his wife's skirt, he displays uncertainty about it, thereby resisting the implication of him being biased about his partner's intentions.

More recently, the idea of stake management has been extended to cover the idea of managing one's 'subjective side' more broadly (Edwards 2007). Subjectivity management refers to warding off stake or prejudice but also to resisting the idea that speakers exaggerate what they see or that they are disposed to be negative. Furthermore, the 'subjective side' is not by definition a threat to objectivity. Interactants may, for example, display themselves as an honest person or as someone with an inclination to speak plainly, and thereby enhance the objectivity of what they say.

In a study on modal expressions in police interrogation – as in: 'I wouldn't hurt an old lady' – Edwards (2006b: 479) shows how suspects use the inferential qualities of 'would' so as to build the subject-side basis of their account:

(1) PW:1:15 (Edwards 2006: 479), S = suspect ; P = police officer

```
13   S:   I didn' push
14        the woman or nothin, (0.5) I really did not do
15   →    that.= I' m not that type of person y ' know what I
16        me:an. .h Fair enough I stole the ciggies, (0.9)
17   →    I wouldn' hurt an old lady.
18        (0.5)
19   P:   [ Right. ]
20   S:   [ No.    ] (.) Not a chance.=
```

The 'would' in the suspect's self-assessment (line 17) invokes both generalized normative and (counter-)dispositional knowledge. As recipients we are invited to place ourselves *prior* to the event described and conclude that the suspect has not done what he is accused of: he recognizes the current moral order – you should not hit elderly ladies – and he is the type of person that would never do such a thing.

Rather than denying head-on, the speaker draws on what Edwards calls the *backdated predictability* of 'would' to manage his subjective side and provide him with the much-needed accountability. Note how the police officer is minimally acknowledging, but not objecting to, the suspect's generalized normative claim (line 19). The police officer's routine orientation to pursuing factual evidence tends to exclude such claims and thereby allows the suspect to produce a robust moral self-assessment.

Sneijder and te Molder (2005) showed how a similar blend of logic and morality was drawn upon in an online forum for vegans. A modal expression, embedded in a script formulation, enabled participants to attribute responsibility for vitamin deficiencies to individual practitioners, rather than to veganism as a whole. As with the backdated predictability of 'would', it was the formulation's design as a factual prediction, and the hidden normativity of the modal construction therein, that permitted speakers to display their attributional work as unmotivated:

(2) Sneijder and te Molder 2005: 685–6

```
Date: May 05
From: Paul
10           You can buy vegan B12 pills under
11           the Solgar brand, but check that
12           suitable for vegans is written on
13           the jar. I use the 100 mg. tablets
14           which I buy from the health food
15           store. You can get D3 by being
16    →      outside regularly. (sunlight). By
17    →      just ensuring you have a varied
18    →      diet you won't easily run the risk
19    →      of any other vitamin deficiency.
```

In lines 16–19, Paul presents a varied diet as a condition for not risking vitamin deficiency, using a scripted formulation (By doing X, you will not Y). 'Risking vitamin deficiency' is reformulated into a logical consequence of individual behaviour rather than something that is inherent in veganism. Note how the future orientation of *won't easily* (line 18) is difficult to distinguish from its reference to the recipient's ability to perform the required action. The suggestion is that 'not running the risk of vitamin deficiency' will (almost) directly follow from ensuring a varied diet. This expectation, however, also attends to the ability and therefore the rational obligation of the recipient to prevent deficiencies by following the proposed guidelines. The rationality of this and similar constructions allowed speakers to project themselves as 'doing description' rather than managing self-interest. It *can* be heard as an attribution of responsibility or blame, while it avoids associations with the need to disguise ideological weakness or to protect one's lifestyle against threats from outside. As with the modal expression in the police interrogation, this script-and-modal construction appeared robust, as it was not pursued or objected to as long as its potentially blaming character could plausibly be denied. It could be seen from the one case in which the formulation attributed blame in a more explicit manner, and evoked a defensive uptake, that its routinely descriptive character was important for the interactional business performed (ibid: 689–92).

From subjectivity management to epistemics-in-action: On rules to follow or rules to use

Discursive psychological research has always been interested in the fact-interest-accountability triangle, that is, in the interplay between mind and world, or subjectivity and objectivity, as seen through the eyes of participants themselves, and in how reports, while handling these matters, attend to the speaker's own accountability (Edwards and Potter 1992). The interest is not limited to what is achieved with managing that interplay but extends to *how* exactly speakers handle the subject-side basis of what they say (Edwards 2007) and what members' objectification methods (Potter 1996) consist of. A discursive psychologist is interested in *that* the action is performed but also *what* is being done to perform it. For example, speakers may underline the spontaneity of their observations, i.e., present them as not in any sense mentally prepared, as to ward off potential accusations of prejudice (Edwards 2003).

This focus on action is sometimes mistaken as a focus on content *per se*. Stivers, Mondada and Steensig (2011: 7–8) distinguish two strands of research that address 'how knowledge is managed in and through social interaction'. The first strand is discursive psychology, focusing on 'how knowledge, cognition, the mind and other psychological constructs are dealt with as topics by participants in interaction'. The second strand is mainly represented by conversation analysts, as Stivers et al. point out, and *'has not focused on the content on what is said* but on epistemic positions taken through language and embodied action' (my emphasis). Discursive psychology is thus defined as focusing on content *rather than* epistemic positioning. While it is not entirely clear what the latter is referring at, it seems to reduce DP to a kind of content analysis that is stripped of its interactional context. Although no hard and fast rule, DP studies usually want to create an *interaction-based* pathway into a relevant domain, rather than transcend that particular domain *per se* and reveal universal language structures. While the first does not exclude an interest in the second, the practical consequence of such an entry point may be that there is a specific interest in what the actions performed precisely entail, and the implications thereof for the field that is studied.

A study of face-to-face meetings between scientific experts and celiac patients about a new gluten-neutralizing pill (Veen et al. 2012), showed how a particular question design regarding the use of the pill suggested primary access to the patient's life by the experts and the irrationality of the person who would refuse the pill. On the basis of this study, recommendations were formulated on how to best interact with patient-users in relation to new therapies in the field of celiac disease. An example from a different domain is Wiggins' (2014) study of family mealtime talk. It demonstrated that the parents typically claimed epistemic primacy over their children's food preferences. The children's claims about 'likes' and (especially) 'don't likes', on the other hand, were frequently countered by their parents or treated as inappropriate. Wiggins concluded that it could be more effective for parents to inquire about, or soften claims about, their child's food preferences, so as to enable the children to claim epistemic primacy over their bodily states.

The crucial aspect to note here is not that the DP approach is distinctly different from CA. There is no question of a difference by principle between CA and DP – they cherish the very same interactional outlook on talk. DP, however, has always had a *simultaneous* interest in conversational normativity as found in adjacency pairs, that is, the relevance of (or preference for) a second pair part (e.g., an answer) as set up by the first pair part (a question), and the normativity of everyday social rules (such as what it is to be a credible expert or a good parent, including their rights and responsibilities).

In the case of the previously mentioned expert questions about the celiac pill, for example, both the conversational normativity is of importance – as the questions were designed to prefer particular answers – and the orientation to rules about what a rational patient or a good expert is (Veen et al. 2012). The following fragment is taken from one of the patient meetings organized by the Celiac Disease Consortium, a Dutch innovation cluster consisting of representatives of scientific research, patient associations, dieticians, general practitioners and industry. The closed questions that were used by the scientific experts (Ex) to ask patients (P) about a pill they were developing, biased the patient's reply to assuming the pill's use, and accepting the presuppositions that were made in the preface regarding the patients' quality of life (problematic) and the safety of the pill (100 per cent):

```
(3) (Veen et al. 2012: 470-1) Group 1, 24:26-26:20
1  P1 So you really want to know what we ↓think of such a pill. (1.5)
2  Ex Yes for us that is a eh very relevant question. (.) °Yes° (0.7) I
3  →  can imagine ↑right. What I hea:r here is of course like yes, the
4  →  diet is fine but it is hard. Hard to accept. Ehhh↓hh. (.)
5  →  Holiday a drag. Ehhh well the question is just (1.8) say such a
6  →  pill is coming. And this pill turns out to be completely safe.
7  →  (2.1) Will patients then ↑use it or ehhh (.) are we just sitting
8  →  around here ehhh developing [ some-
9  P4                              [ I guess we'll see how it ↑turns
10    out, hehehehhh
11    ((laughter))
12 P4 Yea [ hhh]
13 P2     [ Yes] I think it that it really depends on how you use it
```

The patient's turn in line 1 establishes what patients ' think of such a pill' as a new topic on the agenda. While acknowledging the relevance of this question, the expert ends up asking a different set of questions (lines 5–8) that shift the focus to patients' *use* of the pill. This reformulation is prepared by the description of dietary practice as a burden ('hard to accept', 'a drag', lines 4–5), which is presented as based on patients' own characterization of the diet as difficult ('What I hea:r here'). Moreover, the yes/no interrogative 'will patients then ↑use it' (line 7) is embedded between a preface that establishes the pill as a perfect solution to their highly unpleasant situation (lines 3–6), turning patients into irrational creatures if they would not accept it, and a postscript (lines 7–8) that frames a negative response as reducing the innovators' efforts to a waste of time. Hence, the preference is for a 'yes'.

By withholding an affirmative response (line 9), the patient both resists confirming the presuppositions about the problematic dietary practice and the pill's safety, and about what the expert displays as being at stake here. 'Are *we* just sitting around here' (lines 7–8) suggests that if the pill is not accepted, it is the innovators who will be negatively affected. So there are orientations to what a rational patient is and a good expert, including experts' and patients' (contested) rights and responsibilities – all of which are crucial for understanding what happens in this interaction.

Crucially, a DP analysis treats whatever kind of norms and rules '*not as principles governing human actions,* but as a resources that actors might use, or make relevant, in accounting for actions or in arguing about some event' (Edwards 1997: 5, my emphasis). This also applies to the social rules just referred to: notions regarding being a good patient or expert, including their rights and responsibilities, are taken into account in the analysis, but not as something fixed, i.e., as expressed by people's minds or reflecting the world-out-there. They are topicalized, negotiated about and dealt with as part of talk's daily business. Furthermore, DP starts from the ethnomethodological insight that accounts *of* actions are, always and at the same time, accounts *for* actions (Edwards 1997: 8; Garfinkel 1967), which explains why participants' epistemic and normative work are routinely and inextricably bound up with each other. Significantly enough, norms are often couched in descriptive rather than explicitly normative terms (see the earlier discussion about modal constructions).

It is here where the recent strand of work in CA devoted to epistemics at times seems to depart from a discursive psychological approach. While it may be a slip of the tongue, Stivers et al. (2011: 8) define epistemics as a strand that attempts to 'join sociology's interest in knowledge as a norm-*governed* domain'(my emphasis), where DP would define knowledge as a norm-*oriented* domain, in which norms function as resources rather than guidelines. The latter corresponds with a 'traditional' CA perspective, in which norms are seen as the 'grid' by reference to which whatever is done will become visible and assessable (Heritage 1984: 117). Remarkably, recent CA work sometimes shows a different view of the matter, in which knowledge plays a role comparable to that in more conventional sociological approaches.

From a causal to a normative model . . . and back again?

The status of intersubjective knowledge is a case in point. DP views common knowledge (Edwards 1997: 119) as 'inherently indeterminate, or interactionally at issue, rather than treating it as a reservoir of shared factual information which exists prior to, and is built up during, conversations.' CA's recent emphasis is on mutual knowledge as 'fundamentally involved in the production and ascription of action' (Heritage 2013: 559). More specifically, 'epistemic status' is seen as the central pragmatic resource in determining whether an utterance will be understood as requesting or asserting information. Participants' epistemic status refers to the relative access to some knowledge domain of two or more persons at some point in time. Despite the continued focus on the relative and relational nature of that status, there is a simultaneous inclination to resist that, and stress its 'realness'. As Heritage (2013: 558) puts it: 'For many domains of knowledge, the epistemic status of the interactants is an easily accessed, unquestionably presupposed, established, real and enduring state of affairs.' It is this shared knowledge of participants' epistemic access to some state of affairs that, for example, permits speakers to produce a statement with declarative syntax (line 5), which is nevertheless heard as a request for information (line 6):

(4) [MidWest 2.4] (Heritage 2012: 8)

```
1   DOC:            Are you married?
2                   (.)
3   PAT:            No.
4                   (.)
5   DOC:      ->    You're divorced (°cur[rently,°)
6   PAT:                            [ Mm hm,
```

The argument is that the utterance in line 5 (You're divorced (°currently,°)) is treated as an information request (despite its 'informative' syntax), because the interactants share knowledge on their mutual cognitive status or epistemic access. Both participants assume that the utterance concerns information within the patient's epistemic domain and so the doctor is not understood as doing 'informing' but as *searching* for information.

While it may not seem problematic here to assume what participants 'really think' about each other's epistemic status and what this status 'actually is', I would like to argue that it is. First of all, one may wonder what is gained by assuming that participants *know* each other's epistemic status. In order to understand the course of the interaction, it is essential to see that the utterance 'You're divorced (°currently,°)' is *treated as* an information request. For this to observe, we do not need to assume that participants *know* each other's status, only that they deal with each other as if that is the case. By doing the latter, we keep our eyes open for the fact that, not only the 'sharedness' of knowledge is difficult to determine, but also and more importantly, analytically often too readily assumed.

By refraining from judgments about the realness of participants' epistemic statuses researchers are allowed the space to analyse knowledge as *potentially* at stake, and 'simply' look at how everyday talk works. That is, as Edwards (2004: 44) puts it, without having to presuppose that talk is a reflection of speakers' and hearers' best mental guesses (the Honest Jo model), or something Machiavellian, on the basis of which interactants are assumed to scheme and plot all day long. Such a practical and dynamic perspective reminds us of the fact that interactants constantly perform work in order to establish 'the obvious'. Following Sacks and Schegloff, Edwards (ibid.) gives the example of how people *do* recognition rather than simply recognize people, namely by providing some basis for independently knowing the person.

(5) Holt: O88:1:9:2 (Edwards 2004: 46)

Lesley and Ed have been exchanging remarks on what they have each been doing lately. Ed responds to an inquiry by Lesley into whether he (still?) does 'private teaching':

```
1  E:   (...) I teach at uh:: North Cadb'ry a boy call'
2       Neville Cole?
3  L:   Oh↓:[ yes:,
4  E:       [ over there, (perchance yo[u know im?=
5  L:                                  [hn
6  L:   =No I do:[n't
```

Edwards (2004) argues that the orientation to that rule becomes visible in the interaction, for example in line 4, where Ed, despite Lesley's earlier recognition of the boy in line 3, pursues her recognition of the boy's name ((perchance you know im?=), as if Lesley has not yet been clear enough about it. In order to understand the course of the interaction, not only does one not *need* to know about participants' assumptions on each other's actual knowledge states, but such knowledge would also be in the way of a clear understanding of what happens here.

'Epistemic status' seems a fruitful concept as long as we do not take it for granted, i.e., not as given, out-there and constraining, but rather as a participants' resource. In that light, the question is whether we need the distinction between epistemic *status* and epistemic *stance*. Epistemic stance (Heritage 2012a: 6) is defined as the moment-by-moment expression of knowledge relationships, as managed through the design of turns at talk. Heritage argues that the additional concept of epistemic stance is necessary because epistemic status can be dissembled by persons who deploy epistemic stance to appear more, or less, knowledgeable than they really are (2012b: 33). One may wonder, however, how necessary that distinction is when we let go of the analyst's appreciation of how real a particular knowledge state is and remain focused on analysing these matters as participants' business. Stance is all there is, and even then we need (and should) not assume that this is what participants *really* think or know.

Apart from the fact that it is neither necessary nor analytically fruitful to assume the realness of epistemic status for understanding interaction, there are also grounds of principle for dropping the matter and letting the realness of stance and status rest. It dissuades the analyst from reverting to 'ontological gerrymandering' (Woolgar and Pawluch 1985), that is, shifting between different realities according to the analyst's choice.

It should be noted, however, that some CA analysts are more inclined to 'freeze' knowledge states and deploy the representational model, than others. Raymond (2010: 92), for example, argues that by alternating between question-formats, speakers may index (or claim or invoke the salience of) alternative social relations and thus make relevant different response forms. He emphasizes that 'the use of a form is not necessarily constrained by nor does it directly reflect what the participants *actually know, understand, or think they know*'(Raymond 2010: 96, my emphasis). At the other end of the spectrum we find recent work by Stevanovic and Peräkylä (2014: 188), who suggest that social relations are anchored in three orders: the epistemic, deontic and emotional order. The orderliness in people's orientations to these orders is founded on 'participants' shared moral and cognitive presuppositions'. The latter comes very close to pursuing causal explanations rather than normative bases for human practices (Edwards 2012), and seems far removed from the original and provoking ideas that Harold Garfinkel (1967) and Harvey Sacks (1992) once arrived at.

Conclusion

What happened to, and with, the post-cognitive project in interaction analysis? We have seen how the status of cognition has become a serious area of attention for interaction analysts. While discursive psychologists have grown so fond of CA that they like to see themselves as the true followers of Harvey Sacks's motto that one should never worry about how fast people are thinking, or even *whether* they are thinking, conversation analysts themselves maintain a love–hate relationship with cognition. There is, at least, an inclination to fixate matters and return to the solid ground of 'real' knowledge and 'actual' thinking, whereas discursive psychologists would never want to commit themselves to such an endeavour. This is not so much an ingrained and ideologically motivated point of view – see Sacks's advice at the beginning of this chapter – but first and foremost a practical way of looking at things: in order to understand what happens in the interaction it does not seem fruitful, counterproductive even, to deploy a causal and realist model of human action. However attractive the model of the 'hydraulic engine' driving sequences of interaction (Heritage 2012b: 49) may sound, there is no compelling reason to embrace it, especially not when it is at the expense of the far more dynamic, normative model of human action that still offers us vast and exciting undeveloped sites for research.

References

Edwards, D. (1997) *Discourse and cognition*. London: Sage.
Edwards, D. (2003) 'Analyzing racial discourse: the discursive psychology of mind-world relationships', in H. van den Berg, M. Wetherell and H. Houtkoop-Steenstra (eds) *Analyzing race talk: Multidisciplinary approaches to the interview* (pp. 31–48). Cambridge, UK: Cambridge University Press.
Edwards, D. (2004) 'Shared knowledge as a performative category in conversation', *Rivista di Psicololinguistica Applicata*, 4: 41–53.
Edwards, D. (2006a) 'Discourse, cognition and social practices: The rich surface of language and social interaction', *Discourse Studies*, 8: 41–9.
Edwards, D. (2006b) 'Facts, norms and dispositions: Practical uses of the modal verb would in police interrogations', *Discourse Studies*, 8: 475–501.

Edwards, D. (2007) 'Managing subjectivity in talk', in A. Hepburn and S. Wiggins (eds), *Discursive research in practice: New approaches to psychology and interaction* (pp. 31–49). Cambridge: Cambridge University Press.

Edwards, D. (2012) 'Discursive and scientific psychology', *British Journal of Social Psychology*, 51: 425–35.

Edwards, D., Ashmore, M. and Potter, J., (1995) 'Death and furniture: The rhetoric, politics and theology of bottom line arguments against relativism', *History of the Human Sciences*, 8: 25–49.

Edwards, D. and Potter, J. (1992) *Discursive psychology*. London, UK: Sage.

Garfinkel, H. (1967) *Studies in ethnomethodology*. Englewood Cliffs, NJ: Prentice-Hall.

Heritage, J. (1984) *Garfinkel and ethnomethodology*. Cambridge: Polity.

Heritage, J. (2012a) 'Epistemics in action: Action formation and territories of knowledge', *Research on Language and Social Interaction*, 45: 1–29.

Heritage, J. (2012b) 'The epistemic engine: Sequence organization and territories of knowledge', *Research on Language and Social Interaction*, 45: 30–52.

Heritage, J. (2013) 'Action formation and its epistemic (and other) backgrounds', *Discourse Studies*, 15: 551–78.

Potter, J. (1996) *Representing reality: Discourse, rhetoric and social construction*. London: Sage.

Potter, J. (2000) 'Post-cognitive psychology', *Theory & Psychology*, 10: 31–7.

Potter, J. (2006) 'Conversation and cognition', *Discourse Studies*, 8: 131–40.

Raymond, G. (2010) 'Grammar and social relations: Alternative forms of Yes/No-type initiating actions in health visitor interactions', in A. Freed and S. Ehrlich (eds), *"Why do you ask?" The function of questions in institutional discourse* (pp. 87–107). Oxford: Oxford University Press.

Sacks, H. (1992) *Lectures on conversation* (Vols I and II), edited by G. Jefferson. Oxford: Blackwell.

Sneijder, P. and te Molder, H. (2005) 'Moral logic and logical morality: Attributions of responsibility and blame in online discourse on veganism', *Discourse & Society*, 16: 675–96.

Stevanovic, M. and Peräkylä, A. (2014) 'Three orders in the organization of human action and social relations: On the interface between knowledge, power, and emotion in interaction', *Language in Society*, 43: 185–207.

Stivers, T., Mondada, L. and Steensig, J. (2011) 'Knowledge, morality and affiliation in social interaction', in T. Stivers, L. Mondada and J. Steensig (eds), *The morality of knowledge in conversation* (pp. 3–24). Cambridge: Cambridge University Press.

te Molder, H. and Potter, J. (eds) (2005) *Conversation and cognition*. Cambridge: Cambridge University Press.

Veen, M., te Molder, H., Gremmen, B. and van Woerkum, C. (2012) 'Competing agendas in upstream engagement meetings between celiac disease experts and patients', *Science Communication*, 34: 460–86.

Wiggins, S. (2014) 'Adult and child use of love, like, don't like and hate during family mealtimes: Subjective category assessments as food preference talk', *Appetite*, 80: 7–15.

Woolgar, S. and Pawluch, D. (1985) 'Ontological gerrymandering', *Social Problems*, 32: 214–27.

7 From Loughborough with love

How discursive psychology rocked the heart of social psychology's love affair with attitudes

Sally Wiggins

Target article: Potter, J. (1998) 'Discursive social psychology: From attitudes to evaluations', *European Review of Social Psychology*, 9: 233–66.

It is difficult to overestimate the importance of attitudes as a psychological concept. Within social psychology, in particular, their prominence is evident in journal articles, conference papers and undergraduate psychology programmes. Attitudes have, it could be argued, become psychology's most successful commodity (although the term was stolen from art and theatre originally; Danziger, 1997). Despite different academic and everyday definitions, the concept has reached the status of common sense, and this gives psychology leverage within cultural consciousness, for who can deny what is clearly a fact about people and society? Who would challenge attitudes and their political rhetoric?

In a paper that systematically demolished the foundations on which cognitive approaches to attitude research were built, then, there were bound to be aftershocks. In this chapter, I offer a reading of Potter's 'Discursive social psychology: From attitudes to evaluative practices' paper (Potter, 1998; referred to hereafter as DSP98, for brevity). I do not claim to provide a thorough review of all work that has been influenced by – and founded upon – DSP98. Mere citation count (at the time of writing, 158 citations), for instance, captures only those written documents that reference the original, and not the thousands of citations of the earlier works which inspired the paper. My aim, instead, is to prompt readers to read and/or return to DSP98 and to become enthused with the theoretical and analytical implications of the work therein. Like a good film or book, one might read something new each time; there is treasure here and more yet to come.

In the first part of this chapter, I place DSP98 in a specific academic context, highlighting the concerns that the paper was attending to and the perspectives that informed the basis of DSP98. I will also highlight where and how discursive psychological research has developed some of the issues raised in DSP98, and use examples from work that has taken the issue of evaluations a step or two further. For many of us, 'measuring' attitudes will never be the same again. Finally, I suggest ways in which research might continue to develop and challenge our understandings and practices around the concept of 'attitudes'. I will be arguing that we should embrace the topic of attitudes in all its diversity and potential, but that psychology should develop a more practice-focused and sophisticated approach to attitudes than is currently used in psychological research. Discursive psychologists need to re-claim the word and demonstrate its use in ways that are more akin to early definitions of attitude, which blurred the distinction between inner (i.e., cognitive processes) and outer (i.e., bodies, interaction and society) worlds (Danziger, 1997). Attitudes are alive and well in mainstream psychology (Hogg and Smith, 2007; Petty, Fazio and Briñol, 2012), but our understanding of them needs to develop too.

Part 1: Challenging dominant attitudes

At the turn of the twenty-first century, discursive research was gaining momentum. Major research councils were funding doctoral researchers – like myself at the time – and small pockets of activity were developing in an international landscape. More broadly, qualitative research was starting to be recognised within higher education institutions, international conferences and peer-reviewed journals. Such research was, however, still on the back-foot. It was common to have to explain discursive psychology (or other qualitative methodologies) to conference and journal audiences, to defend one's position as justifiable and appropriate in a research context. Being put on the defensive had started to become tiresome, given that research of this kind had been active for around fifteen years and was built on strong foundations that were already well established.

It was within this academic context that DSP98 was published. The paper explicitly positioned itself as '*introducing* a discursive approach to social psychology to people who are more familiar with the *mainstream* experimental social cognition tradition' (p. 233, emphases added). So, why the need for an introduction, given that discursive and critical approaches to psychology had been established for over a decade? That DSP98 aimed to 'introduce' the discursive approach to the 'mainstream' is a testament to the work required to break into the established zeitgeist of the time. Cognitive approaches across psychology – apparent in social, developmental, language and intelligence work specifically – were, at least during the 1990s, the dominant force. In the 1980s, the decade prior to DSP98, social psychology was typically researched exclusively using questionnaires or experimental studies. The political and economic issues being played out in the UK at that time were not just affecting the industrial trades; they were also having an impact on the intellectual and scientific climate. The 1980s had seen a dearth of social psychology jobs across the UK. In the intervening years between the end of the 1980s, and the early to mid-1990s, therefore, social psychologists were beginning to slowly regain resources and recognition for research.

The discursive work developed within DSP98 was, and to a great extent still is, heavily influenced by the sociology of scientific knowledge (SSK) (Gilbert and Mulkay, 1984), post-structuralism and the work of Barthes and Foucault, and by ethnomethodology and conversation analysis (Sacks, 1992). Adopting a relativist meta-theory and constructionist stance, the focus was placed squarely on everyday interaction and social practices as constituting the world. Bringing this approach to the very heart of social psychology – attitude theories – it is not surprising that the paper challenged the dominant cognitivist psychology. The form of discourse analysis developed for Potter and Wetherell's *Discourse and social psychology* (Potter and Wetherell, 1987), and later work, was itself drawn from SSK rather than linguistics. Some of the intellectual origins of discursive psychology and of DSP98 specifically, therefore, were clearly focused on understanding *practices*. DSP98 was advocating interdisciplinary work long before the term became fashionable in higher education. Before we examine how DSP98 brought this practice-focused approach to attitudes, however, it is helpful to consider the emerging conceptions of attitudes to date.

The changing face of attitude(s)

It was noted earlier that the concept of attitudes was not originally a psychological category, and Danziger (1997) provides an illuminating and thorough account of the changes in research on attitude and attitudes. Here, I provide a brief synopsis of Danziger's account to foreground the later discussion.

Research on the attitude concept (singular) has a much longer history than that of attitudes (plural). Its earliest roots lie in the arts and theatre, where an attitude referred to the physical posture of an actor, sculpture or painted figure. From this base, its use by Darwin (Darwin, 1872) in his work on expressions and emotions enabled a shift toward what became known as 'motor attitude', a concept with biological underpinnings (i.e., muscle movements). One of the early moves of psychological researchers such as Titchener (1909) and Allport (1924), was to further shift the focus for attitude research from motor expressions to individual psychology and cognitive functioning, to distinguish more clearly between 'attitudes' and 'expressions'. This was a crucial step for psychology. Attitudes therefore became a product of an internal, cognitive or affective state. The *expression* of an attitude could then be separated clearly from its source, and one could – according to this theoretical sleight-of-hand – distinguish between what people 'say' and what they 'really think' (see Chapter 10, this volume).

During the 1920s and 1930s, the concept of attitudes (plural) was now beginning to become established within psychological research. Perhaps most importantly for our current discussion, it was the emerging usage of the term 'social attitudes' (used, in particular, by brothers Floyd and Gordon Allport) that paved the way for contemporary psychological attitude research. This new term enabled psychologists to gain ground in what had typically been treated as sociological terrain. At the same time, psychology as a discipline was trying to assert itself as an individualistic, experimental science. For the blossoming area of social psychology, it became even more important to distinguish itself from sociological research. What enabled it to do so, sealing the success of 'social attitudes' as a psychological commodity, was the development of procedures for *measuring* attitudes.

The purported ability to measure attitudes – and in doing so, treat them as real, psychical entities – is possibly one of the key features that keeps cognitive approaches to attitudes alive and well in contemporary psychological research. Being able to measure something provides both for the lure of quantification (and by implication, generalizability) and practical application. Within social psychology (where attitude research is most frequently practiced) this is still a driving concern, for there is the potential that this area of the discipline will be the 'soft science'; letting the side down in terms of confirming psychology's place in the scientific world.

What should be clear, then, is that the academic context within which DSP98 was published was (and still is; see Jost and Kruglanski, 2002) alive with angst and political manoeuvring, not only about the status of attitude research, but the status of psychology as a discipline itself. DSP98 challenged not simply a single topic within psychology, but the foundations on which its status and future standing rested.

Re-considering the 'psychological thesaurus'

The DSP98 paper was not the first to challenge cognitive psychology's approach to attitudes. One of the founding texts of discourse analysis – Potter and Wetherell's (1987) *Discourse and social psychology* book – also spent much time unpacking the problems with the attitude concept. These include, for instance, the use of categories in attitude scales, the research context itself, the issue of variability in 'attitude' expressions, and the constitution of the attitude object through the very act of evaluation. One of the implications of this discursive challenge to attitudes was to put into question the assumption that attitude expressions are reflections of underlying cognitive states; that psychology need not be limited to the 'inner' world of cognitions and emotions, nor that such a distinction between inner and outer worlds need be made.

It is also important to keep in mind – as discussed in the previous section – that the attitude concept has itself undergone much debate among social cognitive psychologists too, with disagreement over whether it is a hypothetical construct (Eagly and Chaiken, 1993) or 'evaluative knowledge, represented in memory' (Fazio, 2007: 636). Even Gordon Allport (G.W. Allport, 1935) noted that it was the 'imprecision' of the attitude concept, the lack of an exact meaning, that made it so popular. There is also much variability within cognitive or discursive accounts of attitudes. As Potter himself notes:

> By starting with the notion of attitudes it would be easy to give the impression that there are pre-existing objects – attitudes – which are

understood in one way, or one set of ways, in mainstream social cognition work, and then understood in another way in discursive social psychology. However, this would understate the degree to which the attitude notion is constituted out of social psychological theory, and the extent to which the notion is dissolved in discursive social psychology into a range of other considerations.

(DSP98: p. 250)

Attitudes are thus a perfect example of how the use of nominals in academic writing (by social psychologists, among others) has created concepts; that is, by naming a process (e.g., evaluations, assessments, or judgements), it becomes a 'thing', an object (i.e., attitude) (Billig, 2011; Wittgenstein, 1953). This is problematic if we lose sight of the processes that we were examining in the first place; if the 'thing' is treated as fact without any further evidence that it exists.

There is, however, hope yet. The flexibility and variability of the attitude/s concept itself, from its definition to its application in numerous research environments, therefore, is rich with potential for future researchers. One need not feel constrained to use the term 'attitude' (or attitudes) in one way for cognitive work, and another for discursive work. What is required, however, is more empirical work that does not take the term 'attitude' at face value. Work that explicates and illuminates the 'other considerations' noted by Potter above. The term 'attitude' need not be a bad word for discursive researchers. We just need to re-consider how we orient to it and interpret it in light of empirical research.

To summarise so far, DSP98 is no less than a thorough re-appraisal of attitudes, both conceptually and analytically. It is feisty, yet exceptionally eloquent. It crystallises the many theoretical and methodological holes in cognitive, questionnaire-based studies of attitudes. Here, then, is a paper that captured the critical stirrings of the time; that made these tangible and clearly visible. For many researchers, the discursive challenge to attitudes was enough to question the cognitive interpretation of this concept. Too much was being lost in an attempt to put psychological issues into neat boxes. There was more to be gained by looking elsewhere. As attitude research continued to flourish within cognitive social psychology, therefore, DSP98 became a catalyst for new streams of research that have begun to shake the foundations a little further. It is to these streams of research that we turn next.

Part 2: Pulling attitudes apart

The scope of theoretical and analytical implications covered in DSP98 goes far beyond simply addressing the issue of attitudes, and many issues raised in the paper are addressed in other chapters in this collection. For instance, for issues of cognitivism see te Molder (Chapter 6) and for a consideration of the use of naturally occurring interaction rather than interviews, see Rapley (Chapter 5). This section will focus specifically on the impact of DSP98 in two substantive and inter-related areas: (a) the subtle variation of assessments in social interaction, and (b) subject-object relations and the role of attitudes.

a. *The subtle variation of assessments in interaction*

One of the core arguments of DSP98 was the importance of studying people's *practices*; that evaluations in themselves should be the goal of research, not considered as simply the route to something else (i.e., cognitions). The shift to examining evaluative practices is not only a methodological change; it is also a theoretical one. In other words, through examining the object 'attitude' in different ways, the object itself changes. For example, Puchta and Potter's work (2002; 2004) on focus groups demonstrated not only that we can examine this data collection method as an interactional event (i.e., in terms of how people participate in focus groups rather than using focus groups to access putative internal states), but also that they can be used to examine how evaluations are produced *as free-standing* opinions rather than as part of an interactional context (Puchta and Potter, 2002). This work showed, for instance, how the use of elaborate questions enabled focus group participants to produce the required output: the 'attitudes' of the focus group in a neat and useable package.

The shift in focus to evaluative practices also provided a major contribution to research on assessments (note that the terms 'evaluation' and 'assessment' are at times used interchangeably by researchers as well as in this chapter). This work in turn, of course, feeds back into attitude research. Alongside other established work in this area (Pomerantz, 1978; 1984), DSP98 highlighted the variable and socially-organised way in which assessments are grounded in everyday business and the functions and interactional implications of assessments.

Assessments and evaluations enable speakers to do a whole range of psychological business – from small-scale compliments to the management of speaker identities – in a way that often hides the complexity therein. For example, assessments produced as part of a gifting occasion (the event of giving or receiving a gift) are an intrinsic part of the way in which gifts are received (with delight, for example) and speakers identities are managed (as having provided a carefully-chosen gift, for example; see Robles, 2012). Yet they achieve this without speakers ever having to 'name' the event; 'it's lovely', for example, in a particular context, not only acknowledges the gift-recipient as grateful, but also the gift-occasion *as a gifting occasion*.

By examining evaluations in their everyday and institutional contexts, research has begun to explore the ways in which evaluations are functional[1], that they have consequences. These consequences are two-fold: first, for the immediate interaction (e.g., the example above where 'it's lovely' works to present the gift-recipient as grateful), and second, for our understanding of the process of evaluation/attitudes. In other words, that in examining the functions of evaluations, the 'evaluation' itself – and thus the supposed underlying attitude – is theorised in new ways.

It was noted earlier that part of the charm of the attitude concept was its ambiguous and heterogeneous nature; that research on attitudes can focus on any topic, if we simply consider 'attitudes toward X', replacing X with our topic of choice. Research that has drawn upon DSP98 and the arguments therein, for example, has analysed attitudes about violence towards women (Pease and Flood, 2008), attitudes toward war (Gibson, 2011), and language attitudes (Hyrkstedt and Kalaja, 1998; Saito, 2013). Some of this work has shown how a discursive approach to attitudes illuminates the contextual specificity of evaluative practices. For instance, 'it's lovely' in gift-giving (Robles, 2012) has a different set of functions, identities and accountabilities than 'it's lovely' in a family mealtime interaction (Wiggins, 2001). In the latter case, food may be the gift but there are also different expectations as to how one can make an assessment of food and what form of assessment this might be (Wiggins and Potter, 2003).

My own work on food evaluations in everyday family mealtimes can be used to illustrate the potential implications of DSP98 for research on evaluative practices and attitudes. Food evaluations can work, for instance, to compliment the food provider, to make an offer of or request more food, to assert a particular identity, and to reject food (Wiggins, 2001; 2004). They can also be categorised into different types: subjective (those that foreground the subject, or consumer; e.g., 'I love spinach') and objective (those that foreground the object, or food; e.g., 'spinach is yummy') (Wiggins and Potter 2003). They can also specify a particular item of food (e.g., '*this* spinach') or a wider category of food (e.g., 'spinach'). Furthermore, assessments of food can be performed through prosodic as well as lexical features: such as the gustatory 'mmm' (Wiggins, 2002) and the disgust-marker 'eugh' (Wiggins, 2013).

Evaluations are thus incredibly flexible and powerful interactional devices. In and of themselves, they warrant much greater attention in psychological research. But there is more to it than this. If food evaluations are sequentially and prosodically organised in social interaction, and their precise construction and format is dependent on other speakers, then attitudes must be as much a social product as an individual one. Crucially, though, we are not assuming an underlying cognitive entity; there is enough to be found on the 'surface', in social interaction (Edwards, 2006). Assessments of food that suggest embodied, physiological aspects (such as pleasure or disgust) further trouble the individualistic approach to attitudes. This brings us to our second focus for this section: the role of evaluative practices in understanding subject-object relations.

b. Subject-object relations and the role of attitudes

One of the methodological issues arising from attitude rating scales is the practice of using similar words to replace other words (e.g., 'good' vs. 'like') as if these were interchangeable. As Potter (1998) argued, it is quite possible to state that a particular film is 'a bad film' but also to state – without denying the first claim

– that 'I like it' (cf. Wiggins and Potter, 2003). This work highlights the distinction that evaluative terms make to construct an inner and outer world, a separation of person and the world, of 'internal' processes (such as thoughts, beliefs, attitudes, emotions) and 'external' facts; the subject-object distinction (Edwards, 2007). Taking a DP approach, the crucial phrase here is 'to construct': it is not that there is a subject/object dichotomy that is simply reported upon, but it is through discursive practices (including evaluations, assessments, and so on) that such a dichotomy is constituted as existing *a priori*.

An illustration of this issue can be seen below with an example from a family mealtime interaction. This example draws attention to the subtle work that is achieved through making assessments of other people's psychological and physiological states, such as satiety (Laurier and Wiggins, 2011), gustatory pleasure (Wiggins, 2002) and food disgust (Wiggins, 2013; 2014). That is, claims about others' bodily states. In the extract below, a Scottish family are eating an evening meal together. The family comprises a mother, father, two sons (Samuel, aged seven and Joseph – seated on the far left in Figure 7.1 – aged nine years) and daughter (Emma, aged five years). The main course is risotto; a rice dish which in this case includes bacon, onions and peas. At this point in the meal, most of the family have eaten all the food on their plates, though Joseph still has some food left. Both Mum and Dad then become involved in encouraging Joseph to eat more of his food.

Extract 1

```
1.  Mum:     could you- eat a bit more: (.) ↓Joseph
2.           please (0.2) 'stead of [ staring into space
3.  Joseph:                         [ na::h:
4.           (0.4) I don't °like it°
5.  Samuel:  Joseph-
6.  Mum:     >a little bit more< if you don't mind
7.  Joseph:  no::: ((shaking head))=
8.  Dad:     =I'm surprised
9.  Mum:     n:- >yeh<
10. Dad:     you had all the bacon
11.          (1.0)
12. Mum:     he likes bacon, he likes peas (0.2)
13.          and rice.
14. Dad:     yep
```

Among the complex negotiation of food between parents and children in this excerpt is the delicate issue of food preferences. On line 4, for example, Joseph provides a subjective, item assessment of the risotto ('I don't like it', line 4). This might be seen as a justification for his initial response to his Mum ('nah', line 3), that not liking the food is a valid reason for not eating (more of) it.

Figure 7.1 Family meal interaction

The exchange may have ended there; the request to eat more is turned down with a reasonable response. What follows instead (see Figure 7.1 above), is a differently formulated request (line 6) and a further refusal (line 7). Still the matter does not end and Mum and Dad then become engaged in a commentary between themselves about what Joseph 'likes' in categorical terms: 'he likes bacon, he likes peas, and rice' (lines 12–13).

Note the simple listed format with final falling intonation (line 13), and the immediate confirmation (line 14), which produce this claim as established knowledge. The talk thus moves from Joseph's stated dislike of the food on his plate (subjective item evaluation) to his ongoing food preferences (subjective category evaluations). Following this extract, Joseph's parents then proceed to request that he eat 'three more forkfuls' of his risotto and the negotiation of food-to-be-consumed continues.

The subject-object distinction invoked in this example is that of Joseph's 'likes', his apparent internal food preferences that are hereby claimed as public, and knowable, by his parents. Emerging work in this area has identified the discrepancies between parents and young children when making claims about others' food preferences (Wiggins, 2014). There seems to be a trend, for example, for children to mostly make claims about their own food preferences or dislikes, and for parents to make claims as frequently about their own and their child's food preferences; that parents orient to a right to know these bodily states, *and to use this knowledge* in the negotiation of eating practices. In the world of food preferences, then, the subject-side of physiological or cognitive states can become blurred with the object-side of obligations to eat or to know about children's eating habits.

Stating the likes (or dislikes) of another person, however, is a delicate matter. Work on epistemics in conversation analysis is already beginning to demonstrate the moral and interactional implications of knowledge claims, particularly where these relate to something that the other speaker should have greater access to (Heritage and Raymond, 2005; Stivers, Mondada and Steensig, 2011). This is what Pomerantz referred to as 'Type 1 knowables'; those things that a person *as subject* has the right and responsibility to know (Pomerantz, 1980). Knowledge of one's bodily processes (appetite, for example) or of cognitive processes (attitudes) or those that blur the two (emotions, food preferences) would be Type 1 knowables.

Discursive work on evaluative practices, therefore, is helping to illuminate the subject-object issue; to move beyond the Cartesian dualism that still exists, unstated, in much psychology research and theory. On the one hand, the subject-side is a public event and made available to do interactionally-relevant business, as with emotions research (Edwards, 1999; Hepburn, 2004; Peräkylä and Sorjonen, 2012). On the other hand, however, we might also begin to remove the subject-object dichotomy itself, through assessment research. That there is no clear dividing line between what is 'inside' and what is 'outside'.

So far, then, we have considered the theoretical framing of DSP98 and some of the work that has been inspired by its propositions and possibilities. We now look to the future, to consider what else might be gained from a re-working of the attitude concept and from further inspiration from DSP98.

Part 3: Re-defining attitudes

Since the publication of DSP98, discursive psychology has considerably changed the landscape of psychological research on attitudes. Cognitive psychology research on attitudes, for example, is becoming ever more fragmented and struggles to deal with a problematic core theory: either focusing more closely on putative internal states, such as implicit attitudes research (Petty, et al., 2012) or showing how cognitive attitudes have a wider social relevance while maintaining the distinction between inner and outer worlds (Hogg and Smith, 2007).

While the climate of research has changed, the gatekeeping of social psychology remains a concern. Even in recent textbooks, discursive work is absent or disregarded as being purely descriptive and unscientific. That such gatekeeping is problematic and is based on rather shaky empirical grounds has already been discussed at length (Potter, 2012). There are political and economic drivers that shape research and can marginalise alternative voices, and there have been warnings about the ever-smaller fractals within and between psychologists (Billig, 2012). As a discipline – and as social psychology, a sub-discipline – we need to be cautious about letting theoretical tensions go too far. Academic rigour and debate is important to drive forward theory and research, but this should not be at the cost of marginalisation and bullying tactics. In this spirit, therefore, I argue that the topic of attitudes should be used as a way to inspire innovative and collaborative research among social psychologists. DSP98's charting of an empirical as well as a constructionist approach to language is treated by some as evidence that there may be common ground between social constructionism and experimental approaches after all (Jost and Kruglanski, 2002).

The concept of attitudes is alive and kicking across a range of psychological topics and fields; it is unlikely to wain in the immediate future, and research on evaluative practices may be too easily ignored by cognitive social psychologists as 'not really about attitudes'. And so we can return to where we began. As Danziger (1997) noted, the concept of attitude (or attitudes, plural) has changed in its definition, uses and interpretations through generations of researchers. In the current academic climate, the cognitive interpretation is dominant and taken for granted as 'the' way of understanding attitudes. What may lie ahead is a gradual re-definition of the concept, developing an understanding that focuses more on practices and consequences, then on supposed thought states. As research on attitudes evolves, and the separation of subject/object becomes further troubled, so too will the reliability of measurement of attitudes lose its impact.

Discursive psychology can again take inspiration from conversation analysis, among other fields, in considering issues of 'stance' (Englebretson, 2007; Kärkkäinen, 2006). Stance captures some of the features of attitudes and evaluative practices, while blurring interactional, dispositional and embodied elements. We need not reject the term 'attitudes' therefore, nor baulk at its supposed cognitive existence. What is more promising is a refined and more subtle definition than is currently dominant, based on empirical research and the diversity of evaluative practices in different settings. Attitudes, therefore, are likely to continue as a key research area for some time to come. What DSP98 has contributed to, however, is an alternative way forward for this research. This is just the beginning.

Note

1 Note that this is very different from functional approaches to attitudes.

References

Allport, F.H. (1924) *Social psychology*. Boston, TX: Houghton Mifflin.

Allport, G.W. (1935) 'Attitudes', in C. Murchison (ed.) *A handbook of social psychology* (pp. 798–844). New York: Russell and Russell.

Billig, M. (2011) 'Writing social psychology: Fictional things and unpopulated texts', *British Journal of Social Psychology*, 50: 4–20.

Billig, M. (2012) 'Undisciplined beginnings, academic success, and discursive psychology', *British Journal of Social Psychology*, 51: 413–24.

Danziger, K. (1997) *Naming the mind: How psychology found its language*. London: Sage.

Darwin, C. (1872) *The expression of the emotions in man and animals*. London: John Murray.

Eagly, A.H. and Chaiken, S. (1993) *The psychology of attitudes*. New York: Harcourt Brace Jovanich.

Edwards, D. (1999) 'Emotion discourse', *Culture & Psychology*, 5: 271–91.

Edwards, D. (2006) 'Discourse, cognition and social practices: The rich surface of language and social interaction', *Discourse Studies*, 8: 41–9.

Edwards, D. (2007) 'Managing subjectivity in talk', in A. Hepburn and S. Wiggins (eds) *Discursive research in practice: New approaches to psychology and interaction* (pp. 31–49). Cambridge: Cambridge University Press.

Englebretson (ed.) (2007) *Stancetaking in discourse: Subjectivity, evaluation, interaction* (Vol. 164). Amsterdam: John Benjamins Publishing.

Fazio, R.H. (2007) 'Attitudes as object-evaluation associations of varying strength', *Social Cognition*, 25: 603.

Gibson, S. (2011) '"I'm not a war monger but . . .": Discourse analysis and social psychological peace research', *Journal of Community & Applied Social Psychology*, 22: 159–73.

Gilbert, G.N. and Mulkay, M. (1984) *Opening Pandora's box: A sociological analysis of scientists' discourse*. Cambridge: Cambridge University Press.

Hepburn, A. (2004) 'Crying: Notes on description, transcription and interaction', *Research on Language & Social Interaction*, 37: 251–90.

Heritage, J. and Raymond, G. (2005) 'The terms of agreement: Indexing epistemic authority and subordination in assessment sequences', *Social Psychology Quarterly*, 68: 15–38.

Hogg, M.A. and Smith, J.R. (2007) 'Attitudes in social context: A social identity perspective', *European Review of Social Psychology*, 18: 89–131.

Hyrkstedt, I. and Kalaja, P. (1998) 'Attitudes toward English and its functions in Finland: A discourse-analytic study', *World Englishes*, 17: 345–57.

Jost, J.F. and Kruglanski, A.W. (2002) 'The estrangement of social constructionism and experimental social psychology: History of the rift and prospects for reconciliation', *Personality & Social Psychology Review*, 6: 168–87.

Kärkkäinen, E. (2006) 'Stance taking in conversation: From subjectivity to intersubjectivity', *Text & Talk*, 26: 699–731.

Laurier, E. and Wiggins, S. (2011) 'Finishing the family meal: The interactional organisation of satiety', *Appetite*, 56: 53–64.

Pease, B. and Flood, M. (2008) 'Rethinking the significance of attitudes in preventing men's violence against women', *Australian Journal of Social Issues*, 43: 547–61.

Peräkylä, A. and Sorjonen, M.-L. (eds) (2012) *Emotion in interaction*. Cambridge: Cambridge University Press.

Petty, R.E., Fazio, R.H. and Briñol, P. (eds) (2012). *Attitudes: Insights from the new implicit measures*. London: Psychology Press.

Pomerantz, A. (1978) 'Compliment responses: Notes on the co-operation of multiple constraints', in J. Schenkein (ed.), *Studies in the organisation of conversational interaction* (pp. 79–112). New York: Academic Press.

Pomerantz, A. (1980) 'Telling my side: "Limited access" as a "fishing" device', *Sociological Inquiry*, 50: 186–98.

Pomerantz, A. (1984) 'Agreeing and disagreeing with assessments: Some features of preferred/dispreferred turn shapes', in J.M. Atkinson and J. Heritage (eds), *Structures of social action: Studies in conversation analysis* (pp. 57–101). Cambridge: Cambridge University Press.

Potter, J. (1998) 'Discursive social psychology: From attitudes to evaluative practices', *European Review of Social Psychology*, 9: 233–66.

Potter, J. (2012) 'Re-reading *Discourse and social psychology*: Transforming social psychology', *British Journal of Social Psychology*, 51: 436–55.

Potter, J. and Wetherell, M. (1987) *Discourse and social psychology: Beyond attitudes and behaviour*. London: Sage.

Puchta, C. and Potter, J. (2002) 'Manufacturing individual opinions: Market research focus groups and the discursive psychology of evaluation', *British Journal of Social Psychology*, 41: 345–63.

Puchta, C. and Potter, J. (2004) *Focus group practice*. London: Sage.

Robles, J.S. (2012) 'Troubles with assessments in gifting occasions', *Discourse Studies*, 14: 753–77.

Sacks, H. (1992) *Lectures on conversation* (Volumes I and II). Cambridge: Blackwell Press.

Saito, A. (2013) 'The construction of language attitudes, English(es), and identites in written accounts of Japanese youths'. PhD dissertation, University of Southern Queensland.

Stivers, T., Mondada, L. and Steensig, J. (eds) (2011) *The morality of knowledge in conversation*. Cambridge: Cambridge University Press.

Titchener, E.B. (1909) *Experimental psychology of the thought processes*. London: Macmillan.

Wiggins, S. (2001) 'Construction and action in food evaluation: Conversational data', *Journal of Language & Social Psychology*, 20: 445–63.

Wiggins, S. (2002) 'Talking with your mouth full: Gustatory mmms and the embodiment of pleasure', *Research on Language & Social Interaction*, 35: 311–36.

Wiggins, S. (2004) 'Talking about taste: Using a discursive psychological approach to examine challenges to food evaluations', *Appetite*, 43: 29–38.

Wiggins, S. (2013) 'The social life of "eugh": Disgust as assessment in family mealtimes', *British Journal of Social Psychology*, 52: 480–509.

Wiggins, S. (2014) 'Family mealtimes, yuckiness and the socialization of disgust responses by preschool children', in P. Szatrowski (ed.) *Language and food: Verbal and nonverbal experiences* (pp. 211–32). Amsterdam: John Benjamins.

Wiggins, S. (2014). 'Adult and child use of "love", "like", "don't like" and "hate" during family mealtimes: Subjective category assessments as food preference talk', *Appetite*, 80: 7–15.

Wiggins, S. and Potter, J. (2003) 'Attitudes and evaluative practices: Category vs. item and subjective vs. objective constructions in everyday food assessments', *British Journal of Social Psychology*, 42: 13–531.

Wittgenstein, L. (1953) *Philosophical investigations*. Oxford: Blackwell.

8 Discursive psychology and emotion

Carrie Childs and Alexa Hepburn

Target article: Edwards, D. (1999) 'Emotion discourse', *Culture & Psychology*, 5: 271–91.

Discursive psychology (DP) offers a window onto the way emotion and cognition play out in everyday interaction. As one of the pioneers of DP, Edwards has been instrumental in shaping this approach, and his work on emotion and interaction has been particularly inspiring. In this chapter we consider this impact by providing an understanding of the concerns that motivated Edwards, the contributions of the paper and the lasting impact that his research has had on how emotion is conceptualized. Edwards developed a discursive psychology of emotion that examined two things: the ways in which emotion categories can be threaded through everyday talk, and how people use ascriptions and avowals of emotion to perform actions in talk. This focus on how wonderfully useful emotion categories and descriptions can be for speakers had never been done, and still sits in stark contrast to classic individualist studies that characterize the discipline of psychology.

Academic context

Our lay understanding of emotions is that they are things that emerge within us, sometimes bursting through cultural restrictions – the legacy of a more primitive animal past. This view is the starting point for most traditional psychological research into emotion (e.g., Röttger-Rössler and Jürgen, 2009). However, a number of researchers, inspired by the pioneering research of Edwards, have started to work up a very different image. Emotion is not treated as something underlying and separate from interaction, rather as something invoked, described and made accountable for the purposes of actions in talk.

In developing the discursive psychology of emotion, Edwards had two rhetorical targets. First, the ethological, universalist idea of people sharing the same basic set of emotions, a notion developed by Paul Ekman (1992). Edwards notes that rather than being open to difference in emotions, cross-cultural studies invariably start with English language categories – anger, sadness and so on. This means that typical English emotion terms are treated as the kind of thing that emotion *is*, and the problem is to look for *it* – emotion – cross culturally (Hepburn, 2003). However, Edwards notes that the category 'emotion' is a recent arrival in English:

> the English word *emotion* has only recently acquired its current status as a *superordinate* category under which other words such as *anger, indignation, jealousy,* and *surprise* can be grouped together. As a historically modern concept (at least in English), the word *emotion* starts to look a dubious category under which to group all the ways that other cultures (including our own, in other times) talk about feelings, reactions, attitudinal judgments (if we can use all *these* terms), and related matters.
>
> (Edwards, 1997: 196)

Throughout the 1970s and 1980s anthropological and historical studies challenged the 'basic emotions' approach by raising questions regarding the universality and ahistoricality of emotions. Historical analyses have shown that there are changes in the emotional repertoires of cultures throughout history (e.g., Harré, 1986). Meanwhile, anthropological studies have challenged 'cultural assumptions found in Western thinking about the emotions' (Lutz, 1988: 3), arguing instead that uses of emotion terms are bound up with social structure and moral attributions rather than individual feelings.

Social constructionist and discursive approaches gained momentum throughout the 1980s in the context of these cultural and historical analyses (e.g., Harré, 1986). For these researchers emotions are cultural products that acquire meaning within social structure and, far from being discrete, innate entities, can only be experienced in the context of social encounters. One wide-ranging example is Kenneth Gergen and Jonathan Shotter's relational perspective (Gergen, 2009; Shotter, 1997). They relocate our 'inner lives' and emotions in the relational encounters between people, arguing that 'meaning lies not within the private mind, but in the process of relating' (Gergen, 2009: 98). Emotion words are not to be understood as representations of private states but 'as actions within relationships, actions that gain their meaning through social collaboration' (ibid.).

A second target for Edwards' approach was mainstream psychology's individualist approach to emotion. This developed around the notion that studying what people do and how they communicate means studying the mental machinery by which individuals perceive, code and explain the world around them. Emotions are understood as variables that influence behaviour. Researchers assume that private emotions can be accessed through language. Emotion terms (such as 'angry', 'sad', 'happy') are understood as referring to private entities that exist within individuals' minds. Language is a tool that allows the researcher to access these entities. From the outset DP developed as a challenge to this referential view of language.

A more positive influence is Wittgenstein's linguistic philosophy, which excludes the possibility of a private language that develops as individuals label private emotions. Wittgenstein's work is incompatible with cognitive-semantic models of language. He argues that language functions according to shared norms of life and as such emotion words cannot refer to private, discrete states – they require agreed upon, public criteria to determine their proper use. DP also takes seriously Wittgenstein's observation that 'words are deeds' (1980: 46). That is, rather than communicating a private mental state, any emotion term is a means of performing an action. This is reflected in DP's focus on the action orientation of talk, where the primary issue is the interactional work that is done.

The focus of the discursive psychological approach to emotion is the interactive uses of emotion terms, what individuals are *doing* when they avow or ascribe emotions. Work has shown that emotion terms are used to perform a range of social actions such as ascribing blame, assigning intentionality and motives for actions, offering excuses and accounts. Emotion has been approached as an interactional phenomenon in contexts such as relationship counselling (Edwards, 1995), family mealtimes (Childs, 2014) and helpline interaction (Hepburn and Potter, 2007).

While social constructionist studies of emotion and the philosophy of Wittgenstein cleared the intellectual space for the discursive psychology of emotion, work in ethnomethodology and conversation analysis (CA) (Garfinkel, 1967; Sacks, 1992) was a direct theoretical and analytical precursor. As a non-cognitivist approach to discourse, CA makes problematic any approach that understands talk as the communication of speakers' thoughts and intentions (Edwards, 1997). The work of Sacks and his colleagues in CA highlighted that talk is *action* and that language *does* things, rather than acting as a means of communication; 'it is a form of activity; not a medium for the transmission of thoughts, nor for the realization of some other underlying reality' (Edwards, 1995: 585). This provides a direct challenge to psychological theories of language, with implications for some of the prime topics of the cognitive sciences. A discursive psychology of emotion focusses on how emotions are invoked and put to use by people themselves *in situ*. What psychologists have traditionally seen as personal, individualized notions are now seen in terms of their location in broader social and interactional practices. Mind, reality and emotions are treated as discourse's topics and business and analysis focuses on how participants descriptively construct them (Edwards, 1997).

Emotion discourse: Summary

Edwards' (1999) study has had lasting impact and has spawned an expanding and evolving body of empirical studies of emotion in social interaction. He suggests that whatever semantic and conceptual features there may be to emotions, and whatever similarities there might be between these in different cultures, the flexible potential of emotion terms is crucial. This flexibility makes them ideal for performing a range of actions. In order to capture this flexibility Edwards sets out ten rhetorical contrasts. These are central to the interactional project of 'constructing the sense of events and orienting to normative and moral orders, to responsibility and blame, intentionality and social evaluation' (p. 279). These contrasts do not indicate what emotion terms mean, but list the variety of interactional functions that emotion terms can perform. The point is to study emotion as it appears in human practices – whether counselling, courtrooms or other settings. Rather than moving to abstraction and universalism, this approach stays with the specifics of emotions and their local deployment (Hepburn, 2003). Here we offer brief illustrations of each of the ten rhetorical contrasts using materials from Bill Clinton's discussions of his relationship with Monica Lewinsky under Grand Jury cross-examination (extract 1, from Locke and Edwards, 2003) and relationship counselling sessions (extract 2, from Edwards, 1999).

This first extract is taken from Bill Clinton's discussion of his relationship with Monica Lewinsky. Clinton is being questioned about a particular visit to the Whitehouse made by Lewinsky.

Extract 1

```
1   Q:  A:nd Mrs Currie and yourself were: very i:rate
2       (.) that (0.3) Ms Lewinsky had overhea:rd (0.7)
3       uh tha:t you were in the oval office with a
4       visitor. (.) On that day. (.) Isn't that correct
5       that you and Mrs Currie were (.) very irate
6       about that.
7           (4.5)
8   C:  We:ll (1.0) I don't remember (.) all that (.) uh
9       what I remember i:s that she was very um (0.7)
10      Monica was very upset= she got upset from time
11      to time, (0.8) a:nd u:m (3.5) and I was (0.4)
12      you know (0.4) I couldn't see her I had- (.) I
13      was doing as I re↑member u:m (0.7) I had some
14      other work to do that morning, (.) and sh sh
15      she had just sort of showed up and wanted to be
16      let in, and wanted to come in at a certain
17      ti:me, (.) and she wanted everything to be (.)
18      that way, .hh and we couldn't see her.= Now I
19      did arrange to see her later that da:y. (0.5)
20      And I was upset about (.) her conduct. (0.3) I'm
21      not sure I knew (1.0) or focused o:n at that
22      moment (1.0) exactly the question you ask.=
23      I remember I was- (.) I thought her conduct was
24      inappropriate that day.
```

A number of the contrasts set out by Edwards are concerned with notions of rationality – emotion discourse may be used both to establish and to undermine rational accountability.

Emotion vs. cognition

Emotions contrast to cognition. Actions and words can be constructed as expressions of feelings rather than thoughts. In Extract 1 Lewinsky is described as 'very upset'. Considering Clinton's characterization of Lewinsky reveals the discursive work that such invocations perform. Her reactions are characterized *as emotional*, this undermines her rational accountability and it is implied that she has not made a sensible appraisal of Clinton's character.

Irrational vs. rational

Emotions may be considered irrational and inappropriate or as rational and appropriate. In Extract 1 Clinton manages blame and accountability by depicting himself as rational and sensible in contrast to Lewinsky who is irrational and emotional. Lewinsky is described as getting 'upset from time to time', she is *prone* to getting upset, in contrast to Clinton who is understandably 'upset' about Lewinsky's conduct.

The second extract is taken from relationship counselling with a couple, Connie and Jimmy. Following Connie's description of a particular incident, Jimmy is narrating his version of the events, which contrast with Connie's.

Extract 2

```
1  Jimmy:   Uh: I was (.) boiling at this stage and
2           I was real angry with Connie ( ). And
3           uh went up to bed 'n(.)I lay on the bed.
4           (0.7) °got into bed.° (0.6) I- uh (.) could
5           hear giggling ('n all that) downstairs and
6           then (0.5) the music changed (0.5) slow
7           records. (1.2) And um: (1.2) >and then .they
8           changed to slow records< (0.8) I could
9           hea::r (1.0) that Connie was dancing with
10          (0.2) this blo:ke downstairs. (1.0) And
11          Caroline turned round and said (.) something
12          (.) about it (it was wha-) it was oh Connie
13          look out I'm going to tell (.) Jimmy on you.
14          (1.0) And (.) next thing I hear is (.) °what
15          he doesn't know (doesn't) hurt him.°
16                (0.2)
17 Counsel: °I'm sorry?°
18 Jimmy:   What he: doesn't know: doesn't hurt him.
19          (0.8) Soon as I heard that I went- (1.6)
20          straight down the stairs. (0.8) 'n uh (0.6)
21          threw them out. (1.2) Took Connie up the
22          stairs and threw her on the bed. (1.6) I kept
```

```
23            trying to ru:n to jump out the window. (1.6)
24            But y' know: I I couldn't. (.) I couldn't (.)
25            get myself (0.4) to go out. (.) I couldn't
26            (.) do it.
27 Counsel:   So that's what you felt like.
28 Jimmy:    Oh ye:h. felt
```

Cognitively grounded and/or cognitively consequential

Emotions may rationally stem from cognitive insights. Jimmy's 'as soon as I heard that ...' implies a prior cognitive assessment. On the other hand, cognitive consequences are rational insights that stem from emotional experiences, such as Clinton's thoughts about Lewinsky's inappropriate conduct following her 'upset'.

A further major feature of emotion discourse as is that emotions may be constructed with regard to how routine or exceptional they are. Emotion may be worked up as exceptional or otherwise as routine and dispositional:

Event-driven vs. dispositional

Emotions can be driven by events or dispositions. They may be responses that anyone would have faced with the same event; or they can be characteristic features of the way individuals act. That Lewinsky 'got upset from time to time' implies that she was prone to being 'upset' and that any 'upset' may be caused by her disposition, rather than anything done by Clinton to provoke this.

Dispositions vs. temporary states

Lewinsky's tendency towards 'upset' contrasts with Clinton's reactive upset, which was *caused* by Lewinsky's 'inappropriate' actions. Similarly, that Jimmy was 'boiling at this stage' implies that this was a temporary state caused by Connie's actions, rather than a disposition toward anger.

Spontaneous vs. externally caused

There are different ways of assigning causes – one may be angry *because* of something. On the other hand, 'internal' causes may be invoked, such as Lewinsky's dispositional, internally caused upset in Extract 1.

A number of Edwards' contrasts highlight that the notion that emotions are private, innate states that emerge within us is a useful way of talking.

Emotional behaviour as controllable action or passive action

Emotions can be controllable or can be passive reactions. Feelings can be expressed or acted out, or can flood through the person beyond their control.

In Extract 2, while Jimmy was 'boiling', he controlled his actions 'I didn't hit you'. Similarly, although he tried 'to run to jump out the window' he controls his private emotions and 'couldn't do it'.

Natural vs. moral

Emotions may be considered unconscious, automatic bodily reactions or as moral, social judgements. Clinton 'thought' that Lewinsky's behaviour was inappropriate, implying a logical decision based on Lewinsky's actions. This conscious, moral judgement contrasts with Lewinsky's natural 'upset' that she was unable to control.

Honest (spontaneous, reactive) vs. fake

'Honest' emotions are those uncontrollable spontaneous reactions, versus either cognitive calculation or 'faked', insincere emotions. In Extract 1 Jimmy's 'angry' reaction is spontaneous and sincere – it is what he 'felt like'.

Internal states vs. external behaviour: Private ('feelings') vs. public ('expressions', 'displays')

Individuals may make reports about their own experiences and the contents of their own mind – they may express their emotions. Conversely, emotions may be ascribed to others based on overt behaviour. For example, the Grand Jury questioner asserts that Clinton was 'very irate'. Clinton refutes this by describing Lewinsky's inappropriate conduct, at which he was upset.

This is not a definitive or discrete list and these contrasts are interrelated and flexible. As such, the focus of analysis can be on one or several of these features at once. These rhetorical contrasts highlight the action orientation of emotion discourse – the variety of things that emotion talk does. Emotion discourse is conceptualized as action orientated and contemporary analyses have focussed on specific aspects that derive from this. Emotion descriptions are not understandable because they refer to individual feelings that we all share and recognize, rather they are resources to be deployed to perform a range of actions. These rhetorical contrasts are '*ways of talking* about things, ways of constructing the sense of events, and orienting to normative and moral orders, to responsibility and blame, intentionality and social evaluation' (Edwards, 1999: 279). For example, in Extract 1, the depiction of Lewinsky as someone who gets 'upset from time to time' invokes and ascribes dispositional (rather than *temporary* or *event-driven*) upset. This constructs Lewinsky's behaviour as non-normative, implying that the difficulties at the Whitehouse occurred because Lewinsky is the kind of person to get 'upset'. This also undermines Lewinsky's account and protects Clinton from blame – Lewinsky's upset underlies not only her own behaviour but also her false accounts of Clinton's actions. The description of Lewinsky as someone who is prone to 'upset' contrasts with event-driven upset

– an understandable reaction to Clinton's actions. Thus we should look to Lewinsky herself for the causes of her upset, rather than anything that Clinton may have done to cause this.

Work in DP has been described as focussing only on the uses of emotion and mental state terms, with analysis restricted to instances in which these terms are explicitly invoked (Coulter, 1999). However, studies have focussed on different aspects. The first major strand is the respecification of emotion as a discourse practice. DP provides an analytically based alternative to mainstream approaches to emotion, which is reworked as a discursive practice. Emotion discourse is an integral feature of talk that is approached empirically. A second strand is the 'psychological thesaurus' – a focus on the situated, occasioned uses of emotion terms and how these terms are put to use by people themselves *in situ*. A third strand examines how 'emotion' themes are handled and managed without necessarily being overtly labelled as such (see Attenborough, Chapter 15, in this volume). The focus is how descriptions of events and actions are organized in ways that invoke and manage themes such as caring and empathy. As Edwards (2012) notes 'the analytic interest is talk *as* talk', how notions of mind and emotion are topicalized, handled and managed in specific settings. This is in stark contrast to approaches that view language as a vehicle through which emotion is expressed.

The contribution of discursive psychology

So far we have outlined the disciplinary context of the discursive psychology of emotion and have summarized its general features. We will now go on to consider the lasting contribution and impact of Edwards' work in several interrelated areas.

Discursive psychology and social constructionist studies of emotion

The sociology of emotion, in particular social constructionist studies, were an important precursor to DP. By drawing on the rigorous tools of CA, Edwards' research has brought back into this work a way of developing studies of emotion that is grounded in the 'details of actual events' (Sacks, 1984: 26).

The sociology of emotion emerged as a distinct field in the 1970s as anthropological and historical studies challenged the 'basic emotions' approach. During the 1980s research began to go beyond the development of broad perspectives as researchers started to offer an empirically grounded account (see Thoits, 1989 for a review). However, this early work tended to be descriptive and theoretical, rather than empirical, as studies traced the creation and maintenance of emotions within social relations. While these studies directed attention to language and emotion talk, now recognized as differing from culture to culture, how language should be analysed remained unclear. This work lacked methodological rigour and analytic sophistication, and as such prior to the 1990s the literature on emotion discourse was limited. DP extended social constructionist studies of emotion, developing these in an empirically based way. Edwards set out a rigorous analytical approach for the study of emotions in the context in which they occur. DP's continuing engagement with CA provides a way of a way of grounding analysis systematically with regard to empirical data.

For example, Harré (1986) outlines what he considers to be the basic features of emotions, such the local moral order, the social function performed by emotion displays and the systematic rules that govern social action. There is discussion of how 'certain emotions, such as shame and anger, also function to facilitate social control' (Harré and Parrot, 1996: 3). CA provides the tools needed to explicate the orderly, socially organized, situated practices of which social life is composed. Participant's orientations to the moral order and questions of social control have been approached empirically by the broad programme of work in DP that considers how social influence operates in the family (Childs, 2014; Hepburn and Potter, 2011). This involves close analysis of naturalistic data, drawing on conversation analytic literature that has examined syntactic constraints imposed by first pair parts of adjacency pairs, the sequential design of requests and directives and accounts and their sequential design. Drawing on these tools has allowed researchers to explicate some of Harré's basic features of emotions in an empirically based way. For example, Hepburn and Potter (2011) identify emotional escalation in threat sequences in family mealtimes involving 'increased volume, strong assessments, and sharp intonation' (19).

Discursive psychology, respecification and critique

A distinctive feature of a discursive psychology of emotion is its continuing critical engagement with assumptions in cognitive psychology. DP has developed within and as an alternative to mainstream contemporary psychology and has reworked and respecified 'psychology' in discursive terms. There is a fundamental argument regarding the status of cognition as the driving force behind human behaviour. As Potter notes,

> DP has systematic metatheoretical, theoretical, analytic, and empirical grounds for being opposed to this when it is instantiated in experiments, when it appears in a wide range of ways of generating and analysing interviews, and when it is played out in perspectives such as interpretative phenomenological analysis or grounded theory.
>
> (2010: 694)

A major contribution of DP has been the critique of experimental approaches and the respecification of emotion as interactional phenomena.

An early example is Locke's (2003) examination of uses of emotion terms in athletes' accounts. The study of competitive anxiety has been a dominant area of research as scholars have examined the effects of emotions on performance. Anxiety is typically measured by self-report and as such is placed firmly in the biology and cognition of the individual. Emotions are understood as inner mental states that can be measured. In her study of interviews with athletes Locke argues the importance of examining how emotion terms are used in interaction. The focus is on what speakers, rather than analysts, treat as relevant. Experiencing particular types of emotion, such as 'nervousness' is treated as normal and expectable in competitive sport. As emotion discourse can be related to notions of rationality or irrationality, in their accounts athletes were not only accountable for their emotions but for their ability to control them. To soften this accountability, emotions such as 'anxiety' and 'nervousness' were constructed as 'positive' and as facilitative to performance. This work, which shows how emotion discourse is displayed and made accountable in talk, is a departure from understanding emotions as measurable variables that influence sport performance.

More recently, research has highlighted the limitations of work in 'Theory of Mind'. In an examination of uses of the mental state term 'want', Childs (2014) has mapped out an approach to examining what are traditionally understood as 'desires' in studies of social cognition. A major assumption of work in 'Theory of Mind' is that prior to the age of four, children understand others' actions in terms of their desires. It is not until this age that children understand the concept of belief and are able to explain others' behaviour by utilising a belief-desire framework – others act as they *desire* something and *believe* that they can satisfy this desire. Support for this comes from two main strands of research – experimental studies of children's understanding of desires and studies of children's language. Childs shows how this work is based on several problematic assumptions. Drawing on DP's critique of the tendency to attempt to investigate cognition using materials that have been created for that purpose, a fundamental problem discussed by Childs is the idea that vignettes are an adequate 'stand in' for reality. A second target is the notion that language is a methodological tool that allows access to the contents of children's minds. This referential view of language does not account for how mental state terms are used in talk. Rather than making inferences about references to alleged internal states, a more fruitful approach is to recognize that any invocation of 'wanting' will always be a means of performing an action within a conversational sequence. This discursive alternative represents a move away from understanding 'desire' as an individualized notion.

Discursive psychology and studies of emotion in social interaction

Studies of emotion in social interaction have diverse roots and come from disciplines such as interactional sociolinguistics, linguistic anthropology and CA. Work has documented phenomena associated with affect and has explicated how such phenomena are sequentially organized. DP has made a major contribution to this literature as the work of Edwards is one of the few examples to discuss emotion in social interactions in both a theoretical and pragmatic manner (Pepin, 2008). Further, the focus on the ways in which emotion terms are invoked has underpinned work that examines lexical and prosodic resources for expressing emotion. Hepburn (2004) pioneered a body of research in DP that focuses not simply on the categories or formulations of emotion, but also its interactional display. Initial research argued for the value of careful transcription of crying and the different ways of responding to crying, as this reveals a collection of loosely associated and sometimes escalating practices, facilitating identification of its interactional features. For example, crying is something that can both inflect and replace talk, and so can interfere with, but also dramatize or underscore talk. This can makes its uptake complex and tricky – it involves orientating to something that is oriented to in the manner of its delivery, rather than to an action, claim or proposition. Also, cryers may be unwilling for their emotional state to become part of public discourse, creating challenges in responding.

Extract 3 provides an illustration of this. The caller has become upset while divulging abuse for the first time. As is common in this environment, the business of the call is interrupted by a sequence that is focused on the upset itself.

Extract 3

```
1    Caller:    .H.shihh
2               (0.5)
3    Caller:    HHh
4               (0.4)
5               >°°↑Ghhd- ↑al- (like°°< (0.2) °°↑↑i°° (1.4)
6               °°↑↑bleedin ↑↑k:id°°
7               (1.9)
8    Caller:    °°Ghho' I'm a°° °↑↑grown ↑↑man°
9               (1.7)
10   Caller:         K.HHhh Hh[ h ]
11   CPO:                   [Th]ere's:: a bit of the child in ↑all
12              of us an- (0.7) an [that's the h(h)urt chi(h)ld]
13   Caller:                      [ .H h h h     H h h h ]
14   CPO:       there is↑un' it. with you at the moment.
15   Caller:         °.Hhhhh° >hh< >h< >h<
16              (3.5)
17   CPO:       ↑Dohn't worry, °th- i-° tahke your ti:me.
```

The caller illustrates a number of the classic elements of crying: increased aspiration, whispered delivery, sobbing, elevated pitch and long silences. Similarly the child protection officer's (CPO) turns display some characteristic features: first an account for the upset is provided in lines 11 to 14. This normalizes the upset as something that anyone might feel in this situation – a way of providing reassurance for the caller. Hepburn and Potter (2010) also discussed the role of turn medial tag questions in response to upset, such as that on line 14. Tag questions are useful, as they both mark the fact that the prior elements of the turn are something that the caller has epistemic priority over, and also provide a weakened requirement for confirmation. The CPO then delivers a turn that licenses the caller's disruption to the business of the call on line 17. In addition, 'take your time' is delivered with sympathetic sounding intonation, having elements of elevated pitch, stretch and aspiration.

Relatedly, Hepburn and Potter (2007; 2010) show the value of taking a more procedural approach to topics such as sympathy and empathy. They suggest that in their helpline interaction, empathic actions are typically formed from two key elements: a formulation of the crying party's business or emotional state (e.g., 'I can hear that you are very upset'); and some kind of epistemic marking of the contingency or source of that formulation, for example by using yes/no interrogatives or by tag formatting. This dual feature allows crying recipients to claim some access to this type of experience while deferring to the rights of the upset party to define the nature of their troubles.

The work of Hepburn and Potter is part of a larger programme of work that considers talk in institutional settings such as therapy, helplines and legal settings. Emotion terms and orientations have institutional roles in particular settings and a major aim of DP is to show the way in which institutions are characterized by 'psychological business' (Potter, 2005). Early work explicated the uses of emotion and mental state terms in settings such as relationship counselling (Edwards, 1995) and legal discourse (Locke and Edwards, 2003) and a recent major focus has been developing these themes for the possibility of applied work.

Emotion and the future of discursive psychology

Many areas of discursive psychological studies of emotion await further development. For example, the study of crying as an interactional phenomenon has only just started. Future research might explore interaction where there is no outright sobbing and disruption to the progressivity of talk, and yet there are elements such as croaky or tremulous voice, increased delay and so on. At what point should different institutional interlocutors respond to these features? There may be massive differences in the way crying is managed in 'therapeutic' environments, and environments of heightened conflict such as hostile cross-examinations.

Other studies in CA will be useful in developing ways forward, for example in their discussion of empathy, Heritage and Lindström (2012) show it is important to distinguish between the different levels of access that a would-be empathic recipient has to whatever events, sensations or activities are underway, as this will be reflected in their entitlement to offer their own comments or evaluations. Although our examples of crying raise more stark issues of empathy and alignment for respondents, it is nonetheless useful to engage with the developments that Heritage and Lindström's work allows.

In Heritage and Lindström's terms, crying would be something that raises the 'problem of experience' because the experiencer has primary access to their own intense emotions. In this view an empathic dilemma arises for responders to upset, as although they ostensibly lack such rights of ownership, they are nevertheless required to affirm speakers' experiences, and affiliate with the speaker's stance towards them. We can speculate based on this that Heritage and Lindström's empathic dilemma is magnified in proportion to two things: the intensity of the emotional experience and the recipient's lack of access to the other person's experiences. Hepburn and Potter (2012) contrast calls to the NSPCC child protection helpline, with an everyday example involving two sisters, which allow us to begin exploring how this dilemma plays out. In institutional environments, there may be a conflict between focusing on the upset person themselves and concentrating on the institutional task at hand. In earlier research Hepburn and Potter (2010) proposed the value of CPO practices that affiliate, encourage participation, but do not make failure to participate a strongly accountable matter, such as formatting responses to upset with tag question that are placed mid-turn. Further research could develop these issues and tease out the difficulties raised, and possible interactional solutions to these competing demands.

Another area for development is the interactional features that make talk hearable as emotional. Our own work has just begun to examine the interconnection between sequential features of talk and prosody in the production of 'angry' talk (Childs and Hepburn, 2014). We have started to identify the activity types that play a role in producing talk that may be heard as 'anger' such as directives, complaints and admonishments – turns that remove recipients' rights to direct their own behaviour. Common prosodic features are high pitch, elevated volume and stretch. Importantly, our future work will explicate how these sequential and prosodic features combine. While work has identified the sequential features of 'conflict talk', on the one hand (e.g., Dersley and Wootton, 2000), and the significance of intonation, on the other (e.g., Yu, 2011), there is a lack of research that explicates the interconnection between these. How talk that is hearable as 'anger' is responded to is also an important issue. How do interlocutors respond to these features? How is the prospect of unfolding conflict reduced? This line of development may usefully contribute to discursive studies of emotion and to the growing body of literature in CA that has documented the sequential organisation of phenomena associated with affect.

In general, Edwards' work reflects a dual focus on methodological innovation in psychology and a call for greater theoretical sophistication in research on emotion. In spite of being a relatively young approach, the discursive psychology of emotion has had a lasting impact on how emotion is conceptualized. However, there is much that awaits development.

References

Childs, C. (2014) 'From reading minds to social interaction: Respecifying theory of mind', *Human Studies*, 37: 103–22.

Childs, C. and Hepburn, A. (2014) '"Anger" in interaction: Sequential and prosodic properties', paper presented to International Conference on Conversation Analysis, Los Angeles, 25–9 June 2014.
Coulter, J. (1999) 'Discourse and mind', *Human Studies, 22*: 163–81.
Dersley, I. and Wootton, A. (2000) 'Complaint sequences within antagonistic argument', *Research on Language & Social Interaction, 33*: 375–406.
Edwards, D. (1995) 'Two to tango: Script formulations, dispositions, and rhetorical symmetry in relationship troubles talk', *Research on Language & Social Interaction, 28*: 319–50.
Edwards, D. (1997) *Discourse and cognition.* London: Sage.
Edwards, D. (1999) 'Emotion discourse', *Culture & Psychology, 5*: 271–91.
Edwards, D. (2012) 'Discursive and scientific psychology', *British Journal of Social Psychology, 51*: 425–35.
Ekman, P. (1992) 'An argument for basic emotions', *Cognition & Emotion, 6*: 169–200.
Garfinkel, H. (1967) *Studies in etnomethodology.* Upper Saddle River, NJ: Prentice-Hall.
Gergen, K. (2009) *An invitation to social construction* (second edn). London: Sage.
Harré, R. (1986) *The social construction of emotions.* Oxford: Basil Blackwell.
Harré, R. and Parrot, W.G. (1996) (eds) *The emotions: Social, cultural and biological dimensions.* London: Sage.
Hepburn, A. (2003) *An introduction to critical social psychology.* London: Sage.
Hepburn, A. (2004) 'Crying: Notes on description, transcription and interaction', *Research on Language & Social Interaction, 37*: 251–90.
Hepburn, A. and Potter, J.A. (2007) 'Crying receipts: Time, empathy and institutional practice', *Research on Language & Social Interaction, 40*: 89–116.
Hepburn, A. and Potter, J.A. (2010) 'Interrogating tears: Some uses of "tag questions" in a child protection helpline', in A.F. Freed and S. Ehrlich (eds) '*Why do you ask?': The function of questions in institutional discourse.* Oxford: Oxford University Press.
Hepburn, A. and Potter, J.A. (2011) 'Threats: Power, family mealtimes, and social influence'; *British Journal of Social Psychology, 50*: 99–120.
Hepburn, A. and Potter, J.A. (2012) 'Crying and crying responses', in A. Peräkylä and M.L. Sorjonen (eds) *Emotion in interaction.* Oxford: Oxford University Press.
Heritage, J. and Lindström, A. (2012) 'Knowledge, empathy, and emotion in a medical encounter' in A. Peräkylä and M.-L. Sorjonen (eds) *Emotion in interaction.* New York: Oxford University Press.
Locke, A. (2003) '"If I'm not nervous, I'm worried, does that make sense?": The use of emotion concepts in accounts of performance', *Forum: Qualitative Research, 4*: ISSN 1438-5627.
Locke, A. and Edwards, D. (2003) 'Bill and Monica: Memory, emotion and normativity in Clinton's Grand Jury testimony', *British Journal of Social Psychology, 42*: 239–56.
Lutz, C. (1988) *Unnatural emotions.* Chicago: University of Chicago Press.
Pepin, N. (2008) 'Studies on emotion in social interactions', *Bulletin Suisse de Linguistique Appliquée, 88*: 1–18.
Potter, J. (2005) 'Making psychology relevant', *Discourse & Society, 16*: 739–47.
Potter, J. (2010) 'Disciplinarity and the application of social research', *British Journal of Social Psychology, 49*: 691–701.
Röttger-Rössler, B. and Jürgen, H. (eds) (2009) *Emotions as bio-cultural processes.* Springer: New York.
Sacks, H. (1984) 'Notes on methodology' in J.M. Atkinson and J. Heritage (eds) *Structures of social action: Studies in conversation analysis.* Cambridge University Press, Cambridge.

Sacks, H. (1992) *Lectures on conversation.* Oxford: Blackwell Publishing.
Shotter, J. (1993) *Conversational realities.* London: Sage.
Shotter, J. (1997) 'The social construction of our inner lives', *Journal of Constructivist Psychology, 10*: 7–24.
Thoits, P.A. (1989) 'The sociology of emotions', *Annual Review of Sociology, 15*: 317–42.
Wittgenstein, L.W. (1980) *Culture and value.* Chicago: University of Chicago Press.
Yu, C. (2011). 'The display of frustration in arguments: A multimodal analysis', *Journal of Pragmatics, 43*: 2964–81.

9 Recasting the psychologist's question

Children's talk as social action

Carly W. Butler

Target article: Edwards, D. (1993) 'But what do children really think? Discourse analysis and conceptual content in children's talk', *Cognition & Instruction*, 11: 207–25.

Studies of children's development have long been dominated by an interest in children's cognition. Thought is central to models of development, with children's talk, perceptions and behaviour all understood to reflect and be shaped by their cognitive capacity and functioning. Debates around the status and measurement of cognition in children aside, the central role of thought and understanding remains firm. In his 1993 paper, 'But what do children really think? Discourse analysis and conceptual content in children's talk', Edwards presents an empirical, theoretical and methodological recasting of this preoccupation within developmental psychology. Edwards outlines an alternative conception of cognition and talk, with implications for studies of children's development, learning and education, social interaction, and social and cultural worlds.

The focus on cognition was cemented by the work of Jean Piaget, who became interested in children's minds as a result of the particular quality of children's answers to questions designed to measure intelligence. Piaget thought their common errors reflected common ways of understanding the world. Piaget's subsequent use of clinical interviews to find out how children answered such questions as 'how does the sun move?' formed a crucial element of his model of children's cognitive development. That is, by asking children what they thought, it was possible to gain access to their ways of thinking and understanding. For Piaget, children's understandings of the world, people, themselves and so on are structured by their cognitive representations, relatively stable schemes that are used to assimilate similar information and accommodate to incorporate understandings that don't fit with existing representations. Children are understood to have theories about the existence, nature, actions of things in the world, and to test these out through their natural inclination towards experimentation and trial and error.

This conceptualization of children's cognition is reflected and produced through traditional psychological theory and method. Understanding children's cognitive states and processes and how these are developed and shaped (both independently of, and in relation to, social and environmental factors) is at the heart of the developmental psychology enterprise. Other aspects of children's behaviour and abilities are viewed in light of how they can explain, predict, be produced and shaped by, or reveal thought and understanding. So, when children's talk is examined, it is primarily in order to explore their individual cognitive capacity and processes.

Edwards describes this as treating children's talk as a 'window' into their minds, hoping to reveal both *what* and *how* children think and understand. However, this window is a dirty one. The variability, and therefore the lack of reliability, in children's talk is problematic for developmental science. As such, children's natural discourse is rarely examined in contemporary developmental research, with experiments and surveys prevailing in attempts to get a 'clean' view of the child's mind. Even while language may feature in experimental explorations of children's cognition, it is 'tidied up' within published accounts of the research with the results informing the reader of the percentage of children who got something 'right' or 'wrong' – not what they said or how they said it. In this approach, children's talk is silenced, irrelevant.

Edwards sets out a critique of the psychological focus on cognition, and the status of children's talk within developmental psychology. Through an empirical examination of some classroom data and a rich theoretical discussion of the issues around the use and interpretation of such data, the paper contributes to studies of children, their development, cognition, education – and more generally to methods for studying such things. However, its reach and influence is far greater than this alone. In this article, Edwards offers one of his clearest and most compelling descriptions of the basic philosophy underpinning discursive psychology, by exemplifying its core element – the 'recasting of the psychologist's question'.

Discursive psychology (hereafter DP) has a different start and end point from non-discursive approaches to psychology. It fundamentally respecifies psychological topics and methods, but this does not entail a rejection of non-discursive aspects of the mind. Edwards's paper very clearly illustrates how psychological phenomena, such as what children and adults think, can be studied as and when they are made visible, used, and talked about in actual moments of social interaction. If we take these visible, verbal and embodied, presentations of mental phenomena as the data and the phenomenon, there is no need to make assumptions about or develop theories about the representative value of language or use it as a mere conduit into abstract mental processes.

Edwards's paper is written in a quasi-dialogic style, set up in response to the 'psychologist's question' that was regularly asked of Edwards on reading or seeing presentations of his work. The rhetorical framing of the paper involves Edwards directly engaging, both responsively and pre-emptively, with the objections of those working outside of the discursive social-constructionist realm. While finding the data and discussion 'interesting', the psychologists were puzzled by Edwards's failure to address what was, to them, the obvious and crucial question – 'what do children really think?'. Understanding children's *actual* cognitive processes, structures and status was fundamental to the developmental psychology enterprise. Along with another standard response to his work – 'when are you going to turn this into an experiment?' (Edwards, personal communication) – this question represented not only the primacy of cognition, but an inability to grasp the idea of an approach that took children's talk seriously, as a topic in its own right.

Edwards presents an empirical, theoretical and methodological recasting of this preoccupation within developmental psychology. The paper exemplifies the application of the underpinning influences of the methodological and theoretical contributions of contemporary DP: Wittgensteinian (1953/1958) notions of language as action; social studies of science (Gilbert and Mulkay, 1984) that explore how reality and knowledge are defined and produced by people rather than pre-existing (see Potter, 1996); and ethnomethodology and its offshoots, conversation analysis and discourse analysis, with an interest in how talk is used to produce and make sense of the social world (Atkinson and Heritage, 1984; Garfinkel, 1967; Potter and Wetherell, 1987). Bringing these together, Edwards outlines the potential of DP's conception of cognition and talk for developmental psychology.

Central to Edwards's recasting of the psychologists' pre-occupation is that he does not ignore or reject mind, reality and context, but treats them as participant's matters. Reflecting the ethnomethodological underpinnings of the work, this means that analysis explores what participants themselves 'treat as interactionally significant and accountable' (p. 220), and as such examines

> [. . .] participants' categories of mind and reality, to reveal what counts for them as real, or observable, or as the appearance that belies a deeper reality, or what is a proper basis for claims to knowledge, what is a useful and clever, or wrong contribution, and so on.
>
> (1993a: 220)

In studying children's talk as social action, Edwards attends to matters of the mind, understanding, conceptual understandings, knowledge, and so on as children's own matters, there for all to see, as and when it happens. Further, it is *on the basis of* being 'there for all to see' that children's (and everyone else's) understandings are themselves understood, and responded to, taught, assessed, corrected, approved, and so on.

Understanding as public, practical and accountable

Substantively, Edwards's paper is a study of classroom interaction. It is situated among other early studies of talk and social interaction in educational contexts that examined the discursive patterns and social organisation of classroom interaction (e.g., McHoul, 1978; Mehan, 1979; Payne, 1976; Payne and Hustler, 1980; Sinclair and Coulthard, 1975). While the social context of learning was acknowledged and discussed by both Piaget and Vygotsky, these empirical studies began to study classrooms as social and interactional spaces, with 'learning' being something accomplished in talk between teachers and students, through specific discursive structures and practices.

The paper is one of several of Edwards's works during this period that focused on educational issues and classroom interaction (Edwards, 1990; 1993b; Edwards and Mercer, 1986; 1989). His book *Common Knowledge*, written with Neil Mercer (1987), predated Edwards's working relationship with Jonathan Potter, and represents one of the strands that made up the 'Loughborough school' of DP (see Augustinos and Tileaga, 2012; Edwards, 2012). Based on recordings of classroom interaction, this book described the production and organisation of classroom practices, focusing on how knowledge and conceptual understandings came to be produced as shared and known in common. The ideas and methodologies were developed in related papers, but this 1993 publication stands out as one of the clearest and emphatic discussions of psychology and development, education, and cognition.

The data Edwards (1993a) examines comes from a classroom discussion about plant growth following a class trip to a greenhouse. The teacher elicits the five-year-old children's ideas about how plants are grown, based on what the gardener had told them. The aim of gathering the children's contributions was to produce an official record in the form of a 'book about herbs'. The data primarily involves the teacher asking the children 'what they learned at the greenhouse'. One way of approaching this data – if we were to treat children's talk as a window into their mind – is to view their responses as evidence of their knowledge about plant growth, biology and the like, and their conceptual understanding and reasoning more generally. That is, we could see what children think.

Edwards recasts this. Rather than treating talk as expressions or representations of conceptual understandings and reasoning, Edwards studies talk in its own right, as social action. The paper both argues and illustrates how to deal with children's naturally-occurring talk as 'situated discursive practice' (p. 213). From this perspective, and by applying the analytic methods of DP, researchers can recast a study on children's 'conceptual thinking' into one that examines the 'discursive organization of thought' (p. 214), exploring how conceptual understandings are 'done' in actual moments of everyday life. Via this respecification of cognition as a members' matter, done in and through situated social interaction, Edwards shows how education, knowledge and understanding are public, practical and accountable accomplishments.

The analysis examines interaction between the teacher and children during the classroom discussion, and identifies a number of ways in which understandings and interpersonal concerns were discursively produced and constructed. Edwards notes that the overall structure of the discussion was not one in which children were invited to report back what they 'think or know', but was organised as a 'joint recall session' (cf. Edwards and Middleton, 1986), where the children's contributions were their 'rememberings' of what Mark the gardener had said: 'I'm going to call on every single person and ask you what you remember about what Mark said' (ex 2, lines 18–20). It is suggested, then, that the exercise was about the children 'remembering somebody else's words rather than in formulating their own conceptual understandings' (p. 213). While this might pose a problem for the psychologist who actually wants to find out what children think rather than what they remember, Edwards argues that 'all discourse has a history' (p. 213). Drawing on his work on remembering (e.g., Edwards and Middleton, 1986; 1988), and related discursive work on the rhetorical and argumentative organization of thought (e.g. Billig, 1987; Edwards and Potter, 1992), Edwards argues that this dirty window in fact opens up opportunities for exploring how children's conceptual 'thinking' is socially shaped and organised within locally situated interactional contexts:

> [. . .] the very features of discourse that render it opaque with respect to individual cognitions are just the ones that are especially revealing about the social shaping of thought and the local, situational, and pragmatic organization of conceptual thinking. Let us pursue, therefore, the notion that children's concepts can be studied as formulations that occur within and are to some extent constituted as situated discursive practices.
>
> (1993a: 213)

Reconceptualising concepts as practices, perhaps as a surface to be examined rather than a window into something else, takes away the problems the psychologist faces with the messiness of children's talk. Children's cognitions are social accomplishments, done in, and as part of, the messiness of everyday life interaction.

The analysis considers both the structure of the discussion and the design of turns within it to explore the situated discursive practices through which the children's concepts were formulated and displayed. This exploration is rich with observations about the rhetorical, social and sequential organisation and production of 'knowledge'. I focus here on three key analytic points.

First, the accumulation of knowledge about how plants grow was built as a collection of 'discrete contributions', in that each child was expected to provide a separate piece of information. As such, the knowledge was 'sequentially accumulated' (p. 214) via the teacher's organisation of the session and turn-taking within it. One particularly lovely example of this is shown when the teacher highlights her 'need' for nineteen pieces of information – one from each child:

Extract 1

(from Example 3, simplified)

```
((T Reads list))
    OK. that's one, two, three, four, five, six, seven, eight, nine,
    ten. That means I need nine more, and not two from you yet
    Sally, 'cause I want to see what everyone else can (do) [. . .]
```

The teacher's organization of the session therefore not only organises the children's participation in the lesson, but discursively constructs what counts as knowledge and how it is to be produced. The displays of children's conceptual understandings are thus social rather than cognitive products.

Second, the knowledge was jointly produced between the students, and between the students and the teacher. Not only did each child provide a piece of information so that the knowledge was collectively constructed; but the talk itself was designed in a way that encouraged or required the production of an observation, item of information, or memory of 'what Mark said' to be collaborative. This was accomplished via the students completing the utterances of the teacher:

Extract 2

(Example 4)

```
265  Lisa:  Plants take, umm, three days to have roots.
266  T:     When they're under what?
267  Lisa:  Uh, soil
```

The design of the teacher's turn elicits a word search that invites Lisa to complete her utterance. It treats Lisa's initial display of knowledge as incomplete and provides a structure for addressing the adequacy of the conceptual understanding shown. As later discussed in more depth by Lerner (1995), a teacher's use of incomplete turn-constructional units such as these provide opportunities for particular types of participation by students. Thus, both participation and the production of knowledge are practical and social issues.

Finally, the use of an incomplete utterance as in Example 4, and the overall production of the collaborative list, could be considered as examples of 'scaffolding' (Cazden, 1988) through which the children's understanding is structured by the teacher's ways of speaking. This concept builds on Vygotsky's notion of a zone of proximal development, through which an adult or more competent peer helps children perform better than they would independently. Edwards notes that the design of the teacher's turns also provide a kind of 'contextual scaffolding' that sets the contributions within a wider 'conceptual order' providing links between the discrete bits of information via narrative frames and 'contrasts, denials and argument'. The teacher thus highlights the relationships between the pieces of information and the understandings in a way that scaffolds not simply single pieces of information, but how to *do* conceptual thinking.

These observations of the design and structure of the lesson demonstrate the social construction of both the lesson itself and of knowledge and conceptual understandings. However, the psychologist's question remains unanswered. This sort of analysis tells us nothing about what the children are really thinking. Edwards suggests that this isn't a problem with the method or the theory, but a problem with the question:

> [. . .] it is not clear that they 'really think' anything, at least not in the sense of carrying around in their heads ready-made explanations that merely await discursive opportunities to be revealed.
>
> (1993a: 220)

Edwards emphasises that talk (and 'thought') are always produced in some setting, for specific interactional purposes, such that content and context cannot be divorced from one another. This inseparability of content and context causes problems for the psychologists as it inevitably results in variability. As such, cognitive and developmental psychology try to exclude variability altogether. Inconsistencies reveal either change within an individual (i.e., a developmental change) or a lack of reliability in the findings. However, if the interest is in situated action and the contexts (both interactional and cultural) in which talk is produced, then variability becomes precisely what interests Edwards and others working in the discursive tradition; it becomes the 'signal instead of the noise' (p. 217).

> [. . .] the very features that make the content of talk difficult to map onto underlying cognitive representations are just those features that bring to life a study of how such verbal formulations of mind and world are occasioned phenomena.
>
> (1993a: 219)

So in terms of studying children – whether we look at their social worlds, their development, their education and learning – we look to what they are doing, the social actions they perform, how their talk is produced by and produces a situated context. As Edwards suggests:

> We become interested in how children's versions of the world vary as a function of the context for which they are produced, of the question asked, of considerations of intersubjectivity, and of the various social actions performed by speaking.
>
> (1993a: 217)

Developmental psychologists might protest that this focus on the social and discursive organization of action simply ignores or tries to undermine the goals of cognitive science. If it can't provide an answer and focuses on what talk does rather than what it expresses, why should this approach be of any value at all to psychology? Edwards argues that it 'may turn out that whatever underlying neural bases there are to conceptual activities such as thinking and remembering [. . .], will turn out to be organizations for situated actions, rather than for representational abstraction and reflection' (p. 219). As such, it is worth underlining, again, that Edwards, like his colleagues, has 'no objection to there being mechanisms underlying the production of talk' (p. 208). The work does not reject cognition *per se*, but the idea that this is expressed in talk. It offers a reconceptualization of 'relations among language, mind and world' (p. 208), one aspect of which holds that 'the analysis of discourse provides a description of performance for which any model of underlying competence must account' (p. 219). In the process of recasting the psychologists' question, Edwards respecifies where the absence lies – not in the failure to identify children's *true and actual cognition*, but in models of development and competence that fail to account for cognition- and talk-in-action in everyday life, as *situated discursive practice*.

Children's talk as social action

Edwards's paper makes multiple contributions, on the level of topic, methodology, and theory. Topically, it tells us something about classroom discourse; about education practices and processes; about children's talk. Methodologically it illustrates and argues for working with recordings and transcripts of children's everyday interaction and subjecting that to discursive analyses that treat talk as social action. Theoretically it outlines the psychological relevance of discourse via a treatment of talk as social action. Bringing these together, is the paper's argument for the psychological relevance of children's talk as social action and call for psychologists to consider the kinds of questions studies of children's social interactions can ask.

As an undergraduate in psychology, I had a particular interest in developmental psychology and had been considering doing my fourth year Honours dissertation on children's moral development. To do this, I hoped to use Aesop's fables and discuss with the children what they thought about the issues raised in these, notions of right and wrong and so on. That is, I wanted to 'get into children's heads' and make sense of how they viewed and understood the social world. However, I was then introduced to the work of Edwards and colleagues in a module on language and social psychology (run by Ann Weatherall), and found this perspective challenging, compelling and ultimately mind-blowing (in more than one sense!). DP offered an approach that meant that if one wanted to find out about children's understandings and social worlds, one could record children in their ordinary everyday encounters. Furthermore, this data could be analysed rigorously and robustly using sophisticated qualitative methods. I began to see that psychology could accomplish a lot more than finding out 'what children really think', and was sold on the idea that the 'scientific study of human behaviour' that psychology purported to deliver was missing something vital – detailed, empirical studies of actual human behaviour in real-life encounters.

Thus began my studies of children's social worlds and social understandings, not by asking children to tell me about them or devising tests to access their minds, but by recording, transcribing, and analysing what they did in everyday life. This approach not only afforded a treatment of children as human beings rather than 'becomings', but also brought children into the realm of social psychology whereby their actual social practices could be examined. My research involved collecting recordings of children in the school classroom and playground (Butler, 2008; Butler and Weatherall, 2006). By treating children's talk as social action, rather than a window into their heads, I was able to observe and understand how issues of justice and fairness, right and wrong, knowledge and understandings were *done* as situated discursive practices, during children's play and games.

At the time Edwards's work on classroom interaction and family remembering was published, there was little *psychological* research that treated children's talk as social action. Work in linguistics, anthropology and education shared an interest in children's everyday interaction and social worlds (e.g., Garvey, 1984; Ochs, 1991; Goodwin, 1990; Keenan, 1974; Payne, 1976; Speier, 1971; and others), and touched on issues such as children's knowledge and understanding, but there was little direct engagement with psychological models and arguments about what children did and thought (but see Forrester, 1992; Keenan, 1974). As interactional studies of childhood that treat children's talk as social action continue to proliferate, the gap between this work and psychology is arguably becoming larger. While the truly interdisciplinary nature of DP is one of its great strengths, developmental psychology has not benefitted from its methods and findings as much as it could – or should – have.

Those working in the discursive psychological and ethnomethodological tradition now rarely find themselves asked the psychologist's question. As the field has grown and matured it has taken on an identity in its own right, rather than simply being a type of psychology that bothers and concerns 'mainstream' psychology. Discursive psychologists can find welcoming arms among ethnomethodologists, conversation analysts, and those working from critical approaches within psychology. They talk to interaction analysts who, from the outset, have no interest in what children really think, and publish in journals that are built on an assumption that language and social interaction are accomplishments. A success for the field, perhaps, but this is a mixed fortune. Interaction analysts happily recast the psychologist's question, but the psychologists have stopped asking it. They are not in the same rooms or in the same journals, so the dialogue of the sort Edwards recounts simply doesn't happen anymore.

It could be argued that DP's gains within social psychology and interactional studies come with a loss for developmental psychology. The dialogue opened up by Edwards's 1993(a) and related papers is unfinished and one-sided. There remains a need for ongoing and sustained conversation between DP and developmental psychologists so that the potentials of the recast question to address and further the aims and scope of more traditional approaches can be realised.

In the following section, I illustrate how Edwards's approach to children's talk as social action can be used to explore the production and use of understanding in interactions between peers in a classroom, and in play between a young child and her mother at home. The analyses demonstrate the public and accountable nature of understanding within specific sequences of action, and illustrate how ostensibly psychological phenomena is produced and invoked in everyday social interactions.

Knowledge-in-action

The following excerpt is taken from a collection of recordings of Year Five children working in peer-pairs and groups during maths and English lessons collected as part of an undergraduate final-year dissertation (Ramskill, 2013). This piece of data involves Callum and Marie sitting at a desk for two, each working on a maths worksheet.

Extract 3

```
Ramskill CM Maths 01-05
1    Callum:   Oh no:::. ((gaze at paper))
2              (2.2)
3    Marie:    What you do:ne wrong. ((looks at C's work))
4              (2.0)
5    Marie:    You got mixed up di:dn't
6              you.
7              (6.3)
8    Marie:    I know what we have to do.
9              (1.5)
10   Callum:   Don't need help.
11   (25.5) ((Marie calculating under breath))
```

The two children are engaging in the educational activity of completing a worksheet. It could be argued that there is little conceptual talk here, and little to tell us what the children are 'thinking'. Indeed, there doesn't even seem to be much talk about maths. However, if we shift from looking to the content of children's talk, to the interaction between the children and what they are *doing* with that talk; we can see that issues of knowledge and understanding, being correct/wrong, and 'doing maths' are practical issues for the children.

Callum initially displays some trouble ('oh no') but keeps his gaze directed at the worksheet. This verbal trouble display is in the interactional space and responded to by Marie who pursues an explanation. After her enquiry gets no response, she proffers an account of the trouble and seeks confirmation of this from Callum – 'you got mixed up didn't you'. Still without any response from Callum, Marie asserts she knows 'what we have to do', which Callum treats as an offer for help, as seen in his rejection of that offer (line 10). As the interaction lapses Marie continues with a public display of 'doing maths' by making calculations under her breath as she works.

The maths work is thus both public and accountable. States of understanding and competencies are recognised and produced through the children's talk, and silence. Having trouble with the work is something that requires an explanation and a remedy, and the children themselves treat their understandings and performances as visible and accountable. Unlike Edwards's data where the knowledge construction was scaffolded by the teacher, here the children self-construct their participation in educational activity.

Throughout their work, the children display conceptual understandings in ways that flag up knowledge as both public and accountable:

Extract 4

```
1    Marie:    Erm:::, (0.6) is that a se:ven:
2              that's gonna be;
3              (0.8)
4    Marie:    Or eight.
5              (5.5)
6    Marie:    Ten: nine eight se:ven. Yeah.
7              (0.4)
8    Callum:   No: wait¿
9              (1.1)
10   Marie:    Take away three from te:n.
11             (1.5)
12   Callum:   No::, (2.8) [ T hi:r ] ty, equa- zero,=
13   Marie:                [ (Y' ju-)] / (yeah)
14   Callum:   =you don't put a o:ne.
15             (1.2)
16   Marie:    'Kay?.
17             (2.3)
18   Marie:    °*ep° h:ehiheh .hh
19             (2.4)
20   Callum:   Or am I wro:ng.
21   Marie:    I'm not su:re;
```

Marie's out-loud calculations make her work public and accountable, and invites the participation of Callum in the calculations. She asks 'is that a seven', and then provides an alternative 'or eight' (line 4). With no response from Callum, she verbally calculates 'ten nine eight seven' then self-confirms her answer with 'yeah'. At this point Callum projects a disagreement (line 8), to which Marie responds with an account for having arrived at that answer. Callum counters that with an alternative calculation, but then displays doubt – 'or am I wrong' (line 20), with Marie replying 'I'm not sure'. Each child, then, relies on the other to assess their calculations and to back up claims with accounts for arriving at their answer. However, the situation is more complex than simply establishing right or wrong. There are social norms associated with discussing knowledge and correctness. It would be misguided to hear Marie's lack of certainty about whether Callum was wrong or not to be evidence of what she actually 'thinks'. In fact, this demonstrates how muddy the window into the mind is – we see only uncertainty and doubt. Knowing more or less than a peer is an interactionally delicate issue, and the lack of clarity as to what exactly Callum or Marie think is the correct answer, or method for calculating the answer, highlights the local, pragmatic and situational organisation of 'conceptual thinking'.

The pragmatic consequences of displays of uncertainty are evidenced not long after this, when Callum asserts that 'we need help' (line 3):

Extract 5

```
1   Callum:   *M:::Hmmm*  ((Groan))
2   Marie:    Ehehheheh[he
3   Callum:            [We nee(h)d he(h)lp don't
4             we.
5   Marie:    Ah::
6             (3.3)
7   Callum:   ↑[Miss [ Jones?
8   Miss:      [Sh   [ sh °°°Sh. Don't call out.°°°
9             (3.2)
10  Marie:    Next one's gonna be sixty.
11            (2.8)
12  Callum:   What that's gonna be sixteen.
13  Marie:    Yea:h- si:xty:.
14  Callum:   °(Why?)°
15            (0.4)
16  Marie:    'Cos that's only twe:n::[ty up] there.
17  Callum:                           [>gonna put-<]
18            (0.4)
19  Marie:    Don't forget we're doing ta:ke awa:y.
```

In asserting 'we need help' Callum treats Marie's understanding as visible and shared, similar to Marie's recognition of Callum being 'mixed up' in Extract 3. Marie neither agrees nor disagrees with Callum's claim, but after Callum's summons is 'shushed' (line 8) her declaration that the 'next one's gonna be sixty' (line 10) does not position her as someone in need of help. On the contrary it suggests an epistemic certainty, for which she is subsequently held accountable by Callum as he pursues a justification for this claim (lines 12–17). Marie then treats this pursuit of an account for her answer as suggesting a problem in Callum's understanding. She does an assessment of where his conceptual understanding has gone wrong when she offers a reminder, 'don't forget we're doing take away' (line 19). Making sense of Callum's understanding as an issue of memory is a wonderfully delicate way of handling his error; demonstrating the use of psychological states as a resource for handling social interactional issues, and the mutuality of the mind and discourse.

That states of knowledge and ways of understanding are made visible, public and accountable is an utterly mundane feature of everyday classroom life. It clearly demonstrates that what children 'really think' is in fact a participants' matter – it is for the children themselves, or the teachers, to see what each other are thinking or to treat certain actions and practices as accountable evidence of understanding. This recasts the psychologist's question into one that is truly *social*-psychological, not asking what or how children think, but asking how children *display* their thought, reasoning, and understandings *in social interaction*.

The psychological relevance of this is that children's development relies on them not simply developing cognitive capacities and working within the limitations of their cognitive stage, but on producing and seeing cognitive actions as visible and recognisable. The public and accountable status of cognition and action is evident also in the following excerpt in which a mother and three-year-old child are setting up a machine that uses Play-Doh to 'make ice-cream'. The extract begins with Mum asking Emma which colour Play-Doh she would like to make her ice-cream with.

Extract 6

```
1    Mum:    Which colour d' ya want.
2            (4.2)
3    Mum:    ↑Which colour?
4            (0.7)
5  · Emma:   I don' t kno:w.
6            (0.7)
7    Emma:   I thi:nk I want gre:en.
8            (0.6)
9    Mum:    Gre:en.
10           (0.7)
11   Emma:   An' d' you want green too:?
12   Mum:    O:h green is mi:nt icecream isn' t it?
13           (0.8)
14   Emma:   Do you want mint i:cecream too:?
15           (0.6)
16   Mum:    ↑I↑ gue:ss so:.
```

The sequence in lines 1 through to 7 involves Emma making a colour selection. She designs her selection process *as a decision* – by first claiming uncertainty, and then by hedging the certainty of her decision via the modal 'I think I want green'. It matters little what Emma is actually thinking during this 'decision-making process', but whatever is going on should be able to account for what is visibly and accountably being done – 'doing deciding'. Emma does this publically by expressing uncertainty and then accounting for this uncertainty by showing less than a 100 per cent commitment to her choice.

In terms of Emma's understandings, she clearly recognises selection of Play-Doh to be part of the sequence of getting ready for play and that it is now her mother's turn to make a choice, as she proposes Mum might 'want green too' in a turn designed as an offer rather than an option. However, Mum's oh-prefaced response ('Oh, green is mint ice-cream isn't it?', line 12) treats Emma's offer as inapposite (Heritage, 1998). Mum's assertion translates a Play-Doh colour into an ice-cream flavour, and her tag question treats Emma as having epistemic authority over this (Heritage, 2010). But Emma doesn't treat Mum as seeking confirmation of the colour-flavour association – instead, she re-does her offer, 'do you want mint ice-cream too?' with a design and intonation that perfectly matches the delivery of her initial offer. So Emma has treated Mum as initiating repair on her initial offer, and Emma has self-repaired, by replacing green with mint (see Schegloff, 2007).

Repair sequences offer a rich source for seeing children making sense of the meaning, intentions and actions of other people (e.g., Forrester and Cherington, 2009; Laakso, 2010). In this instance, Emma analysed not simply what Mum *said*, but what she was *doing* with her question. By framing her repeat as a repair, she shows that she heard the question as looking for a correction. Seeing what Emma does and how she 'reads' her mother's intentions means that we can see psychologically relevant activity without, ourselves, trying to read her mind or test her on her conceptual understanding or ask her what she thinks her mum is thinking.

Discursive psychology, conversation analysis and developmental psychology

The examples above, and the body of interactional work that explores similar issues, reinforce and extend Edwards's arguments about psychological matters being situated discursive practices. Conversation analytic studies of children's interactions have explored a wide range of topics, including the development of children's interactional practices and understandings, as well as studies of non-verbal interactional practices, turn-taking, social action, socialization, and children's social worlds (see Kidwell, 2012 for a review). However, these topics and issues are rarely discussed in terms of their relevance for psychology, even though the competencies that interactional research reveals are precisely the kinds of competencies that any model of children's socio-cognitive development should be able to account for (but see Kidwell and Zimmerman, 2007).

The implications of this approach to understanding children's development is clearly demonstrated by Wootton (1997), who emphasises the importance of recognising and exploring children's *sequential knowledge*. The empirical description of children's sequential knowledge as local, public and moral resonates with Edwards's claims about children's conceptual understandings, and the situated nature of educational practices. Wootton (2006) argues that the sequential understandings children demonstrate from a young age reveals that they can organize their 'conduct in relation to alignments taken up in preceding interaction, alignments that can touch on such things as people's wishes, desires, plans and preferences' (Wootton 2006: 194). While not making claims about what is actually going on inside children's minds, Wootton, like Edwards, highlights the implications of this sort of analysis for 'the workings of what might be called the child's cognitive apparatus' (p. 195), including short-term memory and a psychological 'theory of mind'.

Wootton (2006) acknowledges the parallels with his work and research within DP, although no link is made to Edwards's papers that address the relevance of this shared research agenda for developmental psychology. Citing a classic description of DP's subject matter, 'the ways in which psychological states, actions, events, beliefs, dispositions, motives, and so on are conceptualized, invoked and talked of' (Edwards, 1997: 296), Wootton suggests that in practice analysis is restricted to instances where explicit mentions of psychological states are made. He argues that as young children rarely use psychological words such as 'remember', DP is ill-equipped to realize the 'broader range of ways through which conduct is designed with reference to accountable, psychologically-linked understandings and attributions' (p. 196).

It is true that one aspect of discursive psychological research on children and young people has involved consideration of the 'psychological thesaurus', which remains part of the mainstay of DP approach. However, the notion that DP *only* looks at the use of psychological words is a common misconception. Edwards's 1993a paper illustrates the theoretical and methodological grounds from which DP can explore children's social interaction to address psychological issues. It addresses the kinds of sequential understandings and the conceptualisation of social action that Wootton argues is unique to his conversation analytic work and identification of the 'orderly properties of interaction processes themselves'. In fact, this is precisely what Edwards argues for in his paper.

The common thread is, of course, that DP uses conversation analysis and as such shares a primary interest in the production and organisation of social action. Edwards's (1993a) paper has a strong methodological and theoretical argument, and the analysis itself may seem 'CA-lite' in comparison to more straightforward empirical articles on interactional phenomena. Yet the discussion of children's talk as social action and of the public and accountable nature of knowledge and conceptual understanding captures and illuminates the intellectual heritage not only of DP but of contemporary conversation analysis. Edwards deals with issues such as the construction of knowledge, reality, mind-world connections and culture that underpin interaction analysis independent of the sub-disciplinary labels people choose to use.

Edwards's recasting of the psychologist's question opens up potential for more dialogue between discursive and developmental psychologists. While the success of discursive approaches within the interdisciplinary field of interaction studies means that analysts now rarely face these kinds of questions, Edwards's classic paper serves as a reminder of the distinctiveness and importance of this approach within a much broader intellectual context. This revisiting of the paper comes with a plea that we don't lose sight of this broader context, and that we pick up on conversations that remain unfinished. What is needed is a clearer recognition of, and engagement with, the intellectual debates that fuelled DP as a discipline. By treating children's talk as social action, appreciating (rather than erasing) the variability of children's talk, and exploring the ways in which children's talk and cognition are done publically and accountably; those who study children's interactions have much to offer the scientific study of children's development and behaviour. At the same time, the field of children's interactions has much to gain from a stronger engagement with the methods, theories and debates that dominate research within their disciplinary homes.

References

Atkinson, J.M. and Heritage, J. (1984) (eds) *Structures of social action: Studies in conversation analysis*. Cambridge: Cambridge University Press.

Augoustinos, M. and Tileagă, C. (eds) (2012) 'Twenty five years of discursive psychology'. Special Issue of *British Journal of Social Psychology*, 51: 405–12.

Billig, M. (1987) *Arguing and thinking: A rhetorical approach to social psychology*. Cambridge: Cambridge University Press.

Butler, C. (2008) *Talk and social interaction in the playground*. Aldershot: Ashgate.

Butler, C. and Weatherall, A. (2006) '"No we're not playing families": Membership categorization in children's play', *Research on Language & Social Interaction*, 39: 441–70.

Cazden, C.B. (1988) *Classroom discourse: The language of teaching and learning*. Portsmouth, NH: Heinemann.

Edwards, D. (1990) 'Classroom discourse and classroom knowledge', in P. Kutnick and C. Rogers (eds) *The social psychology of the primary school*. London: Routledge.

Edwards, D. (1993a) 'But what do children really think? Discourse analysis and conceptual content in children's talk', *Cognition & Instruction*, 11: 207–25.

Edwards, D. (1993b) 'Concepts, memory and the organization of pedagogic discourse: A case study', *International Journal of Educational Research*, 19: 205–25.

Edwards, D. (1997) *Discourse and cognition*. London: Sage.

Edwards, D. (2012) 'Discursive and scientific psychology', *British Journal of Social Psychology*, 51: 425–35.

Edwards, D. and Mercer, N.M. (1986) 'Context and continuity: Classroom discourse and the development of shared knowledge', in K. Durkin (ed.), *Language development in the school years*. London: Croon Helm.

Edwards, D. and Mercer, N.M. (1987) *Common knowledge: The development of understanding in the classroom*. London: Routledge.

Edwards, D. and Mercer, N.M. (1989) 'Reconstructing context: The conventionalization of classroom knowledge', *Discourse Processes*, 12: 91–104.

Edwards, D. and Middleton, D. (1986) 'Joint remembering: Constructing an account of shared experience through conversational discourse', *Discourse Processes*, 9: 423–59.

Edwards, D. and Middleton, D. (1988) 'Conversational remembering and family relationships: How children learn to remember', *Journal of Social & Personal Relationships*, 5: 3–25.

Edwards, D. and Potter, J. (1992) *Discursive psychology*. London: Sage.

Forrester, M.A. (1992) *The development of young children's social-cognitive skills. Essays in developmental psychology*. Hillsdale, NJ, England: Lawrence Erlbaum Associates, Inc.

Forrester, M.A. and Cherrington, S.M. (2009) 'The development of other-related conversational skills: A case study of conversational repair during the early years', *First Language, 29*: 166–91.

Garfinkel, H. (1967) *Studies in ethnomethodology*. Englewood Cliffs, NJ: Prentice-Hall.

Garvey, C. (1984) *Children's talk*. Cambridge, MA: Harvard University Press.

Gilbert, G.N. and Mulkay, M. (1984) *Opening Pandora's box: A sociological analysis of scientists' discourse*. Cambridge: Cambridge University Press.

Goodwin, M.H. (1990) *He-said-she-said: Talk as social organization among black children*. Bloomington: Indiana University Press.

Heritage, J. (1998) 'Oh-prefaced responses to inquiry', *Language in Society, 27*: 291–334.

Heritage, J. (2010) 'Questioning in medicine', in A.F. Freed and S. Ehrlich (eds) *'Why do you ask?': The function of questions in institutional discourse* (pp. 42–68). New York: Oxford University.

Keenan, E. (1974) 'Conversational competence in young children', *Journal of Child Language, 1*: 163–83.

Kidwell, M. (2012) 'Interaction among children', in J. Sidnell and T. Stivers (eds) *The handbook of conversation analysis* (pp. 511–32). West Sussex: -Blackwell.

Kidwell, M. and Zimmerman, D.H. (2007) 'Joint attention as action', *Journal of Pragmatics, 39*: 592–611.

Laakso, M. (2010) 'Children's emerging and developing self-repair practices', in H. Gardner and M. Forrester (eds) *Analysing interactions in childhood: Insights from conversation analysis* (pp. 74–100). Oxford: Wiley-Blackwell.

Lerner, G. (1995) 'Turn design and the organization of participation in instructional activities', *Discourse Processes, 19*: 111–31.

Mehan, H. (1979) *Learning lessons: Social organization in the classroom*. Cambridge, MA: Harvard University Press.

McHoul, A. (1978) 'The organization of turns at formal talk in the classroom', *Language in Society, 7*: 183–213.

Ochs, E. (1991). Misunderstanding children. In N. Coupland, H. Giles, & J.M. Wiemann (Eds.). *Miscommunication and Problematic Talk* (pp. 44-60). California: Sage.

Payne, G. (1976) 'Making a lesson happen: An ethnomethodological analysis', in M. Hammersley and P. Woods (eds) *The process of schooling: A sociological reader* (pp. 33–40). London: Routledge and Kegan Paul.

Payne, G. and Hustler, D. (1980) 'Teaching the class: The practical management of a cohort', *British Journal of Sociology of Education, 1*: 49–66.

Potter, J. (1996) *Representing reality: Discourse, rhetoric, and social construction*. London and Thousand Oaks, CA: Sage.

Potter, J. and Wetherell, M. (1987) *Discourse and social psychology: Beyond attitudes and behaviour*. London: Sage.

Ramskill, R. (2013) 'Cooperative learning classroom interactions: How do children manage their speech in naturalistic cooperation?' Unpublished BSc (Hons) Dissertation, Department of Social Sciences, Loughborough University.

Schegloff, E. (2007) *Sequence organization in interaction: Volume 1: A primer in conversation analysis*. Cambridge: Cambridge University Press.

Sinclair, J. and Coulthard, M. (1975) *Toward an analysis of discourse: The English used by teachers and pupils*. London: Oxford University Press.

Speier, M. (1971) 'The everyday world of the child', in J.D. Douglas (ed.) *Understanding everyday life: Towards a reconstruction of sociological knowledge* (pp. 188–217). London: Routledge and Kegan Paul.

Wittgenstein, L. (1953/1958) *Philosophical investigations*. Edited by G.E.M. Anscombe and R. Rhees. Translated by G.E.M. Anscombe. Oxford: Blackwell.

Wootton, A. J. (1997) *Interaction and the development of mind*. Cambridge: Cambridge University Press.

Wootton, A.J. (2006) 'Children's practices and their connections with "mind"', *Discourse Studies*, 8: 191–8.

10 Seeing the inside from the outside of children's minds

Displayed understanding and interactional competence

Karin Osvaldsson

Target article: Antaki, C. (2004) 'Reading minds or dealing with interactional implications', *Theory & Psychology, 14*: 667–83.

Introduction

It is something of a truism to say that psychology has a long-standing interest in explaining the capacity humans have to 'understand' one another. One specific tradition, which explains this skill with the development of a capacity labelled Theory of Mind (henceforth ToM), has received more and more research attention during the past decades (Baron-Cohen, Leslie and Frith 1985; Bartsch and Wellman 1995; Gopnik and Wellman 1995; Premack and Woodruff 1978; Surian and Leslie 1999; Wellman 1990).

The term ToM is spreading and also becoming part of people's everyday language. Today one can hear not only psychologists, but also pre-school teachers, social workers and perhaps even parents using it with reference to children's actions and behaviour. In this chapter, I intend to briefly outline some central ideas from Antaki's (2004) paper entitled 'Reading minds or dealing with interactional implications?' and discuss how the criticism of ToM advanced in that paper has paved the way for later research on the concept of mind and talk in interaction. I also intend to discuss why this critique must be a concern for psychology. While critical voices had already been heard from ethnomethodology in relation to the concept of mind (Coulter, 1989, 1999) prior to the publication of Antaki's paper, similar voices from within the discipline of psychology had been almost non-existent. But this does not mean that Antaki was alone in his concerns about language and mind and how they were understood in psychology. In 2004, discursive psychology (Edwards and Potter, 1992) was well established. A few years before 'Reading minds . . .', Derek Edwards had published his seminal achievement *Discourse and cognition* (1997). At about the same time as 'Reading minds' was published, contemporary DP work covered a wide range of topics, all addressing and respecifying traditional concerns within psychology. These range from how gender categories operate in disputes (Stokoe, 2003); how 'cognitive distortions' may be understood as an accomplishment in talk rather than a mere character trait of sex offenders (Auburn and Lea, 2003) to accounts for success or failure in sport psychology (Locke, 2004) or how 'normality' is interactionally achieved in interviews with young women in detention homes (Osvaldsson, 2004), to name a few. In conclusion, a critique against a referential view of language or against cognitivism was not new when 'Reading minds' was published. It had been put forward by both discursive psychology and ethnomethodology. The strong contribution of the paper is therefore its target. Antaki directs his critique towards a growing and very influential psychological school – ToM.

Ever since it began, the measurement of individual human capabilities has been a core concern and central marker for the discipline of psychology. In aid of this concern, psychologists rely on a vast tradition of using tests and psychometric instruments. In 'Reading minds', Antaki offers a highly critical argument showing how psychology fails to sufficiently grasp its own key concepts, such as cognition and mind, and the consequences this failure entails. The article presents an epistemological critique that is unusual in the sense that it is not only built as a theoretical argument, but is continuously supported through close analysis of empirical data. This empirical anchoring makes Antaki's critique of ToM particularly forceful.

The gist of Antaki's critique is that instead of actually investigating how people in interaction accomplish or fail to accomplish mutual understanding, ToM merely helps us constitute the presence of different capacities within certain groups of people. In 'Reading minds', Antaki restates some of the key epistemological presuppositions of discourse and conversation analytical work. This allows him to spell out the shortcomings of a representational perspective on language, and to replace this with the benefits of an approach to language as social action. Antaki's critique of ToM is therefore an example of a much wider problem that almost all psychology hosts.

Using examples of actual interaction between psychologists and clients, Antaki's paper describes the shortcomings of a theoretical model that fails to take human interaction into consideration. Instead ToM seeks evidence of this capacity through hypothetical models of inner mental states. Herein lies a paradox: One central task for the ToM tradition is to explain normal cognitive development and functions in terms of the capacity to understand and reflect upon other persons' points of view. Therefore, it is not particularly farfetched to believe that an interest in human interpersonal understanding should also require a research focus on the interpersonal and social spheres of life. But like most other traditional psychological research, the ToM tradition is firmly grounded in an interest in intra-individual mental capacity. The problem this mismatch creates is but one of the matters that Antaki's paper brings to a head.

Antaki's work is part of an established and rapidly growing radical branch of psychology that has taken as its task to level the bias of mentalistic dominance in psychology by introducing a strong focus on interaction. Discursive psychology (Edwards and Potter, 1992) is continuously respecifying not only the ToM tradition, but a wider and wider array of psychological matters, substituting cognition and mentalism for a focus on psychology as action and performance (Potter, 2010). I will return to this, but first a very brief description of ToM from the point view of its promotors.

Theory of Mind

In psychology, ToM denotes the ability to think about other people's mental states, and to use this capacity to try to explain and predict other people's behaviour. The term was originally coined by Premack and Woodruff (1978) in an article that reported a series of experiments on a chimpanzee. In humans, this same capacity is usually tapped into through testing, such as with the 'Sally-Anne procedure of false belief' (Baron-Cohen, Leslie and Frith, 1985), designed to measure whether children are able to distinguish and separate their own knowledge (true belief) from the knowledge of another person (in this case a false belief). In the test, the child is presented with two dolls, named Sally and Anne. There is also a basket containing a marble and an empty box between the dolls. The doll named Sally is asked to leave the room, and when this has happened, Anne moves the marble from the basket to the box. Then Sally returns and the test leader asks the child where Sally will look for the marble.

According to ToM proponents, in the typical case, children from around the age of four will correctly report that Sally will look for the marble in the basket, as she was out of the room when the marble was moved. This capacity to take another person's point of view when coming to conclusions is seen as an indication of the development of a ToM.

Yet after the age of four, there are still some, who often fail on such tests. Persons who are diagnosed with autism or related syndromes belong to one such category (Surian and Leslie, 2009). The same applies to some psychiatric diagnoses, such as schizophrenia (Corcoran, Mercer and Frith 1995; Frith 1992; Frith and Corcoran 1996; Mazza et al. 2001).

Today, mainly two different theoretical traditions exist that account for the origins and development of ToM: the 'Theory-Theory' and the 'Modular Theory', which bases its explanation on the idea of a specific innate mechanism. According to the Theory-Theory, the way children develop a ToM is similar to the way scientists develop and change their theories, that is, through a continuous process of developing, testing, and retesting hypotheses (Bartsch and Wellman, 1995; Gopnik and Wellman, 1995, Wellman, 1990).

The Modular Theory, on the other hand, claims that the capacity for a ToM is based on an innate and central device in the brain that needs a trigger. After the triggered onset, the mechanism continues almost independently (German and Leslie, 2001; Leslie, 1987, Leslie, Friedman and German, 2004). There are theoretical similarities with Chomsky's notion of a Language Acquisition Device (LAD) (Chomsky, 1969[1965]: 30–7) here.

Both of these traditions are experimental in nature, but there is also a smaller strand of developmental psychology that criticizes such experiments for their lack of ecological validity, arguing instead for the need to observe children in natural settings (cf. Dunn, 1991).

As different as these strands may be, they nonetheless share a strong cognitivist position, where development is largely explained by referring to changes taking place within children's maturing brains.

Moves on the interactional table

Within ToM, there are other crucial aspects of language and social interaction that are either taken for granted or ignored. Antaki's paper 'Reading minds or dealing with interactional implications?' picks up on some of these aspects, fleshes them out and reveals the problems inherit in them. Of special importance is the idea within ToM that the basic function of language is to signify or represent objects out there in the world, rather than to be a means for action.

'Reading minds', which appeared in a special issue of *Theory & Psychology* dedicated to critical examination of ToM, is firmly grounded in an epistemological critique, put forward by a particular strand of Discursive Psychology (DP) concerned with the 'respecification' of cognition (see also Antaki, 2006; Edwards 1997; Edwards and Potter, 2005; Edwards and Potter, 1992). As such, his article is a central part of DP's cumulative body of anti-cognitivist critique.

I will introduce my reading of 'Reading minds' with a quote from the paper – a quote that identifies two central problems underpinning ToM and other psychological theorizing based on mentalistic models:

> ToM proponents put inverted commas around 'mind- reading', as if they mean the term only figuratively, but then proceed essentially as if people do actually read minds. That is to say, they presume two things. First they presume that it is philosophically uncontroversial to assume a referential theory of language: that is to assume that phenomena such as private beliefs, wishes and intentions mean something (and are accurate, plausible, etc.) by comparison against some referred to object. Second, they presume that people can (and must) tell what these supposed referred to objects are. One might reasonably argue with both claims.
>
> (Antaki, 2004: 667–8)

From this quote, we can see that Antaki's 2004 paper can be read as, essentially, a philosophical critique of some of ToM's basic assumptions. It identifies a crucial gap between theoretical statements and actual research practice and conclusions.

Something that I particularly like about the paper is his discussion of the human capacity to 'read minds'. Proponents of ToM, Antaki argues, always carefully point out that an actual human capacity to read minds is naturally impossible, and that the concept is to be understood metaphorically. But despite this, in analyses and discussions of human capacities and shortcomings, it is as if the metaphorical status of the concept disappears and gives way to a form of actual mind-reading capacity that is described as something both real and built into normal psychological development.

Antaki's second critique concerns the representational view of language and how this view both presupposes and reproduces neglect of the fundamental importance of social interaction. All standardized psychological tests, including tests of a ToM, have to neglect the importance of situated social interaction, otherwise standardization becomes impossible. It has to be presumed that all test situations can be made equal and thus possible to compare. From this follows that performance on a test must be understood as reflecting the tested individual's inner capacity. The impossibility of psychology's position on these matters is what is so convincingly demonstrated in the empirical examples provided in Antaki s paper.

However, a performative view of language places other demands on the presentation of findings and analysis:

> It holds that phrases like 'what Jane thinks John believes' are really shorthand for something like 'what Jane is saying and doing so as to allow, or force, a range of public implications that would follow from her being understood to think such-and-such about John, in the circumstances'. Of course this is more laborious than saying she can read someone's mind. But it is more sensible, and likely to be more helpful.
>
> (Antaki, 2004: 669)

Antaki here pre-empts the critique often directed at interactional studies for being too detailed in their descriptions of 'what's going on'. According to him, it is only within such detailed analysis and laborious explanations that the possibility for an interactional understanding may be investigated instead of taken for granted. Otherwise, interactional understanding is at risk for being reified as a mind-reading capacity. In a sequential analysis of the interaction between a psychologist and a client diagnosed with schizophrenia, Antaki is able to show how different and more qualified an elaborated versus a glossed analysis of the unfolding interaction becomes. Without referring to any internal mental states of the client (or for that matter of the psychologist), the reader is nonetheless able to follow an analysis of how the client manages to work out what the therapist is displaying and succeeds in responding in a preferred way, with 'moves dealing with what the interlocutor laid on the interactional table' (p. 681). To conclude, what the reader is offered in Antaki's 'Reading minds' is a convincing framework and analysis of how to describe the achievement or lack of achievement of mutual understanding.

Sympathetic views from other traditions

Discursive psychology is not alone in its criticism of cognitivism, nor is Antaki alone in his criticism of ToM. Conceptually ToM is an analyst's project, not easily compatible with participant's concerns, and so pertinent criticism has been raised from ethnomethodology, to which Antaki's form of discursive psychology is related. Scholars such as Jeff Coulter (1989, 1999, and 2005) have for long argued against the concept of 'mind' in a broad sense, questioning whether it is at all relevant to an analysis of human interaction and interpersonal understanding.

Moreover, while Antaki's contribution to the special issue of *Theory & Psychology* is grounded in a detailed analysis of actual interaction, other papers in the issue trace the philosophical roots of ToM. Sharrock and Coulter (2004) use philosophers Ryle and Wittgenstein to argue for a performative view on language, concluding that ToM's referential view of language in fact causes ToM to lose its coherence and usefulness altogether. They also, like Leudar and Costall (2004, same issue), call attention to the problematic dualism between mind and behaviour, which is not limited to ToM but permeates most of psychology. Leudar and Costall (2009) have also pointed out the rather loose correspondence between achievements in experimental settings and interactional management in everyday life (see also McCabe, 2004 and Schegloff, 1999 on these matters).

The impact of 'Reading minds' has hitherto especially been noted in relation to psychotherapy. Clark (2009) and Georgaca and Avdi (2009) have both taken up Antaki's ideas and demonstrated their fruitfulness in relation to an analysis of psychotherapeutic interaction as well as the assessment of outcomes of psychotherapy. When it comes to mental health and especially schizophrenia, McCabe (2004) has convincingly argued against the idea that difficulties with inferring other's mental states would be a strong component in psychotic symptoms such as delusions. In line with Antaki (2004), she also found that patients with a diagnosis of schizophrenia do not display a ToM deficiency when their participation in naturally occurring interaction is analysed. This is in contrast to results on tests designed to measure ToM, and may indicate more of a problem with the experimental design, than an actual 'deficiency'.

Children's interaction and child development

It needs pointing out that the work discussed above is mostly concerned with adults. For this reason, I intend to emphasize the contemporary relevance of 'Reading minds' with reference to psychological research concerning children and child development. I will do this especially concerning its implications for the psychometric approaches to children.

Psychological development has always been a substantial part of psychological theory. The relation between discourse and development was an issue that was targeted very early on in the formation of discursive psychology. Already in 1988, Edwards and Middleton discussed learning to remember as an interactional activity, and Edwards (1993) developed this further in an analysis of discourse in a kindergarten class, framing knowledge and education as a participant's concern, including both children and teachers.

One of the most profound attempts to investigate children's interaction with a specific interest in the development of 'mind', has come from sociology and conversation analysis. Anthony Wootton (1997; 2006; 2007) has dedicated most of his research to a sequentially based interactional account of developmental change. Instead of theoretical models of internal capacities, public understandings are what is understood to come to inform the child's ongoing lines of action. For cognitive psychologist Jean Piaget (1923), the notion of an internal conflict within the child was crucial for development and the acquisition of more advanced levels of thinking. In Wootton's studies, the focus is instead on agreement. Children construct and consequentially develop their actions so as to be compatible with and understandable in their immediate context. Wootton's conversation analytic work has developed in parallel but seemingly without much contact with the project of discursive psychology.

From very early on, Harvey Sacks (1995) had an interest in children's learning of interactional skills. In a lecture on the necessity of acquiring the competence both to deceive and to reveal deceit, Sacks says:

> [. . .] it's of course nonsense to say that thoughts are things that can't be seen, unless you want to take some notion of 'thoughts' which Members do not employ, since they certainly do take it that one can see what anybody is thinking. Not in every case, certainly, but you can see what people are thinking, and there are ways of doing it. And you must learn to do it.
> (Sacks, 1995: LC1, 364)

At a first glance, this quote may look contradictory to the argument that is being advanced throughout this chapter. Isn't he saying the exact opposite to what Antaki has argued? That it is in fact both possible and necessary to learn how to see what others are thinking? But the crucial difference from ToM proponents is of course the notion of thoughts as an issue for participants (*members* in ethnomethodology's terminology) in interaction. Learning to observe that people sometimes do not overtly tell the whole truth, but may lie or have other hidden agendas, are important social skills, which are complicated but have to be acquired.

There is now a substantial body of research investigating knowledge and cognition from an interactional point of view. Likewise there is no lack of studies that take an interest in children as participants in interaction (see, for example, Butler 2008 and Čekaitè *et al.* 2014 on peer talk and interaction; Butler and Weatherall 2011 and Cromdal 2011 on gender; Butler, Potter et al. 2010 and Cromdal, Daniel Persson-Thunqvist *et al.* 2012 on helpline and emergency interaction; or Danby and Theobald 2012 on disputes). While my own work does not directly address ToM, it is nonetheless indebted to the systematic critique and epistemological concerns that underpin Antaki's argument. It could be characterized as an application of the central concerns that his paper raises: a performative view on language in relation to questions concerning mind and mental states. I am interested in finding and analysing examples of the kind of knowledge that a participant's orientation towards other persons' states and conditions may yield. If you wish, a form of 'mind telling' through 'reading actions' (cf. Osvaldsson 2011; Osvaldsson et al. 2013).

Displaying understanding and affection

In a project[1], examining children's calls to emergency services, I have investigated how children and emergency operators jointly co-construct incident descriptions that are sufficient for adequate emergency rescue responses[2].

Extract 1: He's havin sumthin. [B11. 0–00.34]

```
000        ((line open))
001 op     essoess ettetttv<_å:=>vaint<räffat?
           essoess oneonetwowhat' sccurred
002        (2.1)
003 op     essoess>ettett<_två=>varint<räffat?
           essoessoneonetwowhat's ocurred
004 cl     >hej< >kan ni skicka< en ambulans
           hi couldya send an ambulance
005        ti landtorpsgatan hundraåttiett.=
           to hundredeightyone landtorp street
006 op     =>va är de som< händer dä:r?
           what is happpening there
007 cl     ö:ja tror de hjärtinfarkt ellenåt.=
           I think its a cardiac arrest or summat
008 op     =ä:r de nån som har ↑o:nt i bröste:t.
           has someone got chest pains
009 cl     A::[::han ha] fått nånting.=
           Ye he's havin sumthin
010 op     [ä dä- ]
           is it
011 cl     =han >bara< ↓<låter>=_han::
           he's justmaking this sound he
012        .hH javet inte=>han har bara<
           .hH I dunnohe's just
013        ramlat ihop nu.=
           collapsed now
->014 op   =ahokej .hhm-min arbetskam↑↑rat
           ahokey .hhm- my colleague
015        ↓hä:r
           here
016        (.3)
017 cl     [a::
```

```
                    ya
018  op      [ hon ↑SKIckar ambulans under
               she's sending an ambulance
019          ↓ti:den >sådu-ff< (.25) de:
               while we're talking so you
020          dröjer inte att du åja pra:tar
               you an' me talkin won't hold
021          på nåt vi:s.=>utan hon< skickar
--00.30--      us up in any way so she's sendin
022          ambulansen me en gång hä:r.=
               out the ambulance right away here
023  cl      =[ mm
024  op      [ .här de din ↑pappa som har
               is that your dad having
025          ont i bröstet?=
               the chest pain
026  cl      =a:. hh.
               yeh
```

(Cromdal, Osvaldsson and Persson-Thunqvist, 2008: 932–3)

The caller's report that the patient has 'collapsed' in line 13 clearly indicates an acute situation. What we want to consider here is that the operator's receipt of the report and her ensuing actions (lines 14–22) do not merely concern the nature of the emergency, but also handle the emotional state of the caller. This is hearable in line 14. From a ToM point of view (Leslie, 1987), the operator can be said to be able to form a ToM – to have the capacity not just to comprehend the caller's talk, but to understand the caller's situation and emotional state. No doubt, these are important and desirable competences for an emergency operator. But this is as far as a ToM approach may take us. It tells us nothing about the sequential build-up of the emergency report by its parties and the inferential work that this piece of interaction involves. Following Antaki's call for an analysis of the '*interactional implications*' of emotional work we can trace the operator's assurance to the details of the caller's report, where his struggling descriptions of the patient's symptoms (lines 9 through 12) also display a degree of helplessness. And it is precisely to these manifestations of the caller's emotional state that the operator attends in handling the emergency report. Such feedback on emotional states routinely occurs in situations where the callers show signs of immediate distress. These situations provide explicit examples of the type of interactional implications which, according to Antaki, comprise crucial elements of the display of a candidate understanding another person's thoughts and feelings. The operator continues her inquiry into the caller's situation by asking about the relation between the caller and the patient ('is that your dad', line 24), which further testifies to her reading of the caller's affective state. While mundane categorizations of people as dads or children may be of little value for the understanding of emergency incidents *per se*, operators' sensitivity towards emotional displays in callers' talk may be crucial for the successful progression of calls and adequate emergency response operations.

Repair and understanding

In recent years, there has been a renewed interest in the relation between interaction, child development and ToM. In this section, I present some studies that all express a dissatisfaction with standardized test situations and question their adequacy as contexts for studying the development of mind. They are all important contributions and testimonials to the intellectual impact of Antaki's work.

The first study, by Plejert and Sundqvist (2013), reports on children who use augmentative and alternative communication (AAC), such as Bliss[3], for their communication. While research focusing children with an atypical development often approaches the ways in which these children are impaired by comparing them to children who develop in typical ways, Plejert and Sundqvist (2013) instead set out to examine actions that were taken up by the children in order to achieve mutual understanding. Working from a dialogical perspective, they stress the collaborative aspects of actions. One specific cluster of actions in focus was these children's engagement in repair sequences. Such an engagement is claimed to be 'dependent on the ability to understand that another person experiences a trouble of some kind' (Plejert and Sundqvist, 2013: 183).

Plejert and Sundqvist are very careful in their critique of ToM, claiming that they merely wish to complement the theory with an interaction-oriented perspective. However, they also argue that a focus on interaction may better account for the frequent imbalance between these children's results on formal tests of ToM and more everyday assessments of their social skills.

Formulating wants versus acting on them

Childs (2014) argues for a respecification of ToM, based on detailed analyses of interaction during family mealtimes, targeting children's use of 'I want' expressions. As one example, she shows that formulating wants by no means implies acting in line with one's wants. In fact, people do the opposite. In line with Edwards (2008), she argues that formulations of an intention rather make relevant a possible gap between a formulation and possible action. This analysis further supports Antaki's (2004) critique of the limitations of a referential view on language, that such a view understanding and/or formulation must equal action.

One hypothesis within ToM is that children develop an understanding of others' desires before they develop an understanding of their own thoughts and beliefs (Wellman and Woolley, 1989). In experimental studies, one task for children may be to predict the future actions of characters based on knowledge they have received about the test characters' desires (cf. Cassidy *et al.*, 2005). Like Plejert and Sundqvist's (2013) study, Child's analysis demonstrates how the standardized experimental situation combined with a referential theory of language fails to sufficiently account for the variety of ways in which mental state terms are used in ordinary social interaction. She also argues that most methodology used for investigating children's desires is based on problematic taken-for-granted assumptions – assumptions that detailed analyses of naturally occurring interaction must question.

Moral implications

Iversen (2014) has analysed a corpus of research interviews, originally collected within a project examining the psychological impact on children of witnessing violence against their mothers. Her analysis targets a particular question posed in the interviews ('What do you believe the perpetrator thinks about what he has done') (p. 5). The question was formulated with the intention to obtain information on the psychological concept of mentalization (Fonagy, 1991), which refers to the ability to conceptualize others' mental states, based on own thoughts and observations of others' behaviour. As such, the concept is very closely connected with ToM. The children were asked to provide accounts for the feelings and thoughts of the person who was responsible for the violence they had witnessed against their mothers. This person was their father, or in some cases another person they were close to. Her conclusion was that the perpetrator must be believable – recognized as both credible and knowable – for the children to claim access to his thoughts. The research team was interested in the possible damage that these children's experiences may have done to their capacity for mentalization – Iversen's main argument is that both the concept of mentalization and the referential view on language used in the research interview fail to take into account that such assumptions most often also have moral implications.

> It is noteworthy that the coding manual's four categories, which consider a perpetrator's confession to be the best evidence of regret, did not resonate with the interviewees' descriptions, which challenged the idea that talk necessarily expresses thoughts, and instead stressed the importance of their fathers' (believable) behaviour.
>
> (Iversen, 2014: 382)

Concluding discussion

Antaki's paper, and other more recent studies, demonstrate how a discursive approach to psychological topics is an important contribution to psychology. The strongest contribution of this work is perhaps that is demonstrates, in lived detail, the steps and actions that people take to make themselves understandable to each other.

One of the promising features of this strand of research is its scope for application, not only for research, but for actual social encounters, especially encounters with children who are developing in an atypical manner. ToM research points to possible reasons for trouble with mutual understanding, but does not offer the participants any tools for troubleshooting *in situ*. What may be of help, therefore, is detailed knowledge of the contextually bound ways in which people accomplish social interaction in their everyday lives.

Clearly, there is many a stone unturned concerning the relation between interaction, development, and cognitive issues, and it would seem likely that scholars within discursive psychology and allied disciplines will continuously face up to the challenge posed by decades of mind reading in mainstream psychology.

Notes

1 This work was made possible through a research grant from the Swedish Council for Working Life and Social Research (grant #2005-0236).
2 Due to space constraints, only a brief sketch of the analysis is possible here. For a full account see Cromdal, Osvaldsson and Persson-Thunqvist (2008).
3 Bliss: A graphic language using symbols (Blissymbol Communication UK (2014), Bliss – for people who need to communicate with symbols (2010).

References

Antaki, C. (2004) 'Reading minds or dealing with interactional implications?', *Theory & Psychology*, 14: 667–83.
Antaki, C. (2006) 'Producing a "cognition"', *Discourse Studies*, 8: 9–15.
Auburn, T. and Lea, S. (2003) 'Doing cognitive distortions: A discursive psychology analysis of sex offender treatment talk', *British Journal of Social Psychology*, 42: 281–98.
Baron-Cohen, S., Leslie, A. and Frith, U. (1985) 'Does the autistic child have a "theory of mind"?', *Cognition*, 21: 37–46.
Bartsch, K. and Wellman, H.M. (1995) *Children talk about the mind*. Oxford: Oxford University Press.
Bliss – for people who need to communicate with symbols (2010) Stockholm: National Agency for Special Needs Education and Schools. Blissymbol Communication UK. Available at www.blissymbols.co.uk (accessed 29 April, 2014).
Butler, C. (2008) *Talk and social interaction in the playground*. Aldershot: Ashgate.
Butler, C. and Weatherall, A. (2011) 'Accomplishing a cross-gender identity: A case of passing in children's talk-in-interaction', in S.A. Speer and E. Stokoe (eds) *Conversation and gender*. New York: Cambridge University Press.
Butler, C., Potter, J., Danby, S., Emmison, M. and Hepburn, A. (2010) 'Advice-implicative interrogatives: Building "client-centered" support in a children's helpline', *Social Psychology Quarterly*, 73: 265–87.
Cassidy, K.W., Cosetti, M., Jones, R., Kelton, E., Rafal, V.M., Richman, L., *et al.* (2005) 'Preschool children's understanding of conflicting desires'. *Journal of Cognition & Development*, 6: 427–54.
Čekaitè, A., Blum-Kulka, S., Grover, V. and Teubal, E. (2014) *Children's peer talk: Learning from each other*. Cambridge: Cambridge University Press.

Childs, C. (2014) 'From reading minds to social interaction: Respecifying Theory of Mind', *Human Studies, 37*: 103–22.
Chomsky, N. (1965/1969) *Aspects of the theory of syntax*. Cambridge, MA: MIT Press.
Clark, S.J. (2009) 'Getting personal. Talking the psychotherapy session into being'. Unpublished PhD thesis. The Australian National University, Canberra.
Corcoran, R., Mercer, G. and Frith, C.D. (1995) 'Schizophrenia, symptomatology and social inference: Investigating "theory of mind" in people with schizophrenia', *Schizophrenia Research, 17*: 5–13.
Coulter, J. (1989) *Mind in action*. Atlantic Highlands, NJ: Humanities Press International.
Coulter, J. (1999) 'Discourse and mind', *Human Studies, 22*: 163–81.
Coulter, J. (2005) 'Language without mind', in H. te Molder and J. Potter (eds) *Conversation and cognition*. New York: Cambridge University Press.
Cromdal, J. (2011) 'Gender as a practical concern in children's management of play participation', in S.A. Speer and E. Stokoe (eds) *Conversation and gender*. New York: Cambridge University Press.
Cromdal, J., Persson-Thunqvist, D. and Osvaldsson, K. (2012) '"SOS 112 what has occurred?" Managing openings in children's emergency calls', *Discourse, Context & Media, 1*:183–202.
Cromdal, J., Osvaldsson, K. and Persson-Thunqvist, D. (2008) 'Context that matters: Producing "thick-enough descriptions" in initial emergency reports', *Journal of Pragmatics, 40*: 927–59.
Danby, S. and Theobald, M. (eds) (2012) *Disputes in everyday life: Social and moral orders of children and young people*. Bingley, UK: Emerald.
Dunn, J. (1991) 'Understanding others: Evidence from naturalistic studies of children', in A. Whiten (ed.) *Natural theories of mind*. Oxford: Basil Blackwell.
Edwards, D. (1993) 'But what do children really think?: Discourse analysis and conceptual content in children's talk', *Cognition & Instruction, 11*: 207–25.
Edwards, D. (1997) *Discourse and cognition*. Thousand Oaks, CA: Sage Publications.
Edwards, D. (2008) 'Intentionality and *mens rea* in police interrogations: The production of actions as crimes', *Intercultural Pragmatics, 5*: 177–99.
Edwards, D. and Middleton, D. (1988) 'Conversational remembering and family relationships: How children learn to remember', *Journal of Social & Personal Relationships, 5*: 3–25.
Edwards, D. and Potter, J. (1992) *Discursive psychology*. London: Sage Publications.
Edwards, D. and Potter, J. (2005) 'Discursive psychology, mental states and descriptions', in H. te Molder and J. Potter (eds) *Conversation and cognition*. New York: Cambridge University Press.
Fonagy, P. (1991) 'Thinking about thinking: Some clinical a theoretical considerations in the treatment of a borderline patient', *International Journal of Psychoanalysis, 72*: 639–56.
Frith, C.D. (1992) *Cognitive neuropsychology of schizophrenia*. Hove, UK: Lawrence Erlbaum.
Frith, C.D. and Corcoran, R. (1996) 'Exploring "theory of mind" in people with schizophrenia', *Psychological Medicine, 26*: 521–30.
Georgaca, E. and Avdi, E. (2009) 'Evaluating the talking cure: The contribution of narrative, discourse, and conversation analysis to psychotherapy assessment', *Qualitative Research in Psychology, 6*: 233–47.

German, T.P. and Leslie, A.M. (2001) 'Children's inferences from "knowing" to "pretending" and "believing"', *British Journal of Developmental Psychology*, 19: 59–83.

Gopnik, A. and Wellman, H.M. (1995) 'Why the child's theory of mind really is a theory', in M. Davies and T. Stone (eds) *Folk psychology: The Theory of Mind debate*. Oxford, UK and Cambridge, MA: Blackwell.

Houtkoop-Steenstra, H. (2000) *Interaction and the standardized interview. The living questionnaire*. Cambridge: Cambridge University Press.

Houtkoop-Steenstra, H. (2002) 'Questioning turn format and turn-taking problems in standardized interviews', in D.W. Maynard, H. Houtkoop-Steenstra, N.C. Schaeffer and J. van der Zouwen (eds) *Standardization and tacit knowledge. Interaction and practice in the survey interview*. New York: John Wiley.

Iversen, C. (2014) '"I don't know if I should believe him": Knowledge and believability in interviews with children', *British Journal of Social Psychology*, 53: 367–86.

Leslie, A.M. (1987) 'Pretense and representation: The origins of "theory of mind"', *Psychological Review*, 94: 412–26.

Leslie, A.M., Friedman, O. and German, T.P. (2004) 'Core mechanisms in "theory of mind"', *Trends in Cognitive Sciences*, 8: 528–33.

Leudar, I. and Costall, A. (2004) 'On the persistence of the "problem of other minds" in psychology: Chomsky, Grice and Theory of Mind', *Theory & Psychology*, 14: 601–21.

Leudar, I. and Costall, A. (eds) (2009) *Against Theory of Mind*. Basingstoke: Palgrave Macmillan.

Locke, A. (2004) 'Accounting for success and failure: A discursive psychological approach to sport talk', *Quest*, 56: 302–20.

Mazza, M., De Risio, A., Surian, L., Roncone, R. and Casacchia, M. (2001) 'Selective impairments of theory of mind in people with schizophrenia', *Schizophrenia Research*, 47: 299–308.

McCabe, R. (2004) 'On the inadequacies of Theory of Mind explanations of schizophrenia: Alternative accounts of alternative problems', *Theory & Psychology*, 14: 738–52.

Osvaldsson, K. (2004) '"I don't have no damn cultures": Doing "normality" in a "deviant setting"', *Qualitative Research in Psychology*, 1: 239–64.

Osvaldsson, K. (2011) 'Bullying in context: Stories of bullying on an Internet discussion board', *Children & Society*, 25: 317–27.

Osvaldsson, K., Persson Thunqvist, D. and Cromdal, J. (2013) 'Comprehension checks, clarifications, and corrections in an emergency call with a nonnative speaker of Swedish', *International Journal of Bilingualism*, 17: 205–20.

Piaget, J. (1923) 'The language and thought of the child', in H. Gruber and J. Jacques Voneche (eds) *The essential Piaget*. London: Routledge and Kegan Paul.

Plejert, C. and Sundqvist, A. (2013). 'A dialogical approach to Theory of Mind in aided and non-aided child interaction', in N. Norén, C. Samuelsson and C. Plejert (eds) *Aided communication in everyday interaction*. London: J&R Press.

Potter, J. (2010) 'Contemporary discursive psychology: Issues, prospects, and Corcoran's awkward ontology', *British Journal of Social Psychology*, 49: 657–78.

Premack, D. and Woodruff, G. (1978) 'Does the chimpanzee have a theory of mind?', *Behavioral & Brain Sciences*, 1: 515–26.

Sacks, H. (1995) *Lectures on conversation. Volumes I and II*. Edited by Gail Jefferson with introductions by Emanuel A. Schegloff. Oxford: Basil Blackwell.

Schegloff, E.A. (1999) 'Discourse, pragmatics, conversation, analysis', *Discourse Studies*, 1: 405–35.

Sharrock, W. and Coulter, J. 2004, '"ToM", A critical commentary', *Theory & Psychology*, 14: 579–600.

Stokoe, E.H. (2003) 'Mothers, single women and sluts: Gender, morality and membership categorization in neighbour disputes', *Feminism & Psychology*, 13: 317–44.

Suchman, L. and Jordan, B. (1990) 'Interactional troubles in face-to-face survey interviews', *Journal of the American Statistical Association*, 85: 232–41.

Surian, L. and Leslie, A.M. (1999) 'Competence and performance in false belief understanding: A comparison of autistic and normal 3-yr-old children', *British Journal of Developmental Psychology*, 17: 141–55.

Wellman, H.M. (1990) *The child's Theory of Mind*. Cambridge, MA: Bradford/MIT Press.

Wellman, H.M. and Woolley, J.D. (1989) 'From simple desires to ordinary beliefs: The early development of everyday psychology', *Cognition*, 35: 245–75.

Wootton, A.J. (1997/2005) *Interaction and the development of mind*. Cambridge: Cambridge University Press.

Wootton, A.J. (2002/2003) 'Interactional contrasts between typically developing children and those with Autism, Asberger's syndrome and pragmatic Impairment', *Issues in Applied Linguistics*, 13: 133–59.

Wootton, A.J. (2006) 'Children's practices and their connections with "mind"', *Discourse Studies*, 8: 191–8.

Wootton, A.J. (2007) 'A puzzle about please: Repair, increments, and related matters in the speech of a young child', *Research on Language & Social Interaction*, 40: 171–98.

11 From script theory to script formulation

Derek Edwards' shift from perceptual realism to the interactional-rhetorical

Neill Korobov

Target article: Edwards, D. (1994) 'Script formulations: An analysis of event descriptions in conversation', *Journal of Language & Social Psychology*, 13: 211–47.

For nearly two decades, Derek Edwards' work on scripts and script formulations has stood out as both a conceptual pillar and analytic exemplar in the field of Discursive Psychology (hereafter, DP). Although a topic of inquiry rich in its own right, Edwards' work on scripting (1994, 1995, 1997, 2004) represents a quintessence of Edwards' early unique contribution to the Loughborough school's development of DP. It respecifies a traditionally *cognitive* psychological concept as a discursive one, showing concretely how putatively cognitive/mental phenomenon are not so much brought to the scene to direct interaction as they are constituted in and for interaction as an accountable and transactional business item of talk for cultivating the normative bases for human sociality. Although DP has for some time been in the business of reformulating various psychological constructs, Edwards' work has been particularly notable for reconceptualizing the *cognitive* or mental armamentarium of psychology. His early research has addressed topics such as memory/remembering (Edwards *et al.* 1992a; 1992b, 1993), attributions (1993, 1999), perception (1997), thinking (1997, Edwards and Potter 2005), emotions (1997, 1999), and scripts (1994, 1995, 1997, 2004), to name a few. In so doing, he paved the way for a radical rethinking of the relationship between discourse and cognition. As much (or more) than any other of the leading DP researchers, Edwards has thus brought the sharp-edged corrective of DP to the intersection of language and social cognition, with his work on scripts/scripting serving as a case exemplar.

Setting the scene: Reworking the relationship between discourse and cognition

Before addressing Edwards' specific work on scripting, it is important to couch it within Edwards' early discursive psychological reworking of the relationship between cognition and discourse, particularly as that project gained traction in the early to mid 1990s. While there is not sufficient space here to address Edwards' full application of DP to issues related to cognitive science/psychology and cognition/mental states (for this, see Edwards 1997; Edwards and Potter 1992), there are several key ideas worth addressing that directly lay the groundwork for his reformulation of scripts. First, as is reflected in the title, Edwards' work on scripts details a broad theoretical move of shifting the focus from perceptual realism to the interactional rhetorical. Although this theoretical move is built on the shoulders of decades of poststructural, postempiricist, ethnomethodoogical, social constructionist, and hermeneutic philosophical thought, Edwards' DP application of it to *both* cognitive psychological assumptions and raw empirical data in the early 1990s was particularly trenchant and original.

At the heart of these arguments is a rejection of the modern cognitivist idea that knowledge derives from the internal operations of minds. Edwards (1997) problematizes psychology's long-standing commitment to a *dualistic metaphysics*, which assumes an interior mind that both influences and is influenced by an external real world. In any dualism where the mind is posited as interior and casual, a preference for abstraction emerges, where the focus is on context independent nodes of ideational information (e.g., scripts) and how such nodes are turned on or off by experiences in the external real world. This requires a faith in the psychological reality of cognitive processes and representations that are organized, modular to varying degrees, amenable to models and theories, and measurable through experimental means (see Potter and te Molder 2005). Instead, Edwards envisioned DP as a kind of *social epistemology* in which the distinction between 'internal' and 'external' is collapsed. The locus of knowledge is not in individual minds, but in social/interactional patterns of sense-making. Edwards' work on scripts would thus part ways with a perceptual-realist model of cognition for an interactional-rhetorical view. This new approach would advance an idiosyncratic (not abstract) view of language as a specific and locally fined-tuned tool and an emic perspective that focuses on participants own 'realities' as oriented-to practical and performative doings. Here, the analytic fodder is not processes, representations, or other ideational material, but actual descriptions and evaluations that are rhetorically responsive to constantly evolving interactional contingencies.

Second, Edwards' work on scripts reflects a radical double move that involves rethinking the status of cognition and, subsequently, resuscitating the status of discourse from its impoverished view in cognitive work. Edwards is not interested in offering a rival theory of mind or a new 'discursive mind' where mental states and cognitions are taken to be fundamentally discursive. Rather, Edwards rejects the necessity of conceptualizing mind in the traditionally psychological way – i.e., as a 'product-and-process psychology of mental development' (Edwards 1997), where mind is viewed as an objective developmental outcome and causal/directive force on sociality. Instead, Edwards asks that we treat 'minds' as a range of participant's categories and ways of talking, deployed in the action-oriented service of engaging in social life. This, in turn, shifts the way we see discourse. Discourse is no longer the product or expression of underlying cognitive/mental states, nor is it a transparent methodological route to studying cognitive processes. Rather, discourse is an active and constitutive tool. The central advantage of such a reorientation is that it keeps the focus fresh and alive on the ongoing procedures that people actually use to create social life, rather than punting endlessly back to an inner control room beneath the skull.

Some will argue that Edwards is simply offering a complementary theory to the traditional cognitive psychological view, and that whatever DP may reveal about how people use the discursive categories of 'minds' to engage in social action, there still surely must be some underlying ideational realm of cognitive competence (like scripts) that makes discursive action possible. Edwards (2006) is deft to point out the problematic circularity of such a speculation. In a way akin to the idea that it requires language to imagine a world behind or beyond language, Edwards argues that the evidence that there might be an inner cognitive world beneath or beyond discourse *requires the very domain of discursive practices* that such an inner world is supposed to explain. Anything ostensibly cognitive is always part of some local discursive business. People do not adhere to a belief, plan, or script simply for its own sake; they do so as part of some pressing interactional business. Put simply, it requires discourse to theorize about an inner cognitive realm that would make discourse possible. This stands as a radical observation in Edwards' application of DP to cognitive psychological theory.

The final foregrounding pillar in Edwards' application of DP to cognitive concepts such as scripts is his allying of DP's reorientation of cognition with an ethnomethodologically-inspired conversation analytic (CA) methodology. Edwards' reformulation of cognitive states as discursive topics for (rather than causes of) human interaction requires the kind of close and detailed examination of people's talk that was scarce in the broad field of qualitative methods and somewhat nascent in discourse studies in the late 1980s and early 1990s. When Edwards began his work on scripts (as well as other cognitive phenomena) in the early 1990s, the DP/CA partnership was still emerging. His work on scripts represents an early and important bit of connective tissue between the broad field of discourse studies and the ethnomethodologically-inspired programme of conversation analysis.

Edwards (1997) credits Sacks' (1992) and Garfinkel's (1967) ethnomethodological work in the late 1960s for being curious about how people show that they share understanding – that is, that their cognitions are in sync. Sacks thought it pointless to speculate *that* people are thinking similarly or differently, but rather thought that we ought to be concerned to understand *how* it is that people *show* that they understand and share (or don't share) knowledge. Schegloff (1991) would further develop the idea of 'socially shared cognitions/ understandings' for conversation analysis, and would work to specify a detailed set of procedures that speakers use to display congruent or incongruent understandings of one another. Rather than becoming preoccupied with wanting to dig beneath discourse to the inner psychological world of the mind, Edwards

(1994) would ask, in Sacks'-type fashion, and with Schegloff's style of precision: what are the procedures that participants have for dealing with notions of the mind? Those detailed analytic procedures are the focus of Edwards' work on scripts, and their analysis borrows heavily from CA's rich analytic toolbox. As we will see in Edwards' work on scripting, there are specifiable procedures and conversational devices (e.g., the iterative present tense, idioms, event pluralisation, etc.) that people routinely use to create a normative or shared sense of action, understanding, and also, importantly, their own and others' dispositions.

Edwards' shift from scripts to scripting/script formulations

Not only is Edwards' seminal work on scripts (Edwards 1994) an exemplar of a DP reworking of a cognitively ensnared psychological concept, it is also, broadly, part of an expansive empirical project for studying the spontaneous production and receipt of event descriptions. It just so happens that events tend to be described as more or less routine, ordinary, or expected. That is, the scriptedness of talk about happenings and people's actions is a central and highly regular feature of them. Edwards' (1994) dual focus is thus both to advance the DP agenda of reworking the relationship between discourse and cognition, as discussed above, and to study how events and actions are described by actual participants as more or less scripted, and how such script formulations manage accountability and construct dispositions. His goal is not to do away with traditional thinking on scripts, but to instead begin by asking how it is that scripts feature as discursive tools in participants' own explanatory apparatuses.

Background influences

Edwards' project is prompted by a range of influences. Prior to his own work on scripts, Edwards (1994) notes that there was already a body of meta-theoretical work on the scriptedness of event reports (see Reddy 1979), as well as the ways that consensus formulations are brought off, in part, by scripting (Kelly 1967). With respect to the disposition-warranting work that scripting accomplishes, Edwards (1995) points to Gale's (1991) study of the ways that couples sometimes script their partners as dispositionally flawed in some way, and how such tendencies are used to account for relational difficulties. Also influential was Buttny's (1990, 1993) work on blame-accounts sequences that involve reciprocating dispositional scripting sequences in which one person connects a scripted event description (e.g., 'person X can't talk about things') with a dispositional tendency (e.g., 'person X is a very introverted and private person'), only to then have that blaming countered with a dispositional scripting by the other person ('person Y likes to talk and reiterate on things a large number of times'). In addition, Stenner (1993) wondered why it was that couples often present themselves in ways that contrast markedly from the ways their partner describes them. He concluded that such dispositional divergences were not simply a reflection of the couple's lack of knowledge of one another, but rather were conversational resources for accomplishing some bit of relevant social action. It could be that couples are quite attuned to each other, and that part of the relational dance involves using dispositional constructions and contrasts in rhetorically-honed or strategic ways to get something done.

Perhaps the most relevant body of background literature for Edwards' project is the rhetorical foil provided by traditional script theory. Edwards (1994) launches his work on scripts by advancing a thorough critique of traditional script theory. Although Edwards (1994, 1995, 1997) routinely links script theory to the work of Schank and Abelson (Schank 1982; Schank and Abelson 1977), and to a lesser extent Nelson (1986), Edwards' critique is actually much broader in scope. His critique could be applied with equal force and relevance to Bartlett's (1932/1961) seminal work on scripts/schemas, Bateson's (1955/1972), Minsky's (1974), Frake's (1977), Gumperz's (1982), Goffman's (1974) and Tannen's (1993) development of frames/framing, as well as Fillmore's (1976) and Chafe's (1977) hybrid of frame, scene and categorization, just to name few other potential protagonists. Common in this multi-disciplinary lineage of thinking is the idea that human action derives from cognitive capacities that are stored internally in some form or another as cognitive/mental representations (scripts, frames, schemas, rules, etc.) and processes. Much of the DP platform rests on challenging this exact paradigm and, as Edwards (1997) himself notes, though the rhetorical contrast provided by cognitive script theory is useful, it is not necessary.

Nevertheless, Edwards directs his critique mainly at Schank and Abelson's perceptual-cognitive metatheoretical work on scripts and their application of it to models of artificial intelligence in the late 1970s and early 1980s. Schank and Abelson (Schank 1982; Schank and Abelson 1977) theorized that we have specific detailed knowledge (perceptually derived schemas/scripts) of certain situations and of the many different results of different possible actions in those situations. The idea, quite literally, is that we encounter situations equipped with thousands of such scripts. These scripts are *internally* stored and once they are indexed they can direct behavior. We are cognitively outfitted with inference mechanisms that index the relevant script(s) for the situation, interpretive mechanisms for understanding that script, and script appliers for manipulating the casual chain of events (or filling in missing events in that chain) in order to complete the meaning-making process. Understanding thus proceeds like a computer programme. Input-directed linear and causal networks index relevant cognitive scripts. Scripts generate understanding by connecting different segments (or by filling in left-out information) of event sequences in the overall process of meaning-making. People are thus construed as information processors, with our ability to act socially a product of the efficacy of our casual chains firing along the paths of relevant scripts.

In general, scripts are designed to handle stereotypical everyday situations, and it is in that sense that Schank and Abelson (1977) rely on Minsky's (1974) notion of *static* data structures and, subsequently, abstract exemplars to study script assemblage and use. Although Schank's (1982) later work would attempt to account for more variability in script use, scripts are generally speaking not subject to much change, nor has it been shown how they handle complex, idiosyncratic, or novel situations. They work best as predetermined, stereotyped sequences of actions that define a well-known situation, such as 'ordering food at a restaurant', 'going to a birthday party', or 'giving a gift'. Contexts, interactions and language act simply as triggers for already pre-established cognitive data structures that internally direct understanding. Though cognitive research on scripts do acknowledge the variability of contexts, Edwards (1994) notes they often deal quite tentatively with the fact that there may be many different meanings and that each person's 'gift giving script', for instance, may vary (in both content and form) quite tremendously depending on how the script is being put to use.

Edwards' reworking of script theory

Edwards' (1994) critique works to undermine the traditional conceptualization of scripts and how they operate in contexts of meaning-making. To do this, he specifies three possible ways that we might understand scripts, as well as the relation between them. The first are *scripts-w*, which refer to features of the real world that are ordered, such as the concretely ordered ways in which a grocery store checkout aisle is physically set up. *Scripts-w* reflect the assumption that events in the world are fundamentally ordered and that the recognizable features of such order may then trigger what may be called *scripts-pc*, which refer to the ordered features of an individual's perception/cognition of the world. *Scripts-pc* are sets of abstract propositional representations of actions in an individual's mind that are triggered in real-world contexts, such as the features of perception and cognition that arise in the context of grocery store checkout aisles. Finally, *scripts-d* are the ways that events and actions are described as more or less ordered, routine or expected. In a grocery store checkout aisle, *scripts-d* are the live descriptions of events and actions by actual people participating in the social activities that happen in actual checkout aisles. In traditional script theory, the ontological order of these three levels of scripting is as follows (see Edwards 1994; Potter and te Molder 2005):

scripts-w → scripts-pc → scripts-d

Such an ordering make *scripts-d* by-products of perceptually-refined cognitive scripts derived from experience with real-world events (*scripts-w*). Edwards (1994) wants to challenge this order. His solution is not to ontologically privilege *scripts-d* (although there is some debate and confusion surrounding the extent to which DP seeks to invert/reverse, rather than simply subvert, the ontological relationship between discursive and non-discursive phenomena – for debates and discussion, see Coulter 1999, 2004; Edwards and Potter 2003). Edwards' (1994) reformulation involves treating scripts as pragmatically formulated constructions (or 'script formulations'). Edwards's analytic interest is in *scripts-d*, approached as participants' own categories of talk that construct events in particular ways – as more or less routine, ordinary, predictable or exceptional. *Scripts-d* provides the normative bases for accountability, rather than acting as a cognitive programme or perceptual process (*scripts-pc*) for generating social action.

This notion of scripts as creating and sanctioning the normative bases of social action and accountability is perhaps one of the more striking and interesting aspects of Edwards' (1994, 1995, 1997) work on script formulations. *Scripts-d* sanctions and/or subverts consensus formulations. They tell us what everybody knows (or ought to know), and thus either legitimize otherwise non-normative actions or de-legitimize what have been taken to be normative actions, ideas, thoughts or dispositions. Edwards (1997: 144) argues:

> At stake in such descriptions are the normative basis of actions, and the accountability of the actors. That is to say, moral and normative issues of appropriateness, responsibility, and blame are at stake in how a person's actions or involvement is described.

In short, script formulations do more than construct actions or events as more or less normative; they may also paint a picture of the actor's disposition or mental state. Script formulations thus have an enormously rich and important place in psychological inquiry. Script formulations are delicately intertwined with the psychology of dispositional attributions, or what may be glossed as 'personality'. When one's actions or participation in events is scripted as aberrant or abnormal, that person's personality becomes morally accountable. This also works in reverse; if one's disposition is scripted as more or less expected or ordinary, their social actions, by extension, are also seen as more or less normal, rational or reasonable, and are thus more or less morally accountable.

As such, script formulations perform important rhetorical work. They attend to the fact that they are likely to be countered (see Billig 1987; Edwards 1994). They orient to both actual and alternative descriptions, and in so doing, infer a variety of implications about the kind of person the speaker is taken to be or about their participation in certain groups (racial, sexual, political, etc.). Seen this way, *scripts-d* have an enormous *constitutive* potential that undermines the 'scripts-w ‡ scripts-pc ‡ scripts-d' sequence. Their use, especially repetitively or iteratively in certain contexts, may *creative*ly shape the ways we perceive order in the world (*scripts-pc*), and thus the ways that the world is taken to be ordered (*scripts-w*). It is in this spirit that we may return to a Sacks'-type observation in asking, as Edwards (1994, 1997) does: what are the scripting procedures that people use that have, as a result of their repetitive formulations within and across contexts, a showing of people as having certain orderly perceptions and cognitions of an ostensibly ordered world? Or more simply, how is it that our scripted descriptions have, as a consequence, the creation of orderly 'minds' and 'worlds'? This is not to privilege discourse in an ontological reversal, but rather is an invitation to reverse the analytic trajectory of traditional psychological inquiry. Edwards asks that we begin with an investigation of *scripts-d* and see what is created, sustained, or normalized (or undermined/negated) by their actual use.

Edwards' analysis of script formulations

Edwards' analysis of script formulations spans two data sets – the first, in his seminal work (Edwards 1994), focuses on spontaneous telephone conversations, while subsequent work (Edwards 1995, 1997) deals additionally with conversations from counselling sessions. Because this chapter is dedicated primarily to Edwards seminal work (Edwards 1994), what follows is a sketch of the analytic import from that particular article. Edwards (1994) begins by noting that the precise details of scripts are often formulated as script fragments, as a feature of local interactional contingencies, rather than being a result of perceptual expectation failures. And further, while there may very well be *scripts-w*, such as 'beach routines', Edwards shows how imprecise the actual content of such routines is, and instead how they are worked up interactionally for some relevant social business. In so doing, Edwards stresses the constitutiveness of script formulations. Script formulations *construct* events as scripted, which problematizes the cognitive idea of scripts with pre-packaged content.

Edwards' analyses reveal the limitations of traditional script theory in handling the sheer volume and randomness of exceptional script details. Were we to attempt to build cognitive models to bear such weight, it would be ad hoc and cumbersome, and the script would be overwrought and overspecified. Instead, Edwards focuses on how the content of scripts is produced inventively in the performance of some social action (such as complaining). Edwards wants to champion the challenge of working with the messy details of script talk produced on the fly, which highlights the rhetorical design of script formulations. In actual interactions, alternative versions of events, actions and people lurk, and must be dealt with, which requires a range of scripting moves, the logic of which is located in the intersubjective affiliative work it accomplishes and not so much in an orthogonal relation to *scripts-pc*.

Finally, Edwards broaches a topic that is further developed in his 1995 and 1997 work on scripts. He analyzes how script formulations manage accountability not only interactionally but also morally. Script formulations make moral sense of the world. While engaging in social action (i.e., trying to convince someone of something), certain aspects of the world (i.e., a vocation, an illness or a disposition) get portrayed in morally appealing and/or unappealing ways. Edwards shows how script formulations, built as an interplay between discursive items, instances and generalities, coalesce to construct the moral, personal and pathological traits or dispositional patterns of people, all designed, of course, to bring off particular social actions (blaming, complaining, justifications, etc.). In his 1995 work on relationship troubles talk between couples in counselling sessions, Edwards amplifies this focus, honing in on the ways event descriptions make inferentially available the dispositions, moral traits and character (or 'personality') of the participants. The syncing of script formulations with the disposition-warranting work it accomplishes is arguably one of the most sanguine and exciting applications of Edwards use of script formulations to address issues that lie at the heart of not only cognitive psychology (and its interest in 'mind'), but also more broadly with psychology's overwhelming interest in the development of personality.

Impact on subsequent work in DP

Over the last two decades or so, Edwards' (1994, 1995, 1997) work on scripting has ignited a glut of fascinating discursive research. There are two ways to discuss its impact. First, and more broadly, Edwards' work on script formulations has served as a case exemplar in a range of introductions to discursive psychology (e.g., see Wood and Kroger 2000; te Molder and Potter 2005), even appearing as the lone analytic illustration in the Wikipedia entry for 'discursive psychology'. This is likely due, in part, not only to Edwards' stature in the field of DP, but also because Edwards' scripting project is a parsimonious and elegant piece of analysis, widely applicable to a range of metatheoretical, methodological and topical issues in DP. The devices that bring off script formulations have been discussed alongside conversation analytic principles (such as sequence organization and turn design) for discursive psychological inquiries into topics such as 'experiences' (see Potter 2012), 'private thoughts' (Barnes and Moss 2007), or 'states of mind' attributions (see Stokoe and Edwards 2008). Script formulations have also been a central discursive resource/device cited in the broad project of resurrecting membership categorization analysis and grounding it in an orderly and structured conversation analytic methodology for DP (see Stokoe 2012).

Most exciting, however, are the specific ways that select aspects of Edwards' scripting project have been picked up by other DP researchers. In combing through the extant literature that applies Edwards' work on scripting, arguably the most routinely cited and developed aspect of his work on scripting has to do with the way script formulations are used to legitimize, normalize, or otherwise manage the accountable features of certain identities or dispositions, or the actions and beliefs that accompany certain identities and dispositions. In one vein of research, this focus appears in a collection of what might be glossed as sociocultural issues, ranging from sexual identity disclosures among LGB individuals (Chirrey 2011, 2012), the justification of polygamy and extramarital affairs (de Kok 2009), interethnic solidarity (Grancea 2010), mitigations of racism (Benwell 2012), and inoculating gender identity displays from charges of sexism and new sexism (Korobov 2009, 2011a; Korobov and Bamberg 2004). A subsection of this first line of research focuses specifically on the use of script formulations in accounts, descriptions and justifications related to sexual and physical violence (LeCouteur and Oxland 2011; Firth and Kitzinger 2011; Stokoe 2010; Wells 2012). Finally, a second vein of research considers the use of script formulations among romantic couples in the maintenance or negotiation of affiliation in relationships (Korobov 2011b, 2011c; Muntigl and Choi 2010).

Chirrey (2011, 2012) has documented the ways that lesbian, gay and bisexual (LGB) individuals use script formulations to normalize the ways that they construct 'coming out' in various advice columns, websites, pamphlets and so on. Script formulations allow LGB individuals to manage the accountable nature of an LGB disposition by construing 'coming out' as a routine, normal, rational and emancipatory social and personal action. In de Kok's (2009) analysis of Malawi people talking about cultural ways of handling fertility problems, he shows how polygamy and extramarital affairs are presented as normative solutions, and how they are scripted to appear normal and to thus downplay negative attributions to the people who engage with them. Grancea (2010) shows how Romanian and Hungarian speakers create a shared sense of inter-ethnic group identity/solidarity by jointly scripting complaint sequences which both ethnicities can relate to, thereby treating complaints as common sense knowledge, normalized through references to personal experiences. Benwell (2012) focuses on how members of a British book club routinely script an enlightened, non-racist disposition by creating category-based denials of the 'racist other' (through collective rebuffs of the racist other's reported speech), revealing that 'anti-racism' is an accountable matter that requires impression management.

The disposition-warranting work of script formulations has also been applied to discursive research on the management of the accountable features of gender identities. Korobov and Bamberg (2004) show how young men create scripted dispositional accounts of their experiences with young women that mitigate hearably immature, sexist or misognysitic motives and actions in their talk about physical attraction, desire and young women's bodies. Korobov (2009) also shows how young men account for behaviour that is potentially sexually inappropriate by scripting their actions according to a pervasive and stable dispositional and interpersonal tendencies. The young men often claimed either that their ostensibly boorish behaviour actually reflects a kind dispositional playfulness (i.e., 'it's just for fun') or else a scripted interpersonal repartee between themselves and their female friends that involve mutual collusion around what may appear to be inappropriate banter. The effect of such scripting is that it situates the young men's actions within a pre-established and scripted frame of playfulness, thus mitigating the potential for their actions to appear perverse, harassing or desperate.

Relatedly, in Korobov's (2011a) work on 'new sexism', he analyzes how script formulations work as resources that young men use in narrating stories about their experiences with girlfriends who resist traditional femininity norms that would encourage women to be passive, docile or subordinate. Rather than ratcheting up traditionally heroic and macho masculine responses, the young men managed women's resistance to traditional femininity either by scripting an anti-heroic and ordinary masculine disposition of nonchalance or by negatively scripting the woman's disposition vis-à-vis the irrational or 'crazy bitch' trope. In narrating stories about women who actively responded with aggressive retaliation (rather than passivity) for being treated poorly, the young men engaged in dispositional scripting of the female as routinely 'out of control' or generally 'irrational'. In other instances, the men normalized women's retaliation, not as a way of normalizing women's general right to reject men's boorish behavior, but as a way of working up the gender-normative script that suggests men generally make mistakes and women generally get angry about it (see Gilmartin 2007). Normalizing this script allows men to script a victim identity. Further, by celebrating or nonchalantly laughing off women's resistance to traditional femininity, young men seemed adept at normalizing the new sexism found in contemporary forms of 'lad-masculinity'.

Within the realm of sociocultural issues, script formulations have also been analyzed within the context of research on sexual and physical violence. Stokoe (2010) has shown how men accused of battery use scripting to create category-based denials ('I'm not that sort of man') to resist the accountable disposition of a man who acts violently towards women. Similarly, in analyzing the situated identity categorization work of men who have engaged in domestic violence, LeCouteur and Oxland (2011) have found that when men overtly acknowledge the wrongness of their violence, they often script the female as routinely breaching the normative moral order, which indirectly warrants their consequential violence. In Wells' (2012) analysis of judicial attribution practices about battered women who were convicted of killing their abusive partner, she noticed that judges tended to mitigate the seriousness of previous partner violence by formulating past events as discrete episodes due to alcohol consumption, rather than scripting them as broader habitual patterns of domestic violence. Firth and Kitzinger (2011) have studied young women's talk about refusing unwanted sex, noting the ways that the progression of events in sexual encounters gets scripted, which makes saying no to unwanted sexual advances challenging because it involves breaking such scripts. Further, the women work to mitigate the negative dispositional inferences that come with such resistance.

A second vein of research considers the use of script formulations among romantic couples in the negotiation of affiliation in relationships. In studying conversations from couple's therapy, Muntigl and Choi (2010) showed how couples routinely used 'not remembering' as an interactional resource. One partner would often ascribe not remembering to the other, thus scripting the other as aberrant. Not remembering also served as a routine form of resistance to the therapeutic agenda, and one-off instances of not remembering were used to downplay the suggestion that one may have a general interest or agenda for not remembering. Korobov's (2011b, 2011c) analysis of affiliation practices in speed-dating conversations between prospective romantic partners found that mutual coordinated affiliation tended to occur when partners delayed giving explicit accounts of their mate preferences or desires. Delays were often formulated using scripted accounts of general preference about generic relationships or generic guys/girls. The resulting delays engendered topic expansive sequences where partners could ease into the process of offering and proffering mutual disclosures. Similarly, Korobov and Laplante (2013) found that potential romantic partners would often affiliate when one speaker would construct a scripted disposition or action pattern of an imagined romantic partner. Such imagined and scripted dispositional qualities often involved exaggerated and undesirable features of men and women, which tended to prefer a 'no' answer, with their extremity inoculating against any damage disagreement might do. Such scripted imaginings of potential romantic partners served as a preliminary for mutual dissatisfaction. The couple was thus able to affiliate through coordinated resistance.

Conclusion: Future trajectories for scripting in DP

One of the critiques of DP (see Kitzinger 2006) is that it has historically been an oppositional research programme, defined in part by its constructive debates with the perceptual-cognitive assumptions of mainstream cognitive/social psychology. Kitzinger (2006) argues that DP ought to begin from a post-cognitive perspective, rather than repeatedly arguing for it. Repeated demonstrations that cognitions are produced and made relevant in talk may result in DP missing out on broader analytic opportunities, such as the development of a 'rigorous and cumulative research programme of empirical findings on its own terms' (Kitzinger 2006: 68). What most of the research above has done with Edwards' scripting work is simply apply it to a range of topical areas rather than develop it or couch it within a distinctive arena of study. In coupling the bulk of the subsequent work discussed above with his own follow-up application of scripting to relationship troubles-talk (Edwards 1995), it is clear that one of the most wide-reaching aspects of Edwards' work is the disposition-warranting work that script formulations accomplish. Unfortunately, this particular application of scripting is far from a coherent or organized body of research. There are really just pockets of it here and there. In short, the disposition-warranting work of script formulations would benefit were it couched in a larger and more systematically organized research programme.

There are at least two obvious possibilities. The first would be to more concretely ally it with the work that has sought to more closely align membership categorization analysis with CA methodology for the analysis of identity categories (see Stokoe 2006, 2008, 2012). A systematic discursive analysis of the ways membership categories are scripted could be useful in the analysis of the ways speakers conduct interaction and engage in not simply social action but also the creation of relationships as members of particular identity categories. It would be fascinating to see an organized series of studies that detailed the ways speakers in various types of relationships (cultural, institutional, etc.) script relational categories as part of the business of creating topic alignment and affective affiliation. Second, the disposition-warranting work of scripting could be richly synced with work in positioning theory for identity analysis (see Korobov 2010). The disposition-warranting work that script formulations accomplish could stand as a very helpful contribution to positioning analysis' central aim to provide a rhetorical account of the ways particular social actions create social identities. Script formulations are highly common forms of social action that allow speakers to create, resist and modify their own and others' social identities. Both of these possibilities allow DP to extend beyond the realm of analyzing local social action to the broader and arguably more psychologically relevant realm of identity analysis.

One of the other robust features of script formulations is the way they work as consensus formulations. Examined up close or locally, as they typically are, formulations of consensus create a sense of what is and is not normative for a local interaction. But when we pull back and look at such work from a more critical or macro-discursive perspective, the iterative ways that formulations of consensus and normativity sediment in and across various contexts are valuable entry points to talk about power. To date, distinct applications of scripting to issues of cultural/social power are only marginally developed. When it is addressed, the recommendation is often in reverse. For instance, Stokoe (2010) uses scripting as one part of what she calls the much-needed process of unpacking of the component pieces of what some studies call the 'discourse of gendered violence'. Similarly, LeCouteur and Oxland (2011) note how mainstream psychological research on domestic and intimate partner violence focuses on *broad* features of descriptive accounts of victim precipitation, but not as much on how such matters are routinely and regularly built to make the speakers appear credible or their actions warranted. These types of mandates for more grounded, micro analysis are certainly warranted. What is missing, however, are both (a) broader research programmes that interrogate such micro-processes across larger data sets and larger contexts so that we are left with a clearer picture of the play of broader power dynamics; or (b) research that feeds these micro-findings back into broader work on, for instance, the 'discourse or gendered violence' so that these researchers might carefully apply it to social, cultural and institutional issues. The longevity of research on script formulations depends, in part, on taking steps to expand its scope.

And finally, script formulations have relevance in psychological inquiry that extends beyond its importance as an instance of DP's respecifying of the cognitive realm. Script formulations are directly apropos in the social psychology of impression management. Managing the accountable features of certain identities *is*, arguably, impression management. Rather than conceptualizing impression management as an internally-directed perceptual-cognitive process for establishing and maintaining impressions that are congruent with internally held perceptions, scripting theory would empirically demonstrate its interactional logic as a rhetorical response strategy (see Hobbs 2003; Stapleton and Hargie 2011). Similarly, the disposition-warranting work of scripting is pertinent for personality psychologists interested in showing how dispositions, characters or personalities are interactive accomplishments. Such work would square nicely with emerging neo-Eriksonian work that takes seriously Erikson's (1980) and Vygotsky's (1978) belief in the centrality of social contexts and social interactions for the establishment of identity. It would prove ingredient in developmental psychological work that calls for empirical demonstrations of the rich and nuanced links between personal identity development and interactional contexts (see Korobov, in press). However, it is taken up, Edwards' work on script formulations has enormous but yet largely untapped promise in the broader field of psychology. And there is no doubt that it will, as it has for nearly two decades, continue to evolve as one of the more creative, clear and applicable vanguards for discursive psychology.

References

Bartlett, F.C. (1932/1961) *Remembering: A study in experimental and social psychology*. Cambridge, MA: Cambridge University Press.
Bateson, G. (1955/1972) 'A theory of play and fantasy'. Reprinted in *Steps to an ecology of mind* (pp. 117–93). New York: Ballantine Books.
Barnes, R. and Moss, D. (2007) 'Communicating a feeling: The social organization of "private thoughts"', *Discourse Studies*, 9: 123–48.
Benwell, B. (2012) 'Common-sense anti-racism in book group talk: The role of reported speech', *Discourse & Society*, 23: 359–76.
Billig, M. (1987) *Arguing and thinking: A rhetorical approach to social psychology*. Cambridge: Cambridge University Press.
Buttny, R. (1990) 'Blame-accounts sequences in therapy: The negotiation of relational meanings', *Semiotica*, 78: 219–47.
Buttny, R. (1993) *Social accountability in communication*. London: Sage.
Chafe, W. (1977) 'Creativity in verbalization and its implications for the nature of stored knowledge', in R. Freedle (ed.) *Discourse production and comprehension* (pp. 41–55). Norwood, NJ: Ablex.
Chirrey, D.A. (2011) 'Formulating dispositions in coming out advice', *Discourse & Society*, 13: 283–98.
Chirrey, D.A. (2012) 'Reading the script. An analysis of script formulation in coming out advice texts', *Journal of Language and Sexuality*, 1: 35–58.
Coulter, J. (1999) 'Discourse and mind', *Human Studies*, 22: 163–81.
Coulter, J. (2004) 'What is "Discursive Psychology"?', *Human Studies*, 27: 335–40.
de Kok, B.C. (2009) '"Automatically you become a polygamist": "Culture" and "norms" as resources for normalization and managing accountability in talk about responses to infertility', *Health*, 13: 197–217.
Edwards, D. (1993) 'Concepts, memory and the organization of pedagogic discourse: A case study', *International Journal of Educational Research*, 19: 205–25.
Edwards, D. (1994) 'Script formulations: A study of event descriptions in conversation', *Journal of Language & Social Psychology*, 13: 211–47.
Edwards, D. (1995) 'Two to tango: Script formulations, dispositions, and rhetorical symmetry in relationship troubles talk', *Research on Language & Social Interaction*, 28: 319–50.
Edwards, D. (1997) *Discourse and cognition*. London: Sage.
Edwards, D. (1999) 'Emotion discourse', *Culture & Psychology*, 5: 271–91.
Edwards, D. (2004) 'Discursive psychology', in K. Fitch and R. Saunders (eds) *Handbook of language and social interaction* (pp. 257–73). London: Psychology Press.
Edwards, D. (2006) 'Discourse, cognition and social practices: The rich surface of language and social interaction', *Discourse Studies*, 8: 41–9.

Edwards, D. and Potter, J. (1992) *Discursive psychology*. London: Sage.

Edwards, D. and Potter, J. (2003) 'Rethinking cognition: On Coulter on discourse and mind', *Human Studies*, 26: 165–81.

Edwards, D. and Potter, J. (2005) 'Discursive psychology, mental states and descriptions', in H. te Molder and J. Potter (eds) *Conversation and cognition* (pp. 241–59). Cambridge: Cambridge University Press.

Edwards, D., Middleton, D. and Potter, J. (1992a) 'Remembering, reconstruction and rhetoric: A rejoinder', *The Psychologist*, 5: 453–5.

Edwards, D., Middleton, D. and Potter, J. (1992b) 'Toward a discursive psychology of remembering', *The Psychologist*, 5: 441–6.

Erikson, E. (1980) *Identity and the life cycle*. New York: Norton.

Fillmore, C. (1976) *The need for a frame semantics within linguistics. Statistical methods in linguistics*. Stockholm: Skriptor.

Firth, H. and Kitzinger, C. (2011) 'Reformulating sexual script theory: Developing a discursive psychology of sexual negotiation', *Theory & Psychology*, 11: 209–32.

Frake, C. (1977) 'Plying frames can be dangerous: Some reflections on methodology in cognitive anthropology', *The Quarterly Newsletter of the Institute for Comparative Human Development*, 1: 1–7.

Gale, J.E. (1991) *Conversation analysis of therapeutic discourse*. Norwood, NJ: Ablex.

Garfinkel, H. (1967) *Studies in ethnomethodology*. Englewood Cliffs, NJ: Prentice-Hall.

Gilmartin, S. (2007) 'Crafting heterosexual masculine identities on campus', *Men & Masculinities*, 9: 530–9.

Goffman, E. (1974) *Frame analysis*. New York: Harper & Row.

Grancea, L. (2010) 'Ethnic solidarity as interactional accomplishment: An analysis of interethnic complaints in Romanian and Hungarian focus groups', *Discourse & Society*, 21: 161–88.

Gumperz, J. (1982) *Discourse strategies*. Cambridge: Cambridge University Press.

Hobbs, P. (2003) '"Is that what we're here about?": A lawyer's use of impression management in a closing argument at trial', *Discourse & Society*, 14: 273–90.

Kelly, H.H. (1967) 'Attribution theory in social psychology', in D. Levine (ed.) *Nebraska Symposium on Motivation* (Vol. 15, pp. 192–238). Lincoln: University of Nebraska Press.

Kitzinger, C. (2006) 'After post-cognitivism', *Discourse Studies*, 8: 67–83.

Korobov, N. (2009) '"He's got no game": Young men's stories about failed romantic and sexual experiences', *Journal of Gender Studies*, 18: 99–114.

Korobov, N. (2010) 'A discursive psychological approach to positioning', *Qualitative Research in Psychology*, 7: 263–77.

Korobov, N. (2011a) 'Young men's vulnerability in relation to women's resistance of emphasized femininity', *Men & Masculinities*, 14: 51–75.

Korobov, N. (2011b) 'Gendering desire in speed-dating interactions', *Discourse Studies*, 13: 461–85.

Korobov, N. (2011c) 'Mate-preference talk in speed-dating conversations', *Research on Language & Social Interaction*, 44: 186–209.

Korobov, N. (2014) 'Identities as an interactional process', in McLean, K.C. and Syed, M. (eds) *Oxford handbook of identity development* (pp. 210–27). Oxford: Oxford University Press.

Korobov, N. and Bamberg, M. (2004) 'Positioning a "mature" self in interactive practices: How adolescent males negotiate "physical attraction" in group talk', *British Journal of Developmental Psychology*, 22: 471–92.

Korobov, N. and Laplante, J. (2013) 'Using improprieties to pursue intimacy in speed-dating interactions', *Studies in Media & Communication, 1*: 15–33.

LeCouteur, A. and Oxland, M. (2011) 'Managing accountability for domestic violence: Identities, membership categories and morality in perpetrators' talk', *Feminism & Psychology, 21*: 5–28.

Minksy, M. (1974) 'A framework for representing knowledge', in P. Winston (ed.) *The psychology of computer vision* (pp. 211–77). New York: McGraw Hill.

Muntigl, P. and Choi, K.T. (2010) 'Not remembering as a practical epistemic resource in couples therapy', *Discourse Studies, 12*: 331–56.

Nelson, K. (ed.) (1986) *Event knowledge: Structure and function in development.* Hillsdate, NJ: Lawrence Erlbaum.

Potter, J. (2012) 'How to study experience', *Discourse & Society, 23*: 576–88.

Potter, J. and te Molder, H. (2005) 'Talking cognition: Mapping and making the terrain', in H. te Molder and J. Potter (eds) *Conversation and cognition* (pp. 1–54). Cambridge: Cambridge University Press.

Reddy, M. (1979) 'The conduit metaphor. A case of frame conflict in our language about language', in A. Ortony (ed.) *Metaphor and thought* (pp. 284–324). Cambridge: Cambridge University Press.

Sacks, H. (1992) *Lectures on conversation* (ed. G. Jefferson, two vols). Oxford and Cambridge, MA: Blackwell.

Schank, R. (1982) *Dynamic memory: A theory of reminding and learning in computers and people.* Cambridge: Cambridge University Press.

Schank, R. and Abelson, R. (1977) *Scripts, plans, goals, and understanding: An inquiry into human knowledge structures.* Hillsdale, NJ: Lawrence Erlbaum Associates.

Schegloff, E.A. (1991) 'Reflections of talk and social structure', in D. Boden and D.H. Zimmerman (eds) *Talk and social structure* (pp. 44–70). Berkeley, CA: University of California Press.

Stapleton, K. and Hargie, O. (2011) 'Double-bind accountability dilemmas: Impression management and accountability strategies used by senior banking executives', *Journal of Language & Social Psychology, 30*: 266–89.

Stenner, P. (1993) 'Discoursing jealousy', in E. Burman and I. Parker (eds) *Discourse analytic research: Repertoires and readings of texts in action* (pp. 114–32). London: Routledge.

Stokoe, E. (2006) 'On ethnomethodology, feminism, and the analysis of categorical reference to gender in talk-in-interaction', *Sociological Review, 54*: 467–94.

Stokoe, E. (2008) 'Categories and sequences: Formulating gender in talk-in-interaction', in K. Harrington, L. Litosseliti, H. Saunston and J. Sunderland (eds) *Gender & language research methodologies* (pp. 139–57). Basingstoke: Palgrave.

Stokoe, E. (2010) '"I'm not gonna hit a lady": Conversation analysis, membership categorization and men's denials of violence towards women', *Discourse & Society, 21*: 59–82.

Stokoe, E. (2012) 'Moving forward with membership categorization analysis: Methods for systematic analysis', *Discourse Studies, 14*: 277–303.

Stokoe, E. and Edwards, D. (2008) '"Did you have permission to smash your neighbour's door?" Silly questions and their answers in police-suspect interrogations', *Discourse Studies, 10*: 89–111.

Tannen, D. (1993) 'What's in a frame? Surface evidence for underlying expectations', in D. Tannen (ed.) *Framing in discourse* (pp. 14–54). New York/Oxford: Oxford University Press.

te Molder, and Potter, J. (eds) (2005) *Conversation and cognition.* Cambridge, UK: Cambridge University Press.

Vygotsky, L.S. (1978) *Mind and society: The development of higher mental processes.* Cambridge, MA: Harvard University Press.

Wells, E. (2012) '"But most of all, they fought together": Judicial attributions for sentences in convicting battered women who kill', *Psychology of Women Quarterly, 36*: 350–64.

Wood, L.A. and Kroger, R.O. (2000) *Doing discourse analysis. Methods for studying action in talk and text.* London: Sage.

Part III
Social categories, identity and memory

12 Reorienting categories as a members' phenomena

Richard Fitzgerald and Sean Rintel

Target article: Edwards, D. (1991) 'Categories are for talking: On the cognitive and discursive bases of categorization', *Theory & Psychology*, *1*: 515–42.

Edwards' paper, 'Categories are for talking' (1991), is a critical dissection of the static role of categories as conceived in traditional Cognitive Psychology and the then-recent work of Lakoff's *Women, Fire and Dangerous Things* (1987) through the use of Harvey Sacks' (1974; 1992) work on membership categorisation. Edwards uses Sacks to take aim at the prominent theoretical and methodological trends at the time, seeking to liberate members' category work from ironically external conceptions of a shrouded realm located inside the head. However, while the focus for Edwards was on psychology, his detailed understanding of Sacks' work served to open a conceptual space for those working in discursive psychology to engage with members categorisation work as fundamental to the epistemological and methodological repertoires of Discursive Psychology (DP) in ways that ally with the emergence of Membership Categorisation Analysis (MCA: Eglin and Hester, 1992; Watson, 1994; Hester and Francis, 1994).

In the discussion below we focus on how the paper shows three areas of intersection in the emergence of DP and MCA. First, we outline how the initial use of Sacks' category work in the paper was directed towards psychological topics at a time when his ideas were largely confined to the sociological fields of ethnomethodology and conversation analysis. Second, we trace Edwards' work to embed Sacks' categorial work as an analytic method for DP while running parallel to the emergence and development of MCA. Finally, we situate the contemporary influence of Edwards' paper and use of Sacks' work in the creation of a rich confluence and openness to ideas that have become a hallmark of the contemporary DP approach – an approach that not only incorporates a deep understanding of Sacks' categorisation work but, in turn, contributes significantly to the further development of MCA.

Social categories are social actions

In 'Categories are for talking', Edwards (1991) sets out to engage critically with the notions of categorisation derived from and reflecting mental semantic schema. Focusing on the way that categories and categorisation are used in Cognitive Psychology, including Lakoff's *Women, fire and dangerous things* (1987), Edwards introduces ideas from ethnomethodology and conversation analysis, in particular Sacks' work on membership categories. Edwards argues that the then-current models of Cognitive Psychology treat the person speaking as simply a conduit for their (somehow) held in common semantic schema, rather than treating the speaker as a complex social actor for whom descriptions and categorisations are context sensitive and locally occasioned.

The paper comes in the early stages of Edwards' work with Potter and others fleshing out DP's principles and focus. Coming four years after *Discourse and social psychology* (Potter and Wetherell, 1987), the paper initially adopts a more conciliatory and collaborative tone than the intense critique of Cognitive Psychology found in Potter and Wetherell. In his discussion of categories Edwards tracks a path between treating categories as derived from mental schemas on the one hand and the more discursive understanding of social categories argued by Potter and Wetherell. Edwards' opening gambit is that each could learn from the other. Only later in the paper does he take a more critical stance towards theories of categories and categorisation and language found in cognitive psychology. At the heart of the paper, then, is a subtle and skilfully argued critique of the prevailing view from Cognitive Psychology of how categorisation resides in the head and how it is manifest in language.

Edwards begins by acknowledging the then-recent shifts in conceptualising categorisation sparked by Lakoff and particularly the view that language is not only a vehicle for expressing mental classifications, but also that the act of linguistic categorisation is important in and of itself. He then charts a conciliatory path between these two positions through a critique of Cognitive Psychology's semantic schemas and a conceded critique of DP's focus on stereotypes, rather than a more subtle form of categorisation and social action. By suggesting this middle way, Edwards begins to shift the locus of attention from the brain towards social action: 'One of the aims of this paper is to develop the discursive perspective on categorization while recognizing the well-documented and even 'obvious' referentiality of categories' (Edwards 1991: 516).

As he suggests, it is possible to accommodate both perspectives as travelling side by side, one explaining categorisations in the head; the other explaining the occasioned linguistic categorisations. From this middle position it simply becomes a matter of the researcher deciding on a socio-linguistic focus or cognitive-linguistic focus. However, as he then goes onto point out, either way the meeting point is the *utterance* – or rather a person uttering forms of categorisation drawn from mental schemas in response to experiential stimuli. Edwards, in writing this, is developing DP's position that language is primarily a medium for accomplishing social action, and thus opens up the necessary condition of this position that the semantics of categories cannot be analysed from imagined artificial cases but only through the collection and study of naturally-occurring situated cases.

From this Edwards then returns to how 'categories' are commonly understood in Cognitive Psychology with a view to examining them in relation to their use in language. The first type of categorisations identified are words that classify and label objects, events, space etc., which are referred to as a semantic schema of categorisations. The second type of categorisation in Cognitive Psychology is propositional, where a named entity is collected with another one such that 'dogs are animals', 'I am a truck driver'. For cognitive psychology, according to Edwards, the two are inextricably linked and hierarchically organised, whereby the verbalisation of categories in the world presupposes a semantic schema from which such propositional categorisations are to be constructed.

The theory of a hierarchically organised semantic schema is then explored by Edwards in relation to emerging arguments from DP, especially Billig (1987). Edwards relates the argument that the natural inclination to classify objects into ever simpler categories *necessarily* leads to social stereotyping and prejudice as an inevitable outcome of *normal* mental functioning. That is to say our mental categorial schema is naturally inclined to reflect a categorisation process where people are categorised into large groups for cognitive ease. However, as Billig points out, people not only have the ability to treat people as belonging to large groups they also have the ability to particularise an individual ('the exception that proves the rule'). Therefore, analysis of categorisation needs to reflect a more subtle locally reactive experiential categorisation rather than just a generalised stock of common knowledge that draws upon an elementary mental schema. With the role of language given more prominence and the subtlety of categorial expression raised, Edwards then begins to tease out further the tension between a 'stock of knowledge' and how this knowledge is manifest in any particular situation. This shifts the locus of attention to *language in use*.

In the next phase of the paper Edwards begins by recounting Lakoff's argument that while mental categories are seen to be arranged through different levels, basic (chair), super (furniture) and subordinate (dining chair) of organisation, when an object is identified through this schema the categorisation is able to be modified in any particular encounter. If this is so for any particular object or category then the categories in the schema must be 'fuzzy' as they need to allow for further parsing work and exceptions. This provides Edwards with an opening to focus the argument towards the actual lived encounter where a person in the world *expresses* these forms of categorisation:

> The idea that semantic categories have fuzzy membership boundaries, inequalities of membership and permit multiple and even contrasting possibilities for description suggests that language's category system functions not simply for organising our understanding of the world, but

for talking about it in ways that are adaptable to the situated requirements of the description, and the differences of perspective, and to the need to put words to work in the pragmatics of social action.

(1991: 523)

From this point Edwards then shifts the focus of categorisation squarely to the person producing categorisations in response to a specific context of the occasioned situation and interactional purpose based upon selection from the relevant fuzzy mental categories. Thus, descriptions of the world and their linguistic vehicle cannot simply be treated as 'see (select from schema) say' but involve what is said about what, to whom, and for what locally occasioned purpose. Thus *occasioned relevance* becomes the center of analytic interest. That is to say categorisations are not simply labels attached to objects but motivated interactional work *invested* in by the participant at any particular time and where stake and outcome shape the selection and interactional engagement of participants. Thus the occasioned work of categorisation is an accountable matter with possibilities flowing from the particular descriptions or categorisations produced. Through this shift Edwards positions talk, hitherto treated largely as a resource for seeing into the head, as the topic of analysis; a topic where the focus becomes the flexibility of category use in any particular instance, as well as the accountable normative reasoning underpinning particular categorial choice.

It is at this point that Edwards introduces Sacks' discussion of normativity and sequentiality underpinning category use in the child's story 'The baby cried. The mommy picked it up' (Sacks, 1974). Treating references to 'baby' and 'mommy' as *normative* categories, he goes on to shows how these categories involve assumptions of attributes and behaviour, and expected behaviour between the categories. Likening these category references to Lakoff's 'Idealized Cognitive Models' (ICM), Edwards argues that Sacks provides a way of analysing how idealisations are both observable through descriptions where such references are used and, more importantly, how to examine the divergences and flexibility expressed in response to such 'norms'.

Edwards then moves on to develop his argument further by suggesting that any understanding of the deployment of categorisations in situated talk requires attention to both its situatedness (indexicality) and its orientation (rhetoric). He illustrates this with the category 'car'. While 'car' may serve as an idealised category for Lakoff, he points out that there are not only many *types* of car but also that different cars have socially deployed semiotic significances of what it means own them, i.e., what the object 'says' about the owner or driver. Here Edwards introduces Sacks' discussion of 'hotrodding' as discussed by a group of 1960s teenagers (1992: Vol. 1, 169–74). For the teenagers a 'Pontiac station wagon' is not a 'hotrodder' but rather an ordinary adult car, or the more negatively evaluated 'mommy's car' (p. 137). However, this category is also a category for any police officer happening upon the scene with a different set of assumptions about the object (car) and activity (hotrodding) (1992: Vol. 1,

182–7). The indexicality of local categorisation practices thus also allows the teenager to rhetorically appreciate how the police officer would categorise the station wagon as 'not a hotrodder', the driver as 'not doing hotrodding', and consequently not 'stopping the hotrodder' because car and driver can be treated as not in a category necessitating law enforcement. Of course the point is that categories are inherently flexible and so trying to preconceive mental idealisation prior to any particular use is of little analytic value.

What this highlights is that while the teenagers in Sacks' data were able to shift around and play with different descriptions for the same object, Cognitive Psychology has difficulty accounting for such categorial variation between different people's descriptions of an object or event or even the same person describing the object differently at different times. That is, ICM's or mental models and schemas cannot account very well for different descriptions of the same object because they are based on there being an *accurate or correct* description. As Sacks' transcript demonstrates this is an erroneous pursuit because people are quite able to shift between descriptions have different descriptions and even see the object from someone else's viewpoint, or indeed deliberately not. Thus, Cognitive Psychology's models are left to argue that while the linguistic expression may include fuzziness, the mental model provides a base-line categorisation that may never be actually described. If the ICM category system is only ever idealised then it is a theory based on projecting what the world is *expected to be* rather than how it *actually unfolds* in any particular situation. This is more than a concession to categorial fuzziness in spoken expression, argues Edwards, it is more akin to folk theorisation.

The overall aim of the paper is thus to advance DP's remedial critique of psychology using Sacks' categorial work with, one can imagine, the hope of challenging Cognitive Psychology's focus on mental schemas of categorisation and shifting towards a focus that treats categorisation as a *social* action.

Following 'Categories are for talking', Edwards continued to embed Sacks' categorial work as a thread through DP's project (1995). What is notable about this period is that, in 1992, Sacks' lectures became available for the first time in published form. The impact of this is clearly seen in Edwards' subsequent detailed writings on Sacks (1995; 1997) and also in the emerging systematic development of Sacks' approach to categorisation in interaction, eventually known as Membership Categorisation Analysis (MCA) (Hester and Eglin, 1997a).

Sacks as remedial respecification of psychology and the emergence of MCA

Sacks' lectures were first fully published in 1992 in two volumes. Previous to this there were a few publications (e.g., 1974, 1986), a short collection of his lectures in the journal *Human Studies* (1989), and some photocopies shared between those who knew who to ask. Following his introduction of Sacks' work in 'Categories are for talking', Edwards provides an extended review of Sacks' lectures (1992) in 'Sacks and psychology' (1995), introducing more aspects of Sacks' work as they relate to some conceptual, analytic, and programmatic areas of Cognitive Psychology.

The overall aim of 'Sacks and psychology' (Edwards, 1995), building on 'Categories are for talking', is to argue how Sacks directs our attention towards understanding members' category work as social action rather than mental schemas, i.e., that it is erroneous to view language simply as a *vehicle for thought*. Instead language, or rather the activity of *talking*, should be the focus of understanding categorisation. Edwards reiterates that categories are not to be seen as residing in the head, awaiting stimulation by some experiential object to then return in verbalised form, that they are always *categories in use*. The locally produced interactional work of description reveals the way categories are used, assembled, deployed, negotiated and managed in particular situations. As such they are not so much a fuzzy representation of a typological schema in the brain but are in themselves a reflection of a society's culture, i.e., a culture *in action*. Edwards goes onto explore what the payoff would be for treating talk as a *topic* of enquiry rather than a *resource* by which to gain access to inner mental schemas. For Edwards this 'respecification' of topic and resource falls into three main areas; what 'member' and 'membership' entails as part of any locally accomplished membership category work; the value of using transcripts of naturally occurring talk to examine how intersubjectivity is displayed; and the use by Sacks of a metaphor of machinery to understand how local category work is put together.

Members, intersubjectivity and machinery

The notion of 'member' for psychology, and some other social sciences, is often used by analysts to group sections of populations together, often for research purposes. For Sacks, however, 'member' and 'membership' are seen as routine actions used to accomplish social organisation in such a way as to display local sense-making to each other. As such everyday categorisation work is part and parcel of enacting and engaging with the world. As Edwards points out in Sacks and psychology, to take this seriously means orienting to how people categorise or describe themselves and others, and understanding this as always contingent and occasioned against possible alternatives within a purposeful orientation.

The second theme that Edwards raises is the use of transcripts of naturally occurring interaction, rather than invented or imagined interactional events. Edwards' argument is that even for psychology the use of naturally occurring transcripts of actual interaction provide another version of the 'second turn proof procedure (Edwards, 1995) for people's descriptions and categorisations. Obviously this also serves to respecify intersubjectivity as a members concern, as it shifts the focus from what analysts can say about achieving intersubjectivity to how a display of intersubjectivity is attended to and achieved for the members talking. Edwards, of course, steers clear of suggesting that this is a window into 'intersubjectivity' by emphasizing how intersubjectivity is displayed and attended to *in situ*.

The third major theme Edwards raises is Sacks' metaphor of the machine for analysing sense-making in interaction. The treatment of this metaphor is interesting for our discussion because it intersects with the emergence of MCA. The metaphor is described by Sacks:

> [. . .] the image I have is of this machinery, where you would have some standardized gadget that you can stick in here and there and can work to in a variety of different machines. And you go through the warehouse picking them up to build some given thing you want to build.
> (Sacks: Vol. 1, 158, in Edwards, 1995: 588)

Edwards notes how this metaphor could sound very much like a feature of Cognitive Psychology's 'script-based remindings' (1995: 588). Sacks even extends the metaphor to individuals whereby the task of the analyst is to try and reassemble the sense-making through identifying the components and rebuilding the machine. Edwards downplays this possible understanding of Sacks by noting that the machine metaphor is belied by the overall thrust of Sacks' emphasis on talk as overwhelmingly produced for and contingent upon the local orientations of participants.

In summary, from 'Categories are for talking' (1991), through the extended review in 'Sacks and psychology' (1995), and the subsequent work including *Discourse and cognition* (1997), Edwards increasingly embeds Sacks' categorial work as an essential component of DP. However, while increasingly drawing upon Sacks' work, his orientation is primarily focused on using Sacks to critique Cognitive Psychology through DP. Moreover, while Sacks' work is used to great effect as part of DP's project, Edwards tends to treat Sacks' observations largely uncritically. For example, the problems with the machinery metaphor are raised but are not given systematic critical examination. Thus, while some of Sacks' observations might lead in ostensibly opposite analytic directions, these implications tend to be raised only in passing. In the developing parallel field of MCA, however, where Sacks' lectures provide an equally rich source of interest, some of his ideas were subject to further critical re-examination.

Discursive Psychology and Membership Categorisation Analysis

Edwards' goal, as part of DP, is the respecification of psychological concepts, especially around the use of language as a window into the brain. With this stated goal Edwards uses Sacks' work and insights to offer a skillful critique of Cognitive Psychology and the understanding of how categorisation is used. However, at the same time that Edwards engages in remedial respecification of psychology, ethnomethodologists in sociology working with Sacks' ideas took a different tack. While Sacks' work provided an illustrative critique of sociology his work was also beginning to be considered as a coherent approach to understanding how social categories were embedded in social action rather than a foil for a critique of sociology or a useful methodological addition to conversation analysis. For Watson (1994, 1997), and then Eglin and Hester (1992), Hester and Francis (1994), Hester and Eglin (1997b), Sacks' work was something to build upon, develop and critique where necessary. An interesting illustration of this emerging development is the way the machinery metaphor is tackled by Edwards in 'Sacks and psychology' (1995) and by Hester and Eglin in their Introduction chapter to *Culture in action* (1997a, b). Both of these discussions come after the publication of Sacks' lectures (initially in 1992, and in paperback in 1995) and both draw upon them. For Edwards the focus is on psychology, for Hester and Eglin the focus becomes Sacks' work itself.

As mentioned above, in 'Sacks and psychology' (1995) Edwards discusses Sacks' 'machinery' metaphor and the image of someone going through a warehouse selecting various bits to build a machine, according to the task at hand. The *analytic* task is to disassemble the parts of the machine into their components to be able to then reproduce the machine that produced the observations in context. Edwards observes that this may sound like it is compatible with 'straightforward cognitive science' (p. 588), in that it suggests a background standard stock of knowledge that is then able to be re-selected and assembled in explaining the way categories are used in any particular occasion. As Edwards points out, this potential schema model reading of Sacks, which Schegloff also raises (Schegloff, 'Introduction to Sacks', 1992: Vol. 1, xxi), belies the emphasis on occasioned-ness that Sacks gives his observations. Hester and Eglin (1997b), also drawing on the then recently published *Lectures on conversation* (1992), take up a similar exploration though their emphasis becomes somewhat different as they tackle some of Sacks' own writings head-on.

In their Introduction to the book *Culture in action* (1997b) Hester and Eglin undertake a shift towards treating Sacks' work as offering a more programmatic method of analysis. The Introduction covers three main parts, each of which serves to move attention to Sacks' work in itself rather than in service for a different task. In outlining this programmatic orientation to Sacks' 'method' they include a critique of some aspects of Sacks' work, including the 'machinery' metaphor.

Before embarking on their critique of Sacks, Hester and Eglin first offer a step-through introduction of Sacks' (1974) observations in 'On the analysability of children's stories'. The authors largely delimit Sacks' 'method' to this one paper, thereby curtailing the large amounts of observations contained in the lectures while also creating a framework from which to further examine the wealth of analysis in the lectures. Indeed, while the *Lectures* offer a vast array of brilliant observations they suffer from a lack of systematic coherence as Sacks works through various observations with some subsequent iterations over the semesters and years. They are, however, an excellent insight into Sacks' working through these occasioned observations.

The 'method' discussion is followed by a list of previous work using Sacks' category ideas. While each of these research papers uses Sacks' observations, for the most part they are largely single papers employing an aspect drawn from

Sacks. This ad hoc collection is assembled together with a number of people who have used Sacks' work extensively (for example Caroline Baker, Lena Jayyusi and Rod Watson). By assembling this work Hester and Eglin provide a recognisable corpus, both establishing a device and one that is able to be added to.

Having provided a coherent method and a collection of research that uses Sacks' category work, the third part of the chapter identifies and explores three areas where Sacks' work seems problematic. Particularly where his observations could be seen as suggesting a 'decontextualised' model of category analysis. Here Hester and Eglin identify the machinery metaphor as being problematic in the same way that Edwards had done. For Hester and Eglin, however, this is reason to explore Sacks' work further and offer a critique of Sacks' 'analytic stages'. The stages identified by Sacks are first to see some action being done, second to make these categories strange for analysis, and finally in the third stage, to try to reassemble the category work using a selection of pre-existing device. While Hester and Eglin agree with the first two stages they contend that the third stage is problematic. Here there is a potential reification (cf. Watson, 2015) of members *in situ* category through the possible separation of the analysis from the local context in which it occurs. That is, at this point there is a danger of analysts producing decontextualised accounts of category work. Or, as Schegloff argues, there is the potential to be analytically *promiscuous* where such analysis relies upon the analyst's understanding rather than the participants' (see also Stokoe, 2012; Fitzgerald, 2012; Fitzgerald and Rintel, 2013). Thus, the sense-making metaphor of a 'warehouse full of pre-existing gadgets', serves to undermine Sacks' insistence on always locally occasioned work. In order to maintain the locally occasioned emphasis, Hester and Eglin argue that rather than a static 'stock of knowledge' it would be better to conceive of social knowledge as 'knowledge *in action*', or indeed as '*culture in action*'. Hester and Eglin then go onto critique a number of specific points that lead from this. First that there are 'natural' and 'occasioned' collections of categories, whereby 'natural' are treated as pre-formed prior to their use and occasioned are treated as produced in situ. If this were the case it would again suggest static forms of categorisation that pre-exist their use in any particular occasion. Thus if categories are always and in every case assembled and deployed in the occasion of their use then the idea of pre-existing 'natural' collections cannot be sustained.

Although acknowledging that Sacks' own words contribute to the perceptions of static forms of knowledge and analytic decontextualisation, Hester and Eglin's critique re-emphasises the always occasioned thrust of Sacks' in his analysis of social categorisation. Moreover, this discussion and critique of Sacks' ideas provides the groundwork for the approach they introduced as MCA. From this *reconsideration* (Housley and Fitzgerald, 2002) of Sacks' category work, MCA begins to emerge as a workable method capable of building cumulative findings and observations as well as a stable methodological framework from which to further mine Sacks' lectures (Fitzgerald and Housley, 2015).

Contemporary influences on MCA

While Edwards' use of Sacks ran largely parallel to Hester and Eglin's development of MCA, it can argued that Sacks' influence on DP was an openness to different approaches (of which Sacks' work was a part). Moreover, that this openness influenced later DP research through a sensitivity to membership categories which in turn reflexively contributes to MCA.

Edwards' insistence of inserting Sacks' category work as a methodological attentiveness within DP can be seen as contributing to a repertoire of analytic approaches to the occasioned production of social meaning. This in turn provides a space for, rather than simply incorporating, related language and talk-focused fields approaches such as Conversation Analysis, Membership Categorisation Analysis, Multimodal Analysis, and more broadly Discourse Analysis. In some respects this separate yet collectable group of approaches resembles some of the different elements of ethnomethodology brought together in Roy Turner's (1974) edited collection *Ethnomethodology*. In this collection Ryave and Schenkein's *Notes on the art of walking* (1974) sits alongside Schegloff and Sacks' *Opening up closings* (1974), Turner's *Words, utterances and activities* (1974), and Sacks' *On the analyzability of stories by children* (1974). What remains remarkable about this collection of studies under the heading of 'Ethnomethodology' is that philosophical, theoretical, and empirically detailed studies are brought together under the one heading, *Ethnomethodology*. In many ways this collection provides a salutary contrast to recent trends where these approaches have become separate, distinct, and even hostile to each other. However, DP's agnosticism towards disciplinary boundaries has established an openness to various approaches and a willingness to move between and across multiple approaches. In turn it can be argued that this has provided an increasingly rich and detailed approach to the study of language in use, which has contributed *back* to these approaches, including MCA.

DP, underpinned by Edwards' interest in Sacks, informs and now contributes to the developing methodological richness to MCA both as an approach in itself and in combination with other approaches. By focusing on the approaches as tools for analysis it is notable how DP demands a level of understanding across all the approaches it utilises. For categorisation work this means both a sensitivity to locally displayed social categorisation in action as well as relevant category work being combined with related approaches, depending of the analytic focus. While this is evident in much of the recent work in DP a number of particular examples where MCA is used in combination with other approaches to great effect is found in Butler's (2008) work on children's play, in Stokoe and Edwards' (2007) on race, and Stokoe's (2003; 2010) work around gender and more recently Reynolds' multi-dimensional examination of arguments (Reynolds, 2013).

Reynolds' use is particularly interesting, coming as it does very much as DP is in an ascendant period. Reynolds examines how his found practice of 'enticing a challengable' relies on the occasioned deployment of proposedly normative membership categories (and associated membership actions) of the target interlocutor by the challenger to trap the target into a position of hypocrisy, and thereby forward an argumentative goal of the challenger. In his chapter exploring the frames of this proposed normativity, he demonstrates how the analytical flexibility of DP's treatment of the deployment of norms as accountable resources allows for a more principled explanation of social action than other similar psychological approaches, specifically Social Categorisation Theory (Turner, 1987).

Most interestingly for the purposes of this discussion, Reynolds captures both the distinctions and interconnections between the concepts of normativity in MCA and DP.

Reynolds uses MCA to illustrate the way in which challengers categorise targets in the preface phase in order to make the enticing questions more 'obvious', and then how challengers:

> employ the 'second viewers' maxim' as a resource for both constituting that a norm, a moral 'rule', is relevant and also that the arguable constitutes the basis of a challenge to the status of the target's adherence to the norm enacted in the pre-challenge phase.
> (Reynolds, 2013: 15)

However, to more fully flesh out the description of the practice, Reynolds turns to DP 'to illustrate the way in which challengers *employ "generic" norms, as well as the category-related norms* [...] as resources for challenging the target's normativity,' highlighting 'the important role of consensus in the work of enticing a challengeable and the way in which norms, specifically normative challenges, are the central thrust of the practice of enticing a challengeable' (p. 15, emphasis added). This combination provides Reynolds with principled and detailed tools to demonstrate his central claim that 'the practice of enticing a challengeable is enacted to challenge the target's adherence to a norm, at once making the challenger an agent of social order, and the target a violator of social order' (ibid.: 15).

Finally then, these examples, and other work, demonstrate not only an open analytic ease within DP but also reflexive contribution to the development of MCA and ongoing interaction between analytic approaches. Indeed it is then testament to Edwards' initial and ongoing understanding of Sacks' category work, while others focused on his contribution to sequential analysis, that DP continues to be one of a vibrant and rich area engaged in interactional analysis.

References

Billig, M. (1987) *Arguing and thinking: A rhetorical approach to social psychology.* Cambridge: Cambridge University Press.

Butler, C. (2008) *Talk and social interaction in the playground.* Aldershot: Ashgate Publishing.

Edwards, D. (1991) 'Categories are for talking: On the cognitive and discursive bases of categorization', *Theory & Psychology, 1*: 515–42.

Edwards, D. (1995) 'Sacks and psychology', *Theory & Psychology, 5*: 579–96.

Edwards, D. (1997) *Discourse and cognition.* London: Sage.

Eglin, P. and Hester, S. (1992) 'Category, predicate and task: The pragmatics of practical action', *Semiotica, 88*: 243–68.

Fitzgerald, R. (2012) 'Membership categorization analysis: Wild and promiscuous or simply the joy of Sacks?', *Discourse Studies, 14*: 305–11.

Fitzgerald, R. and Housley, W. (eds) (2015) *Advances in Membership Categorisation Analysis.* London: Sage.

Fitzgerald, R. and Rintel, S. (2013) 'From lifeguard to bitch: How a story character becomes a promiscuous category in a couple's video call', *Australian Journal of Communication, 40*: 101–18.

Hester, S. and Eglin, P. (eds) (1997a) *Culture in action: Studies in membership categorization analysis* (No. 4). Lanham, MD: University Press of America.

Hester, S. and Eglin, P. (1997b) 'Membership categorization analysis: An introduction', in S. Hester and P. Eglin (eds) *Culture in action: Studies in membership categorization analysis* (No. 4) (pp. 1–23). Lanham, MD: University Press of America.

Hester, S. and Francis, D. (1994) 'Doing data: The local organization of a sociological interview', *British Journal of Sociology, 45*(4): 675–95.

Housley, W. and Fitzgerald, R. (2002) 'The reconsidered model of membership categorization analysis', *Qualitative Research, 2*: 59–83.

Lakoff, G. (1987) *Women, fire, and dangerous things: What categories reveal about the mind.* Chicago, IL: University of Chicago Press.

Potter, J. and Wetherell, A. (1987) *Discourse and social psychology: Beyond attitudes and behaviour.* London: Sage.

Ryave, L. and Schenkein, N. (1974) 'Notes on the art of walking', in R. Turner (ed.) *Ethnomethodology: Selected readings* (pp. 265–74). Harmondsworth: Penguin Education.

Reynolds, E. (2013) 'Enticing a challengeable: Instituting social order as a practice of public conflict'. Unpublished PhD Dissertation. The University of Queensland.

Sacks, H. (1974) 'On the analysability of children's stories', in R. Turner (ed) *Ethnomethodology* (pp. 216–32). Harmondsworth: Penguin Education.

Sacks, H. (1986) 'Some considerations of a story told in ordinary conversations', *Poetics, 15*: 127–38.

Sacks, H. (1989) 'Lectures 1964–1965' with an Introduction/Memoir by E.A. Schegloff. In Gail Jefferson (ed) *Human Studies. 12*(3/4), 211–393.

Sacks, H. (1992) *Lectures on conversation* (two volumes) (hardback). Edited by Gail Jefferson with introductions by Emanuel A. Schegloff. Oxford: Basil Blackwell.

Sacks, H. (1995) *Lectures on conversation* (two volumes). Edited by Gail Jefferson with introductions by Emanuel A. Schegloff. Cambridge, MA: Blackwell.

Schegloff, E. (1992) 'Introduction', in Harvey Sacks, *Lectures on conversation*, Volume 1 (hardback) (pp. ix–lxiii). Edited by Gail Jefferson with introduction by Emanuel A. Schegloff. Oxford: Basil Blackwell.

Schegloff, E. and Sacks, H. (1974) 'Opening up closings', in R. Turner (ed.) *Ethnomethodology: Selected readings* (pp. 233–64). Harmondsworth: Penguin Education.

Stokoe, E.H. (2003) 'Mothers, single women and sluts: Gender, morality and membership categorization in neighbour disputes', *Feminism & Psychology, 13*: 317–44.

Stokoe, E. (2010) '"I'm not gonna hit a lady": Conversation analysis, membership categorization and men's denials of violence towards women'. *Discourse & Society*, *21*(1): 59–82.

Stokoe, E. (2012) 'Moving forward with membership categorization analysis: Methods for systematic analysis', *Discourse Studies*, *14*: 277–303.

Stokoe, E. and Edwards, D. (2007) 'Black this, black that': Racial insults and reported speech in neighbour complaints and police interrogations', *Discourse & Society*, *18*: 337–72.

Turner, R. (1974) 'Words, utterances and activities', in R. Turner (ed.) *Ethnomethodology: Selected readings* (pp. 197–215). Harmondsworth: Penguin Education.

Turner, J.C. (1987) 'The analysis of social influence', in J.C. Turner, M.A. Hogg, P.J. Oakes, S.D. Reicher and M.S. Wetherell (eds) *Rediscovering the social group: A self-categorization theory* (pp. 68–88). Oxford: Blackwell.

Watson, R. (1994) 'Harvey Sack's sociology of mind in action', *Theory, Culture & Society*, *111*: 169–86.

Watson, R. (1997) 'Some general reflections on "categorization" and "sequence" in the analysis of conversation', in S. Hester and P. Eglin (eds) *Culture in action: Studies in Membership Categorization Analysis* (pp. 49–76). Lanham, MD: University Press of America.

Watson, R. (2015) 'De-reifying categories', in R. Fitzgerald and W. Housley (eds) *Advances in Membership Categorisation Analysis* (pp. 23–50). London: Sage.

13 Some relevant things about gender and other categories in discursive psychology

Sue Widdicombe

Target article: Edwards, D. (1998) 'The relevant thing about her: Social identity categories in use', in C. Antaki and S. Widdicombe (eds) *Identities in talk*. London: Sage.

Introduction

Edwards' chapter, 'The relevant thing about her: Social identity categories in use' (1998) outlined an alternative approach to category use in interaction. This played an important role in helping social and discursive psychologists among others move forward in understanding when, how and why speakers make particular categories relevant. To fully appreciate its significance, it is important to outline the academic terrain in which it was written; to trace ways in which those ideas grew; and show how they paved the way for a revolutionary, situated and empirical social psychological approach to membership categories and identities.

Edwards drew on conversation analysis (CA), and in particular Sacks' (1979, 1992) study of therapy sessions with a group that could be described as teenagers. Sacks observed the use by participants of the 'membership category' 'hotrodder' to describe themselves and what they did (namely customizing cars or 'hotrods'). This category ascription was used to rule others in or out as legitimate members, and contrasted with adults' (i.e., outsiders') terms like 'teenager'. 'Hotrodder' was thus a participant's rather than an analyst's category. The title of the chapter was, however, inspired by Sacks' (op. cit.) analysis of a different fragment of data from the same group session. In a discussion about the absence of a member of the group, one participant (Ken) switches from calling her by name (Louise) to using the gendered categories, 'the opposite sex' and 'a chick'. In this way, he selects gender as the relevant thing about her, and Sacks shows how this functions as a safe compliment. Edwards (op. cit.: 19) notes that 'for both persons and situations, if they did not have to be described that way (or described at all), then the way they are described can be examined for what it might specifically be doing'. There were three key features of Edwards' approach. First, he adopted a set of assumptions about categories and identities; specifically, that membership categories are discursive, action-oriented and 'fuzzy' in that various conventional attributes may potentially be tied to category membership on particular occasions. Second, he argued for a focus on the use by, and relevance of, categories to *participants*, and this differed from the tendency in other social scientific approaches to treat categories as *analysts'* resources (see Widdicombe, 1998). Third, the approach Edwards advocated was a thoroughly empirical and open-minded one, in that it focused on the data to hand, rather than generating data to test *a priori* theories about the functioning of categories and identity.

Edwards' observations were derived from a close examination of a relationship counselling session with a couple he gave the pseudonyms Connie and Jimmy. In the first part of the analysis, he showed how the counsellor invoked age and longevity of marriage as resources for making sense of the couple's problems. For example, he examined the way that length of marriage was used to characterize the state of their marriage (as basically good with problems, or as problematic with consistent rows from the beginning). He concluded that 'even the most ostensibly obvious, factual, trivial, demographic kinds of person-identifying categories can be invoked, worked up and played down and otherwise used by participants as part of the discursive business at hand' (op. cit.: 24).

In the second part of the analysis, Edwards turned to the gender-related categories, 'girls' and '(married) women'. He examined how they were used alternatively in attributing responsibility for relationship breakdown. For example, at one point in the session, Connie said she found Jimmy 'living with someone else' after he walked out and she attributed the cause of his leaving to this relationship:

Extract 1 (from Edwards, 1998: 25)

```
81 Connie  I can't accept (1.0) I can't accept (1.0) y' know: (.)
82         what he's telling me, (0.5) y' know?= =I just belie:ve
83         that this girl was here all alo:ng, (0.2) and that's why
84         (0.5)
```

Edwards suggested that Connie's use of 'this girl' (line 83) served to downgrade her status and implied, perhaps, further attributes such as being unattached and unmarried. Jimmy described the circumstances of his moving in quite differently:

Extract 2 (from Edwards, 1998: 26)

```
98  Jimmy  [. . .] U::m (0.8) it's >not right< to sa:y that (0.5)
99         >I didn't leave Connie for another woman.<
100        (0.6)
101        But (0.4) I was liv- sleepin' away for (0.5) 'bout
102        three- three weeks (.) four weeks three weeks (0.4)
103        whatever, (0.6) when I moved in: (.) with a wo- girl,
104        which I did have (1.0) uh: a bit of a fling with (.)
105        when Connie went on holiday last year.
```

Edwards observed that Jimmy's denial that he left Connie 'for another woman' is consistent with his attribution of relationship breakdown to longstanding difficulties and Connie's flirtatious behavior. He also showed that the repair 'wo(man)' to 'girl' downplayed the status of that relationship (cf. 'another woman'), along with other descriptions such as 'bit of a fling' (cf. 'affair') and 'moving in' (cf. 'living with').

Edwards described how Connie's behaviour, too, is the subject of complaint in that Jimmy attributed their problems to Connie's flirtatious behaviour. He examined how, in describing her social activities, Connie uses 'friends' and 'girls', a description of infrequency ('every six weeks'), and the purpose and 'trigger' (to chat when a friend has a problem) to characterize nights out as harmless. On the basis of his claimed experience of being out with her, Jimmy recycled her reference to a 'girls' night out' but deleted her description of how such evenings come about. Instead, he implied the sexual nature of Connie's social activity. She later reformulated this, replacing 'girls' with 'married women' and this, together with a set of associated activities (talking about children or problems), works to reject the accuracy and reasonableness of Jimmy's complaint. Edwards' analysis is thus a clear demonstration of the way categories and associated activities may be invoked in the service of rhetorical and interactional business.

Edwards provided us with a way of addressing the question of why *this* category *now* with respect to some counselling data. His chapter contributed significantly to the development of discursive psychology (DP), by reconceptualizing the core social psychological concepts of categories and identities and how they should be studied. This approach was set in contrast to an alternative, more conventional, social psychological way of addressing the same questions, namely Self-categorization Theory (SCT; Turner, 1987). For SCT, relevance depends on which of the potentially applicable categories (say gender or occupation) fit better with (and make sense of) observed variations between people. In more technical terms, under certain conditions, our aim is to maximize the perceived or cognitive 'meta-contrast' between 'ingroup' and 'outgroup' category members, and minimize within-category differences (i.e., for which potentially available category are 'we' most distinct from 'them'). When a particular membership category becomes the (perceptually) salient one, individuals may self-categorize and self-stereotype in terms of that category. Self-categorizations are thus psychological, private, mental processes that influence thought and behavior (e.g., discrimination or preferential treatment of a fellow ingroup member).

SCT, like DP, treats group membership and categorization as a members' concern in that individuals are regarded as categorizing themselves, rather than having categories imposed on them. DP and SCT also both recognize variability, although they conceptualize it very differently. For SCT, individuals *have* numerous identities; these are derived from the categories they belong to and are stored as cognitive representations. They are switched on according to perceptual factors and other variables. For DP, categories are invoked, attributed, and 'built' according to the work they are required to do, and variability is thus an inescapable adjunct of the ways identities are 'situated practices' (Edwards and Potter, 2001). In SCT, candidate categories are treated as obvious or are provided by the experimenter who thereby defines the social field; DP by contrast looks to see what categories speakers make relevant and how these help define the local context of interaction. Moreover, in DP categories are worked up and shaped for the current purposes, it is not a question of, say, recognizing Connie as a 'girl' or 'married woman' on sight. SCT's key empirical questions are to do with specifying the causes and consequences of self-categorizations. DP is concerned with how we shape, manage, and use categories in the local contexts in which we do. In contrast to SCT, then, DP provides an empirical approach to the categories that people use, how they use them, and where they are spontaneously used (in interaction). It takes seriously the idea that just because a category *can* be applied to a person it does not follow that it *is* so (e.g., Edwards points out that Jimmy and Connie could be described as Irish and the counsellor as English but these categories are not invoked in the session examined above).

Edwards was not alone in treating categories as primarily participants' business or concern in the late 1990s. Antaki, Condor and Levine (1996) contrasted different ontological notions of identity, including identity as a feature of perception or cognition ($SI^{perception}$ or SI^p), exemplified by SCT, or of how people describe themselves ($SI^{description}$ or SI^d), exemplified in Edwards' analysis and their own. Drawing also on Sacks' (1992) 'hotrodder' analysis, they examined how participants made different identities relevant through the course of a dinner party interaction. They argued that analyzing occasions on which social identities 'loom large and disappear' (op. cit.: 478) during the course of a social interaction provides an empirical way in to the idea that different identities are made relevant and used as resources at different times. They traced the mobilization of identities of one participant in particular, Charly, as 'newly qualified', as a 'successful if cynical medical student', as an abstract reasoner, a fellow professional and a doctor, and how these were produced and used in stories, accounts, acknowledgement of stories and in arguments. The meaning or sense of these categories is derived from the local frame of reference and the interactional work they were made to do. They are tied to the occasion and differ from those conventionally analyzed in social science (e.g., gender and race), but they are no less relevant; indeed, their relevance is determined by the participants' orientation rather than imposed or assumed by the analyst. They argue that this approach is therefore better able to address the flexibility and variability in category ascriptions and identities that SCT has tried to resolve with notions of identities being 'switched on' in a social field or context that is usually set up by the experimenter.

Antaki *et al.* show how we can get an empirical handle on the longstanding social psychological question of how it is that social identities are sometimes, but not at all times, relevant to us. Outside social psychology, Schegloff (1997) was similarly concerned with questions of 'whose categories?' and 'who decides?' in contrast to the sociological preference of assuming the relevance of demographic categories. He outlined three key analytic concepts to help analysts determine category relevance in a piece of interaction: participants' orientation, procedural consequentiality and being open-minded. Participants' orientation refers to the interactional occasions when participants treat something (e.g., gender) as significant for, or pertinent to, the ongoing talk. '[Thus] I can 'orient to' you as my sister, a teacher, or as a feminist, and so on' (Speer, 2001: 113). 'Procedural consequentiality' refers to the requirement that the particular category has consequences for the ongoing talk, or some 'visible effect on how the interaction pans out' (Antaki and Widdicombe, 1998: 5). Finally, adopting a data-led approach means that analysts should allow categories to emerge rather than using them to determine in advance what is relevant or interesting. Each of these key concepts can be seen in 'The relevant thing about her'. For example, the speakers invoked the gendered categories 'girls' and 'married women' spontaneously, selecting these as the relevant descriptions for the business at hand. Their consequentiality was shown in the role they played in building different accounts of Connie's social life. It was also displayed in the way that both Connie and Jimmy reformulated the categorical descriptions in their ex-spouse's prior account, thereby implicitly recognizing in practice, and rejecting, the work done by those terms. Finally, Edwards explicitly avoids treating demographic categories as explanatory devices for him as analyst; instead, he inspected the data to see whether, when and how speakers used them as resources for action.

Edwards, Antaki *et al.*, Schegloff, and Sacks all advocated an open-minded, empirical approach that placed participants' orientation in interaction as an important analytic criterion for knowing which categories are relevant and when. This notion offered a promising alternative to other analyst-led approaches to situated category use but it was not unproblematic. Addressing its limitations along with other issues, however, has led analysts such as Stokoe (e.g., 2012a, b) to develop a promising approach to membership categories, and a body of work that has helped define discursive psychology (DP) as a distinctive enterprise rather than 'just' a reconceptualization of concepts like categories and identities. The area where questions of relevance were taken up most explicitly was in developing an alternative, feminist approach to gender and language (e.g., Stokoe, 2011, 2012b; Stokoe and Smithson, 2001; Kitzinger, 2000; Speer, 2001; Weatherall, 2002). My concern in what follows is not specifically with how this represented a new perspective on gender and language, nor whether (or not) it was a feminist approach; rather I want to examine the ways that the question of relevance was refined over more than a decade in this context.

Telling when gender is relevant

Like Edwards, Stokoe and Smithson (2001: 243) were interested in occasions where 'gender categories . . . crop up in the interactions' and how they work to accomplish particular actions. They suggested that CA provides analysts with a principled and systematic way of examining gender relevance, rather than relying on the researcher's cultural knowledge to 'spot' instances of gender or to assess concordance with observed behaviour. Stokoe and Smithson's (2001) work on gender and language made two important contributions to an analytic approach to 'category relevance'. First, they expanded our appreciation of *when* gender is made relevant by specifying the types of occasions when it is. Second they examined critically the limitations of participants' orientation as an analytic tool.

In their analysis of young adults' focus group discussions about the future, and university seminar discussions, Stokoe and Smithson observed that gender was made relevant in three interactional contexts. First, in repair work where the speaker hearably corrects his or her use of a term. For example, the repair 'four girls (.) at erm (.) four women at erm (.)' (op. cit.: 257) displays the initial categorization ('girls') as a source of potential interactional trouble that is addressed by re-categorizing them as women. Edwards observed a similar repair in the other direction,'wo- girl' (see Extract 2 above), and I discussed above how this arguably addressed problematic status inferences that might follow the use of the term 'women'. Weatherall (2002) similarly showed that gender was made relevant through repairs in pre-school children's talk. Second, Stokoe and Smithson (op. cit.: 258) identified the use of generic terms: for example, 'reduce the hierarchy so that your boss is not (.) some guy that you don't (.) you hate talking to'. Here, a masculine term 'guy' is used to refer to a hypothetical male or female boss. Weatherall also found the use of generic gender references such as 'guy', and how gender was made relevant when there was 'trouble' over a doll's gender. Third, Stokoe and Smithson observed that speakers oriented to gender when the claim of being sexist was denied or resisted:

Extract 3 (from Stokoe and Smithson, 2001: 261)

```
1 M: But er what I find (.) like I said (.) no detriment to women you
2     know I'm not a chauvinist or anything (.) but er say you've got a
3     single mother [ ]
```

In this extract, a disclaimer is used as a preface to talk which could be glossed as chauvinist, and displays awareness that the following talk is problematic.

To summarize, the idea of participants' orientation is a central one, methodologically and in terms of what is novel or distinctive about the CA/DP approach in relation to determining the relevance of categories to speakers. An accumulating body of work in the early 2000s identified interactional occasions *when* gender was made relevant by participants. Interestingly, all pointed to how gender becomes relevant in the context of some interactional difficulty (e.g., that merits repair work or a disclaimer). This empirical approach seemed to have much to offer feminist gender and language research and social psychological understanding of participants' category use. Nevertheless, the issue of 'participants' orientation' remained a troubling one, because it was not clear how analysts could determine participants' orientation, and because participants' orientation may be limited and limiting. That is, the notion of participants' orientation is rather vague. How can the analyst tell, in a rigorous and empirical way, that gender is relevant, and how can we decide that certain attributes are bound to the category on a particular occasion of its use? The idea of relevance thus demands practical specification.

The limits of participants' orientation

Previous work such as Edwards' (see also Hopper and LeBaron, 1998; Schegloff, 1997) focused on instances where there was an explicit use of a gendered term (e.g., girl, woman, he or guy). However, other studies indicated that gender may also be made relevant through descriptions of activities that are taken to be gendered on the occasion of use, rather than through the explicit use of the category label (e.g., Wowk, 1984). Moreover, a speaker may use a gendered term such as 'woman' or 'she' but the subsequent talk shows that gender goes unnoticed: it is not picked up by participants in subsequent turns, and is therefore not oriented to (Stokoe and Smithson, 2001). The question remains, therefore, if it is not through an explicit utterance, how can we decide that gender *is* relevant for the speakers? How do we know that certain category-bound attributes are being invoked (i.e., that 'girl' implies sexy and 'married women' are non-flirtatious on this occasion)?

Furthermore, if analysts stick to participants' orientation, are they then restricted to analyzing *how* gender is relevant, not *why* it is so in this bit of interaction (Stokoe and Smithson, op. cit.). I described above Edwards' (1998) observations about Jimmy's use of 'another woman' and 'wo-girl' (Extract 2 above). Sticking to participants' orientation, we can say that the speaker uses both 'girls' and 'women' and we can therefore see that gender is relevant to this interaction. But Stokoe and Smithson observe that this is all we can conclude without drawing on background cultural knowledge. Edwards proposes that 'girl' downgrades the gendered membership category ascribed to the 'other woman' because of the categories' relative status (in Extract 2). Although this seems a reasonable inference, it requires the analyst to draw on extra-discursive knowledge of the status of different category terms and their category-bound attributes. Similarly, in order to determine that the reference to certain activities is a way of making a particular category relevant, we need to draw on the background knowledge that Schegloff (1997) argues we need to put aside in the interests of analytic rigour. Stokoe and Smithson note that generally analysts do not acknowledge their role in making links between categories and attributes; deciding that some categories and attributes go together is treated as 'everyone's knowledge' or common sense.

Despite its utility conceptually then, analytically, the idea of participants' orientation requires further refinement in order to fulfill its potential as a resource for analysts. More recent work has attempted to do just this. I want to examine in particular Stokoe's (2011, 2012a, b) efforts to refine the analytic method, and how this approach has been applied to other categories.

Refining the analytic approach to category use

I begin with Stokoe's (2011) work on self-initiated self-repair (SISR) in which she revisits her earlier work on how gender is made relevant. This work is significant because she begins to identify conversational practices that provide evidence for speakers' orientation to gender, thus enabling a more thoroughly grounded, empirical basis for the analyst's claim that gender is being made relevant *here*. In the process, Stokoe also begins to address the 'why' question that, I noted earlier, appeared to be beyond the boundaries of the techniques conversation analysis could strictly deliver. In her paper, Stokoe distinguishes several 'formats' of the within-turn SISRs, and this then allows her to identify cases where gender *is* clearly made relevant (because it is marked), where a gendered category is used but gender is not made relevant, and where there is ambiguity regarding whether the speaker is orienting to gender or not.

As a starting point, Stokoe notes that on occasions where two terms (e.g., 'woman' and 'girl') are both seemingly *referentially* adequate, a SISR implies that there is something *functionally* inadequate about the repaired term because, for example, of the inferences that follow (e.g., 'girl' may in some contexts suggest sexy or available). She examines how marked the repair is, as an indication of 'commitment to the repair solution' (p. 102). A repair may be marked, for example, by repeated term(s) used in pre- and post-framing as in the following extract. This is taken from a university tutorial discussion in which a student, Sam, is talking about *a cappella* singing:

Extract 4 (from Stokoe, 2011: 96–7)

```
5  S:  Brilliant (I-) but I saw f:our girls, (0.4)
6      at um:: ((looks away from other students))
7      (0.2)
8  S:  four wo:men ((rolls eyes)) (0.7) at um:: (1.0) >Por' obello Road
9      market.<
```

The repair is marked by the speaker's pre- ('four') and post-framing ('at um') of the gender references, as well as gestures, eye-rolling and body movements. In Stokoe's other examples, the gender repair is marked by an apology ('girl-woman-sorry'). These demonstrate an orientation to gender. Moreover, they suggest that one function of marked repairs is self-presentational, in that they attend to the 'subject-side management' (Edwards, 2005) of what is said. In other words, terms used display a sensitivity to the way that they may be taken as saying something about the speaker (e.g., they are 'gender aware' in the example above) as well as serving an affiliative function.

In other cases, gendered categories are used in an X or Y format ('girl or woman'). In the extract below, for example, the suspect (S) is describing his neighbour's actions to a police officer.

Extract 5 (taken from Stokoe, 2011:102)

```
4  S:   Then the woman (0.4) or the girl that lives there:
5       is coming chargin' down the stairs.=goin' come on
6       then if that's what you wanna do: we'll get it on.
```

Here S's use of 'or' in a list of alternatives demonstrates a lack of epistemic knowledge (and thereby a lack of any relationship with her). Sometimes, however, there is ambiguity as to whether the initial referent is repaired or not. For example:

Extract 6 BBC Radio 4 Woman's Hour 12.11.07
(taken from Stokoe, 2011: 105)

```
1  MEP:  .hhh uh an' think it's (.) te:rrible that uh young
2        ladies are .hh or young women are discri:minated
3        against in this wa:y.
```

Here, pre- and post-framing ('young' and 'are') is indicative of repair (possibly managing the 'subject-side' concern to be seen as 'gender aware'). On the other hand, the use of 'or' makes both categories viable descriptors. Stokoe's point is that, rather than treat this kind of ambiguity as an analytic problem, we can regard it as a participant's resource; because the ambiguity regarding whether the speaker is doing a repair or listing alternatives, 'makes him less readily accountable for either' (p. 105).

Repair is one kind of occasion in which gender is made relevant. However, one of the difficulties faced by analysts concerned with gender (or any other particular category) is knowing when such categories are likely to occur spontaneously in naturalistic interaction and without this, it is difficult to see if there are common patterns of use. Stokoe's (2012b) work begins to address this issue by combining membership categorization analysis (MCA) and CA. MCA focuses on how categories and their inferential attributes are involved in action; how they may be used as resources; and the practical reasoning that informs the ascription of category membership to self or others. It provides a way of showing how participants treat categories as part of collections (e.g., 'family' or 'sex') or as paired with another category (e.g., 'men', 'husband'), and of analyzing the work done by drawing on relationships between categories. On the other hand, CA's sequential analysis identifies 'robust, repeatable, patterned categorical practices' (op. cit.: 238) and looks at how action unfolds, thereby revealing the 'consequential' things people do with (gender) categories. Identifying how certain categories are predictably invoked to accomplish a particular action (see also Stokoe, 2003, 2006; Kitzinger, 2007), can help build a collection of instances and through this contribute further to the analysis of when gender is relevant.

Using this combination of sequential and membership categorization analysis, she identified further occasions on which gender is made relevant, relating to the sequential environment and the doing of particular actions. For example, Stokoe (2006, 2012a) observed the use of gender categories by suspects in police interviews, following yes/no interrogatives about a specific incident or person. For example:

Extract 7 (from Stokoe, 2012a: 297)

```
1  P:  You threaten 'er at all.
2          (0.4)
3  S:  No I didn't threaten 'er.
4          (1.1)
5  S:  .hh I've got no reason to threaten 'e:r, I've never 'it a
6       woman in my life. =an' I never will 'it a woman in my life.
           (0.8)
```

The category reference 'woman' is used at lines 5 and 6 in denying the action that the suspect is implicitly accused of through asking the question, 'you threaten 'er at all'. In this and other extracts, Stokoe examines the sequential pattern: a yes/no response followed by an account in which a category based denial is produced. She notes that speakers move from the particular case or person to the general via categorization ('I've got no reason to threaten 'e:r' to 'I've never 'it a woman in my life' on lines 5–6). The speaker then extends the denial ('an' I never will') and Stokoe (2012a: 298) cites Edwards' (2006) observations about the related term 'would' and how it allows speakers to make a dispositional claim that is inconsistent with the offence they are accused of. The reasoning is that if the suspect does not possess a disposition to hit women in general, he did not do it this time. Police officers do not, however, acknowledge or take up these character-related self-assessments in the following turns.

There are other predictable occasions when gender references occur: for example, in advice giving and in producing an account of action in category based responses to questions. In relation to giving advice, Stokoe shows how speakers may treat a third party as behaving as a member of a category rather than an individual behaving in a situation-specific way in making sense of a third party's action (or non-action). For example 'whether 'e's jus' bein' 'oh: I'm a man I'm so ca:s(h)ual, (0.2) which they a:re' (Stokoe, 2012a: 285), and the use of categorical idiomatic formulations, such as 'but *all* men are *ba*stards' (op. cit.: 286). These expressions work to produce the claim about category members as normatively correct and therefore difficult to challenge, and they tie predicates (e.g., 'casual') to categories (e.g., 'man') for local purposes.

In other contexts, Stokoe (2012a: 290) observed the systematic way in which in giving accounts, speakers 'invoke categories and generate category-bound features in the course of accomplishing a particular action'. For example, the following account is given by a pharmacist in response to a radio presenter's question about a new scheme to sell Viagra in pharmacies.

Extract 8 (from Stokoe, 2012b: 239)

```
1   I:   What sort've people (.) have been co:ming
2        t'you.
3              (0.2)
4   Ph:  .hh we've had a: wi:de variety of ↑gentlemen
5        coming to see us:. To access the Viagra
6        thro:ugh our programme .hh a lot of men when
7        we ta:lk to them have said I've been meaning
8        to do something about this for a:ges an' I've
9        just never got round to it, (0.2) ↑typical
10       guy response. =re(h)ally y'know.=.hh an'
11       eventually they think w'll I really do need
12       to do something about it now.=
```

From this and other extracts, Stokoe (op. cit.) identifies what she calls a 'categorial practice', which comprises a description, categorization and an orientation to common knowledge ('y'know'). In this extract, the pharmacist first refers to a 'wide variety of gentlemen' in response to a question about the nature of her customers, and she describes the accounts given by '*a lot* of men' when they ask for Viagra, thus making gender relevant (note that the prior question asks about 'people' and is therefore non-gendered). Second, she produces an upshot of the prior description that again indicates its category-relevance: '↑*typ*ical guy response'. She thereby ties an activity ('putting health needs off') to the category ('guy') to accomplish (here) an account of their action. Third, there is a common knowledge component, 'y'know', which is said with some laughter ('re(h)ally y'know). This portrays the category-related account and the category-boundedness of the activity as recognizable common knowledge. In other extracts the status of the associated claim as common knowledge is worked up through 'y'know' or tag questions ('don't they') and laughter particles add to the shared category knowledge appeal (Stokoe, 2012b: 244). In turn, the common knowledge component orients to shared category membership of speaker and recipient, and therefore has an affiliative function. Stokoe (2012b) shows how a similar practice also occurs in narratives, produced in diverse locations, including calls to an antisocial behaviour officer; a call to a mental health helpline; police interviews; and speed-dating interaction, not just in response to questions that invoke categorical responses. However, she also shows how recipients can align, affiliate, resist, and co-construct the categorial practice.

The 'categorial practice' identified by Stokoe allows her to pin down how common sense notions (about categories and their members) are achieved and managed and how shared cultural knowledge about gendered behaviour and attributes is produced in, through and for situated action. Category-relevant environments are initiated, for example, through the design of questions, or produced in response to them, and categorical formulations follow descriptions of individual activities or events. An important point is that people treat categories as inference-rich, as having attributes that are for that moment, oriented to as typical, recognizable and shared. Thus, 'what counts' as gendered behaviour is built by participants in tying activities and predicates to categories, which are treated as common sense knowledge. This in turn helps address one question raised earlier: whether it is possible for analysts to say what the relevant attributes *are*, if they are not stated explicitly. Stokoe's (2012a: 300) point is that speakers orient to the inference-rich nature of categories collaboratively 'by building into categorical formulations devices for saying "there-is-more-to-this-category-than-I-need-to-describe-here"' such as 'common knowledge components' and idiomatic expressions.

The issue of omnirelevance

Klein (2011) takes a similar approach to another gender-relevant issue: the apparent omnirelevance of gender. Feminist researchers often assume that gender is pervasive or 'omnipresent' in our lives; it is relevant to all social interactions, relations and so on. The focus on participants' orientation and relevance for them, however, means that 'it is incumbent on the researcher to show *how and that* gender as omnirelevant is produced and oriented to' (Weatherall, 2002: 768). Previous work by Hopper and LeBaron (1998) proposed a three-part sequence in which, first, something is said that 'touches off' or provides a 'pre-text' for 'noticing' gender in the second part. This makes relevant features that may be taken up later as a resource for interaction, in the third part of the sequence.

Klein's (2011) work provides a further basis for examining gender omnirelevance and for understanding why it seems ubiquitous and natural, not just tied to specific occasions. Klein's (2011) particular analytic interest was in non-recognitional person reference, that is, references like 'this guy' that signal to a recipient that they do not know the non-present third party who is being talked about. Klein argues that a gender categorization constitutes a 'minimum basic form of non-recognitional reference' (op. cit.: 66). However, she also observed a difference between action-relevant and system-relevant references to gender. Gendered references are action-relevant when treated as relevant to a story or other conversational action; they are system-relevant when the reference is treated as 'only referring' or connecting initial and subsequent person references. She suggests that a gendered reference is omnirelevant when it is action-relevant.

Weatherall, Hopper and LeBaron, and Klein provide us with empirically grounded ideas of how we can turn the assumed omnirelevance of gender into an empirical issue. The apparent pervasiveness of gender in conversation can be addressed via the sequences and mechanisms through which gender categories or terms crop up in conversation. These developments, moreover, allow a practical understanding of how the 'flagging' of gender is done in everyday interactions (to borrow the term Billig (1995) uses to capture a similar feature of national identity). This in turn presents a very different way of understanding the 'other side' of social psychologists' conceptual dilemma regarding social identity, which is that although identities are not always salient, they are always 'there', stored in SIT (Social Identity Theory)/SCT as cognitive representations waiting to be activated at the appropriate moment (Turner, 1987).

This kind of thinking can be and has been extended to other kinds of categorizations. For example, Whitehead and Lerner (2009) adopt a similar approach, in looking at how, when and why speakers make relevant often invisible, racial categorizations such as whiteness, in interactions.

Beyond gender: Making racial categories relevant

Previous work on 'race talk' focused on its ideological aspects, and on how locally-produced expressions of racial prejudice help maintain 'broader patterns of racism' (van Dijk, 1992; Wetherell and Potter, 1992). Whitehead and Lerner (2009), however, note that 'race talk' depends on making race categories relevant and their use as a resource. It is therefore useful to identify how racial categories are used in the ordinary, sequential contexts in which they are invoked. They examine instances from a large corpus of data in which the often taken-for-granted category 'white' is used explicitly, and identify and analyze three interactional environments in which it is made relevant by speakers.

One interactional context is in providing an account for action. In their analysis, Whitehead and Lerner (2009) show how, in a story about an attack on the storyteller's friend, race categories are not produced until just before the key events of the story, where 'white' is used as an account for action. That is, 'white' is produced just in time to render that account meaningful (i.e., to make the story one in which his friend was attacked because he was white). The racial categories of the attackers are not made explicit.

Second, they show that 'white' is expressed in referential repairs, that is, where there is prior ambiguity with respect to race and a resolution is achieved through a repair involving direct reference to a racial category. In the extract below from a therapy session with teenagers, for example, Roger's immediately prior description of 'coloured guys' and 'many fights' (lines 1 and 8, not shown) implies that these incidents are, on this occasion, bound to the racial category 'coloured guys'. He then connects himself to fighting on line 15 below.

Extract 9 (from Whitehead and Lerner, 2009: 624)

```
15  Roger:  Mosta the time I was kicked out fer fightin,
16          (2.5)
17  Ken:    Yer going,
18          (1.2)
19  Roger:  I'm gone.
20  Al:     Hah
21          (1.8)
22  Dan:    Fighting with whom?
```

```
23  Roger:  White kids.
24          (0.5)
25  Roger:  I only once hadda fight with a coloured guy.
```

Roger does not specify who he fought with, although the implication, in this sequential context, is that this was with black guys. The therapist, Dan, seeks clarification of the ambiguity (line 22) and Roger treats Dan's question as a request for the antagonists' racial category and thus he makes explicit the usually unstated category, 'white kids'. The normally taken-for-granted status of 'white', is disrupted here by the prior mobilization of race.

A third context in which 'white' is made relevant is, by contrast, where race does not seem relevant and a racial category is therefore used gratuitously. The category, once made relevant, is then available for other participants to use opportunistically. This point also ties in nicely with Hopper and LeBaron's (1998) in relation to omnirelevance and gender: that once gender has been made relevant in a conversation, it is available for later use. Whitehead and Lerner note similar observations have been made by Land and Kitzinger (2005) in their analysis of telephone calls in which self-attributing the membership category, lesbian, early in the interaction heads off possible trouble later as a result of participants incorrectly assuming the person's heterosexuality.

This work demonstrates the potential of seeking answers to the question of when categories other than gender are made relevant. Whitehead and Lerner suggest that understanding how the invisibility of whiteness is achieved in everyday interaction can also indicate ways to disrupt that invisibility, and hence resist 'society's hegemonic whiteness' (op. cit.: 634). It provides a further example of how close attention to the details of talk is not incompatible with bringing about social change. Future work might extend this to other categories that seem pervasive such as age-related ones.

Conclusion

Edwards' chapter and the work it stimulated generated useful debates about participants' orientation as an important resource for analysis, and its limitations in the search for ways to tell that, when, and why a category is relevant. Stokoe (2012a: 282) cites Edwards' argument (personal communication) that sometimes there is ambiguity, and this is 'designedly so', and we should recognize that we cannot as analysts always be definitive about categories and their attributes; we should not expect to produce a definitive version of what is going on for every occasion. Instead, we can fruitfully recognize that ambiguity and treat categories as 'provisional'. These theoretical and methodological debates were not present in Edwards' chapter for his aim was very different, as was the literature within which he situated his analysis. The impact of the chapter has, then, moved beyond the context in which the ideas were first construed. The question remains, of course, what can social psychology, especially in the area of social identity, learn from the development of Edwards' work?

'Traditional social psychology', such as social identity and self-categorization theories, are replete with theories and experiments on social identity and its functioning largely in researcher-generated contexts with reference to researcher-generated questions. We know less about the functioning of identity categories in everyday contexts, as used and oriented to by participants. SCT provides a theoretical and empirical approach to categories which aims to generalize via establishing causal regularities (under certain conditions). MCA/CA promises to deliver regularities, but grounded in interaction and what happens. One advantage of this is that researchers do not need to be concerned about how their findings can be applied to the 'real world' because they are derived from an examination of naturalistic data. Furthermore, Whitehead and Lerner, Stokoe and others demonstrate there are important practical applications of this understanding. Edwards' chapter made an important contribution to precisely these questions, and Stokoe has extended this by providing a promising analytic combination of MCA and CA, and by showing that it is possible to build a collection of identity work (for a particular identity category or the range of invoked identities). Analysts are beginning to build a repository of examples, findings and insights, in other words a body of empirical work, that helps develop an alternative vision of category use not dictated by reacting to or defining as an alternative to the established ways of seeing, as Edwards in a sense was. SCT/SIT made claims about the functioning of group members in society in ways that made social life happen. DP now has an approach and the basis for extending and building further an understanding of society and its categories through interactions of members. We can now see the kinds of contexts in which identities may be invoked, as well as having an empirical approach to the kinds of questions of relevance raised in traditional, feminist, and constructionist and CA approaches. Edwards' (1998: 33) point, of course, still stands: 'Categorization is approachable discursively as something we actively do, and do things with [...]'

References

Antaki, C. Condor, S. and Levine, M. (1996) 'Social identities in talk: Speakers' own orientations, *British Journal of Social Psychology*, 35: 473–92.
Antaki, C. and Widdicombe, S. (1998) *Identities in talk*. London: Sage.
Billig, M. (1995) *Banal nationalism*. London: Sage.
Edwards, D. (1998) 'The relevant thing about her: Social identity categories in use', in C. Antaki and S. Widdicombe (eds) *Identities in talk*. London: Sage.
Edwards, D. (2005) 'Managing subjectivity in talk', in A. Hepburn and S. Wiggins (eds) *Discursive research in practice: New approaches to psychology and interaction* (pp. 31–49). Cambridge: Cambridge University Press.
Edwards, D. (eds) (2006) 'Facts, norms and dispositions: Practical uses of the modal *would* in police interrogations', *Discourse Studies*, 8: 475–501.
Edwards, D. and Potter, J. (2001) 'Discursive psychology', in A.W. McHoul and M. Rapley (eds) *How to analyse talk in institutional settings: A casebook of methods*. London: Continuum International.

Hopper, R. and LeBaron, C. (1998) 'How gender creeps into talk', *Research on Language & Social Interaction*, *31*: 59–74.

Kitzinger, C. (2000) 'Doing feminist conversation analysis', *Feminism & Psychology*, *10*: 163–93.

Kitzinger, C. (2007) 'Is "woman" always relevantly gendered?', *Gender & Language*, *1*:39–49.

Klein, N.L. (2011) 'Doing gender categorization: Non-recognitional person reference and the omnirelevance of gender', in S.A. Speer and E. Stokoe (eds) *Conversation and gender*. Cambridge: Cambridge University Press.

Land, V. and Kitzinger, C. (2005) 'Speaking as a lesbian: Correcting the heterosexist presumption', *Research on Language & Social Interaction*, *38*: 221–65.

Sacks, H. (1979) 'Hotrodder: A revolutionary category', in G. Psathas (ed.) *Everyday language: Studies in ethnomethodology*. New York: Irvington Press.

Sacks, H. (1992) *Lectures on conversation* (edited by G. Jefferson, 2 vols). Oxford: Blackwell.

Schegloff, E.A. (1997) 'Whose text? Whose context?' *Discourse & Society*, *8*: 165–87.

Speer, S.A. (2001) 'Reconsidering the concept of hegemonic masculinity: Discursive psychology, conversation analysis and participants' orientations', *Feminism & Psychology*, *11*: 107–35.

Stokoe, E. (2003) 'Mothers, single women and sluts: Gender, morality and membership categorization in neighbor disputes', *Feminism & Psychology*, *13*: 317–44.

Stokoe, E. (2006) 'On ethnomethodology, feminism, and the analysis of categorical reference to gender in talk-in-interaction', *The Sociological Review*, *54*: 467–94.

Stokoe, E. (2011) ' "Girl – woman – sorry!": On the repair and non-repair of consecutive gender categories', in S.A. Speer and E. Stokoe (eds) *Conversation and gender*. Cambridge: Cambridge University Press.

Stokoe, E. (2012a) 'Moving forward with membership categorization analysis: Methods for systematic analysis', *Discourse Studies*, *14*: 277–303.

Stokoe, E. (2012b) ' "You know how men are": Description, categorization and common knowledge in the anatomy of a categorical practice', *Gender & Language*, *6*: 233–55.

Stokoe, E. and Smithson, J. (2001) 'Making gender relevant: Conversation analysis and gender categories in interaction', *Discourse & Society*, *12*: 243–69.

Turner, J.C. (1987) 'A self-categorization theory', in J.C. Turner, M.A. Hogg, P.J. Oakes, S.D. Reicher and M.S. Wetherell (eds) *Rediscovering the social group: A self-categorization theory*. Oxford: Basil Blackwell.

Van Dijk, T. (1992) 'Discourse and the denial of racism', *Discourse & Society*, *3*: 87–118.

Weatherall, A. (2002) 'Towards understanding gender and talk-in-interaction', *Discourse & Society*, *13*: 767–81.

Wetherell, M. and Potter, J. (1992) *Mapping the language of racism: Discourse and the legitimation of exploitation*. Hemel Hempstead: Harvester Wheatsheaf.

Whitehead, K.A. and Lerner, G.H. (2009) 'When are persons "white"?: On some practical asymmetries of racial reference in talk-in-interaction', *Discourse & Society*, *20*: 613–41.

Widdicombe, S. (1998) 'Identity as an analysts' and a participants' resource', in C. Antaki and S. Widdicombe (eds) *Identities in talk*. London:Sage.

Wowk, M. (1984) 'Blame allocation, sex and gender in a murder interrogation', *Women's Studies International Forum*, *7*: 75–82.

14 Dilemmas of memory

The mind is not a tape recorder

Steven D. Brown and Paula Reavey

Target article: Edwards, D. and Potter, J. (1992) 'The Chancellor's memory: Rhetoric and truth in discursive remembering', *Applied Cognitive Psychology*, 6: 187–215.

Introduction

Many researchers who have gravitated towards Discursive Psychology can produce very vivid accounts of when exactly it was that they 'lost their faith' in cognitive-experimental psychology. For one of us, it was during a lecture at the University of Reading, listening to an eminent psychologist describe the relationship of cognitive architecture to the brain using the well-known metaphor of software running on hardware. Perhaps the metaphor was striking and innovative when it was freshly minted. But by the late 1980s, it seemed quite impoverished. Is that it? Is that what the rich contours of human experience come down to? Could it really be so simple?

Edwards and Potter's (1992) critique of 'truth' in cognitive-experimental approaches to memory and their alternative formulation of a discursive treatment of remembering, arrived at a fortuitous moment. Rather like the embattled Conservative government of the time, whose Chancellor, Nigel Lawson, is one of the central figures of the piece, so it felt that the dominant regime – the dreaded cognitivists – were losing their grip on the discipline. A new intellectual force was emerging, not from the heartlands of power, but from highly unlikely places such as Manchester, Milton Keynes, and most surprising of all, Loughborough. Change was coming, or at least that is how things felt in the early 1990s. In what follows we will try to describe exactly why 'The Chancellor's Memory' offered such a rewarding challenge to theoretical and methodological sensibilities, one that continues to shape and inform our own work today. But we will also try to make clear how that piece formalized the terms of engagement with cognitive-experimental psychology in a way that has ultimately been highly unproductive. We can see in this early work the effort to elevate discourse and conversation analysis beyond the status of mere methodology to the foundations for a new form of psychology itself. And it is here that the Loughborough approach came to be somewhat peculiarly modeled on the regime it sought to supplant, the Blairist New Labour to the Thatcherism of cognitive-experimental psychology, if you like. The challenges of working through this difficult legacy will be one of our major themes.

Context

Critical (Social) Psychology in the 1980s had reached something of an impasse. The classic early works of authors such as Ken Gergen, Rom Harré and John Shotter had performed extensive diagnosis of just what was wrong with the discipline, but they were less than illuminating as to what would need to be done to create a viable alternative. As Brown and Locke put it:

> The key texts of the crisis literature had all called for change in social psychology. To some extent 'experiments' became seen as emblematic of all that was wrong with the discipline. The search for new methods then became at the same time shorthand for doing social psychology differently. However, the majority of the crisis literature proved to be very thin in terms of specific recommendations for appropriate methodologies. This left a generation of researchers in the unfortunate position of being 'against' experiments but with little sense of the alternatives (i.e. what they were actually 'for').
>
> (Brown and Locke, 2008: 376)

It was in this very particular context that a 'turn to language' became so appealing. Mick Billig's (1987) work on rhetoric and Jeff Coulter's (1979) application of ethnomethodology had both been instrumental in nudging debates about the problem of imputing mental states away from philosophical discussion and towards the issue of methods. We can see this clearly in Derek Edwards's work in the 1980s. Edwards and Goodwin (1985) argue that lexical development in children is poorly grasped when it is treated in terms of gradual conceptual understanding, because this implies that 'thinking' precedes 'doing'. However, by looking at 'real world' instances of children's social interactions, it is clear that language is deployed pragmatically by the child to 'do things' before its referential function can be said to be established. This leads, in Edwards and Mercer (1987), to a concern with how the language of instruction in a classroom setting can construct understanding as a shared, communicative accomplishment.

Dave Middleton's early work shared this concern with the linguistic steering of children's activities, having been part of the group that refined the experimental demonstration of 'scaffolding' in parent-child interactions (see Wood and Middleton, 1975; Wood, Bruner and Ross, 1975). These studies were critical to a move in developmental psychology of placing cognitive development in a socio-cultural context. Together, Edwards and Middleton took these varied ingredients of pragmatics, communicative settings, interaction and 'thinking through doing', and applied them to the study of memory. Why exactly it is that they chose to focus on memory, rather than any of the other key topic areas of either developmental or social psychology, is a little unclear. There appears to be a certain arbitrariness here, much as there is with Potter and Wetherell's (1987) treatment of attribution theory or Potter and Litton's (1985) engagement with social representations, where the point of the exercise is to deconstruct 'traditional' approaches by showing the viability of a rhetorical and discursive alternative, rather than a sustained effort to move the topic on per se (see also Edwards, Middleton and Potter, 1992: 445). To this end, Edwards and Middleton conducted a series of studies using both quasi-experimental methods (the 'E.T.' study – Edwards and Middleton, 1986) and semi-naturalistic data collection (the family photographs study – Edwards and Middleton, 1988). These studies generated transcribed interactional material that Edwards and Middleton analysed to show how versions of past events were jointly negotiated in an argumentative context using a variety of discursive devices (see Middleton and Edwards, 1990).

The 'Chancellor's memory' paper builds on the work of Middleton and Edwards by refining the focus. In the edited volume, *Collective remembering*, a fairly wide-ranging agenda had been set out that included themes such as the 'social practice of commemoration', the 'social foundation and context of individual memory' and 'social institutional remembering and forgetting'. These themes are fairly marginal to Edwards and Potter (1992), who concentrate instead on the wholesale 'bracketing out' of subjectivity and experience, along with the methods of experimental psychology. If the earlier work had implied that discourse analysis and pragmatics expanded the toolkit of psychology, here Edwards and Potter were clear that it was instead intended to replace them:

> [I]n any account of conversational remembering, what is required is not merely an extension of traditional cognitive concerns into real-world settings, but a re-focusing of attention upon the dynamics of social action, and in particular, of discourse.
>
> (Edwards and Potter, 1992: 188)

The argument turns upon an initial critique of Ulrich Neisser's (1981) paper on 'John Dean's memory'. Neisser's career, like that of Jerome Bruner, straddled the emergence of cognitive psychology in the 1970s. Both had been trained in the heady mix of Gestalt psychology and perceptual research and had arrived at the conclusion, contra the dominant behaviourist paradigm, that it was necessary to study 'thinking' as an active, reflexive force in shaping human action, rather than the residual echo left by stimulus-response chains. As Graham Richards (2009) and Jean-Pierre Dupuy (2000) have shown, it is difficult for us to now properly appreciate just how radical information theory and cybernetics was to 'pre-cognitive' psychologists. Notions such as feedback loops and signal/noise pairings made it possible to envisage a psychological subject embedded in an informational ecology in which she or he could operate as an active agent. However, it is to Neisser's very great credit that, despite having drawn together the implications of information theory for a *Cognitive Psychology*, he later came to see (as did Bruner) the limitations of the dogmatism of the 'standard model' of cognitive processes that he had initially formulated.

In the 1981 paper, published in *Cognition: The International Journal of Cognitive Science*, Neisser is performing a rather delicate act. He is, in effect, telling an audience of committed cognitive-experimentalists that they have been getting something very important wrong. Because they have studied memory solely in laboratory settings, they have blinded themselves to the complexity of how memory actually functions in daily life:

> In a psychological experiment, it is relatively easy to determine whether what the subject says is true. The experimenter knows what really happened because she staged it in the first place, or because she kept a record with which the subject's report can be compared. Because life does not keep such records, legal testimony is usually evaluated in more indirect ways: corroborative witnesses, cross-examination, circumstantial evidence. For some of Dean's testimony, however, it is now possible to compare what he said with a factual record: the *Presidential Transcripts*. This comparison will enable us to assess the accuracy of his memory rather precisely. In addition, it may clarify our theoretical conceptions of memory itself.
>
> (Neisser, 1981: 2)

This passage is interpretatively rich. Neisser contrasts what happens inside the laboratory with what happens outside of it (i.e., the vast majority of human experience). Experimentalists are correct to be confident in the findings of memory experiments, he states, because they have 'staged' events in such as way as to have a clear point of comparison. But outside of the laboratory, this is simply not possible. However, all is not lost! Sometimes institutions create records of their own that may act in ways analogous to experimental practices. If the audience is willing to hear, Neisser will go on to demonstrate just what can be done if one cares to look closely at these records.

In this invitation to follow him 'outside the laboratory', Neisser simultaneously flatters and entices his audience. At the time he was already a grandee figure in the discipline, a world-renowned figure and founder of the paradigm in which the audience were deeply embedded. But he was also a figure who had become, suddenly and unexpectedly, rather controversial. Three years earlier, Neisser had attempted to engage this same audience of hardcore cognitivists with rather less enticing statement – 'If X is an interesting or socially important aspect of memory, then psychologists have hardly ever studied X' (Neisser, 1978: 4). The 1981 passage needs to be set alongside the 1978 statement. By the time of 'John Dean's memory', Neisser has blown a great deal of his professional capital, he can no longer demand his audience's attention, he has instead to work to whet their appetite with a taster of what might await them if they were prepared to suspend their prejudices.

This is not the way that Edwards and Potter (1992) read Neisser's invitation. They take it as demonstration that while he is making a 'significant and welcome departure' (p. 189), in the end a leopard never really changes its spots. He remains fixated on the idea that it is, somehow, possible to establish the 'truth' of what happened, and thereby assess the veridicality of what is remembered. The alternative analysis that Edwards and Potter (1992) conduct is developed first in relation to John Dean's testimony and then further fleshed out using the 'Lawsongate' example. Their key argument is that throughout his testimony, 'Dean's *truth* is indistinguishable from his mode of accounting' (p. 194). The various claims he makes around what he can and cannot remember and the way in which he organizes his accounts of the meetings with Nixon are treated as rhetorically organized to attend to the ongoing interactional pragmatics of the hearings. Edwards and Potter make a very compelling case that variation in the accounts that Dean offers – sometimes appearing to make 'verbatim' recall, at other times decrying that his 'mind is not a tape recorder' – can be understood as contextually occasioned. In building this argument, Edwards and Potter draw support from Molotch and Boden's (1985) work, which focused on a different set of data to that used by Neisser, made of up of transcripts of the hearing Dean attended where he was questioned by a US Senator widely considered to be 'Nixon's man', who was as a consequence hearably antagonistic towards Dean. Neisser is then seen as having only 'half the story'.

The Lawsongate material gets a very similar treatment, although one that probably benefits from the cultural knowledge that Edwards and Potter bring to the material (e.g., how the Parliamentary 'lobby' system works; background knowledge on the political fortunes of the ruling Conservative Party). One of the key aspects to the analysis is how the issue of the 'missing tape' is treated in the exchanges. Here there is apparently no possibility of establishing a 'bottom line' account of 'the truth of what happened'. Edwards and Potter thus demonstrate that pragmatically oriented claims to 'truth' are central resources to the unfolding of social action, rather than matters that lay in the hands of the analyst. Here we see an empirical working through of what would come to be, for a time, a very particular preoccupation in Discursive Psychology – the absence of 'bottom line' accounts – which would go on to be developed in its own right in 'Death and furniture'.

A number of other stylistic and methodological details of the piece are worth remarking on here. The analysis is initially framed with the three themes of 'function', 'variation' and 'construction'. This loose framing of the way that discourse works is found in both *Discourse and social psychology* and *Collective remembering*, before becoming superseded by the more tightly organized Discourse Action Model (DAM) in *Discursive psychology*. Whether or not the apocryphal story is correct that DAM was created to satisfy the demands of the reviewers of Edwards and Potter's *Psychological Review* piece ('where's the damn theory then?'), it seems reasonable to suppose that nascent Discursive Psychology became more formalized as a consequence of the effort to communicate the approach to a cognitive-experimental audience. 'The Chancellor's memory' is, after all, published in the journal *Applied Cognitive Psychology* – the first and last time its avid readers were offered such a methodological joyride outside the laboratory, we imagine.

What happened next

The response to the effort made in 'The Chancellor's memory' to engage with the cognitive-experimental community can best be gauged by looking at the published commentaries to an invited paper that Edwards, Middleton and Potter contributed to *The Psychologist*. The Edwards *et al.* (1992) piece opens by repeating many of the objections to the laboratory study of memory discussed by Middleton and Edwards (1990) and Edwards and Potter (1992), before briefly summarizing recent work at Loughborough using DAM as a guide. The tone is interesting. If Neisser, in 'John Dean's memory', attempts to lure psychologists from the laboratory with the promise of the delights in store outside, Edwards *et al.* are telling cognitive-experimentalists that their jobs have been outsourced to more effective workers and they might as well leave the laboratory before it is closed down. Unsurprisingly, the responses range from the nonplussed to barely restrained fury. Some reject discursive work on the grounds that is simply unscientific:

> If you cast your lot in with the empiricists in the seventeenth century, and feel a thrill at trouncing the rationalists, then the study of memory in the twentieth century imposes a simple criterion to determine the truth of a hypothesis: systematic, controlled observation yielding replicable results. Can discourse analysis provide such data?
> (Banaji, 1992: 448).

On this count, Discursive Psychology does not meet the bar for an empirical science. But the argument is reversed by Roediger and Wheeler, who see a potential 'gold mine' of data but with very little theoretical coherence:

> we have tried several times to comprehend the nine tenets of DAM . . . but . . . fear that we have failed. The model seems so general that is excludes nothing . . . At one point in our efforts to understand discursive remembering we looked up *discursive* in the *Oxford American Dictionary* (1980) and were informed discursive means 'rambling from one subject to another'. Just so.
> (Roediger and Wheeler, 1992: 453)

These two arguments – Discursive Psychology as neither sufficiently empirical nor convincingly theoretical – would be repeated time after time in the coming decades. And the response would eventually harden into a mantra: Discursive Psychology is rigorously empirical, but the nature of this rigor exceeds the narrow and naïve definitions of scientificity used by cognitive-experimentalists (e.g., Edwards, 2012); Discursive Psychology rejects ungrounded theorizing, instead producing descriptions of the pervasive features of social life that are superior to mere conceptual deduction (e.g., Potter, 2012a).

One further response is worth considering. Alan Baddeley – the Godfather of British psychology of memory – asks whether discursive work properly concerns memory at all:

> What emerges then is that the authors are interested in the social interaction between members of groups, and its verbal expressions, and that they find remembering a useful topic for generating such interaction. Hardly a model of memory, but potentially a very interesting topic.
> (Baddeley, 1992: 447)

We might see this simply as Baddeley displaying his displeasure at the lack of respect he and his work had been shown by these upstarts whose names were barely known in the hallowed circles of the Experimental Psychological Society – 'In conclusion then, while I do not propose to give up cognitive psychology, I am intrigued to know what Dr Edwards and his colleagues have been finding out about groups reminiscing' (p. 448). But he also has a point. 'The Chancellor's memory', along with the Edwards et al. (1992) piece, is not, strictly speaking about 'memory' at all. It is an attempt to show how the subject matter parsed by cognitive psychology can be lifted wholesale into a discursive approach. This will be the long-term project of Discursive Psychology – setting out a way of doing psychology as the study of the discursive practices in which 'mental life' is rendered operant in the pragmatics of communication. As Edwards and Potter (1992) conclude:

> Our recommendation is to let go of a commitment to mind as a pre-existing, independently knowable explanation of talk and action . . . Like the 'truth', the cognitions that are thought to apprehend and distort it are also researchable as discursive formulations, as versions of mental life, framed in talk and text, and oriented to the pragmatics of communication. The study of how conceptualizations of cognitive processes are deployed in everyday and scientific discourses will be a major focus of further work.
> (Edwards and Potter, 1992: 211)

Even if one is sympathetic to what is being said here (as indeed we are!), it is difficult to see what purpose is served by 'recommending' to cognitive-experimentalists that they 'let go' of the paradigmatic basis on which their intellectual commitments, and indeed careers, are formed. Everything we know about paradigms, since Kuhn (1962), suggests that communities of researchers are not simply persuaded into new modes of working, they are reluctantly forced to do so when the groundswell of evidence makes current practices untenable. Interestingly, in the decade that separates 'John Dean's memory' from 'The Chancellor's memory', a movement had begun – the 'everyday memory' tradition (Conway, 1991) – that is now, arguably, building to the kind of groundswell that might bring about the sort of conceptual re-orientation that Edwards and Potter called for. It was within this emergent body of work that Neisser rebuilt his reputation after the 1978 comments (Neisser, 1982; Fivush and Neisser, 1994).

It is unclear what, if anything, is gained in epistemic terms by making unequivocal assertions about what is and what is not to be properly called 'Psychology' given the diverse and complex historical emergence of the discipline. But Baddeley's barb that Discursive Psychology has no 'model of memory' does stick. To treat remembering as primarily researchable in terms of the interactional formulation of descriptions and claims about the past is to miss what is, for all of us, a crucial aspect of 'memory'. We all feel a connection between what we are doing now and our personal and collective histories. That felt connection, which we might gloss as a 'flow of experience', is a critical resource that we all draw upon in making sense of any given interaction. While it most certainly does not drive how we 'frame versions of mental life in talk and text' in any causal way, and most definitely is not adequately grasped with the kinds of 'models of memory' associated with Baddeley, the flow of experience is a significant issue for any putative psychology of memory.

Critique

In this last section, we want to begin by pointing to a division within Discursive Psychology that occurs around the publication of 'The Chancellor's memory'. Following the reception of *Collective remembering*, Dave Middleton signed a contract with the publisher, Sage, to author a research monograph, provisionally entitled *Social remembering*, by 1992. As is the way with such projects, there was some drift in the timeline . . . In fact, the book was not published until many years later, in 2005, with a different title *The social psychology of experience*, and with one of us attached as a co-author.

Why did it take so long to complete this book? If one reads the second half of the Edwards et al. (1992) piece, there are various indications of what *Social remembering* might have looked like, had it been completed as planned. It would most likely have focused on remembering as a process for producing collectivity or 'communities of memory' through a work of 'becoming members again' ('re-membering'). Middleton would come to describe this process as the interdependency of the individual and the collective (see Middleton, 2002). By this he meant that it was analytically important to keep a hold of the notion of 'the individual', but just not in the way that cognitive-experimental psychology had come to define it. This concern with personhood had, he felt, been jettisoned by Discursive Psychology in its move to 'let go' of the philosophical and operational difficulties implied by the concept of 'mind'.

In order to explain why Middleton felt this was important, we have to consider where the project of 'letting go of mind' has gone since in Discursive Psychology. Potter's (2012b) short commentary on Creswell (2012) provides a good summary. In this piece, Potter responds to the resurgent interest in the term 'experience' in contemporary social science. He cites the later Wittgenstein's (1958) classic argument on thinking as language as having sufficiently addressed all relevant philosophical matters, and then details a range of foreboding methodological issues that confront the researcher who is nevertheless determined to find a means of engaging with experience as an extra-discursive matter. Particularly, ire is (justly) reserved for 'Interpretative Phenomenological Analysis' (IPA) (see Smith, Flowers and Larkin, 2009), which is seen as ducking the issue entirely by conflating talk about mental states with these states themselves. Discursive Psychologists, by contrast, start with 'practices and people acting in relation to one another, and bracket off issues of cognition' (p. 577). In detailing these difficulties, Potter performs himself as somewhat exasperated by 'a common but unnecessary nostalgia for a more classic form of "interiority"' (p. 586). This he names as either 'dualism' or 'cognitivism'. The alternative is to respecify psychological categories as interactionally occasioned descriptions made in particular communicative settings. He finds himself incredulous that 'even after some 20 years since the publication of *Discursive Psychology* . . . researchers of all flavours still have difficulties in accommodating this radical move' (p. 577).

But what is the nature of this 'radical move'? It consists of reifying the very dualism it seeks to unpick. If there is something called 'experience' that differs from discursive practice, then, the argument goes, it can only be located in the 'interior' realm of the Cartesian subject. Cognition is either a discursive matter or an 'in-the-head' matter (in which case it is probably either inaccessible or uninteresting and can be safely bracketed out). This is a version of cognition that is not altogether recognizable to contemporary cognitive science. The 'extended mind' hypothesis of Clark and Chalmers (1998), for example, applies the term 'cognition' to activities that occur 'outside the head' as well as 'inside'. John Sutton and colleagues have developed 'distributed cognition' approaches to social remembering that point to the crucial role of material mediators such as diaries or electronic devices (Sutton *et al.*, 2010). Recent work in 'enactive' and 'embodied' cognition aims at pushing further at the boundaries between self and world to see thinking as fundamentally a matter of doing (Colombetti, 2014). And in contemporary philosophy, the displacement of cognition from a Cartesian version of mind continues apace with the renewed interest in the process philosophies of A.N. Whitehead (1985) and Henri Bergson (1991).

The issue here is that there is nothing terribly radical at all about the move of respecifying the psychological in interactional terms (as Ian Hacking 1999 once noted in relation to Coulter's work).The impact of post-dualist approaches such as Actor-Network Theory and the double whammy of Foucauldian and Deleuzian philosophies as the metaphysics of choice for social scientists who see themselves on the cutting edge, has left contemporary work completely unfettered by any notion of interiority across vast swathes of Sociology, Human Geography, Cultural Theory, Management Studies, International Relations, Science and Technology Studies . . . and the list goes on. Discursive Psychologists are really pushing at an open door outside of the discipline with arguments such as the following:

> Clearly language, or discourse, is not all that there is in the world, not all that psychology and society are made of, and not the same thing as experience, or reality, or feelings, or knowledge. It is just language, discourse, or talk-in-interaction: not those other things. But *it is the primary work of language to make all those 'other' phenomena accountable.*
>
> (Edwards, 2006: 42)

Few readers of outlets such as, say, *Environment and Planning D: Society & Space* or *Journal of Cultural Economy*, would find anything here objectionable. In fact they might very well see themselves as taking a similar tack in their own empirical work, namely getting at 'psychology' or 'society' through the interactional work through which these things are constituted. And this brings us to the central problem. Given the spread of post-dualist thinking across the social sciences, what is it exactly that makes Discursive Psychology particularly 'psychological'? Or put another way, if discourse is 'not the same thing' as 'experience' or 'feelings', then whose task is it to explore this difference in a post-cognitive framework if not psychologists? Why keep strictly to the project of purifying any extra-discursive conception of subjectivity, experience or mind from a psychology of memory?

In a curious way, Edwards and Potter seem to have swapped places with Neisser. Where the latter once appeared to be attempting to prolong an ageing paradigm beyond its natural lifespan by proposing a move outside the laboratory, it is Potter who now claims that the increasing focus on naturalistic data in Discursive Psychology 'promotes innovative analyses, pushes researchers off well-worn social science agendas, and promotes powerful leverage for real-life problems and issues' (2012b: 577). If Neisser seemed to be suggesting that there was little that cognitivism could not explain, then Potter appears to be currently attracted to the same position – 'Despite the burgeoning evidence of supposed "phenomenological" research, it is not clear that any other perspective provides as nuanced an account of psychological matters as they are threaded through people's lives and provides a more systematic, rigorous and repeatable analysis' (2012b: 586). This last phrase is particularly striking. Discursive Psychology has its roots in the Sociology of Scientific Knowledge, a discipline that was acutely aware of the vacuous nature of claims to 'systematicity', 'rigor', and most notoriously 'replication' (see Ashmore, 1989; Collins, 1992; Gilbert and Mulkay, 1984). To see these terms repeated here without any apparent irony is most peculiar (compare with Edwards *et al.*, 1992: 454).

The main thrust of Edwards and Potter's (1992) critique of Neisser is that he treats the *Presidential transcripts* as a 'bottom line' against which the veridicality of Dean's testimony can be established. But what are we to make of the centrality of the methodological drive towards more 'systematic' and 'rigorous' data collection in current Discursive Psychology, where only recorded 'naturalistic data' is deemed adequate for analytic purposes, and other forms of data are dismissed as 'got up' (see Potter, 2012b)? Ashmore *et al.* (2004) refer to this as 'tape fetishism' – the idea that the tape functions as a kind of time machine that transports the analyst back to 'where the action is' and thereby serves as a hotline to getting in touch with the 'richness' and 'intricacies' of actual people interacting with each other in real time' (Potter, 2012b: 448). If the psychology of memory is arguably at its strongest when it entertains methodological pluralism and makes a concerted effort to constructively engage with analytic and epistemic differences, in precisely the manner that Edwards and Potter (1992) asked of their readers, then the spirit of early cognitivism, its dream that the difficult questions around the psychological were simply methodological issues to be overcome by better techniques, lives on proudly in contemporary Discursive Psychology. Neisser, at least, thought there was a way out of his laboratory.

And that is why, we think, Middleton never published the planned version of *Social remembering*. He came to appreciate that the difficulties of constituting a genuinely social approach to the psychology of memory involved more than purely technical questions. The kind of analysis required, while still grounded in the evidential base supplied by 'the tape', could not be reduced to its re-description, in the same way that his earlier work on 'scaffolding' could not be hung entirely on experimental data. In his work after the Edwards *et al.* (1992) piece, Middleton engaged with sociocultural psychology, an area where his many contributions continue to be celebrated (e.g., Middleton, 1997; 2002). He found here an intellectual project where memory was not treated as an arbitrary term for marking certain kinds of descriptive practices, but instead referred to substantive human activities for making use of the past in the present, and connected together important figures in the discipline, such as Bartlett and Vygotsky. Curiously, sociocultural psychology also offers a connection back to Neisser's work, through the 'sociocultural model of autobiographical memory' formulated by his former colleague, Robyn Fivush (Fivush *et al.*, 2011). It turns out that the meeting of cognitivism with discourse analysis announced by Edwards and Potter ended up taking place elsewhere.

The book Middleton did eventually publish, *The social psychology of experience*, was yet another turn. The problem of how to think continuity and interdependence, how we turn around on the past in the present, is tackled through readings of Bergson, Halbwachs and Bartlett. While there is ample transcribed data to be found throughout, theory is used to 'amplify' and transform what is on the tape to situate a given interaction in an account of a broader flow of experience. That text was one of the points of departure for our own current work (Brown and Reavey, 2015), where we argue that in the case of difficult or distressing experiences, it is incorrect to assert that there a multitude of possible versions of events that are interactionally available to survivors. It seems to us that the problem is rather that persons feel 'locked into' very specific versions of events. However, the dynamics of memory in play are broadly distributed across relationships, institutions, material affordances and – of course – discursive practices. What interests us is developing 'post-cognitive' accounts of remembering that nevertheless do not deny that we have a felt connection to our past that shapes the versions of events we are able to muster.

We are not alone in wanting to expand the 'rich surface' of human conduct around memory that is so celebrated by Edwards and Potter to include 'extra-discursive' matters. Kyoko Murakami's (2012) work has begun to explore how a re-thinking of temporality impacts on an interactional analysis of remembering. Lucas Bietti (2014) is involved in an audacious project to connect discursive approaches to memory with cognitive and linguistic models. David Kaposi (2011) has sketched out a view of the psychology of memory as a 'political and moral science' based on a rereading of Edwards and Potter (1992). And closer still to home, Cristian Tileagă's (2009; 2011) ongoing research is mobilizing a concept of ideology in relation to the joint-construction of the biographical and the historical. Much as we appreciate the purist connoisseurship of the way Discursive Psychology handles the 'exquisite', 'intricate' and 'rich' conversational practices that are – of course! – at work in remembering, we find these searching explorations of the messy and dirty meshwork of discursive and extra-discursive relations more to our taste.

References

Ashmore, M. (1989) *The reflexive thesis: Wrighting sociology of scientific knowledge*. Chicago, IL: The University of Chicago Press.

Ashmore, M., MacMillan, K. and Brown, S.D. (2004) 'It's a scream: Professional hearing and tape fetishism', *Journal of Pragmatics*, 36(1): 349–74.

Baddeley, A. (1992) 'Is memory all talk?', *The Psychologist*, 5: 447–8.

Banaji, M. (1992) 'The lures of ecological realism', *The Psychologist*, 5: 448.

Bergson, H. ([1908]1991) *Matter and memory*. New York: Zone.

Bietti, L. (2014) *Discursive remembering: Individual and collective remembering as a discursive, cognitive and historical process*. Berlin: Walter De Gruyter.

Billig, M. (1987) *Arguing and thinking: A rhetorical approach to social psychology*. Cambridge: Cambridge University Press.

Brown, S.D. and Locke, A. (2008) 'Social psychology', in *The Sage handbook of qualitative methods in psychology* (eds C. Willig and W. Stainton Rogers) (pp. 373–89). London: Sage.

Brown, S.D. and Reavey, P. (2015) *Vital memory and affect: Living with a difficult past*. London: Routledge.

Clark, A. and Chalmers, D. (1998) 'The extended mind', *Analysis*, 58(1): 7–19.

Collins, H. (1992) *Changing order: Replication and induction in scientific practice*. Chicago, IL: University of Chicago Press.

Colombetti, G. (2014) *The feeling body: Affective science meets the enactive mind*. Cambridge, MA: MIT Press.

Conway, M. (1991) 'In defence of everyday memory', *American Psychologist*, 46: 19–26.

Coulter, J. (1979) *The social construction of mind*. London: Sage.

Cresswell, J. (2012). 'Including social discourses and experience in research on refugees, race and ethnicity', *Discourse & Society*, 23(5): 553–75.

Dupuy, J.-P. (2000) *The mechanization of mind: On the origins of cognitive science.* Princeton, NJ: Princeton University Press.

Edwards, D. (2006) 'Discourse, cognition and social practices: The rich surface of language and social interaction', *Discourse Studies,* 8: 41–9.

Edwards, D. (2012) 'Discursive and scientific psychology', *British Journal of Social Psychology,* 51: 425–35.

Edwards, D., Ashmore, M. and Potter, J. (1995) 'Death and Furniture: The rhetoric, politics and theology of bottom line arguments against relativism', *History of the Human Sciences,* 8: 25–49.

Edwards, D. and Goodwin, R.Q. (1985) 'The language of shared attention and visual experience: A functional study of early nomination', *Journal of Pragmatics,* 9: 475–93.

Edwards, D. and Mercer, N.M. (1987) *Common knowledge: The development of understanding in the classroom.* London: Methuen.

Edwards, D. and Middleton, D. (1986) 'Joint remembering: Constructing an account of shared experience through conversational discourse', *Discourse Processes,* 9: 423–59.

Edwards, D. and Middleton, D. (1988) 'Conversational remembering and family relationships: How children learn to remember', *Journal of Social and Personal Relationships,* 5: 3–25.

Edwards, D., Middleton, D. and Potter, J. (1992) 'Towards a discursive psychology of remembering', *The Psychologist,* 5: 56–60.

Edwards, D. and Potter, J. (1992) 'The Chancellor's memory: Rhetoric and truth in discursive remembering', *Applied Cognitive Psychology,* 6: 187–215.

Fivush, R., Habermas, T., Waters, T.E.A. and Zaman, W. (2011) 'The making of autobiographical memory: Intersections of culture, narratives and identity', *International Journal of Psychology,* 46: 321–45.

Fivush, R. and Neisser, U. (eds) (1994) *The remembering self: Construction and accuracy in self-narrative.* Cambridge: Cambridge University Press.

Gilbert, G.N. and Mulkay, M. (1984) *Opening Pandora's box: A sociological analysis of scientists' discourse.* Cambridge: Cambridge University Press.

Hacking, I. (1999) *The social construction of what?* Cambridge, MA: Harvard University Press.

Kaposi, D. (2011) 'Truth and rhetoric: The promise of John Dean's memory to the discipline of psychology', *Journal for the Theory of Social Behaviour,* 42: 1–19.

Kuhn, T. (1962) *The structure of scientific revolutions.* Chicago, IL: University of Chicago Press.

Middleton, D. (1997) 'The social organisation of conversational remembering: Experience as individual and collective concerns', *Mind, Culture and Activity,* 4: 71–85.

Middleton, D. (2002) 'Succession and change in the socio-cultural use of memory: Building-in the past in communicative action', *Culture & Psychology,* 8: 79–95.

Middleton, D. and Brown, S.D. (2005) *The social psychology of experience: Studies in remembering and forgetting.* London: Sage.

Middleton, D. and Edwards, D. (1990) *Collective remembering.* London: Sage.

Molotch, M.L. and Boden, D. (1984) 'Talking social structure: Discourse, domination and the Watergate hearings'. *American Sociological Review,* 50: 273–88.

Murakami, K. (2012) 'Time for memory: Beyond spatial metaphors?', *Culture & Psychology,* 18: 3–13.

Neisser, U. (1978) 'Memory: What are the important questions?' in M.M. Gruneberg, P.E. Morris and R.N. Sykes (eds) *Practical aspects of memory* (pp. 3–24). London: Academic.

Neisser, U. (1981) 'John Dean's memory: A case study', *Cognition*, 9: 1–22.
Neisser, U. (1982) *Memory observed*. Oxford: WH Freeman.
Potter, J. (2012a) 'How to study experience', *Discourse & Society*, 23: 576–88.
Potter, J. (2012b) 'Re-reading Discourse and Social Psychology: transforming social psychology', *British Journal of Social Psychology*, 51: 436–55.
Potter, J. and Litton, I. (1985) 'Some problems underlying the theory of social representations'. *British Journal of Social Psychology*, 24: 81–90.
Potter, J. and Wetherell, M. (1987) *Discourse and social psychology: Beyond attitudes and behaviour*. London: Sage.
Richards, G. (2009) *Putting psychology in its place: Critical historical perspectives* (third edn). London: Routledge.
Roediger, H.L. and Wheeler, M.A. (1992) 'Discursive remembering: A brief note', *The Psychologist*, 5: 452–3.
Smith, J.A., Flowers, P. and Larkin, M. (2009) *Interpretative phenomenological analysis: Theory, method, research*. London: Sage.
Sutton, J., Harris, C.B., Keil, P.G. and Barnier, A.J. (2010) 'The psychology of memory, extended cognition and socially distributed remembering', *Phenomenology & the Cognitive Sciences*, 9: 521–60.
Tileagă, C. (2009) 'The social organization of representations of history: The textual accomplishment of coming to terms with the past', *British Journal of Social Psychology*, 48: 337–55.
Tileagă, C. (2011) '(Re)writing biography: Memory, identity and textually mediated reality in coming to terms with the past', *Culture & Psychology*, 17: 197–215.
Whitehead, A.N. ([1929] 1978) *Process and reality*. New York: Free Press.
Wittgenstein, L. (1958) *Philosophical investigations*. Oxford: Blackwell.
Wood, D., Bruner, J.S. and Ross, G. (1975) 'The role of tutoring in problem solving', *Journal of Child Psychology & Psychiatry*, 17: 89–100.
Wood, D. and Middleton, D. (1975) 'A study of assisted problem solving', *British Journal of Psychology*, 66: 181–91.

15 A forgotten legacy?

Towards a discursive psychology of the media

Frederick Thomas Attenborough

Target article: MacMillan, K. and Edwards, D. (1999) 'Who killed the princess? Description and blame in the British press', *Discourse Studies*, 1: 151–74.

Introduction

At the time of its publication, MacMillan and Edwards's 'Who killed the princess?' (henceforth WKP) represented one of the first attempts to show that and how an approach inspired by discursive psychology (DP) could contribute to the project of a discursively oriented media studies (also see Ashmore, 1993). But it was also one of the *last* such attempts. In the years that followed, the potential for such cross-disciplinary engagement was all but lost: while DP was turning away from texts and towards the study of talk-in-interaction, media studies was becoming ever more familiar with textual methods such as critical discourse analysis (e.g., Richardson, 2007). And so although WKP now stands as one of many articles comprising a body of research in which media texts are analysed for their discursive, rhetorical and performative features, it is one of the few in which DP features as the analytic method of choice. This is unfortunate. The 'generally applicable discourse analytic approach' (MacMillan and Edwards, 1999: 151) demonstrated in WKP provided for a novel understanding of something discursive psychologists and ethnomethodologists would recognise as the 'reflexive adequacy' of textual descriptions (e.g., Garfinkel, 1967), but that media-centric critical discourse analysts have only recently begun to analyse, *and to analyse from a very different methodological position*, as 'recontextualisation' (e.g., Fairclough, 2010). In order to 'remember' DP's 'forgotten' ability to address the analytic concerns of a textually-focused media studies, this chapter considers WKP as if it were a contribution to the study of 'recontextualisation'.[1]

For any study of recontextualisation, a basic premise is that when 'events' happen, discourse happens to those events. For an event to be reported in a media text is also for that event to be recontextualised in and through the linguistic, visual and graphological choices of that text's author. It was something of this order that WKP caught 'in-flight' (Garfinkel, 1967: 79) during its study of press reportage of Princess Diana's death in 1997. This was an event rich with recontextualising possibilities. In that the British print-press was reporting the death of Tony Blair's 'people's Princess' in a context where many people, including Diana's family, had been accusing 'them' of having played a part in causing that death, issues of blame and culpability had to be handled with care. One of the first things that WKP did was to show that this 'handling' rarely required a journalist to be seen to be publicly handling anything at all. There did not, in other words, need to be any active, first-party deflection, denial or repudiation of blame for that blame to become deflectable. Why? Because the critical accounts provided by Diana's family could be used to do the job on the media's behalf, thus providing for an apparently unmotivated, stake-free deflection of blame. This might initially seem counter-intuitive. But, as MacMillan and Edwards went on to make clear, the trick to this reportage was its third-party narratorial format. We, as readers, got to read accounts that were presented to us by journalists *as if* the accounts of critical family members. But what we actually got – yet could never tell from the newspaper reportage itself that we *were* getting – were subtly recontextualised versions of those accounts. Family members could still be seen to be blaming 'the media', of course . . . *just not where 'the media' included the paper we happened to be reading*; and they could still be seen to be denouncing the media . . . *just as they were 'irrationally' 'lashing out' at everyone else because they were 'bitter' and 'grief stricken'*; and so on and so forth.

The chapter is divided into three sections: the first considers how MacMillan and Edwards' 'generally applicable discourse analytic approach' cut into descriptions of Diana's death; the second shows just how 'generally applicable' the method is, applying it to a very different empirical context; and via a comparison with critical discourse analysis, the final section considers the 'added value' that DP can bring to the project of a textually oriented media studies.

Descriptions as recontextualisations

WKP's discourse analytic method developed out of various, broadly ethno-methodological approaches, including DP (see Edwards, 2012), the sociology of scientific knowledge (henceforth SSK; Ashmore, 1993, 1995; Attenborough, 2012a), and membership categorization analysis (henceforth MCA; Edwards, 1995). What it shares with those approaches is a rejection of a referential understanding of language in which *words-in-here-on-a-page* name *things-out-there-in-the-world*. On this view, the question of *how* descriptions are put together is only relevant when separating accurate from inaccurate accounts; where the former are held to escape their contexts of production, with language acting as a passive receptacle for the transmission of 'world' onto 'page', the latter are adjudged so tainted by the biases/prejudices of their contexts of production that they end up deploying language to actively distort the way world appears on page (Woolgar, 1988). In the wake of Diana's death, for instance, it was just such a process of 'referential judgement' that helped people establish who was to blame: across courtrooms, police investigations, newspaper front pages and living rooms, the aim was to locate a definitive once-and-for-all version of what *really did* happen over and above the many other inaccurate accounts (Edwards, 2006: 45). But for DP, SSK and MCA this everyday approach to the work of description is *analytically* problematic. To assume some natural link between an accurate description and the event so described is to assume a non-linguistic sense of the world as a final arbiter of accuracy. Yet for these approaches there is no socially meaningful sense of the non-linguistic without the founding, constitutive force of language (Edwards, 2012). Although language might not be all there is in the world, it is, nevertheless, all there is in the world *that allows for the world to become accountable to ourselves and others* (see Edwards, 2006: 42). Once you reject, as these approaches reject, the possibility of some non-linguistic arbiter of accuracy, it follows that *all* descriptions – whether those we end up deciding to treat as referentially accurate or those we do not – have to be understood as products of particular, locally specific contexts. WKP's method of analysis stems from this basic proposition. The interest was not in whether mediated reports transmitted accurate, context-free information, but how they became 'vehicles for action' (Stivers and Sidnell 2013: 3) in a context where actions might include 'deflecting blame', 'denying culpability', and so on. In this way, MacMillan and Edwards were able to locate descriptions as not *just* descriptions, but also, and at the same time, as attempts at *just the right kind* of description for a particular context.

So how did these principles inform the practice of analysing data in WKP? Let us start by considering the residual bits of referentially-oriented description that MacMillan and Edwards *themselves* had no choice but to develop in order to provide readers with a sense of the context within which all the other, referentially oriented descriptions that they wanted to analyse had emerged.

Extract 1: WKP's referential description of Diana's death

```
1. 'On 31 August 1997, Diana, Princess of Wales, died in a car crash underneath
2. the Pont de L'Alma, Paris. According to media reports, the car she was
3. travelling in went out of control and smashed into the central reservation
4. of a tunnel alongside the Seine' (1999: 152) having been 'pursued' by
5. 'photographers' (1999: 155)
```

Details and facts have been assembled. Sources that the authors chose to regard as reputable have been deployed in order to create a seamless account of 'what really happened'. Sources regarded as disreputable/hyperbolic have been ignored. What we get, then, is a vehicle for action where the action intended is something like pulling off a neutral, objective and factual account of what *really did* happen. Consider, for instance, the category 'photographers' (line 5). Precisely *as* a category it provides us, as readers, with a set of inferential resources, via which we may start to understand the people so categorised as likely to perform a certain set of pretty neutral, uncontroversial actions: taking pictures, using cameras, investigating events, pursuing public interest stories, and so on. Unlike, say, 'paparazzi', 'MI6 agents' or 'murderers', it stands as the right kind of description, and categorization, for an academic context in which the aim is to do being neutral. But in the aftermath of Diana's death, 'photographers', or any variant thereof, was no longer the right kind of categorization for the British tabloids as they sought to describe 'those kinds of people'. To be sure, in the weeks leading up to the crash the relationship between tabloid press and photographers had been innocuously symbiotic. Coverage of Diana stories had been extensive, with various reports detailing 'her romantic involvement with Fayed [and providing] pictures of them on holiday together (taken with long-focus lenses)' (1999: 152). As potential front-page material, British tabloids were even 'competing for the most "exclusive" stories and pictures' (ibid.: 155) – indeed, just two weeks before Diana's death, a *Sunday Mirror* editorial announced that 'the Sunday Mirror has won the battle to publish the Di pictures', comparing their '16 stunning photos' to those of the *News of the World* who were 'reduced to printing an embarrassing series of computer-generated fakes' (ibid.: 155).

Unsurprisingly, in the days and weeks following her death, this symbiotic relationship was no longer quite so innocuous. For the tabloid press, to tie the people being accused, blamed and denounced in relation to Diana's death to the label 'photographers' was to do something far too neutral, objective and factual. As a category, it was incapable of fully backgrounding another action that *any and all* such incumbents might readably have been expected to undertake, namely, engaging with, and working for, the tabloid press. That is why, immediately after the car crash, 'the obtaining of such pictures, and the people involved in that, were widely denounced in the national media and (according to the media) by the general public' (ibid.: 155). These denunciations, however, were not always explicit and forceful. Often they were subtle, unobtrusive and bound up with the supposedly neutral, objective and factual work of categorizing people as *certain kinds of people*. In this way, descriptions of 'them' became vehicles for actions such as deflecting blame. For instance, if the category 'photographers' can be read to collect exactly the same kind of (now unpalatable) people together on the basis of a standard set of characteristics, values and capabilities, then in Extracts 2–4, from WKP, we find categories that allow for this global category to be opened-up, complicated and differentiated (Jayyusi, 1984: 166).

Extract 2   (Express, 1 September, in MacMillan and Edwards, 1999: 155)

```
1.   They are predominantly freelance - not employed directly
2.      by newspapers - and sell their scoops to the highest bidder
```

Extract 3 (*News of the World*, 14 September, ibid.: 156)

```
1.   Yobs with cameras masquerading as photo-journalists
```

Extract 4 (*Daily Mail*, 4 September, ibid.)

```
1.  Most of them are the journalistic equivalent of cowboy
2.  mini-cab drivers and some are not even real photographers
3.  - they simply flash off their expensive gear and hope for
4.  the fuzzy best
```

In Extract 2, 'freelance' serves to detach the people so categorised from any readable attachment to 'the press'. That they are 'predominantly' freelance helps first to differentiate, and then to distinguish between, the sorts of people that we do and do not need to be blaming for what happened. Moreover, 'predominantly' is a word that helps to imply that this sort of generalization is not a 'gross, all-or-nothing kind of generalization, but something ostensibly more careful': it acknowledges possible exceptions, thereby ensuring that any such exceptions remain exceptional, 'proving rather than disproving the rule' (ibid.: 156; and cf. Extract 4's 'most of them' (line 1), and 'some' (line 2)). With Extracts 3 and 4, we move even further from an undifferentiated term such as 'photographers'. There are yobs that '*masquerade* as photo-journalists', and 'cowboy mini-cab drivers ... some [of whom] are *not even real* photographers'. This contrast between 'appearance' and 'reality' helps to position its authors as possessing the kind of professional vision (Goodwin, 1994) to enable an accurate focalisation, and dissection, of a complex media landscape. In this way, space for *legitimate* criticism of the media's role in Diana's death is curtailed. To differentiate not just between photographers, freelancers, and so on, but also between 'real' photo-journalists and 'fake' yobs and cowboys, is to create nuance and subtlety where nuance and subtlety are rhetorical significant: 'they', as the tabloid print-press, can still be accused of being part of a media that employed photographers, of course; *but just not 'that kind' of photographer*. Finally here, let us note that it is the freelancers, yobs and cowboys that represent grammatically active agents in each extract. The rhetoric here 'is in what this denies', namely, that it might be the tabloids who actively sought their products, or even, as the *Sunday Mirror* put it, 'won the battle' to do so (ibid.).

So far we have looked at first-person descriptions in which the roles of principal, author and animator all coalesce in the same person (see Goffman, 1979). But MacMillan and Edwards also analysed another form of description, and one that is just as crucial to and for the genre of news reportage. Let us refer to this as the 'third-party recontextualisation'. Here, a journalist passes on a description produced by someone else. In this way, the 'someone else' in question may end up ceding the roles of author and animator to the journalist-reporter. This changes entirely what it means to think of descriptions as vehicles for action. In settings where people write/speak for themselves, they formulate their descriptions – that is, their *vehicles for action* – to and for one another, either turn-by-turn or line-by-line, in an unfolding interaction. In any mediated report about those descriptions, however, a journalist reformulates those points of view on behalf of the original interactants. As a result, only that which a journalist decides is relevant to understanding someone's talk/text will appear in the report. Now, when people talk or write about their own experiences in ways that we, as analysts, might unflinchingly characterise as, say, 'an accusation of blame', we are accepting the trajectory of *their* description, and *their* vehicle. But in any subsequent newspaper article about that vehicle, how *they* sought to shape it, and drive *their* reader in a certain direction, is relatively unimportant. Participants do, of course, retain some control over the reportage: if their words are to be represented, then a journalist is limited to choosing among direct, indirect and free indirect modes of recontextualisation (see Wales, 2011). But there is more to the media than the reportage of talk/text: from lexical, syntactical and rhetorical details, through to the graphology of the page/screen upon which it appears, these things will be recontextualised as part of a journalist's description of 'what actually happened'. In this way, people can lose control over their own descriptive vehicles, whilst all the while appearing to their respective audiences as if still in control of them. This is how accusations levelled against 'the media' and/or 'the press' by Diana's family ended up getting glossed such that any given newspaper's audience could read their accusations as if 'accusations . . . *levelled against some other part of the media*', or 'accusations that were false . . . *but perhaps understandable given the emotionally fraught circumstances*', and so on.

Take, for instance, Extract 5. It is part of a statement made by Diana's brother, Earl Spencer, which was broadcast across various television channels in the wake of her death.

Extract 5 (ITV, 31 August, in MacMillan and Edwards, 1999: 158)

```
1.  I always believed the press would kill her in the end.
2.  But not even I could imagine they would take such a
3.  direct hand in her death as seems to be the case.
```

As the principal, author and animator of his own description, Spencer is able to construct a description fitted to the action of apportioning blame for his sister's death. In contrast to Extracts 2–4, for instance, Spencer takes us back to the world of global, undifferentiated categories. In this context, it is precisely a *lack* of subtlety and nuance that is rhetorically useful: 'the press' (line 1) is the press is the press; the press is a system, and the entire system, from its photographers through to its editors, is to blame. But now consider Extract 6, in which this statement gets recontextualised as 'this statement'.

Extract 6 (*Daily Star*, in MacMillan and Edwards, 1999: 159

```
1.  Yesterday, Diana's devastated brother, Earl Spencer,
2.  revealed he had a premonition the paparazzi would play
3.  a part in the Princess's death. He told reporters: 'I
4.  always knew the Press would kill her in the end'.
```

To be sure, across lines 3–4, we get Spencer's actual words. Here, there is very little scope for those words to be diverted from the originally intended action of blaming 'the press'. In this sense, Spencer retains control of his descriptive vehicle. But note: everything that precedes this direct quote, starting from 'Earl Spencer' (line 1) and ending with 'the Princess's death' (line 3) is not transmitted via Spencer's words, but a journalist's gloss on those words. Spencer is still readably the principal of this gloss: it is he that 'reveals' and it is he that has a 'premonition' in which 'the paparazzi play a part in the Princess's Death'. But it is our journalist, as animator and author (and presumably also as one of the 'reporters' (line 3) who is now readably distinguishable from 'the paparazzi' (line 2)), who chooses these specific words. And these choices matter. They cannot but affect what it is that we, as readers, end up getting invited to see as that which Spencer, the supposed principal of this description, actually suggested. What he himself appears to be revealing across lines 1–3 effectively minimises the force of the accusation he is then seen to present directly, in his own words, across lines 3–5.

A comparison between the mediated recontextualisation (Extract 6) and Spencer's initial recontextualisation (Extract 5) shows three important ways in which this effect is created. First, there is the word 'premonition', which tends to be associated with 'mysterious kinds of divinations, warnings, omens and intuitions, rather than, say, inferences based on and justified by observed events' (1999: 158). As an interpretation of Spencer's 'always believed', 'premonition' is thus able to 'loosen any justified, observational basis his belief might have had' (ibid.). Second, the word 'paparazzi' is substituted for 'press'. This effectively interprets the word 'press' such that the 'referential aim' of the statement is redirected, 'deflecting blame away from the newspapers themselves' (ibid.). Finally, 'kill' (line 5) is downgraded to 'play a part in' (line 3). In these ways, press responsibility in the princess's death is 'descriptively downgraded, shifted to the paparazzi, and its rational basis undermined' (ibid.). The *Daily Star*, as part of 'the press' in general, is able to disappear from the original epicentre of Spencer's accusation. Rhetorically, what is crucial here is that it is not the *Daily Star*, but *Spencer himself* – as the principle to his own descriptive vehicle – who suggests that they were never actually there in the first place. Or, as MacMillan and Edwards put it, 'all [of] this is produced not as any kind of disagreement with Spencer, but as a version of what he actually said' (ibid.). In this way, 'both the respectful relaying of an opinion, and its undermining as unworthy of serious consideration, were possible almost simultaneously' (ibid.: 170).

Discursive psychology and media texts

In the introduction to this chapter I noted how it was possible to read WKP as an early attempt to show that a DP-inspired analytic approach could underpin a discursively oriented media studies. But this was not to suggest that DP was somehow uninterested in texts. Although most recent DP-oriented studies take talk-in-interaction as their primary data, it is not difficult to find DP-related research in which texts are approached as sites for the active literary/narratorial management of matters such as agency, intent, doubt, culpability, belief, prejudice, and so on (e.g., Attenborough, 2014a; Antaki *et al.*, 2006; Horne and Wiggins, 2009; Lamerichs and te Molder, 2003; Sneijder and te Molder, 2005; Tileagă, 2011). What it *was* to suggest, however, was that studies like WKP, in which 'the media' is considered as a distinctive site for this kind of management, are few and far between (e.g., Attenborough, 2014b; Antaki and Leudar, 2001; MacMillan, 2002; Romaniuk, 2009). This is unfortunate. WKP was not just a one-off empirical case study. It was also a general demonstration that mediated texts allow for a particular form of third-party representation in which journalists can actively manage someone else's management of culpability without appearing to be doing anything other than simply reporting what that 'someone else' had said/done.

In order to show how 'generally applicable' WKP's 'discourse analytic method' really is, this section develops a case-study in which we see third-party recontextualisations at work in a very different setting, yet performing similar, *and similarly consequential*, rhetorical work. The study in question focused on an incident of sexism in the English Premier League (henceforth EPL) involving Andy Gray and Richard Keys, a well-known football punditry team (see Attenborough, 2012b; 2013). Their shows, in which they presented live coverage of EPL football for the television channel *Sky Sports*, had been huge ratings successes. But in January 2011, however, it was suddenly they, and not the football they commentated upon, that became the story for the British press. The first piece of evidence for this story came from a video extract apparently leaked into the public domain by a *Sky Sports* employee. While commentating on an EPL football match earlier that month, Gray and Keys had been recorded, off-air, discussing one of three on-pitch match officials, assistant referee Sian Massey. The video showed a live transmission being streamed *out* to viewers, but also back *in* to Gray and Keys in their studio. As the match officials led the two teams onto the pitch prior to kick off, Massey appeared in a momentary mid-shot. Unaware that their microphones were still recording, Gray and Keys began talking about Massey. Extract 7 is a transcript of the video recording. 'Her' refers to Massey, and 'Kenny' refers to Kenny Dalglish, the manager of one of the football teams.

Extract 7

```
Keys: Well somebody better get down there and explain offside to her
Gray: Yeah, I know. Can you believe that? A female linesman. That's
      exactly what I was saying; women don't know the offside
      rule. Why do we [ call them linesman?
Keys:                [ Course they don't
Gray: Somebody's fucked up big.
Keys: I can guarantee you there will be a big one ((offside decision))
      today. Kenny will go potty. This is not the first time, is it?
```

```
                Didn't we have one before?
        Gray:   Yeah.
        Keys:   Was it Wendy Toms?
        Gray:   Wendy Toms, or something like that, yeah. And she was fucking
                hopeless as well.
        Gray:   Pretty much. It just makes yo [ u
        Keys:                                 [ No. No. It's gotta be done. It's
                good. Ugh. The game's gone mad.
```

The second piece of evidence comprised another video extract, this time released directly by *Sky Sports*. Captured at the same football match a few hours before the first exchange, it shows Gray standing pitch-side with another reporter, Andy Burton. In Extract 8 they are moments away from recording a piece to camera.

Extract 8

```
        Burton: Apparently, a female lino today, bit of a looker according to Steve
                the cameraman
        Gray:   A female linesman?
        Burton: That's what he said to me. He says she's alright, now I don't know
                if I should trust his judgement on that.
        Gray:   Nah I wouldn't
        Burton: (Laughs)
        Gray:   I definitely wouldn't
        Burton: Right, ready? Ready boys?
        Crew 1: Standing by.
        Gray:   Do you want permission to carry on, John?
        Crew 2: Footage.
        Burton: Female assistant, Andy, any good to you?
        Gray:   Nah, I can see her from here. Fuck! [ What do fucking women know
        Burton:                                    [ This, yeah, it's broken mate.
        Gray:   about the offside rule?
```

It was on the basis of these recordings that various parties constructed their complaints about Gray and Keys' sexist behaviour. Later that same week, and apparently as a direct result of the release of these recordings into the public domain, *Sky Sports* terminated Gray's contract. A few days later, Keys resigned his position.

So, how to analyse these events? Following WKP's approach to 'culpability', the aim was to understand how newspapers sought to mediate this account, acting as author, animator and surrogate-principal to each of these characters such that the events become 'one thing' rather than 'any other kind of thing'. Here, for instance, and having seen Extracts 7 and 8, it is plausible to imagine a recontextualisation of Gray and Keys' actions as deliberately and unambiguously sexist. At a very general level, both pundits could be described as treating women – that is, women *in general* – as incapable of understanding football precisely because they are women. If, from the analyst's perspective, sexism can be taken to involve 'practices whereby someone foregrounds gender when it is not the most salient feature' (Vetterling-Braggin, 1981), then any such recontextualisation could claim their actions as readably 'sexist'. The point of imagining this particular recontextualisation here is not to suggest that it presents the definitive version of 'what actually happened'. It is to suggest that, as with any recontextualisation of an incident as specifically sexist, a description of what happened is also, and at the same time, the vehicle for an evaluation of *the inappropriateness* of what happened (Stokoe and Edwards, 2009). Evaluation and description are in alignment: the latter provides a claim of inappropriateness, and the former evidences that inappropriateness (Drew, 1998).

Across this data corpus, however, there were instances of recontextualisation in which description and evaluation were non-aligned. In these cases, a negative evaluation of what happened as 'offensive' and/or 'sexist' would often be formulated by the journalist authoring the article (e.g., Extracts 9 and 10).

Extract 9 (*Daily Mail*, 25 January, p. 6)

```
1. TV bosses reveal what ELSE Gray the soccer sexist said.
```

Extract 10 (*Daily Express*, 25 January, p. 1)

```
1. Now sexist football pair face the boot.
```

More frequently, however, it would be the negative evaluations of 'witnesses', 'friends of the victims', and so on, that got recontextualised via nominalised (Extract 11), attributed (Extract 12) and unattributed (Extract 13) free direct speech.

Extract 11 (*Daily Express*, 25 January, p 3)

```
1. The pair were axed ... amid a growing backlash over their
2. sexist comments
```

Extract 12 (*Daily Star*, 25 January, p. 6)

```
1. Vicki Slee, who played for Arsenal, said: 'they have obviously
2. both been sexist for a long time'.
```

Extract 13 (*Daily Mirror*, 25 January, p. 1)

```
1. The Sky Sports pair were suspended over their 'sexist and patronising'
2. off-air remarks about referee's assistant Sian Massey
```

But while evaluations were authored by witnesses and journalists alike, descriptions would only ever get developed by journalists. And, as will become clear, these journalist-led descriptions failed to provide the sorts of details that could have confirmed the validity of the evaluations alongside which they appeared.

Let us focus here on the issue of 'intent'. One aspect of social interaction that appears 'pretty systematically' to be associated with presenting another's actions in such a way as to warrant a complaint that he or she behaved badly, is a sense that they did what they did *deliberately* (Drew, 1998: 315–16). Descriptions can be formulated such that it becomes difficult to hear the action described as anything other than sexist: 'it' did not just happen, by chance or by accident, but was engineered or knowingly carried out (Wowk, 1984: 77). To be seen to have transgressed, then, is one thing; to be seen to have done so *deliberately* is something else entirely (Edwards, 2008). Across the data, however, one particularly robust finding was the way in which any adequate sense of an intent to offend on the part of either Gray and/or Keys was minimised. What we find instead are recontextualisations in which their actions appear as if not originally intended as sexist. In this way, any evaluation of those actions as unproblematically sexist is rendered readably deniable. Consider Extract 14.

Extract 14 (*Daily Express*, 25 January, p. 3)

```
1. The row erupted after the leaking of their weekend off-air
2. exchange about Ms Massey in which they said women officials
3. 'don't know the offside rule'.
4. Keys, 53, joked: 'Somebody better get down there and
5. explain offside to her'.
```

Of immediate interest here is the action description 'joked' (line 4). Grammatically, the verb 'to joke' functions as a verbal-process-action within the clause beginning 'Keys, 53 [...]'. *Rhetorically*, however, it has another function, hinting at the kind of intent that may well have caused Keys' verbal-process-action. As Marlin (1984: 26) has noted, 'some verbs are ambiguous as to the extent of intentionality implied'. The statements 'James *defaulted*, so that John lost' and 'James *helped* John lose' could both, for example, be used to describe the same end-result: John's loss. But each possibility would bring with it a different understanding of James' role in John's loss: in the former, there would be little implication that James' action – '*defaulting*' – was intended to ensure John's loss, while in the latter there would be a suggestion that his actions – '*helping*' – were intended to bring about that loss. In this case, as Marlin (1984: 28) points out, 'to help' acts as an intention-promoting verb, 'rais[ing] the level of alleged culpability of an agent in relation to some consequence'.

Thinking in terms of intention-promotion is useful when considering the force of 'to joke' in Extract 14. But it is also important to consider the locally specific and situated 'moral work' (Drew, 1998: 295) of choosing this particular action description. In this instance, 'to joke' represents a descriptive possibility *bound up with the reporting of an incident of alleged sexism*. Accordingly, it is not so much the intention-promoting ability *per se* of the action description 'to joke', but its ability to promote a *specific type* of intention that is of analytic interest here. Compare, for example, 'to joke' with 'to ridicule', one of an infinitely extendable number of alternative descriptors. The latter could just as plausibly have been chosen as a way of describing Keys' verbal process action (e.g., 'Keys, 53, then *ridiculed* her knowledge of football [. . .]'). But whereas joking is routinely and unproblematically readable as 'saying or doing something to excite laughter or amusement', ridiculing is routinely and unproblematically readable as saying or doing something 'to make a mockery of someone; or to cause to appear ridiculous' (*Oxford English Dictionary*). Both, then, imply intent. But the intent implied by 'joking', is, *or at least may be readable as,* not quite the same as that involved in the doing of 'ridicule'. To joke is to deliberately intend something, but only where that 'something' is an attempt to make others laugh. Unlike the act of 'ridicule' it may not imply any intent to be *deliberately* hurtful to, or about, some other person(s). In the same way that 'John's loss' could become readable as an unintended consequence of 'James' *defaulting*', then here, in Extract 14, any suggestion of a 'sexist' act can become readable as, at most, the unintended consequence of Keys' '*joke*'.

There is, however, something else about Extract 14 that contributes to this reading: its modal framework. The article from which it is taken has a third-person narrative form. In such a framework, modality can be aligned either with the journalist narrator or located in the viewpoint of a particular character in the story. As a result, and as Simpson (2004: 126) has noted, there is 'considerable scope for ambiguity, and sometimes for irony, in this mode, because we are often less certain about whose point of view exactly is being relayed'. In Extract 14, certain noun phrases (e.g., 'a vile joke'), and certain types of process with evaluative adverbs (e.g., 'embarrassingly, Keys then made a dreadfully sexist joke') would have avoided any sense of ambiguity, making it clear that events were being reported not from Keys' point of view, but from that of the journalist narrator (Halliday, 1994). A verb like 'joked', however, creates uncertainty as to exactly whose point of view is being relayed. Is 'joked' a recontextualisation in which we see the action from Keys' point of view at the time that he made the joke? Or does it represent the journalist narrator's point of view about what Keys had done? Epistemically, there is no way of deciding between these two possibilities. The crucial point here, however, is that *even if we could decide*, neither possibility would provide any sense of Keys' action as intentionally 'sexist': on the one hand, we get something that might plausibly stand as Keys' own interpretation of his actions (i.e., the 'joke' was only ever intended as a 'joke'); and, on the other hand, we get something that might plausibly stand as the journalist's interpretation of Keys' action (i.e., the 'joke' is still, in fact, a 'joke').

By itself, one verb or ambiguous modal framework is not very significant, principally because a series of newspaper articles will usually be varied. But this type of recontextualisation appears throughout the data corpus. In some cases, as in Extract 15 (which has been shortened to avoid copyright issues), the effect is such that Gray and Keys' actions become readable not just as 'unintentionally sexist', but as not even sexist at all.

Extract 15 (*Daily Star*, 28 January, p. 7)

```
1.   Joke gear has pair off to a T.
2.   Clothes firms are cashing in on Gray and Keys
3.   with a series of comedy T-shirts. One says 'Sexist? Do me a
4.   favour, love', which was said by Keys ...
5.   Internet gags include ...
```

What is it that the 'comedy T-shirts' (line 3) and the 'internet gags' (which, according to the *Daily Star*, included photographs of match official Massey holding shopping and a vacuum cleaner) (line 6) take as their direct object? Is it that what Gray and Keys said stands as comedic and/or gag-like? Or is it Gray and Keys themselves and their own peculiarly sexist dispositions? For a number of reasons, the former stands as the most readable possibility. First, because the homographic pun in the headline – 'joke gear has pair *down to a T*' – indexes not just the T-shirts subsequently referred to (line 3), but a sense that those T-shirts, precisely as 'joke gear', have the art of Gray and Keys-esque joking perfected; or, as the idiomatic expression used here would suggest, that they have that art 'down to a T'. Second, because although 'clothes firms' are 'cashing in on' (line 2) Gray and Keys with a series of 'comedy T-Shirts', the extract displays a kind of semantic 'cohesion' that precludes any reading of this as 'cashing in on *their dreadful actions*' (Halliday and Hasan, 1976). The literal, un-modalised re-description of what Keys said (lines 3–4) is tied to the previous, and also un-modalised descriptions of 'comedy T-Shirts' (line 3), and 'joke gear' (line 1). In this sense, the clothes firms appear to be 'cashing in on *Gray and Keys' initial good work*'. Third, and perhaps most importantly, because across this recontextualisation the journalist narrator leaves it unclear as to whether the jokes, and so on, are 'jokes' solely from the point of view of those making the Gray and Keys-esque T-shirts, or whether they are also 'jokes' from the journalist's perspective. As in Extract 14, to use 'comedic' descriptors without then questioning the validity of those descriptors is to allow for Gray and Keys' actions to stand as 'comedic'. And if they were originally intended as 'comedic' then it becomes difficult to read them as having also been intended as 'offensive'. Indeed, the direct invocation of others – 'clothes firms' (line 2) and unnamed internet users (line 6) – who appear to 'get' Gray and Keys' style of humour, provides for an 'externalising device' (Woolgar, 1988: 76): if the 'jokes' are 'jokes' not solely from the idiosyncratic perspective of two lone sexists, but are widely recognised as such by various others, then 'joke' may in fact represent an objective description of what they 'really' are.

Towards a discursive psychology of the media

If, as DP suggests, descriptions are constructive of their objects (Edwards and Potter, 2005: 243), then it is worth starting this conclusion with an acknowledgement that this chapter is itself a description. I have chosen to construct WKP as a *certain kind* of object, deliberately foregrounding just one phenomenon that I claim to have found therein, namely, the 'third party recontextualisation'. Clearly, for other readers, WKP may not 'just' be about this kind of thing; as if 'this kind of thing' were, in fact, the most fundamental and important aspect to the article as a whole. But, as with any topic, to describe is to recontextualise. And so here, on my reading and in my chapter, we can say that an attempt has been made to construct a descriptive vehicle capable of re-appropriating WKP for the project of a *discursive psychology of the media*.

There are at least two good reasons for attempting this re-appropriation. The first has to do with DP's treatment of descriptions/accounts/whatever as the vehicles for social actions exactly like, for instance, '(mis)reading an academic article in a forlorn attempt to boost one's own flagging career and inadequate citations record'. But in the media the stakes are often a little higher than this. If, for instance, a mediated description of [x] (where [x] might represent 'someone's death', 'a case of sexism', or many other things besides) has a large audience and, as a result, a crucial role to play in the public understanding of [x], to treat 'it' as a topic in its own right is to help foreground the discursive, rhetorical and performative strategies, via which that description of [x] has been turned into a vehicle for a particular kind of social action. To know that and how such vehicles are put together matters because they are embedded within the descriptions that help to shape people's understandings of matter; that is, of victims, murderers, journalists, paparazzi, women, 'fucking women', men, bodies, and so on. In this chapter, for instance, we began with the issue of who was to blame for the death of Diana, Princess of Wales, before studying an incident of alleged sexism in the English Premier League. In both cases, we saw how journalists presented other people's accounts of issues like 'culpability' and 'sexism' such that they appeared, to us as readers, as if they really were 'just' those people's own accounts. In neither case did we get any sense that journalists had done anything but pass on descriptive details from their original sources. As a result, we ended up with what looked like those people's own *claims* about culpability/sexism, and those people's own *descriptions* of the actions evidencing the culpability/sexism being claimed. But, as we also saw, those apparently faithful re-descriptions of what people had said had been recontextualised such that *claim* and *description* were no longer in alignment: people could still be seen to be claiming things about culpability and sexism, but only now on the basis of descriptions evidencing actions that we struggled to understand as specifically *culpable* or *sexist* actions. This work of recontextualisation was rhetorically consequential, absolving 'the press' of blame for Diana's death in the first case, and turning 'sexism' into 'just a bit of banter' (or some variant thereof) in the latter. It is an empirical question – and one that any DP-oriented media studies would need to answer on a case-by-case basis – as to whether or not these, or similar, strategies of recontextualisation are at work in other media reports. But given that a large proportion of people get to know about issues like 'who was to blame for Diana's death', or 'an incident of sexism' through precisely the sorts of tabloid generated, third-party vehicles for action that we have analysed here in this chapter, it stands as an empirical question worthy of further study.

The second reason for appropriating DP as a method for studying the media has to do with its attention, across various forms of text and talk-in-interaction, to the situated use of emotion categories and, more generally, our 'rich common sense psychological lexicon' (ibid.: 241). In an era of increasing tabloidization, personalisation and infotainment within and across various forms of media (see Costa Lobo and Curtice, 2015), it is via just such a 'lexicon' that third-party mediated recontextualisations are often developed. To understand why DP is so well suited to the study of this lexicon as a specifically *mediated* lexicon, it is useful to unpack the description produced earlier in this paragraph of DP as a method that attends to 'situated' talk and text. For although well-established textual methods such as critical discourse analysis acknowledge that mediated recontextualisations of things like people's 'internal mental states' (see Machin and Mayr, 2012: 59) may be rhetorically significant, it is usually a curiously un-situated acknowledgement. For instance, and according to Machin and Mayr's otherwise excellent *How to do critical discourse analysis* (2012), 'if we say that someone "cried" and "whispered", the reader is drawn to empathise with them much more so than with a person who only "said"' (ibid.). For DP, however, what 'cried' (for instance) does or does not come to mean is a contextually specific matter. It *could*, of course, be used to pursue empathy. But it could, just as easily, be used to initiate a complaint about someone, to describe someone's unreasonable behaviour, to work up an account of someone's mental health problems, or all of the above at the same time (e.g., see Smith, 1978), or many other things besides. Indeed, as this chapter's analysis of words such as 'grief', 'bitter' and 'joked' has made clear, what mediated words come to mean has less to do with dictionary-style definitions of what they are *supposed* to mean *in most circumstances* than it does with the wider, constantly unfolding syntactical, rhetorical, interactive and/or dialogic and polylogic contexts within which they are used, and within which they absorb and exude situated meanings.

Note

1 This chapter's (not altogether serious) references to the 'remembering' and 'forgetting' of DP's legacy utilises some of Edwards's earlier work (see 1997) on the rhetorical affordances of such terms. Handily, to suggest that all other researchers have 'forgotten' a phenomenon that you yourself have, just this minute, on the back of a fag packet, decided to start labelling as DP's 'legacy' offers you the opportunity to subsequently appear as if initiating the glorious, retrospective (and, of course, highly citable) 'remembering' of that legacy.

References

Antaki, C., Ardévol, E., Núnez, F. and Vayreda, A. (2006) '"For she who knows who she is": Managing accountability in online forum messages', *Journal of Computer-Mediated Communication, 11*: 114–32.

Antaki, C. and Leudar, I. (2001) 'Recruiting the record: Using opponents' exact words in parliamentary argumentation', *Text, 21*: 467–88.

Ashmore, M. (1993) 'The theatre of the blind: Starring a Promethean prankster, a phoney phenomenon, a prism, a pocket, and a piece of wood', *Social Studies of Science, 23*: 67–106.

Ashmore, M. (1995) 'Fraud by numbers: Quantitative rhetoric in the Piltdown forgery discovery', *The South Atlantic Quarterly, 94*: 591–617.

Attenborough, F. (2012a) 'Severe acute respiratory syndrome (SARS) and the rhetorical construction of "bad" scientific work', *Public Understanding of Science, 21*: 211–25.

Attenborough, F. (2012b) 'Sexism re-loaded . . . or sexism re-presented? Irrelevant precision and the British Press', *Feminist Media Studies, 13*: 693–709.

Attenborough, F. (2013) 'Jokes, pranks, blondes and banter: Recontextualising sexism in the British print press', *Journal of Gender Studies, 23*: 137–54.

Attenborough, F. (2014a) 'Rape is rape (except when it's not): The media, recontextualisation and violence against women', *Journal of Language Aggression & Conflict, 2*(2): 183–203.

Attenborough, F. (2014b) 'Words, contexts, politics', *Gender and Language, 8*: 137–145.

Costa Lobo, M. and Curtice, J. (eds) (2015) *Personality politics? The role of leader evaluations in deeocratic Elections.* Oxford: Oxford University Press.

Drew, P. (1998) 'Complaints about transgressions and misconduct', *Research on Language & Social Interaction, 31*: 295–325.

Edwards, D. (1995) 'Sacks and psychology', *Theory & Psychology, 5*: 579–96.

Edwards, D. (1997) *Discourse and Cognition.* London: Sage.

Edwards, D. (2006) 'Discourse, cognition and social practices: The rich surface of language and social interaction', *Discourse Studies, 8*: 41–9.

Edwards, D. (2008) 'Intentionality and *mens rea* in police interrogations: The production of actions as crimes', *Intercultural Pragmatics, 5*: 177–99.

Edwards, D. (2012) 'Discursive and scientific psychology', *British Journal of Social Psychology, 51*: 425–35.

Edwards, D. and Potter, J. (2005) 'Discursive psychology, mental states and descriptions', in H. te Molder and J. Potter (eds) *Conversation and cognition* (pp. 241–59). Cambridge: Cambridge University Press.

Fairclough N. (2010) *Critical discourse analysis: The critical study of language.* Harlow: Pearson Education.

Garfinkel, H. (1967) *Studies in ethnomethodology.* Englewood Cliffs, NJ: Prentice-Hall.

Goffman, E. (1979) 'Footing', *Semiotica, 25*: 1–29.

Goodwin, C. (1994) 'Professional vision', *American Anthropologist, 96*: 606–33.

Halliday, M.A.K. (1994) *An introduction to functional grammar.* London: Edward Arnold.

Halliday, M.A.K. and Hasan, R. (1976) *Cohesion in English.* London: Longman.

Horne, J. and Wiggins, S. (2009) 'Doing being "on the edge": Managing the dilemma of being authentically suicidal in an online forum', *Sociology of Health & Illness, 31*: 170–84.

Jayyusi, L. (1984) *Categorization and the moral order*. London: Routledge.

Lamerichs, J. and te Molder, H. (2003) 'Computer-mediated communication: From a cognitive to a discursive model', *New Media & Society*, 5: 451–73.

Machin, A. and Mayr, A. (2012) *How to do critical discourse analysis*. London: Sage.

MacMillan, K. (2002) 'Narratives of social disruption: Education news in the British tabloid press', *Discourse: Studies in the Cultural Politics of Education*, 23: 27–38.

MacMillan, K. and Edwards, D. (1999) 'Who killed the Princess? Description and blame in the British press', *Discourse Studies*, 1: 151–74.

Marlin, R. (1984) 'The rhetoric of action description', *Informal Logic*, 6: 26–9.

Richardson, J.E. (2007) *Analysing newspapers: An approach from critical discourse analysis*. Basingstoke: Palgrave.

Romaniuk, T. (2009) 'The Clinton cackle: Hillary Rodham Clinton's laughter in news interviews', *Crossroads of Language, Interaction, & Culture*, 7: 17–49.

Simpson, P. (2004) *Stylistics*. London: Routledge.

Smith, D. (1978) 'K is mentally ill: The anatomy of a factual account', *Sociology*, 12: 23–53.

Sneijder, P. and te Molder, H. (2005) 'Moral logic and logical morality: Attributions of responsibility and blame in online discourse on veganism', *Discourse & Society*, 16: 675–96.

Stivers, T. and Sidnell, J. (2013) 'Introduction', in J. Sidnell and T. Stivers (eds) *The handbook of conversation analysis* (pp. 1–8). Oxford: John Wiley & Sons.

Stokoe, E. and Edwards, D. (2009) 'Accomplishing social action with identity categories: Mediating neighbour complaints', in M. Wetherell (ed.) *Theorizing identities and social action* (pp. 95–115). Sage: London.

Tileagă, C. (2011) '(Re)writing biography: Memory, identity and textually mediated reality in coming to terms with the past', *Culture & Psychology*, 17: 197–215.

Vetterling-Braggin, M. (ed.) (1981) *Sexist language*. New York: Littlefield Adams.

Wales, K. (2011) *A dictionary of stylistics*. Harlow: Longman.

Woolgar, S. (1988) *Science: The very idea!* Chichester: Ellis Horwood.

Wowk, M. (1984) 'Blame allocation, sex and gender in a murder interrogation', *Women's Studies International Forum*, 7: 75–82.

Part IV
Prejudice, racism and nationalism

16 Re-theorizing prejudice in social psychology
From cognition to discourse

Martha Augoustinos

Target article: Billig, M. (1985) 'Prejudice, categorization and particularization: From a perceptual to a rhetorical approach', *European Journal of Social Psychology*, 15: 79–103.

This chapter examines the significant impact Billig's (1985) classic paper, 'Prejudice, categorization and particularization: From a perceptual to a rhetorical approach', has had on re-theorizing prejudice in social psychology, and for providing a conceptual and empirical foundation upon which to build an alternative and influential body of discursive psychological research on prejudice. Billig's critical questioning of perceptual and cognitive models of prejudice challenged the commonly held view in social psychology that prejudice was an inevitable, albeit unfortunate, consequence of categorization. In arguing for a rhetorical rather than a cognitive approach to categorization, Billig encouraged the development of a language-based approach to prejudice that examines how prejudice is discursively constituted in both formal discourse and everyday social interaction. This body of work has found that far from being rigid, hostile and dogmatic, everyday prejudice is accomplished by the use of flexible linguistic resources and contradictory rhetorical arguments that reproduce and justify racial and social inequalities. The implications of this discursive research for current and future social psychological theories of prejudice are discussed.

Categorization: 'Prejudice is more than perception'

By the time Billig published this seminal article in 1985 cognitive models of prejudice had become firmly entrenched in social psychology. As Billig emphasised then, this was no small measure to the significant impact of Gordon Allport's seminal work, *The nature of prejudice* (1954). Allport's definition of prejudice as 'an antipathy based upon a faulty and inflexible generalization' (Allport, 1954: 9) about a social group and its members emphasized the prominent role that social categorization and stereotyping were given as 'normal' and 'natural' perceptual-cognitive processes. According to Allport and subsequent social cognition models, categorizing people into their respective group memberships (such as race, gender, age) is driven by our cognitive need to simplify the overwhelming amount of information we receive from our environment. This group-based or category-based perception is seen as distorting reality because people are not viewed as individuals but rather as prototypical group members. In turn, this leads to stereotyping which implicitly is just one step away from prejudice – literally pre-judging someone based solely on their group membership. This inextricable relationship between categorization, stereotyping and prejudice is central to contemporary social cognition models of prejudice and, notwithstanding some of the qualifications that recent research has placed on this directional, and by implication, causative link between these three processes (see below), it is nonetheless the case that categorization in and of itself is seen as the cognitive basis for prejudice, driven primarily by our limited processing capacities.

Billig's concerns about the pessimistic implications of cognitive models of prejudice were to be eclipsed, however, by the automaticity literature that has dominated social psychology since the 1990s (Dijksterhuis, 2010; Dijksterhuis, Chartrand and Aarts, 2007; Wegner and Bargh, 1998). This body of influential work has sought to demonstrate through laboratory experimentation that perception and behaviour that is 'mindless' – that is, occurs spontaneously beyond an individual's conscious awareness – constitutes a significant part of our everyday thinking. More specifically that social psychological processes such as categorization and stereotyping occur automatically and outside conscious awareness through repetition and practice. According to the automaticity literature humans are primarily 'cognitive misers' (Fiske and Taylor, 1991) who engage in conscious deliberate processing only if necessary. Categorical thinking that utilizes heuristic shortcuts and stereotypic expectancies is the default option. Indeed, Bargh (1999) has described stereotyping as a 'cognitive monster' that is difficult to control and claims that up to 99.44 percent of our thoughts and actions are automatically driven (Bargh, 1997).

This even more pessimistic view, that everyone is subject to the automatic activation of stereotypes, regardless of their attitudes and values, was initially reported in Devine's (1989) landmark study. Devine found that negative stereotypes associated with African Americans could be automatically activated outside of conscious awareness among both low and high prejudiced people. During conscious processing, however, low prejudice people inhibit the negative stereotype of African Americans and replace it with their egalitarian beliefs and norms. In contrast, high prejudice people are less likely to inhibit the stereotype, because it is consistent with their beliefs about the group. Devine therefore argued that there was a *dissociation* between unconscious and conscious processing of stereotypes. In a round-about way then, Devine's dissociation model side-stepped the gloomy picture that had previously been painted about the inevitability of prejudice. Yes, stereotyping is difficult to inhibit at the unconscious level, but stereotyping and prejudice, although related, are not necessarily the same thing. Prejudice is a much more complex phenomenon, comprised of a constellation of concerns tied to beliefs, values, and social identity. This is in fact what Billig argued in 1985, that 'prejudice is more than perception' (p. 85) and what early discourse analytic research on prejudice and racism was beginning to highlight (Potter and Wetherell, 1987; van Dijk, 1987).

Particularization: 'For any given psychological process, one should look for an opposing process'

Despite the increasing popularity of Devine's dissociation model of prejudice and its parsimonious account of stereotyping and prejudice by differentiating them as distinct psychological phenomena, there are now many studies challenging the view that category-based perception is mindless and unaffected by perceivers' goals, motivations and beliefs (Macrae and Quadflieg, 2010; Dijksterhuis, 2010). Several studies purport to demonstrate that stereotype activation is indeed moderated by perceivers' prejudiced beliefs: specifically that people high in prejudice are more likely to activate racial stereotypes outside conscious awareness than people with egalitarian beliefs (Johns, Cullum, Smith, and Freng, 2008; Lepore and Brown, 1997; Locke, McLeod and Walker, 1994). Studies have also found that perceivers' intentions, motivations and goals have moderating effects on the automatic activation of group stereotypes (Blair and Banaji, 1996; Macrae et al., 1997), which have tempered some of the extreme claims that have been made regarding the degree to which human thought and behaviour is 'mindless'. Such findings have led to a shift away from the cognitive miser metaphor of social cognition, to a metaphor of the person as a 'motivated tactician': that 'thinking is for doing' (Fiske, 1992). Again, this is precisely what Billig argued for in 1985. Likening categorization models of prejudice to 'bureaucratic models' of thinking that privilege efficiency and order over flexibility and creativity, Billig turns his attention to a psychological process that is the opposite of categorization: particularization.

Indeed one of the enduring enigmas is that in everyday social interaction, outside the confines of the laboratory where stimuli are strictly controlled, people can be categorized in multiple ways; the same person can be categorized as a woman, as black, as a lawyer, as a mother, as a feminist. What determines which category gets activated or used in everyday settings and how does category selection attend to the interactional needs of social interaction? Billig (1985) specifically attends to the problem of category selection, arguing that the process of categorization is closely bound to an opposing force – particularization. He writes:

> Even when the perceptual model is considered, there is no reason for supposing that it is non-problematical which category or schema will be selected for processing incoming information. One should not assume that there is one relevant schema always lurking just behind the eye, waiting to pounce on the unsuspecting iconic image, for that space behind the eyes must be overcrowded with numerous lurking schemas, all with broadly

similar intentions. For any instance, one would need to explain how one schema is able to leap out quicker than its rivals in order to rob the iconic image of its riches.

(Billig, 1985: 90)

Billig's critique of the rigid and inflexible conceptualisation of categorization by both social and cognitive psychologists became a significant precursor to the emergence of an entirely new approach to categorization that has its roots in language and discourse. Potter and Wetherell's (1987) ground-breaking book, *Discourse and social psychology*, offered a conceptual and empirical alternative to the study of categorization, much of it drawing on Billig's 1985 critique. Rather than treating categories as rigid *a priori* cognitive entities lurking in the mind, waiting to be switched on and off, discursive psychology emphasized that people constituted categories in talk and social interaction to do certain things. Potter and Wetherell (1987: 116) argued:

> Instead of seeing categorization as a natural phenomenon – something which just happens, automatically – it is regarded as a complex and subtle social accomplishment ... this ... emphasizes the action orientation of categorization in discourse. It asks how categories are flexibly articulated in the course of certain sorts of talk and writing to accomplish particular goals, such as blamings or justifications.

Building on this work, Derek Edwards (1991) argued that 'categories are for talking', describing categorization as '*something we do, in talk,* in order to accomplish social actions (persuasions, blamings, denial, refutations, accusations, etc.)' (1991: 517; original emphasis). Unlike traditional psychology, that treats categories as uncontested and non-problematic social objects, perceived directly through identifiable physical and social features, discursive psychology emphasised how categories themselves are constituted in discourse in flexible ways. Categorization is not simply a perceptual-cognitive process based on direct and veridical perception, but a discursive practice that actively constructs versions of reality and identities for speakers and others (see also Chapters 12 and 13 in this volume).

In keeping with Billig's maxim regarding the selective and flexible nature of categorization, categories used in talk are expected to be variable, flexible, and shifting, depending on their functional and contextual use. Categorization may be inevitable, but as Billig argues, there is nothing inevitable about the particular category, or the content of the category, that is selected in any instance. The aim of discursive psychology is to examine how categories are used in specific instances and the interactional and rhetorical work they perform in being used in this way (Edwards and Potter, 1992). Thus categories are treated as discursive resources rather than reified cognitive templates to organise or simplify perception (Edwards, 1997).

Discursive psychology's approach to categorization has been strongly influenced by Harvey Sacks' (1995) work in ethnomethodology and conversation analysis, which examines how categories are used in naturally-occurring conversation and social interaction. This is in stark contrast to the experimental stimuli used in laboratory experiments that seek to understand the assumed perceptual and cognitive processes that underlie categorization and stereotyping. Inside the laboratory social categories are used unproblematically as verbal stimuli in experimental procedures designed to elicit either implicit or explicit evaluative responses. Outside the laboratory, however, in everyday talk and social interaction, social categories, even seemingly mundane categories, are used in flexible and context-specific ways. Examining how categories are deployed in everyday talk and what work they perform in social interaction has led to a significant tradition of research known as membership categorization analysis or MCA (Lepper, 2000; Watson, 1997), a tradition that has developed largely in parallel to psychological theories of categorization.

As Sacks (1995) has shown, categorizations are selections from a broad range of possible available alternatives. Unlike social cognition models of categorization, membership categories are not treated as 'storehouses' of decontextualized meaning, but come to have meaning in specific contexts (Lepper, 2000). Membership categorizations are therefore not objective blocks of description or cognitive templates (cognitive schemas) waiting to be activated, but are built up sequentially in interaction in order to accomplish a range of social actions (see Chapters 12 and 13, this volume).

Categories in race talk

In emphasizing the flexible and context-specific nature of categorization and particularization, Billig's paper argued for examining how categories are used in everyday conversation and institutional talk on prejudice. In one of the first and most ambitious social psychological studies of this kind, and drawing extensively on Billig's scholarship, Wetherell and Potter's *Mapping the language of racism* (1992) presents a systematic and detailed analysis of the language of racism and prejudice in New Zealand. Based on a corpus of interviews with Pakeha (white majority) respondents and an analysis of historical texts and documents, one of the aims of this research was to analyze how social categories are mobilized or actively built in discourse to construct different social and 'racial' identities, and to provide accounts that legitimate group differences as 'real' and 'natural'. Wetherell and Potter (1992), found the categories of 'race' and 'culture' were used by the Pakeha majority as contrastive categories to define the Maori people as a distinct biological group of people who shared similar physical characteristics, values and personality characteristics. These categories were used predominantly to contrast Maori with the Pakeha majority, which was represented as the 'norm' of New Zealand society. While many of the respondents spoke favourably of a Maori cultural identity, ultimately this identity was viewed as secondary to a homogeneous and unifying 'national' identity. The category of 'nation' was used in Pakeha talk to limit and constrain the aspirations of a Maori identity, which was seen to undermine and threaten national unity. Indeed, nationalist discourse of this kind is also a ubiquitous feature of contemporary 'race' talk (Rapley, 1998). As Billig (1985: 97) argues: 'any assignment of a particular instance to a general category is potentially contestable, by an argument based on particularization'.

In our own work on race talk in Australia we found similar instances where speakers challenged and contested the category of Indigenous or Aboriginal Australians. In the extract below a participant in a focus group discussion on intergroup relations in Australia argues that the emphasis on social and cultural identities other than 'Australian' is divisive and undermining of national unity: that Aboriginal-Australians and other ethnic minorities must see themselves first and foremost as Australians (group facilitator responses are in parentheses).

Extract 1: Focus group discussion (Augoustinos, Tuffin & Rapley, 1999)

```
I especially think that it's going to be better for
Aborigines if they do get more people like Kathy
Freeman that doesn't look at the racist aspects but
[Mmm] sets her mind to the goal that I'm an
Australian and this is where I want to be [Yes]. And
I think that's a big thing with racism that people
see it as that they're Aborigines or that they're
from a different ethnic group but no one seems to
see that we're Australians? That's a a big point
that that really gets me that everyone's got their
own small minority groups [Mmm] you're either Anglo-
Saxon or you're something else and you seem to fit
nicely into it [Yep]. But the fact that we're
Australians is forgotten and I think that until
people start to realise it that regardless of what
we are, we're Australians, it's always going to
continue.
```

Wetherell and Potter (1992) have described the practice of categorizing at the level of the nation to minimize differences between people and instead highlight commonalities as a 'togetherness repertoire'. Although privileging a superordinate national identity can function to emphasise social inclusion, paradoxically, it can also work to undermine the legitimacy of minority groups having their varied cultural and social identities recognised and affirmed. Thus, existing differences in culture, history, language, and ethnicity are to be subsumed (even negated) by appealing to the nationalist moral imperative to identify collectively at the level of the nation state. As Billig suggests, the flexible and fluid use of privileging the category of nation over race can be occasioned by the prejudiced and the tolerant alike, depending on the context of its use.

A rhetorical and discursive approach to prejudice

By emphasizing the argumentative qualities of categorization and particularization Billig draws on classical rhetorical theory dating back to Aristotle's *Rhetorica* to examine the dilemmatic and contrary structure that is to be found in everyday sense-making practices. Elaborating these ideas further in *Arguing and thinking* (1987) and *Ideological dilemmas* (Billig et al., 1988), Billig gave birth to a new tradition of scholarship in the discipline – rhetorical psychology. By arguing for a rhetorical rather than a cognitive approach to prejudice specifically, Billig paved the way to examining the actual language of prejudice, in both formal discourse and everyday social interaction. Indeed, rhetoric and argumentation became a significant influence in shaping the development of discursive psychology and is today a core feature of discursive research (Augoustinos and Tileagă, 2012; Potter, 1998).

Adorno et al.'s (1950) *The authoritarian personality* reinforced the view in psychology that prejudice and tolerance were associated with distinct cognitive styles. In doing so, the categories of the 'prejudiced individual' and the 'tolerant individual' became reified as personality types with clear definitional boundaries. Indeed, this binary contrast between prejudice and tolerance has continued in recent psychological theorizing such as Devine's (1989) dissociation model of prejudice and in more recent personality approaches such as right-wing authoritarianism (Altemeyer,1998) and social dominance orientation (Sidianius and Pratto, 1999). In sharp contrast, discursive research on prejudice has found that, far from being rigid, hostile and dogmatic, everyday prejudice is accomplished by the use of linguistic resources and rhetorical arguments that are combined flexibly to justify racial and social inequalities in ways that deny or disavow a prejudiced identity. As Billig (1991) emphasizes, the common sense notion of 'prejudice' – to pre-judge – has become associated with irrationality, poor reasoning, and unexamined views. Prejudice is therefore recognised as violating a common sense belief in the values of reason and rationality, which have become the very underpinnings of democratic societies.

Again Wetherell and Potter's (1992) research in New Zealand is perhaps the best exemplar of this work. They detail how Pakeha respondents were proficient in the use of a range of liberal-egalitarian arguments that drew on principles of freedom, fairness, individual rights, and equal opportunity in talk about Maori–Pakeha relations. Their analysis identified how Pakeha talk was organised flexibly around ten common, 'rhetorically self-sufficient' or 'clinching' arguments that were recurrently drawn upon by respondents to justify their views. These arguments were described as providing a basic accountability and possessing a rhetorical robustness based on their common sense appeal to liberal-egalitarian values. These rhetorically self-sufficient arguments included:

1. Resources should be used productively and in a cost-effective manner.
2. Nobody should be compelled.
3. Everybody should be treated equally.
4. You cannot turn the clock backwards.
5. Present generations cannot be blamed for the mistakes of past generations.
6. Injustices should be righted.
7. Everybody can succeed if they try hard enough.
8. Minority opinion should not carry more weight than majority opinion.
9. We have to live in the twentieth (twenty-first) century.
10. You have to be practical.

(Wetherell and Potter, 1992: 177)

These stock devices are described as 'rhetorically self-sufficient' because they required little elaboration or further warrant from speakers. Importantly Wetherell and Potter (1992) argue that these common sense maxims should not be viewed as cognitive templates or schemas that underlie racist discourse, but rather as 'tools' or 'resources' that are combined in variable ways by speakers to do certain things, most notable of which is to avoid a 'racist' identity and to justify existing social relations. Like Billig et al. (1988), Wetherell and Potter argue for the fragmentary, dilemmatic and contradictory nature of people's views, rather than seeing them as enduring, stable and consistent cognitive responses that can be easily categorized as 'prejudiced' or 'tolerant'.

These 'self-sufficient' arguments were also found in the public debate in Australia on whether to apologise to Indigenous Australians for historical injustices and were recurrently drawn upon by the Australian public in letters to a newspaper website (LeCouteur and Augoustinos, 2001) and in political discourse (Augoustinos, LeCouteur and Soyland, 2002) in arguments opposing a national apology. For example, the extract below comes from a speech the then Prime Minister of Australia, John Howard, made to the Reconciliation Convention in May 1997. In this speech Howard justifies his refusal to offer a national apology on behalf of the nation for past injustices against Indigenous people, specifically, for the forced removal of Indigenous children from their families and communities – who came to be called the 'Stolen Generations'. In this extract, Howard draws definitional boundaries around what 'Reconciliation' should mean to Australians by listing what he perceives as 'threats to reconciliation' despite interjections (boos: lines 65 and 70) from the audience and demands that he apologise (l. 82).

Extract 2: Prime Minister Howard's Address at the Reconciliation Convention, May, 1997

```
64  H:  .hhh but this optimism (.3) my friends (.3) about the
65  A:                          [boo]
66  H:  reconciliation process cannot be blind (.3) .hhh we must
67  A:                                              [yeah]
```

```
68  H:  be realistic (.2) in acknowledging some of the threat-s
69      (.2).hhh to reconciliation (.5) RECONCILIAION will not
70  A:                                  [boo]
71  H:  work .hhh (.) if it puts a higher value (.) on symbolic
72      gesture::s .hhh and over (.) b-lowen promises .hhh (.)
73      rather than the practical needs of Aboriginal .hhh and
74      Torres Strait Islanders .hhh in areas like health (.2)
75      HOUSING (.2) education and employment (.4) .hhh it will
76      not WORK if it is premised solely .hhh on a sense of
77      national guilt (.) and SHAME (.3) .hhh RATHER we should
78      acknowledge PAST injustices (.2).hhh and focus our
79      energies on addressing the root causes (.3) of current
80      (.) and future disadvantage .hhh among (.) our Indigenous
81      People (.3).hhh NOR ladies and gentleman .hhh will the
82  A:              [apologise]
83  H:  reconciliation process work effectively (.3) .hhh if one
84      of its central purposes (.2).hhh becomes the
85      establishment of different systems of accountability .hhh
86      and lawful conduct .hhh among Australians on the basis of
87      their race (.) or any other factor (.3).hhh the
88      reconciliation process (.) .hhh will only work
89      effectively (.) .hhh if it involve::s (.) and inspires
90      all Australians (.3).hhh RECONCILIATION is not helped
91      (.2) .hhh if its critics are able to claim .hhh that
92      resources directed towards Aboriginal .hhh and Torres
93      Strait Islander people who are disadvantaged (.3) .hhh
94      have not been well (.) or wisely used
```

Howard constructs a particular version of reconciliation by invoking several self-sufficient rhetorical arguments in succession; all premised on common sense, and all requiring little further elaboration or supportive argumentation. In lines 66–8, there is an appeal to the argument, 'you have to be practical' by emphasising the importance of being realistic. In lines 71–4, Howard sets up a specific contrast between 'symbolic gestures' and 'practical needs', arguing for the importance of the latter: an argument that is unlikely to attract disagreement given the significant importance of Indigenous peoples' needs in 'health, housing, education and employment'. These practical needs, however, are not mutually exclusive to symbolic needs such as a national apology for past practices. This binary contrast between the practical and the symbolic was recurrently used by the government to contrast their preferred approach to reconciliation to that of Indigenous leaders, most of whom represented a national apology as a symbolic *prerequisite* to reconciliation. In arguing that reconciliation will not work if it is based on a sense of national guilt and shame about the past, as opposed to redressing 'current and future' Indigenous disadvantage (lines 76–81) also invokes – implicitly at least – that 'present generations cannot be blamed for the mistakes of past generations'. Indeed this was the government's favoured justification for refusing to apologise: an apology implies guilt and shame, present generations should not be burdened in this way given that they are not personally responsible for things that happened in the past.

An explicit contrast between the past and the present/future is also evident in this argument. Reconciliation will not work if it is based on the shame and guilt associated with past injustices; rather we should focus on the here and now and, of course, the future. This reasoning is implicitly linked to the self-sufficient argument that 'you cannot change the past'. Last, in arguing that reconciliation will not work if it establishes 'different systems of accountability and lawful conduct' (lines 85–7), Howard draws upon the self-sufficient argument that 'everyone should be treated equally'. Again this central tenet of liberal egalitarianism is rhetorically robust given its normative status in liberal democracies.

Thus, we see the mobilisation of four self-sufficient rhetorical arguments in close succession: you have to be practical; present generations cannot be blamed for the mistakes of past generations; you cannot turn back the clock; and everybody should be treated equally. These commonplaces establish the rhetorical boundaries of Howard's version of reconciliation via systematically undermining alternative constructions.

As Wetherell and Potter (1992) so clearly demonstrated in their analysis of Pakeha talk, these arguments can be combined in flexible ways to justify and rationalise positions that ultimately contribute to the continued oppression and disadvantage of minorities. But, in keeping with Billig's emphasis on the dilemmatic and contrary nature of common sense, these arguments can also be mobilised in arguing in favour of an apology. One of the most pervasive arguments in favour of an apology was that 'injustices should be righted', and that an apology was the first step towards this end. The lack of recognition of Indigenous grievances, and the failure to apologise, was represented as preventing the nation from moving forward to a better future.

On 13 February, 2008, newly elected Prime Minister Kevin Rudd finally offered a formal apology to Indigenous Australians. Rudd's apology was a set-piece political address that systematically attended to previous arguments against an apology, often using the same rhetorical arguments but in contrary and flexible ways, in this case to justify the apology (Augoustinos, Hastie, and Wright, 2011; Hastie and Augoustinos, 2012). In the extract below, Rudd constructs the apology as a means by which the nation can fully reconcile with its past and by doing so unify the nation, enabling it to move towards a more positive future.

Extract 3: PM Rudd's Apology: 13 February, 2008

```
201  As has been said of settler societies elsewhere (.4) .hhh
202  we are the bearers of many blessings from our ancestors
203  (.4) and therefore (.5) we must also be the bearer (.3)
204  of their burden::s (.) as well (2) .hhh THEREFORE for our
205  nation the course of action is clear (1) THEREFORE for
206  our people (.3) the course of action (.) is clear
207  (.6).hhh and that is to deal now with what has become one
208  of the darkest chapters in Australia's history (1) .hhh
209  in doing SO (.7) we are doing mor:e than contending with
210  the facts the evidence and the often rancorous public
211  debate (.5) .hhh in doing so we are also wrestling with
212  our own soul (1) .hhh THIS IS NOT AS SOME WOULD ARGUE a
213  black armband view of history (1) it's just the truth
214  (.5) the cold (.5) confronting (.3) uncomfortable (.4)
215  truth (.8) .hhh FACING with it (.7) DEALING with it (.9)
216  moving on from it (1.4) and until we fully confront that
217  truth (.3) there will always be a shadow hanging over us
218  and our future (.) .hhh as a fully united and fully
219  reconciled people (1) .hhh IT'S TIME to reconcile (.4)
220  IT'S TIME to recognise the injustices of the past (.7)
221  IT'S TIME (.3) to say sorry (.6).hhh IT'S TIME (.3) to
222  move forward together
```

By highlighting that the past has brought both 'blessings' and 'burdens' (lines 202–4), Rudd provides a counter to the temporal arguments 'that you cannot change the past', and that 'present generations cannot be blamed for mistakes of past generations'. To deny our connections to the past is then to deny the blessings 'we' have also received. Rather than living in the past, turning the clock back to 'one of the darkest chapters in Australia's history' (lines 207–8), and apologising is constructed here as a 'clear' 'course of action' (lines 205–6) in response to mistakes of the past. The facticity of the Stolen Generations is also constructed as beyond doubt by Rudd: 'the facts, the evidence', 'just the truth: the cold, confronting, uncomfortable truth' (lines 212–13). This contrasts with the Howard government's denial that there was a Stolen Generation' (Augoustinos et al., 2002).

In recognising this 'truth', Rudd also deploys a healing metaphor: Australians must 'wrestle with our own soul' (lines 210–11) in order to 'confront the truth'. Failure to acknowledge this truth will lead to a 'shadow hanging over us and our future' (line 216). Hence, we cannot move forward into the future until we have dealt with the past. Moving forward together is made contingent on recognition and acknowledgment of the past, again resisting the temporal self-sufficient arguments that 'you cannot turn back the clock' and 'you have to live in the twentieth [first] century'.

The historical significance of the apology offered to Indigenous Australians cannot be over-stated and has been described as a watershed moment in Australia's history (e.g., Manne, 2008). The psychological significance of the apology is also of great import, not only for the recipients of the apology – Indigenous Australians – but also as a significant site for examining how rhetorical arguments previously identified as central to formal and informal discourse on 'race' can be effectively undermined.

Conclusion

In arguing for a rhetorical rather than a cognitive approach to prejudice, Billig's seminal 1985 paper sowed the seeds for constructionist and critical approaches to understanding the contemporary nature of prejudice. Significantly, it gave rise to a distinctive discursive psychological approach that examined the linguistic and rhetorical details of both everyday prejudice in social interaction and its articulation and reproduction in institutional discourse. This body of work has provided a contrast to traditional psychological approaches challenging both cognitive and personality theories that have dominated the discipline. As Wetherell and Potter argue (1992: 208), by representing prejudice as a state of mind, as 'a failure of inner-directed empathy and intellect, rather than a social pathology, shaped by power relations and the conflicting vested interests of groups', social psychology has colluded in conceptualizing prejudice as an individual pathology requiring attitudinal change rather than political action and social change. The individualization of prejudice has been referred to by Wetherell (2012) as the 'prejudice problematic', and discursive psychology along with other critical approaches (e.g., Dixon and Levine, 2012; Hopkins, Reicher and Levine, 1997), are producing new forms of knowledge that attend to the interactional and collaborative social practices that reproduce and sustain prejudice. Inspired by Billig, this body of work is challenging the pessimistic assumption that prejudice is a psychological by-product of human cognition and that solutions to its amelioration lie primarily within individual minds. Rather, drawing on Billig's dialectical and rhetorical approach, it emphasizes the fluid and flexible contours of both prejudice and tolerance and how they intersect to produce ambivalent and contradictory argumentative threads. Again this ambivalence should not simply be located in the psychology of individuals as several theories of modern racism have purported, but in the ideological dilemmas inherent in widely shared liberal tropes premised on the principles of rationality, practicality, individual rights and equality: arguments that can be flexibly juxtaposed as we argue and debate notions of fairness and justice.

References

Adorno, T.W., Frenkel-Brunswik, E., Levinson, D.J. and Sanford, R.N. (1950) *The authoritarian personality*. New York: Harper & Row.

Allport, G.W. (1954) *The nature of prejudice*. Reading, MA: Addison-Wesley.

Altemeyer, R.W. (1998) 'The other authoritarian personality', *Advances in Experimental Social Psychology*, 30: 47–91.

Augoustinos, M. and Tileagă, C. (2012) 'Twenty-five years of discursive psychology', *British Journal of Social Psychology*, 51: 405–12.

Augoustinos, M., Hastie, B. and Wright, M. (2011) 'Apologising for historical injustice: Emotion, truth and identity in political discourse', *Discourse & Society*, 22: 1–25.

Augoustinos, M., LeCouteur, A. and Soyland, J. (2002) 'Self-sufficient arguments in political rhetoric: Constructing reconciliation and apologizing to the stolen generations', *Discourse & Society*, 13: 105–42.

Bargh, J.A. (1997) 'The automaticity of everyday life', in R.S. Wyer, Jnr (ed.) *Advances in social cognition* (Vol. 10, pp. 1–61). Mahwah, NJ: Erlbaum.

Bargh, J.A. (1999) 'The cognitive monster: The case against controllability of automatic stereotype effects', in S. Chaiken and Y. Trope (eds) *Dual process theories in social psychology*. New York: Guilford.

Billig, M. (1985) 'Prejudice, categorization and particularization: From a perceptual to a rhetorical approach', *European Journal of Social Psychology*, 15: 79–103.

Billig, M. (1987) *Arguing and thinking: A rhetorical approach to social psychology*. Cambridge: Cambridge University Press.

Billig, M. (1991) *Ideology, rhetoric and opinions*. London: Sage.

Billig, M., Condor, S., Edwards, M., Middleton, D. and Radley, A. (1988) *Ideological dilemmas: A social psychology of everyday thinking*. London: Sage.

Blair, I.V. and Banaji, M.R. (1996) 'Automatic and controlled processes in gender stereotyping', *Journal of Personality & Social Psychology*, 70: 1142–63.

Devine, P.G. (1989) 'Stereotypes and prejudice: Their automatic and controlled components', *Journal of Personality & Social Psychology*, 56: 5–18.

Dijksterhuis, A. (2010) 'Automaticity and the unconscious', in S.T. Fiske, D.T. Gilbert and G. Lindzey (eds) *Handbook of social psychology* (Vol. X, pp. 228–67). New York: Wiley.

Dijksterhuis, A., Chartrand, T.L. and Aarts, H. (2007) 'Effects of priming and perception on social behavior and goal pursuit', in J.A. Bargh (ed.) *Social psychology and the unconscious: The automaticity of higher mental processes* (pp. 51–132). Philadelphia: Psychology Press.

Dixon, J. and Levine M. (2012) (eds) *Beyond prejudice: Extending the social psychology of conflict, inequality and social change*. Cambridge: Cambridge University Press.

Edwards, D. (1991) 'Categories are for talking: On the cognitive and discursive bases of categorization', *Theory & Psychology*, 1: 515–42.

Edwards, D. (1997) *Discourse and cognition*. London: Sage.

Edwards, D. and Potter, J. (1992) *Discursive psychology*. London: Sage.

Fiske, S.T. (1992) 'Thinking is for doing: Portraits of social cognition from Daguerreotypes to Laserphoto', *Journal of Personality & Social Psychology*, 63: 877–89.

Fiske, S.T. and Taylor, S.E. (1991) *Social cognition*. New York: McGraw-Hill.

Hastie, B. and Augoustinos, M. (2012) 'Rudd's apology to the Stolen Generations: Challenging self-sufficient arguments in "race" discourse', *Australian Psychologist*, 47: 118–26.

Hopkins, N., Reicher, S. and Levine, M. (1997) 'On the parallels between social cognition and the "new racism"', *British Journal of Social Psychology*, 36: 305–29.

Johns, M., Cullum, J., Smith, T. and Freng, S. (2008) 'Internal motivation to respond without prejudice and automatic egalitarian goal activation', *Journal of Experimental Social Psychology*, 44: 1514–19.

LeCouteur, A. and Augoustinos, M. (2001) 'Apologising to the Stolen Generations: Argument, rhetoric and identity in public reasoning', *Australian Psychologist*, 36: 51–61.

Lepore, L. and Brown, R. (1997) 'Category and stereotype activation: Is prejudice inevitable?', *Journal of Personality & Social Psychology*, 72: 275–87.

Lepper, G. (2000) *Categories in text and talk*. London: Sage.

Locke, V., MacLeod, C. and Walker, I. (1994) 'Automatic and controlled activation of stereotypes: Individual differences associated with prejudice', *British Journal of Social Psychology*, 33: 29–46.

Macrae, C.N. and Quadflieg, S. (2010) 'Perceiving people', in S.T. Fiske, D.T. Gilbert and G. Lindzey (eds) *Handbook of social psychology* (Vol. X, pp. 428–63). New York: McGraw-Hill.

Macrae, C.N., Bodenhausen, G.V., Milne, A.B., Thorn, T.M.J. and Castelli, L. (1997) 'On the activation of social stereotypes: The moderating role of processing objectives', *Journal of Experimental Social Psychology*, 33: 471–89.

Manne, R. (2008, March) 'Sorry business: The road to the apology', *The Monthly: Australian Politics, Society & Culture*.

Potter, J. (1998) 'Discursive social psychology: From attitudes to evaluations', in W. Stroebe and M. Hewstone (eds) *European Review of Social Psychology* (Vol. 9, pp. 233–66). Chichester: John Wiley.

Potter, J. and Wetherell, M. (1987) *Discourse and social psychology: Beyond attitudes and behaviour*. London: Sage.

Rapley, M. (1998) '"Just an ordinary Australian": Self-categorization and the discursive construction of facticity in "new racist" political rhetoric', *British Journal of Social Psychology*, 37: 325–44.

Sacks, H. (1995) *Lectures on conversation* (Vols I and II; ed. G. Jefferson). Oxford: Blackwell.

Sidanius, J. and Pratto, F. (1999) *Social dominance: An intergroup theory of social hierarchy and oppression*. New York: Cambridge University Press.

van Dijk, T.A. (1987) *Communicating racism: Ethnic prejudice in thought and talk*. London: Sage.

Watson, R. (1997) 'Some general reflections on "categorization" and "sequence" in the analysis of conversation', in S. Hester and P. Eglin (eds) *Culture in action: Studies in membership categorization analysis* (pp. 49–76). Washington, DC: University Press of America.

Wegner, D.M. and Bargh, J.A. (1998) 'Control and automaticity in social life', in D.T. Gilbert, S.T. Fiske and G. Lindzey (eds) *Handbook of social psychology* (Vol. 1, fourth edn, pp. 446–96). New York: McGraw-Hill.

Wetherell, M. (2012) 'The prejudice problematic', in J. Dixon and M. Levine (eds) *Beyond prejudice: Extending the social psychology of conflict, inequality and social change* (pp. 158–78). Cambridge: Cambridge University Press.

Wetherell, M. and Potter, J. (1992) *Mapping the language of racism: Discourse and the legitimation of exploitation*. Hemel Hempstead: Harvester Wheatsheaf.

17 'Race stereotypes' as 'racist' discourse

Kevin Durrheim

Target article: Condor, S. (1988) '"Race stereotypes" and racist discourse', *Text*, 8: 69–89.

Social psychology understandings of stereotypes have changed significantly as the research field has developed. Early stereotyping research was informed by Lippmann's (1922) theory of stereotypes as shared representations that were fashioned in public opinion; and Katz and Braly's (1933) adjective checklist was used to elicit the content of group stereotypes. By the time of Brigham's (1971) review, however, the literature had become 'sterile', overly descriptive, 'littered with reports of stereotypes of Group A by Group B' (Schneider, 2004: 11). Stereotyping research was revitalized in the 1970s by the application of cognitive theory. As stereotypes came to be viewed as being '*inherently* cognitive in nature' (Hamilton and Trolier, 1986: 154, my italics) interest in public opinion and shared stereotype content was replaced by a focus on categorization and the psychological mechanisms of stereotyping.

It is in this disciplinary context that Condor (1988) published her landmark critique of the social psychology of stereotyping and sketched an alternative discursive approach. She was writing in the heady days when British social psychologists were applying social constructionist thinking to challenge cognitive theories of prejudice (Henriques et al., 1984), and produce alternative rhetorical (Billig, 1987) and discursive (Potter and Wetherell, 1987) approaches. Condor (1988) focused on racial stereotypes in order to elucidate the theoretical and political consequences of the cognitive approach, which treated the content and expression of stereotypes as inconsequential. It did not matter whether the stereotypes were about Blacks and Jews or about apples and oranges, the cognitive processes were the same. Not only did discursive social psychology promise to recover an interest in collective representations and the content of public opinion; it also offered a new theory and an approach to studying stereotypes that moved beyond the adjective checklist method and the view that stereotypes were 'pictures inside the heads of these human beings' (Lippmann, 1922: 30).

This chapter will provide an overview of Condor's (1988) understanding of discourse as an 'object of inquiry', outlining her contribution and showing how she anticipated future developments. It will also engage critically with her discourse analysis of racism in cognitive social psychology texts in order to sketch some of the limits of the discursive approach and to propose an alternative project.

Discourse as object of inquiry

Like other discursive social psychologists writing at the time, Condor (1988) highlighted a number of overlapping features of discourse, which I refer to here as rhetoric, language, and interaction.

(a) Rhetoric (and the reification of race thinking)

The first problem that Condor (1988) identified with the cognitive approach was its 'reification of race thinking' (p. 81). Cognitive social psychologists argued that stereotypes were the product of mental mechanisms. They were 'the outcome of normal cognitive processes' (Ashmore and Del Boca, 1981, cited in Condor, 1988: 71), most notably, the 'almost inherent' tendency 'to lump others we encounter together into social groups: females and males; blacks and whites [...]' (Hamilton 1981, cited in Condor, 1988: 82). As the products of the universal capacity for categorization, stereotypes were viewed as being natural and inevitable features of social life, the result of normal cognitive functioning.

There are two consequences of this reification of race thinking. First, it is a short step from naturalizing stereotyping to portraying cognitive mechanisms rather than people or groups as the originators of stereotypes: as Hamilton (1981) suggested, 'aspects of our cognitive functioning may, *by themselves*, constitute the basis for stereotyping and intergroup discrimination' (cited on p. 82, Condor's emphasis). Second, the theory suggests that stereotypes are 'neutral cognitions' (p. 79). Cognitive researchers appreciated that race stereotypes might be fallible 'simplifications of social reality' (Stephan and Stephan, 1984, cited in Condor, 1988: 83), susceptible to bias. However, they regarded them as benign evaluations that were primarily motivated by the 'quest for truth', and were necessary for optimal functioning and ultimately for survival. Thus, any bias that may arise in 'attaching labels to different racial and ethnic groups' is portrayed an innocent and necessary corollary of the imperative for cognitive economy, the attempt 'to impose order on a chaotic social environment' (Stephan and Rosenfield, 1982, cited in Condor, 1988: 79).

The problem with reification of race thinking is that it may 'lead to a lack of critical assessment of the "uses" to which notions of "race" may be put' (Condor, 1988: 79). Attributing stereotypes to the workings of natural mental processes limits our understanding of their strategic nature. Certainly, cognitive social psychologists appreciate that categorization is strategically linked to identity dynamics, but Condor has in mind more social strategies when she highlights the 'essentially rhetorical nature of stereotype articulation' (p. 75).

The cognitive approach treated trait attribution as 'a cognitive rather than a rhetorical phenomenon, as the outcome of automatic cognitive mechanisms rather than a meaningful position in a debate concerning social justice' (p. 84). Much subsequent work in social identity theory (cf. Billig, 2002) and implicit bias (e.g., Greenwald and Krieger, 2006) had continued to reflect this view.

Condor here echoes Billig's (1987) call for a rhetorical approach to social psychology, treating stereotypes as resources for arguments rather than cognitive entities. In particular, she suggests that the content of the traits that people associate with groups are selected and strategically deployed to support arguments about social justice. Treating these representations as products of mental mechanisms would 'lead researchers to overlook the social, and power, element of racism as seen and experienced in social life' (Condor, 1988: 71–2). The rhetorical approach expands and socializes the functions served by stereotypes. By situating stereotypes in a conversational and social context we are able to imagine a wider range of individual, interpersonal, ideological functions that stereotypical representations might serve.

(b) Language (and the reification of race categories)

The second problem that Condor (1988) identified with the social cognitive approach was the 'reification of "race" categories' (p. 82). This is the flip side of the reification of race thinking for, if stereotyping is a neutral cognition, stereotypes must be based on 'neutral observation' (p. 77). Indeed, social psychologists often take the existence of race and race categories for granted, treating racial referents such as 'black', 'white' or 'coloured' as labels of 'natural differences' between people. Condor argues that this is a 'logical extension of the social cognition approach', which treats stereotypes as 'simplifications of social reality' (p. 83). The process of categorization might produce biased perception of the world, but it is nonetheless 'prompted by some stimulus from "the world outside"' (Stephan and Stephan, 1984, cited in Condor, 1988: 83). In practice, race categories are taken for granted when they are treated as descriptive entities, for example, in sample descriptions, research instruments and in experimental manipulations.

Condor (1988) argues that the reification of 'race' is most clearly apparent in the 'supposition that similarity-difference "really" exists as an aspect of the environment independent of the observer' (p. 83). This supposition is evident in theories that highlight the inductive, empirically-grounded emergence of categories 'along the lines of similarity' (Taylor, 1981, cited in Condor, 1988: 83) or according to attributes, such as skin colour, that are 'visually prominent' (Fiske and Taylor, 1984, cited in Condor, 1988: 83). This supposition also informs the idea that stereotypes maximise category differentiation via the processes of comparative fit and the meta-contrast ratio (e.g., Brown and Turner, 2002). In addition to the assumed reality of race categories, social cognitive researchers also subscribe to a realist theory about the traits associated with these categories. For example, Taylor (1981) argued that 'stereotypes, both benign and pernicious, evolve to describe categories of people, just as sunsets are characterized as colorful or balls as round.' (cited in Condor, 1988: 77).

In contrast, like other discursive psychologists writing at the time (van Dijk, 1987; Wetherell and Potter, 1992), Condor (1988) treats race categories and stereotypes as social constructions, not as natural occurrences. This is the reason why she places scare quotes around the word 'race'. Condor's post-structuralist orientation is apparent when she wonders, contradicting Taylor, 'whether the concept of "sunset" does exist independently of "colourfulness"' (p. 77). She here draws attention to the way in which the meanings of concepts originate in the contrasts and associations of language, and in their use. If this is true of such innocuous concepts as sunsets and colourfulness, how much more is it true of the 'way in which notions of "race" are associated (often implicitly) with a host of interconnected symbols which have important functional significance in racist society' (p. 72). Rather than the meaning of race deriving from 'neutral observation' Condor argues that race categories and the 'complex network of emotive ideas' associated with these categories are derived from our language.

Language provides the 'host of interconnected symbols' – the nouns and the adjectives – from which stereotypes are built. Language also provides the 'semantic associations' that link meanings together, and that allows the 'very notion of "race"' to draw upon 'concepts outside its own immediate referents: purity-pollution; national-alien; Christian-Heathen; us-them; superior-inferior' (p. 72). Language allows such associations to be made indexically, in context-specific ways that both reflect the history and use of the terms and brings these connotations to bear in specific situations (cf. Edwards, 1997).

(c) Interaction (and the reification of responses)

Condor (1988) attributes the reification of race thinking and the reification of race categories to 'neglect of the conversational context of stereotyping research' (p. 81) – which we could describe as a third more fundamental reification, namely, the reification of responses. She argues that '"Stereotyping" research may be regarded as a conversation between researcher and "subject"' (p. 81). This conversation begins when researchers ask participants to report their stereotypes. Stereotyping research can thus be viewed as a dialogue in which the researcher is 'intrinsically involved' (p. 75). The problem with researcher involvement in stereotype generation is not that researchers thus introduce bias to the responses, but that dialogical context of responses is lost when social psychologists forget that these responses are *replies* when they 're-present their findings as cognitive rather than discursive phenomena' (p. 75). Social psychologists attribute stereotypes to participants by removing stereotypes from their conversational context.

This leads to the reification of race thinking, making it appear that responses have their origins in the minds of the respondents rather than in the 'conversational context' set up by the interview or the questionnaire (see Billig, 1987 and Potter and Wetherell, 1987 for similar arguments). Social psychologists 'talk about the "results" of their studies as if they occurred spontaneously' – e.g., as cognitive mechanisms 'by themselves' constituting stereotypes (Hamilton, 1981, cited in Condor, 1988: 82). By ignoring the 'role of the question in structuring the answer' and focusing only on subjects' responses – 'one half of the adjacency pair' – researchers may be led to 'reify answers as psychological structures', thereby naturalizing social categorization (p. 82).

Ignoring the dialogical context of responses also results in the reification of race categories. For, by disregarding the,

> *conversational* and social context in which instances of 'racial' categorization and stereotyping are observed, social psychologists are easily led to the conclusion that these images (which apparently emerged 'by themselves') must have been prompted by some stimulus from 'the world outside'.
> (p. 83)

In sum, Condor (1988) advanced a multidimensional and integrated understanding of discourse to explain how stereotypes are deployed strategically in conversational contexts and draw on language resources that have been forged historically in such contexts of use. This view of race stereotypes stood in stark contrast to social cognition theory that prevailed at the time, which argued that stereotypes were the product of mental operations and reflected reality (with possible bias). This view of stereotypes formed the foundation of subsequent discursive research on stereotyping and racism. It has proved especially useful for studying the subtle and indirect expressions that characterize the 'new racism'. In the process, researchers have begun to develop a fuller understanding of the social life of stereotypes. More recent publications by Condor and others have highlighted the power of interaction for perpetuating the language of racial stereotypes in contexts where people disavow racism (e.g., Condor and Figgou, 2012; Durrheim, Greener and Whitehead, 2015). Before reviewing this work, we consider how discourse theory understands the links between race stereotypes and racism.

The social construction of racism

In addition to describing race stereotyping as discursive practice, Condor (1988) advanced a second line of argument about the nature of racism. Her interest in the content of group stereotypes allowed her to develop a critical perspective on racial representations as ideology. In particular, she critiqued an aspect of 'new racism' that she calls 'metalevel racism', that is discourse that 'den[ies] the meaning and implications of the notion of "race"' (p. 69). She then turned the tables on the social cognitive approach, arguing that metalevel racism could be identified in both lay and academic theories that portray '"race" stereotypes and categories as cognitive phenomena which can be traced to an external "reality" of racial distinction' (p. 69). Finally, she outlined the rhetorical and ideological effects of such 'race' discourse, just as Billig's (1988) companion article highlighted the effects of discourse that denied prejudice.

Condor's argument can be broken down into two parts. First, she argues that 'race' and 'racism' are co-constitutive, claiming that '*our way of talking about "racism"* may itself perpetuate racist practice insofar as it obscures or legitimates the meaning and social consequences of the deployment of "race" categories' (my emphasis, p. 73). The discursive construction of 'race' and 'racism' are deemed to be co-constitutive because arguments about 'race' take accusations of 'racism' into account. They do this by developing a serviceable definition of racism against which to contrast current talk as being not racist (Durrheim, Quayle and Dixon, forthcoming). This line of reasoning has much in common with Billig's argument that speakers deny prejudice by developing an idea of '*the* "proper" prejudice' (Billig, 1999: 152) against which to excuse their own arguably prejudiced utterances as being not prejudiced. Condor suggests that a theory of stereotypes as normal cognitions reflecting real-world distinctions similarly serves to exclude some classes of racial stereotyping from the category 'proper racism'.

The second part of her argument follows directly from this: not only does co-constitutive talk about 'race' and 'racism' serve rhetorical functions, but it also has practical effect. The belief that stereotypes are cognitive phenomena that reflect external reality serves to excuse stereotypical accounts as being not racist and may thus inadvertently give these stereotypes the credence they need to support racist practice. Condor's variant of social constructionism incorporates a version of realism. While she argues that stereotypes are socially constructed in discourse, her objective is to delineate the real effects of such construction in practice and in social structure. Racism is not only a rhetorical construction; it is also a feature of the world. The aim of discursive research is to show how the co-construction of 'race' and 'racism' helps to preserve racial inequality. This is metalevel racism, sans scare quotes.

Condor illustrates this theory by representations she found in the *South African Yearbook* of 1985, which depicted 'coloureds' (one of the 'races' defined by apartheid legislation) as having 'a natural feeling for rhythm and a strong love of music' (p. 79). Even seemingly benign representations such as this can have 'pernicious implications' (p. 79). Treating such stereotypes as neutral cognitions ignores the way that they arise from and help to secure particular relations of power. Thus Condor claims: 'To say, for example, that white people are "happy" does not mean the same as to say that black people are "happy"' (p. 80). The difference is that the stereotypical happiness of an oppressed group (as opposed to anger, for example) can serve ideological and system-justifying functions (see Dixon, Levine, Reicher and Durrheim, 2012). It can encourage 'coloured' people to see themselves as happy, and to individualize and pathologize being unhappy or angry. This can undermine the possibility of solidarity between oppressed groups as 'coloureds' distinguish themselves as happy people in contrast with angry 'black Africans'. It can also encourage whites to treat 'coloured' workers as 'happy' as was perpetuated most despicably by the 'dop stelsel' in which South African farmers paid workers wages in wine.

The strategic effects of stereotypes are not restricted to conversation and interpersonal dialogue; it extends to ideology, historical practices and the constitution of racial worlds. Common sense depictions have a history and a politics: They ventriloquate the history of their usage as they supply co-ordinates for meaningful and accountable action and thereby operate to reproduce a racist world. These effects are not necessarily linked to intentions – so the ideological effects of a particular view of stereotypes (e.g., metalevel racism) might arise quite innocently.

Stereotyping by implication

Condor (1988) has a special interest in what has come to be termed 'deracialized' discourse (Augoustinos and Every, 2007). The metalevel racism of social cognitive theory of stereotypes is an exemplar of a broader category of discourse that allows speakers to deny racism while communicating racial stereotypes. Accounts of stereotypes as reality-reflecting natural cognitions are but one way in which 'theories of "race" can be concealed inside apparently innocent language' (p. 72). This can be done even more effectively by using deracialized language to develop implicit 'meanings and implications associated with the use of "race" categories' (p. 72).

This way of communicating stereotypes owes its possibility to the associative properties of language discussed above, the fact that the language of race is comprised of a 'host of interconnected symbols'. In Britain of the 1980s, Condor (1988) claimed, 'the association of the construct of race with notions of "nation", "immigration", "law and order" may both reflect and perpetuate the system of dominance-subordination in which such notions of "race" are developed and employed' (p. 72). The network of stereotypical associations within which race was embedded allowed a racist system of domination–subordination to persist even while people disavowed racism. For example, it would be possible to conjure up racial fears by warning against the threat posed by a rising tide of immigration, without mentioning race. The association with race could remain implicit, allowing the warning to be portrayed as being 'not racist'.

This same effect could be achieved by way of implicit contrasts. Condor cites Rex's (1970) argument that an 'implicit reference to some moral or political code' might be communicated by the seemingly tolerant assertion that 'this is a human being' when it is set implicitly 'against the assertion, "this is a Jew" or "this is a negro"' (p. 78). Bergsieker et al. (2012: 19) have recently called the process whereby 'audiences draw negative inferences from communicators' faint or unidimensional praise of targets' 'stereotyping by omission'. For example, describing a potential 'coloured' work partner as 'happy and fun-loving' can flag an omission about stereotypically poor work ethic and lead to negative evaluation.

Condor (1988) did not develop a theory of how implicit stereotyping occurred – either by association or by contrast. However, she anticipated such a theory in her focus on the conversational and interactive aspects of discourse. Whereas social psychologists have traditionally thought of stereotypes as originating 'in the heads' of individuals, Condor appreciated that they originated in the interactional context between people. It is here, between speaker and hearer, that implicit themes and common sense knowledge circulates, and where implications can be heard while not uttered. The associative powers of language enable stereotypical 'adjectives [to] tap into a system of implicature' (p. 80), but it is in interaction that such implication is set to work.

Implication is evident when speakers deny prejudice, attempting to forestall possible interpretations of prejudice (Billig, 1988). In these situations, speakers presumably anticipate that their utterance could be heard as being racist, and they preemptively disavow racism. The interactional nature of this hearing is also evident when people deny prejudice on behalf of another (Condor et al., 2006), accuse others of racism (Cresswell, Whitehead and Durrheim, 2014), or attribute their actions to their racial category membership (Whitehead, 2012). In all these cases hearers treat speakers' utterances as being racialized, even when they were not explicitly so.

The possibility of hearing race stereotypes when they have not been vocalized allows speakers to use implicit stereotypes as resources for accounting and explaining (Durrheim, Greener and Whitehead, 2015). The norm against making explicit or crude statements of racism and prejudice has not eliminated these race stereotypes. Rather, they circulate as implicit themes in the spaces between speakers and hearers. In a process that Durrheim (2012) calls 'stereotyping by implication', speakers may use the associative powers of language to gesture toward common sense stereotypes without having to utter them. The white beachgoers he interviewed denied that they segregated on racial grounds, arguing that they would not like neighbours of any race that are noisy, inconsiderate and abuse alcohol on the beach. By selecting these adjectives conventionally associated with black beachgoers they invoked race stereotypes implicitly even while they disavowed race thinking. Similarly, Whitehead (2009) has shown how speakers can pose a puzzle – e.g., 'I wonder why s/he reacted like that?' – to prompt hearers to quietly supply racial stereotypes as reasons.

By these arts of suggestion and indirection racial stereotypes can do their work of justification and criticism in deracialized discourse. There is no way of explaining this operation of stereotyping by a cognitive theory that sees stereotypes as originating in an encounter between mind and world. Condor (1988) can be credited with opening up this avenue of research in her groundbreaking discursive understanding of stereotyping. It is by stereotyping by implication and allusion that speakers can simultaneously deploy and disavow racial stereotypes in strategic rhetoric, found 'racial projects' (Omi and Winant, 1994), and mobilize hatred (Durrheim, Quayle and Dixon, forthcoming) in liberal and even anti-racist ideological climates.

The discursive approach to prejudice and stereotyping has led to a fundamental revision of our understanding of racism. In contrast to the traditional psychological and sociological definitions of racism as mental signature or social structure (Durrheim, 2014), racism has come to be seen as a 'collaborative accomplishment' that is produced in interaction (Condor et al., 2006: 458; Condor, 2006; Condor and Figgou, 2012). Because expression is sensitive to the norm against prejudice (Billig, 1988), race categories and stereotypes are often accompanied by denials or are expressed implicitly using deracialized language. Accusations of racism – which themselves can be counter-normative (Augoustinos and Every 2010; Goodman and Burke, 2010) – spark debate in which the nature of racism is contested. What counts as being 'racist' or 'prejudiced' in the end 'ultimately depends upon its acceptance or rejection on the part of an audience' (Condor et al., 2006: 458). It is in this sense that 'racism' is a 'collaborative accomplishment' (Condor et al., 2006: 458; Condor, 2006). What counts as racism is the outcome of a social process and is achieved in the 'moment-by-moment unfolding of interactions' between speakers and hearers (Whitehead, 2012: 1248).

Discursive social psychology and racism critique

The main target of Condor's (1988) critique is cognitive social psychology. She views ' "social cognition" as racist discourse' (p. 76), and identifies 'elements of "metalevel racism" in contemporary social cognition work on "race" stereotyping' (pp. 75–6). We have already considered her reasons: By reifying race thinking and race categories, the social cognitive approach naturalizes race stereotypes as adaptive products of normal cognitive processes and as reflections of reality. In this she finds many 'parallels between social cognition accounts and aspects of "new" racist discourse' (p. 86). By way of evidence, she contrasts the writings of influential social cognitive theorists with a slice of 'new racism' she identified in an editorial comment in *The Sun*, a popular British newspaper. The editorial also treated race as an incontestable basic fact, argued that the perception of racial traits and differences was natural, and thus concluded that 'If, say, the majority of muggers in Brixton are black it is our duty to our readers to say so' (cited on p. 73). And yet the editorial could deny racism by treating stereotypes as reflections of natural human differences. In the process 'race' is removed from its historical context and the role it plays in supporting a system of inequality.

Discursive social psychology has often been used in critical anti-racism projects of this kind, to develop a critique of racism on the basis of text analysis. Following the pattern adopted by Condor (1988), researchers show the way in which 'race' is constructed in order to develop a critique of 'everyday racism' (Essed, 1991), 'racist discourse' (Durrheim and Dixon, 2000; Verkuyten, de Jong and Masson, 1994), or 'the language of racism' (Wetherell and Potter, 1992). The target is racism, sans scare quotes, much like Condor's target is metalevel racism. While discursive social psychologists have celebrated the constructed nature of 'race', they have often been reluctant to embrace the constructed nature of 'racism'. There are good reasons for treating racism this way because the deconstruction of 'racism' tends to undermine the political project that informs the deconstruction of 'race'. It leads to the conclusion that, like the use of race, accounts of racism – including those of discourse analysts – are little more than occasioned constructions that function to produce interested versions of reality (Edwards, Ashmore and Potter, 1995).

From the social constructionist perspective, however, there is nothing (ontologically speaking) to separate 'race' from 'racism'. They are both social categories that are used in occasioned and serviceable ways by drawing on shared interpretive repertoires. They are also both socially constructed realities. Condor is aware that racism does not only exist in talk, but that forms of talk like that of *The Sun* editorial are part of a 'particular system of social inequality within which "race" categories are deployed' (p. 78). Like 'racism', these 'race' categories also exist outside of talk as segregated and unequal social groups. Of course these are not natural categories, but they are socially constructed realities produced by the history and ongoing practices of 'racism'. 'Race' discourse supports racial inequality, but this does not equal racism without scare quotes, just as it does not produce race without scare quotes. The racially segregated and unequal world – populated by 'races' it has produced – is itself a collaborative accomplishment. Moreover, all commentators and analysts are invested in the system in one way or another, often ambivalently, as many contending, allied and overlapping versions of change can strategically deploy notions of 'race' and 'racism'. Consider, for example, the investments that qualitative researchers have in 'racism' when they conduct interviews and knowingly participate in 'racist' discourse as they gather 'good data' for critical, anti-racist scholarship. Or when they align their critiques of racism with the interests of the oppressed, in ways that might not be fully shared by these minorities.

Condor reifies racism by ignoring her own role in its production. We can step back and see Condor in conversation with her social cognitive colleagues, contesting the nature of 'race' and 'racism' in a struggle over ideas as well as influence in the discipline. Her objectification of racism is achieved by ignoring the basic tenets of her own approach. By putting psychology texts alongside *The Sun* article to show the parallels between them and suggest that they both are racist she ignores the conversational context of these texts. Moreover, she ignores her role as analyst in producing the text as part of a debate about the nature of social psychology. 'Metalevel racism' is as much a construction and a resource in this debate as it is an exemplification of the 'new racism'.

This approach to critique has been a hallmark of much discursive research on stereotyping and racism. Just like their cognitive colleagues, discursive social psychologists sometimes presume to have a privileged understanding of what racism is or, at least, they 'often regard the terms of their own debate as lying outside dominant discourses' (see Durrheim, 2014: 85). The anti-racism of the kind expressed by Condor and others, and the conception of 'racism' it develops, also stretches out beyond the academy, as does the conception of 'racism' of her cognitive colleagues. As Condor (1988) says, 'social psychological talk not only reflects, but also feeds back into, forms of discourse located "outside" the discipline itself' (p. 86). At this systemic level, we can see different versions of 'racism' in dialogue with each other as they are taken up in debates about social change. They provide powerful resources for all kinds of projects as they are used in arguments about immigration, desegregation, affirmative action, and (as we have seen) even about the nature and direction of social psychology.

In addition to taking sides in this debate, discursive social psychology is well equipped to analyze the whole conglomerate, to show how different versions of 'racism' are set against each other either implicitly or explicitly in arguments about social justice, change, and other matters. Discursive research can also show how these arguments 'articulate' with discursive practices, rendering particular versions of the world intelligible and defensible. Rather than privileging one or other version of racism, Durrheim, Mtose and Brown (2011) direct attention to 'race trouble', that is, the dynamics of the whole assemblage of discourse and practice that constitute 'race' and 'racism' in any situation. This includes both explicit and implicit use of 'race' stereotypes and ideas about 'racism' to support, justify and criticize a multitude of positions and investments, sometimes ambivalently, and the kinds of worlds and practices that they are part of (Creswell, Whitehead and Durrheim, 2014; Durrheim, Greener and Whitehead, 2015; Durrheim Quayle and Dixon, forthcoming).

Conclusion

Condor's (1988) classic article is rightly part of this celebratory volume. This ground-breaking paper articulated an understanding of discourse that was widely shared by the early writers and came to have enormous influence in the discipline. Like many of her contemporaries, she also made critical use of the theory and methods of discursive social psychology. Her work shows the influence of the thinking of the time. It also anticipated and opened the way for future developments. Most centrally, her focus on interaction and implication – long before the rise of conversation analytic approaches in the discipline – opened the way for a view of racism as a collaborative accomplishment, and an interest in the role of the hearing as much as the uttering of stereotypes.

In addition, in this article and in her other writings, Condor has not been content with an analysis of discourse only. She addresses the world in order to change it. I have argued that an unreflexive critique of racism may be the wrong strategy. Nonetheless, her approach to discourse – focused on interaction, hearing, and the articulation of discourse with 'reality' – provides the keys for an alternative approach to a critical social psychology and analysis of 'racism'. I have suggested that the concept of race trouble can help to remind discursive social psychologists that they are implicated in the production of 'racism'. This does not mean that we have to give up the struggle for social change. But it does mean that we have to interrogate all claims about 'race' and 'racism' – including our own – showing how they co-constitute each other in complex and contradictory ways in debate and in other social practices.

References

Augoustinos, M. and Every, D. (2007) 'The language of "race" and prejudice: A discourse of denial, reason, and liberal-practical politics', *Journal of Language & Social Psychology*, 26: 123–41.

Augoustinos, M. and Every, D. (2010) 'Accusations and denials of racism: Managing moral accountability in public discourse', *Discourse & Society*, 21: 251–56.

Ashmore, R.D. and Del Boca, F.K. (1981) 'Conceptual approaches to stereotypes and stereotyping', in D.L. Hamilton (ed.) *Cognitive process in stereotyping and intergroup behaviour* (pp. 1–35). Hillsdale, NJ: Erlbaum.

Bergsieker, H.B., Leslie, L.M., Constantine, V.S. and Fiske, S.T. (2012) 'Stereotyping by omission: Eliminate the negative, accentuate the positive', *Journal of Personality & Social Psychology*, 102: 1214–38.

Billig, M. (1987) *Arguing and thinking: A rhetorical approach to social psychology*. Cambridge: Cambridge University Press.

Billig, M. (1988) 'The notion of "prejudice": Some rhetorical and ideological aspects', *Text*, 8: 91–111.

Billig, M. (1999) *Freudian repression: Conversation creating the unconscious*. Cambridge: Cambridge University Press.

Billig, M. (2002) 'Henri Tajfel's "cognitive aspects of prejudice" and the psychology of bigotry', *British Journal of Social Psychology*, 41: 171–88.

Brigham, J.C. (1971) 'Ethnic stereotypes', *Psychological Bulletin*, 76: 15–38.

Brown, P.M. and Turner, J.C. (2002) 'The role of theories in the formation of stereotype content', in C. McGarty, V.Y. Yzerbyt and R. Spears (eds) *Stereotypes as explanations: The formation of meaningful beliefs about social groups* (pp. 67–89). Cambridge: Cambridge University Press.

Condor, S. (1988) '"Race stereotypes" as racist discourse', *Text*, 8: 69–89.

Condor, S. (2006) 'Public prejudice as collaborative accomplishment: Towards a dialogic social psychology of racism', *Journal of Community & Applied Social Psychology*, 16: 1–18.

Condor, S. and Figgou, L. (2012) 'Rethinking the prejudice problematic: A collaborative cognition approach', in J. Dixon and M. Levine (eds) *Beyond prejudice: Extending the social psychology of conflict, inequality and social change* (pp. 200–22). Cambridge: Cambridge University Press.

Condor, S., Figgou, L., Abell, J., Gibson, S. and Stevenson, C. (2006) '"They're not racist . . ." Prejudice denial, mitigation and suppression in dialogue', *British Journal of Social Psychology*, 45: 441–62.

Cresswell, C., Whitehead, K. and Durrheim, K. (2014) 'The anatomy of "race trouble" in online interactions', *Ethnic & Racial Studies*, 37: 2512–28.

Dixon, J., Levine, M., Reicher, S. and Durrheim, K., (2012) 'Beyond prejudice: Are negative evaluations the problem? Is getting us to like one another more the solution?', *Behavioral & Brain Sciences*, 35: 1–15.

Durrheim, K. (2012) 'Implicit prejudice in mind and interaction', in J. Dixon and M. Levine (eds) *Beyond prejudice: Extending the social psychology of conflict, inequality and social change* (pp. 179–99) Cambridge: Cambridge University Press.

Durrheim, K. (2014) 'Two histories of prejudice', in C. Tileagă and J. Byford (eds) *Psychology and history: Interdisciplinary explorations.* Cambridge: Cambridge University Press.

Durrheim, K. and Dixon, J.A. (2000) 'Theories of culture in racist discourse', *Race & Society*, 3: 93–109.

Durrheim, K., Greener, R. and Whitehead, K. (2015) 'Race trouble: Attending to race and racism in online interaction', *British Journal of Social Psychology*, 54: 84–99.

Durrheim, K., Mtose, X. and Brown, L. (2011) *Race trouble: Race, identity and inequality in post-apartheid South Africa.* Scottsville: University of KwaZulu-Natal Press.

Durrheim, K., Quayle, M. and Dixon, J. (forthcoming) *The struggle for the nature of 'prejudice': A social identity model of 'prejudice' as identity performance.*

Edwards, D. (1997) *Discourse and cognition.* London: Sage.

Edwards, D., Ashmore, M. and Potter, J. (1995) 'Death and furniture: The rhetoric, politics and theology of bottom-line arguments against relativism', *History of the Human Sciences*, 8: 25–49.

Essed, P. (1991) *Understanding everyday racism: An interdisciplinary theory.* Newbury Park, CA: Sage.

Fiske, S.T. and Taylor, S.E. (1984) *Social cognition.* New York: Random House.

Goodman, S. and Burke, S. (2010) '"Oh you don't want asylum seekers, oh you're just racist": A discursive analysis of discussions about whether it's racist to oppose asylum seeking', *Discourse & Society*, 21: 325–40.

Greenwald, A.G. and Krieger, L.H. (2006) 'Implicit bias: Scientific foundations', *California Law Review*, 94: 945–67.

Hamilton, D.L. (ed.) (1981) *Cognitive processes in stereotyping and intergroup behavior.* Hillsdale, NJ: Erlbaum.

Hamilton, D.L. and Trolier, T.K. (1986) 'Stereotypes and stereotyping: An overview of the cognitive approach', in J.F. Dovidio and S.L. Gaertner (eds) *Prejudice, discrimination and racism* (pp. 127–57). Orlando, FL: Academic Press.

Henriques, J., Hollway, W., Urwin, C., Venn, C. and Walkerdine, V. (eds) (1984) *Changing the subject.* London: Methuen.

Katz, D. and Braly, K. (1933) 'Racial stereotypes of one hundred college students', *Journal of Abnormal & Social Psychology*, 30: 175–93.

Lippmann, W. (1922) *Public opinion.* New York: Harcourt Brace.

Omi, M. and Winant, H. (1994) *Racial formation in the United States: From the 1960s to the 1990s* (revised edn). New York: Routledge.

Potter, J. and Wetherell, M. (1987) *Discourse and social psychology: Beyond attitudes and behaviour.* London: Sage.

Rex, J. (1970) *Race relations in sociological theory.* London: Routledge and Kegan Paul.

Schneider, D.J. (2004) *The psychology of stereotyping.* New York: The Guilford Press.

Stephan, W.G. and Rosenfield, D. (1982) 'Racial and ethnic stereotypes', in A.G. Miller (ed.) *In the eye of the beholder: Contemporary issues in stereotyping.* New York: Praeger.

Stephan, W.G. and Stephan, C.W. (1984) 'The role of ignorance in intergroup relations', in N. Miller and M.B. Brewer (eds) *Groups in contact* (pp. 229–55). Orlando, FL: Academic Press.

Taylor, S.E. (1981) 'A categorization approach to stereotyping', in D.L. Hamilton (ed.) *Cognitive processes in stereotyping and intergroup behavior* (pp. 83–114). Hillsdale, NJ: Erlbaum.
van Dijk, T.A. (1987) *Communicating racism: Ethnic prejudice in thought and talk*. Newbury Park, CA: Sage.
Verkuyten, M., de Jong, W. and Masson, K. (1994) 'Similarities in anti-racist and racist discourse: Dutch local residents talking about ethnic minorities', *New Community*, 20: 253–67.
Wetherell, M. and Potter, J. (1992) *Mapping the language of racism: Discourse and the legitimation of exploitation*. Hertfordshire: Harvester Wheatsheaf.
Whitehead, K.A. (2009) 'Categorizing the categorizer: The management of racial common sense in interaction', *Social Psychology Quarterly*, 72: 325–42.
Whitehead, K.A. (2012) 'Racial categories as resources and constraints in everyday interactions: Implications for racialism and non-racialism in post-apartheid South Africa', *Ethnic & Racial Studies*, 35: 1248–65.

18 Fact and evaluation in racist discourse revisited

John Dixon and Stephanie Taylor

Target article: Potter, J. and Wetherell, M. (1988) 'Accomplishing attitudes: Fact and evaluation in racist discourse', *Text*, 8: 51–68.

Introduction

Jonathan Potter and Margaret Wetherell's 1988 paper, 'Accomplishing attitudes', has a triple significance. First, it is one of the foundational publications in the development of discursive psychology, encapsulating a central argument from their 1987 book *Discourse and social psychology: Beyond attitudes and behaviour* and anticipating some of the argument of their 1992 book (first authored by Wetherell) *Mapping the language of racism*. Second, it is an early contribution to discursive research on racism, one of the areas of research for which the field remains best known. Third, the paper established a new way of understanding what Gordon Allport (1935) once described as psychology's most 'distinctive and indispensable' concept – the concept of 'attitude'.

This chapter aims to summarize, contextualize, and reappraise Potter and Wetherell's paper. We show how this paper transcended several limitations of mainstream work on race attitudes, offering an important new framework for exploring processes of racial evaluation. At the same time, we hold that it simplified some of the assumptions of traditional research on race attitudes and arguably underestimated some of its enduring contributions. The chapter also identifies some potential directions for future work in the discursive psychological tradition and some areas of possible integration with developments in the discipline's mainstream. We begin by setting the scene.

The nature and historical significance of the concept of attitude

Although definitional quibbles could be aired, the core meanings of the term 'attitude' are relatively well agreed in the mainstream literature. To hold an attitude is to rate something on a scale ranging from positive to negative. That 'something' might be a person, a thing, an event or pretty much anything else. Some researchers might distinguish the affective, cognitive, and conative dimensions of evaluation (cf. Rosenberg and Hovland, 1960); others might prefer to work with a more generic conception. Increasingly, researchers might differentiate implicit (unconscious, spontaneous, uncontrolled) from explicit (conscious, deliberative, controlled) evaluations (for a recent review see Van Bavel, Xiao and Cunningham, 2012). Notwithstanding these complexities, the basic concept of 'attitude' remains fairly straightforward: it is an evaluation of an 'object' that expresses a degree of favour or disfavor (cf. Eagly and Chaiken, 1995).

Why has such a simple concept generated so many thousands of studies, becoming a standard 'outcome measure' across such a wide range of psychological research? In part, the historical significance of the concept of attitude derives from its apparent potential to explain behavior. It seems intuitive that if we can understand how individuals evaluate objects, then we can better predict how they will act towards such objects. If, for example, we know that someone hates fruit and vegetables, then we might infer that she will be unlikely to stick to her new 'five a day' diet. In point of fact, the relationship between attitudes and behaviors is more complex than this simple example suggests (e.g., Ajzen and Fishbein, 1980). Understanding the conditions under which it varies has generated intense debate, a tangled mass of empirical research, and various theoretical frameworks. Nevertheless, by and large, 'attitudes' continue to be treated as 'intervening variables' in a lot of psychological work. They are viewed as psychological structures that mediate or moderate the effects of other factors on individual behavior.

Historically, attitudes and their associated patterns of behavior have been seen as especially important for understanding how we treat human objects of evaluation, namely other people. Indeed, the technology of attitude measurement underpins a vast body of research on racial prejudice dating back to the early years of the last century. Using measures such as the Social Distance Scale, the Feeling Thermometer and the Symbolic Racism Scale, among many others, psychologists have sought to describe the nature of intergroup attitudes, to trace their implications for understanding discriminatory behaviours, and to clarify why we come to dislike and mistreat others in the first place. Moreover, by exporting innovations in attitude theory and measurement, they have shaped developments in companion disciplines such as sociology and political science. The current migration of psychological work on 'implicit attitudes' (Greenwald, McGhee and Schwartz, 1998) is continuing this process (e.g., see Quilllian, 2006).

At the same time, the project of changing attitudes has become a cornerstone of our discipline's approach to combating problems such as racism, anti-Semitism and xenophobia. According to the prejudice model of social change (cf. Wright and Lubensky, 2009), if we can get people to like one another more (i.e., improve their attitudes), then this will reduce their tendency to discriminate against others. In turn, wider structures of inequality and exclusion will gradually subside. Interventions to promote intergroup contact, to foster common identification and to arouse intergroup empathy – to name but a few popular techniques of prejudice reduction – are all grounded in this underlying model of social psychological change. All take 'attitude modification' as the key to creating a better society.

As this brief introduction barely illustrates, the concept of attitude is a mainstay of traditional social psychology: a foundational concept through which researchers attempt to understand social problems, predict individual behavior, and improve social life. For this reason, the discursive critique that emerged in the late 1980s was of strategic as well as substantive importance. In questioning attitude research, discursive psychologists struck at one of our discipline's most fundamental constructs. Moreover, by revealing its limits as a way of understanding racism, they highlighted the deficiencies of what Wetherell and Potter (1992) would later call 'the prejudice problematic'. Potter and Wetherell's (1988) paper introduced the nascent discursive critique of mainstream work on race attitudes. It also outlined an alternative perspective grounded in the analysis of the everyday linguistic practices of racial evaluation through which attitudes

Table 18.1 Traditional vs. discursive approaches to attitudes

	Traditional	*Discursive*
Object of study	Individual psychological phenomena or mental states.	Public and social linguistic practices through which (racial) others are evaluated.
Underlying assumptions	Psychological realism; race attitudes are 'expressed' when a pre-established psychological reaction is made visible.	Social constructionism; attitudes are 'constructed' and performed in and through everyday language use.
Key features	• Abstraction of individual responses from particular contexts of expression. • Reduction of contextually variable responses to an overall score that represents the individual's consistent 'race attitude'. • Split between evaluation and attitude object. • Neglect of how participants themselves understand and warrant their 'attitudes'.	• Attitudes understood within the social and rhetorical contexts in which they are accomplished. • Focus on the varying and often inconsistent functions of evaluation. • Attitude object construction is seen as the outcome of (racialized) practices of evaluation based in shared interpretive systems. • Focus on how participants warrant their 'attitudes' as reasonable, moral and grounded in 'fact'.
Method of study	Quantitative scaling and statistical analysis of individual and group responses.	Discourse analysis of the action-orientated functions and consequences of the language of (racial) evaluation within specific contexts.

are shown to be 'accomplished' or produced as an effect of participants' talk, for example, through reference to supporting 'facts' that are themselves warranted in the telling.

From attitude expressions to discursive practices

Table 18.1 above summarizes some key dimensions along which the traditional and discursive approach to race attitudes can be contrasted, capturing the basic elements of Potter and Wetherell's (1988) argument. Their article highlighted three limitations of traditional work on race attitudes, notably limitations in its conceptualization of context, attitude variability and attitude 'objects', and then showed how a discursive approach might help researchers to overcome those limitations. More specifically, they highlighted the rhetorical processes through which the 'attitudes' that sustain racial inequality may be framed as moral, acceptable, and grounded in fact. Before turning to its details, we want to make some general observations about the kind of position Potter and Wetherell were attempting to develop in their paper.

To begin with, they were advocating a shift in the object of traditional attitude research. They argued that such research focused on entities located in the heads of individuals: mental states that remain invisible until they are accessed by the methods of psychological research. By contrast, Potter and Wetherell wanted to highlight the visible, interactional practices of racial evaluation going on all around us: the everyday discourse through which individuals and communities, together, are constantly appraising 'others'. In other words, they wanted to shift the object of attitude research from the *individual's interior life* to the *social practice of evaluation*.

Of course, as other chapters in this volume testify, contrasting objects of study typically reflect contrasting ontological assumptions about the nature of social psychological reality and contrasting epistemological assumptions about how we might best 'know' that reality. Traditional attitude research has typically adopted a form of psychological realism. It has presupposed that attitudes exist as real 'mental states' of individuals, albeit states that can only be known via their 'expression'. Note that this conception institutes a sharp split between attitudes and the primary means through which they are expressed, namely language use. Attitudes are seen as pre-existing and predetermining their expression in language, which is viewed simply as a medium for the transmission of already formed psychological tendencies. By contrast, drawing on a constructionist perspective, Potter and Wetherell (1988) proposed that attitudes should be treated as evaluative practices. They are something *accomplished* rather than *expressed* within everyday language use. Language, in this conception, is not merely a medium through which our interior worlds become exterior. It is the very material through which 'attitudes' are formed, achieved, modified and defended. Moreover, language use is the primary means through which evaluations take effect in the world, producing social, rhetorical and political consequences.

From this general perspective, Potter and Wetherell (1988) advanced a number of more specific arguments, some of which are summarized in Table 18.1 above. A typical race attitude study, they noted, attempts to quantify individual responses to an attitude object, generally by using a set of questionnaire items. Researchers can then construct a summary score (e.g., by calculation of a mean response), which comes to represent the individual's overall evaluation of the attitude object.

Consider, as a simple example, the questionnaire presented in Table 18.2 below, which employs a technique known as the semantic differential. As you can see, each item is anchored by opposing adjective pairs (e.g., cold vs warm), with the individual items yielding an overall mean index that can range from 1 (very negative) to 10 (very positive). Using this and similar scales, researchers working in South Africa have explored the patterning of racial attitudes across members of different groups, continuities and changes in such attitudes over time, and factors that shape them at both an individual and collective level (e.g., see Durrheim et al., 2011). Similar traditions of research have emerged in many other societies, often under the aegis of the concept of 'prejudice'. Indeed, it is not an exaggeration to say that most social scientific knowledge about racial and ethnic attitudes has been based on research that employs this kind of methodology.

Although acknowledging that this approach has yielded important insights, Potter and Wetherell (1988) sought to highlight its limitations, paving the way for an alternative approach. First, they suggested that attitude measurement tends to separate evaluations from the context in which they are performed. The items in Table 18.2, for example, ultimately yield a rather abstract number between 1 and 10 that sheds little light on any actual process of evaluation unfolding within any actual situation. When one restores evaluations to the circumstances of their performance, examining how they are accomplished in everyday talk, a second limitation of tradition attitude research becomes apparent. Those evaluations typically turn out to be complex, messy, variable, and even contradictory. They are marked, for instance, by qualification,

Table 18.2 Measuring racial attitudes

Please describe how you feel about black South Africans in general. Describe your feelings by selecting any number between 1 and 10, where 1 is very negative and 10 is very positive.

Negative	*1*	*2*	*3*	*4*	*5*	*6*	*7*	*8*	*9*	*10*	Positive
Cold	*1*	*2*	*3*	*4*	*5*	*6*	*7*	*8*	*9*	*10*	Warm
Hostile	*1*	*2*	*3*	*4*	*5*	*6*	*7*	*8*	*9*	*10*	Friendly (10)
Suspicious	*1*	*2*	*3*	*4*	*5*	*6*	*7*	*8*	*9*	*10*	Trusting (10)
Disrespect	*1*	*2*	*3*	*4*	*5*	*6*	*7*	*8*	*9*	*10*	Respect (10)

equivocation, the combination of positive and negative elements, and moments when individuals apparently backtrack on an assessment they offered previously. This complexity and variability is lost when attitudes are reduced to a number that stands, once and for all, for the individual's 'racial attitude'. The problem here is not one of simplification *per se*. The problem, as we shall illustrate presently, is that understanding contextual variation in how 'race attitudes' are accomplished is central to understanding their very nature and consequences, as well as the broader ideological contexts through which they are shaped.

A third limitation of traditional attitude measurement concerns its treatment of the target of evaluation, the so-called 'attitude object'. In questionnaire measures, such as that illustrated in Table 18.2, this object is defined in advance by the researcher; in this case, as 'black South Africans in general'. The assumption here is that the object exists independent of the process of evaluation, i.e., there are 'black South Africans in general' and then there are the evaluations that people make of them. Why is this (common sense) idea problematic? Perhaps most crucially, it overlooks a process that Potter and Wetherell (1988) termed 'attitude object constitution', whose significance is revealed when one considers how attitudes are accomplished in real situations where individuals must define for themselves their targets of evaluation. In such situations, there is no easy separation between attitude and object. To the contrary, they are typically part of an indissoluble and mutually reinforcing process through which individuals try to accomplish (racial) evaluations in ways that defend their legitimacy, warrant their morality, and ground their attitudes in the reality of the social world 'out there'.

Before illustrating some of these themes via a practical example, we want to end this section of the chapter on a qualifying note. Mainstream psychological research often involves testing predictive models that use hypothetical constructs designed to 'stand in' for social psychological phenomena, along with quantitative measures designed to operationalize such constructs. However, one should not presuppose that mainstream psychologists necessarily assume that either their constructs or the means through which they are operationalized are somehow isomorphic with those phenomena (see also Taylor, 2007). By implication, we feel that it is simplification to claim that mainstream researchers necessarily buy into the idea that the evaluative processes they label as 'attitudes' exist exclusively as internal psychological structures or that they somehow share the properties of attitude measurement scales. In some more simplistic examples of attitude research (e.g., popular opinion polls) this may be the case, but other work is more sophisticated (e.g., Ajzen and Fishbein, 1980; Manstead, Proffitt and Smart, 1983).

A (brief) worked example: Warranting opposition to 'racial desegregation' in post-apartheid South Africa

Potter and Wetherell (1988) illustrated their arguments using interview research conducted with 'white' New Zealanders (see especially pp. 56–64). Here we draw on research conducted by the first author and colleagues in South Africa during final years of the apartheid system, which was broadly informed by Potter and Wetherell's work (e.g., see Dixon et al., 1994, 1997). Specifically, we consider an account of an event in which a group of people legally classified at that time, under apartheid legislation, as 'black' and 'coloured' established an 'informal settlement' within a town populated mainly by people legally classified as 'white'. The account is one of a campaign of letters published in local newspapers. Mostly written by 'white' residents, these letters sought to evaluate this form of 'racial desegregation', and in so doing, articulated their 'attitudes' towards the new community.

Argus criticized

The article in the Argus of May 17 under the headline of 'Hout Bay's Battle of the Squatters – the Wealthy determined to oust the Poor' is totally misleading. It is irresponsible for the Argus reporter to categorise people in this way.

More accurately, the so-called 'battle' is between legitimate land owners and illegal squatters, many of whom, contrary to statements made in the article, are recent arrivals with no previous Hout Bay connections.

I am, I think, Mr Average Hout Bay Citizen. I am not wealthy, we do not have a live in maid or gardener, and I don't know many people in Hout Bay who do. We came to Hout Bay over ten years ago because we wanted to enjoy the lifestyle that this area offers: a place to bring up our children in safe and beautiful surroundings and ironically enough because we perceived this as an area most likely to achieve racial harmony in the longer term.

Before settling here we lived in a rented flat, had to save hard for many years in order to raise the deposit on our home, and we continue to work hard to pay off the large bond. I believe that it has been worthwhile and we love Hout Bay. I also believe however that it is unacceptable for anyone, regardless of their skin, to move onto someone else's land and squat there.

Let us get it in perspective. If instead of buying a house I had erected a tent on the land presently occupied by squatters, I would have been moved off within hours.

I cannot believe that the police, the Regional Services Council, and private landowners are powerless to act against this violation of the law.

Mr Average Hout Bay

(The *Sentinel News*, June, 1990)

One could analyze this account by exploring how it expresses an internal psychological 'readiness to respond' to a given target group. A case could be advanced, for instance, that the author's attitude towards this group would register on the 'negative' pole of a quantitative rating scale and that this reaction underpins his resistance to social change. That case would be compelling in some respects. A discursive analysis, however, would take a quite different tack. It would seek to reveal what this account is designed to accomplish, what its effects might be in this specific context, and how the varying constructions of the 'attitude object' service this process.

To begin with, the 'attitude object' seems here to be a matter of some controversy. Should we accept that we are dealing with economic relations between a 'wealthy' letter writer and a community of 'poor' people, as the newspaper report cited in the opening paragraph reported? Or are we dealing with legal relations between 'land owners' and 'squatters', as the second paragraph claims? Or, again, are we dealing with relations between 'new arrivals with no connections to the town' and established residents who presumably have such connections? More subtly, why does the writer keep bringing up the category of 'race', if only to affirm that race is irrelevant to his evaluation of events? We would suggest that much of this letter's narrative is designed to construct particular versions of the 'attitude object' and to accomplish particular evaluations of the group who have settled in the town. Defining the attitude object is inextricably part of this process. If we accept, for instance, that events in Hout Bay reflect a struggle between 'illegal squatters' and 'legal landowners', then the author's negative evaluation of the new community means one thing. If we do not accept this form of social categorization, however, then it means something entirely different.

That 'something' haunts the entire letter. Indeed, it is the source of a considerable amount of defensive rhetoric (Potter, 1996) – arguments designed to undermine a potential counter-argument to the evaluation being worked up. Why, for example, does the writer take such pains to establish that he is not a rich man? Why does he tell us that he is 'not wealthy', does not have a 'live in maid or gardener', but does have a 'huge bond' (mortgage) that he has had to 'save hard' to pay off? Why does he imply that, as 'Mr Average Hout Bay citizen', his personal situation can be framed as representative of the situation of the town's other property owners?

We would argue that this sustained process of (self)categorization serves two closely related functions in the account. On the one hand, it defends against the idea that negative reactions to the new informal settlement reflect a class struggle between the undeserving 'haves' and the deserving 'have nots'. On the other hand, it constructs a version of the attitude object in which such reactions become justifiable and accountable. 'They', after all, are people who have illegally appropriated private land from its rightful owners, newcomers who have no prior ties to the town, and people who, if anything, have been unfairly privileged and softly treated by the authorities. If Mr Average had 'erected a tent' on the occupied land, we are told, he 'would have been moved off within hours'. In short, this account shows how the definition of attitude object – and the nature of the relationship between the evaluator and the target of evaluation – is designed to warrant the author's evaluation.

Two additional features of the account are worth noting, for they reveal other aspects of the discursive approach to understanding 'attitudes' that Potter and Wetherell (1988) sought to develop. First, the account shows how individuals are constantly striving to affirm the *factual basis* of their evaluations. To espouse an attitude, as Billig (1987) famously observed, is to take a position in a field of controversy. As such, matters of veracity are constantly on the agenda and must be managed as individuals offer their opinions. This process may entail formal appeals to evidence. As our account illustrates, it may also entail use of more subtle verbal gestures such as use of phrases like 'more accurately' and 'let us get in it perspective', which quietly affirm the reasonable, factual nature of the evaluation offered, while undermining alternative versions.

Second and more specifically, this account shows how people must often accomplish 'racial' attitudes in an ideological context where the spectre of being accused of 'race prejudice' looms large. 'Mr Average' thus conducts rhetorical 'work' to sanitize his own motives, notably by constructing his evaluation of events as neutral, unbiased and, above all, unrelated to racism. To labor the obvious, for example, we would argue that this is the main rhetorical function of the seemingly trivial aside: '[. . .] ironically enough because we perceived this an area most likely to achieve racial harmony in the long term'. In context, this phrase both orients to, and attempts to defuse, the potential accusation that the writer's resistance to the desegregation is racially motivated. It establishes the author's credentials as racially tolerant, while arguing simultaneously for the exclusion of 'squatters'.

Reflections and future directions

Inspired by Potter and Wetherell's (1988) seminal paper, this brief analysis illustrates but a few of their key concerns. In our closing section, we take a step back and evaluate some overall contributions of their approach to the study of attitudes, as well as making a few suggestions for future work. Our aim is not to review general critiques and counter-critiques of discursive psychology or to probe the full range of (meta)theoretical and methodological debates that might be relevant to our chapter.[1] Instead, we want to stick narrowly to the theme of 'accomplishing attitudes' and consider how discursive work might continue to inform, but also be informed by, mainstream attitude research.

Potter and Wetherell's (1988) paper made two kinds of contributions in our view. First, along with the work of Billig (1987) and Potter and Wetherell (1987), it was the vanguard of a new approach that aimed to critique traditional attitude research and transcend its methodological, epistemological, and conceptual limitations. It thus paved the way for a small, but provocative, discursive literature on the nature of attitudes (e.g., Augoustinos, Tuffin and Sale, 1999; Condor et al., 2006), including Billig (1991) on evaluations of the royal family, Wiggins and Potter (2003) on everyday food assessments, and Puchta and Potter (2002) on how focus group dynamics shape 'individual' opinions. Later work explored, for example, how speakers tend to depict counter-positions as extremist or how, conversely, they sometimes downgrade their (commitment to) their own attitudes (e.g., 'that's just my personal opinion') in order to deflect potential challenges. It explored too how attitudes are are accomplished in the hurly burly of everyday talk, often being 'distributed' across individuals and over an unfolding sequence of conversational turns. Moreover, they are marked by such a high degree of contextual variation that the entire project of identifying an individual level, psychologically fixed 'readiness to respond' to specific attitude stimuli, becomes moot.[2]

Second, the discursive perspective contributed more directly to our understanding of how racism operates, exerts consequences in the world, and is then reproduced. This contribution was anticipated in the conclusion of Potter and Wetherell's (1988) paper, which looked towards an approach based on close, situated analysis of how racism is enacted 'in everyday anecdote, argument and account' (p. 65). When they wrote their paper, as we noted earlier, most psychological research on racism operated within the straitjacket of the 'prejudice problematic'. Their paper opened up an equally important agenda that gripped the imagination of an emerging community of researchers.

To begin with, they helped to establish the everyday language of racism as an object of analysis in its own right (and not, for instance, as the mere symptom of an irrational mind). Nearly a quarter of a century later, this idea seems commonplace, but at the time, within social psychology at least, it was radical. Relatedly, they demonstrated how such language may be designed to preempt the allegation that support for racist practices (e.g., exclusion) and institutions (e.g., segregated education) reflect speakers' individual prejudices. As the account we analyzed above began to illustrate, it may appeal to notions of reason and fairness; objectivity and tolerance; the 'facts' of the external world 'out there'. In short, it may be organized rhetorically to deny that inequality reflects racial bigotry. Finally and related, both in their 1988 paper and in later single and co-authored publications, Potter and Wetherell insisted that this complex process of discursive legitimation does not merely express personal motivations (e.g., Wetherell and Potter, 1992). Talk is social. Close analysis of small details of everyday talk, they pointed out, allows us to glimpse the operation of the wider ideology through which inequality is sustained, even as speakers affirm their membership of a 'moral community of the unprejudiced'.

Little wonder, then, that Potter and Wetherell's work subsequently influenced a host of research on racism and other forms of inequality, including our own work (e.g., Dixon et al., 1997; Taylor and Wetherell, 1999). This research continues to emerge in societies as varied as Australia, New Zealand, Spain, Brazil, South Africa, and the UK, and in previously under-researched sociopolitical contexts, such as Eastern Europe. Much of it follows Potter and Wetherell's (1987) injunction to move 'beyond attitudes' in order to consider the varying discursive effects of everyday racial discourse as they play out across a range of social contexts.

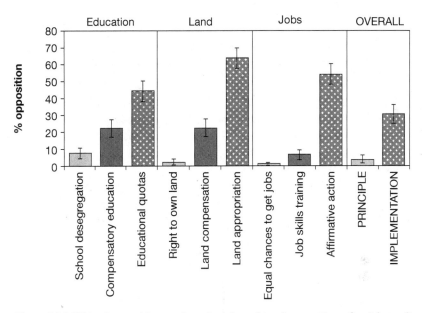

Figure 18.1 Whites' opposition to the principle and implementation of racial equality in post-apartheid South Africa (adapted from Dixon et al., 2007).

Note: The graph shows the percentage of whites opposing principles and practices of different forms racial equality, shown with 99 percent confidence intervals.

The phrase 'beyond attitudes' can, of course, can read in different ways. On the one hand, it might signify that the entire mainstream tradition of attitude research is so deeply flawed, so limited conceptually and methodologically, that it should be jettisoned and replaced with a fundamentally different (and incommensurable) style of work. We suspect that this is the position now adopted by most researchers working under the banner of 'discursive psychology'. For many, the concept of attitude has become a tired anachronism that has been laid to rest (although it is perhaps worth remembering here that mainstream attitude research continues to inspire hundreds of studies per year and remains a cornerstone of psychology teaching throughout the world). On the other hand, the phrase 'beyond attitudes' might signify something intriguingly different: a commitment to exploring the tensions between mainstream and discursive work in the hope not of reconciling them, but of devising a social psychology of racism that might weigh and exploit the contributions of both traditions. It is in this spirit that we offer two examples in conclusion.

(Race) Attitude variability revisited: The principle-implementation gap in attitudes towards inequality

The first example highlights a limit in Potter and Wetherell's (1988) original critique of mainstream attitude research that has unfortunately been carried forward by later researchers. Ironically, this limit is exposed particularly starkly by work on racial attitudes. It concerns the supposed neglect of attitude variability in the traditional literature. To be sure, as Potter and Wetherell highlighted, the psychometric methods commonly used in attitude research often do filter out attitudinal inconsistency and variability by constructing a single statistical index that represents an individual's racial attitude. However, the idea that traditional work is somehow circumscribed by this practice or that traditional attitudes theorists overlook variability is at best a simplification.

In point of fact, understanding the inconsistent, complex and contextually variable expression of race attitudes has been a – perhaps *the* – driving force of mainstream research over the past thirty years (e.g., see Dovidio, 2001). During this period, for example, researchers have increasingly recognized how the same individual may espouse quite different race 'attitudes' depending on the dimensions of evaluation used, the context in which they are expressed, how they are measured, and even how they are discursively framed. Various theories have emerged that attempt to predict and explain this phenomenon: self-presentational accounts, dual process models of explicit and implicit attitudes, symbolic racism theory, and aversive racism theory are a few examples. Similarly, methodological frameworks have been devised that are expressly designed to reveal the variable and sometimes contradictory nature of individual attitude expressions and to trace their implications. The bogus pipeline, the Implicit Association Test, and Dovidio and Gaertner's job selection task are examples.

On a broader level, researchers have also recognized that race attitudes are themselves historically shifting and responsive to wider social and political dynamics, giving rise to emergent distinctions between old-fashioned and symbolic prejudice (Kinder and Sears, 1981), implicit and explicit prejudice (Greenwald and Banaji, 1995), subtle and blatant prejudice (Pettigrew and Meertens, 1995), and Jim Crow and laissez faire prejudice (Bobo, Kleugel and Smith, 1997). What 'counts' as a negative racial attitude has become a target on the move, a point on which both discursive and mainstream researchers agree. As Dovidio and Gaertner (1998: 25) observe, '[. . .] like a virus that has mutated, racism has also evolved into different forms that are more difficult not only to recognize but also to combat.'

Our point here is not that traditional work has become immune to the kind of critique developed by Potter and Wetherell (1988) or, more specifically, that its treatment of the question of attitude variability is adequate. Indeed, Wetherell and Potter (1992) offered some compelling arguments about to the contrary, some of which were revisited and extended by Durrheim and Dixon (2004) in a critique of later waves of attitude research. Rather, our point is that this work is grappling with problems of attitude variability in ways that have the capacity to inform, as well as be informed by, discursive research.

Consider, as a simple illustration, the data presented in Figure 18.1, which is taken from an attitude survey conducted in post-apartheid South Africa. It captures a form of race attitude variation that has been widely researched in the traditional literature, depicting the so-called *principle-implementation gap* in whites' attitudes towards racial equality. Research on this topic has generally highlighted a contradiction between attitudes towards ideals of racial justice and attitudes towards concrete policies designed to achieve such justice (see Dixon, Durrheim and Tredoux, 2007). Thus, as Figure 18.1 illustrates, respondents who show strong 'in principle' support for equality (in domains such as employment, education and land ownership) are often more resistant to actual interventions to promote social change (e.g., affirmative action in the work place, race quotas in schools, and land redistribution). In addition, evidence shows that different kinds policies of attract different levels of opposition. Compensatory policies (e.g., scholarships for underrepresented students) tend to elicit less opposition than preferential policies (e.g., racial quotas in schools), and policies discursively framed as 'race targeted' tend to invoke more opposition than policies framed in more general terms (or as benefitting other groups, such as the elderly).

Attempts to explain the principle-implementation gap are steeped in controversy. As Tuch and Hughes (1996: 724) wryly put it, '[. . .] what accounts for this gap, and what the gap reveals about whites' racial thinking, continues to be hotly debated in the race attitudes literature.' Without going further into the details of this literature, we want to suggest that this is precisely the kind of area of 'traditional' work that would benefit from research in the discursive tradition introduced by Potter and Wetherell (1988). How ordinary people construct the nature, meaning, and relationship between 'racial' principles and policies, how such constructions vary across different discursive and ideological contexts, how such variations are designed to accomplish social and rhetorical goals, how individuals' themselves navigate the apparent ideological dilemmas that the principle-implementation gap entails – these are all the kinds of issues that their approach to 'accomplishing attitudes' was designed to address. They are the kinds of issues, too, that might re-open a productive dialogue between discursive and mainstream traditions. In the next section, we consider another potential area of dialogue.

Beyond talk: Embodiment and racial evaluation

Mainstream research on race attitudes has prioritized their linguistic expressions, which are usually assessed by proxy through use of questionnaire scales. In the past few decades, however, there has been an upsurge in work employing non-verbal measures. This work has shown, for example, that processes of evaluation may be conveyed via a rich array of embodied behaviours, ranging from eye contact to seating distances, from blinking rates to facial expressions. It has shown, too, that attitudes expressed via overt verbal behaviors may sometimes be at variance with those expressed via the more indirect, and arguably less controllable, non-verbal behaviours. Perhaps most intriguing, it seems that the targets of evaluation are themselves highly sensitive to subtle discrepancies between non-verbal and verbal dimensions of evaluation. The work of Jennifer Richeson, Nicole Shelton and Jack Dovido and colleagues elegantly illustrates some of these themes and also the emerging methodological paradigms through which they are being explored (e.g., see Dovidio, 2001; Shelton and Richeson, 2006).

To date, discursive psychological research on attitudes has also had a linguistic emphasis, and in many ways this is understandable. This research has often been designed to challenge the still-widespread tendency for psychologists to use language data uncritically (e.g., by treating talk about others as a transparent reflection of how individuals feel, thereby ignoring its functions in context). Moreover, discursive psychologists have often treated the very distinction between discourse and embodiment as a dualism that dissolves when it looks at how attitudes are 'done' in concrete sequences of social interaction and at what they are designed to accomplish (cf Wiggins and Potter, 2008).

For one thing, they have pointed out that so-called non-verbal 'expressions' cannot be understood simply as the manifestation of an inner psychological state that 'leaks out': they are part of the same rhetorical and action-oriented process of 'attitude object constitution' that occurs in everyday language and must be understood as such. As Wiggin's (2002) witty study of gestures of 'gustatory pleasure' at the dinner table illustrates, saying 'mmm' with a facial expression of pleasure may be read simply as expressing an internal evaluation of the food in one's mouth. In context, however, it may equally function as a reassuring compliment to the cook, a gesture of 'spontaneous' enjoyment, an attempt to convey a shared experience of pleasure, or even a ploy to get little Joey to eat his broccoli. For another thing, they have pointed out that particular bodily 'reactions', including reactions towards others, are rendered meaningful only via their construction in language. If someone pulls their children closer when a black man approaches on the street is that a gesture of racism or a legitimate response to the threat posed by a male stranger? If a 'white' South African moves to another part of the beach when a large group of 'black' South Africans sit nearby, is that an act of illegitimate prejudice that recreates racial segregation or an accountable reaction to feeling 'crowded out' (Durrheim and Dixon, 2005)? In each case, a broadly 'negative evaluation' of others has been performed via an embodied practice. Yet its meaning and consequences is arguably not intrinsic to the practice itself, but emerges only via its second order constitution in discourse.

Even if this is true – and it is not an uncontroversial claim (cf Durrheim and Dixon, 2005) – we believe that further study of embodied practices promises to enrich future work on how attitudes are accomplished. Along similar lines, in a recent discussion of research on affect, Margaret Wetherell (2012) has both vigorously defended the discursive approach and acknowledged the need for research that integrates analysis of linguistic practices with analysis of other kinds of material and embodied practices.

How might this kind of integration be accomplished? Charles Goodwin's (2000) work illustrates one approach to answering this question. Goodwin proposes that within an unfolding interaction the use of bodies can contribute to a complex configuration in which talk is just one of several elements (including 'relevant artifacts, spaces, and features of the material surround', p. 1519). Using the example of a dispute between girls playing hopscotch, Goodwin illustrates the potential importance of bodily stances – as when two of girls turn towards and look at each other – in establishing a space as a field of interaction. He also shows how physical gestures and movements can both mirror communications (e.g., when one girl says 'four' and holds up a hand to show four fingers) or act as a separate sign system (e.g., when one girl steps into another's path to stop her playing). He notes, too, how certain features of the physical environment, like the painted hopscotch grid on the pavement, pre-exist and persist beyond any particular interaction. They serve as semiotic structures that can *potentially* be deployed by actors and that may become essential to certain kinds of 'relevant actions'. A 'body jumping on a surface that does not contain a hopscotch grid', for example, 'is not playing hopscotch' (ibid.: 1517).

Goodwin's study indicates some possible directions for future research on attitudes. Perhaps most obvious, his work shows how evaluation of others might be done through a complex interplay of language, gestures, bodily orientation, etc., unfolding within particular interactional and physical settings. In this sense, the discursive approach has the potential to take attitude research in new directions (e.g., by exploring the action-oriented nature of particular sequences of verbal and embodied activity in context; see also Wiggins, 2002).

Researchers might also explore how physical environments enable our evaluations of others. In work rooted in a conversational analytic perspective, as favoured by researchers such as Goodwin, this means exploring the role played by such environments within the immediacy of unfolding interactions, as revealed by participants' own orientations and situated practices. Discursive researchers might additionally attempt to establish links between the physical environments in which evaluations are constructed and wider power relations within a society. As such, they might seek to explore the shared meanings that become associated with the concrete and relatively persistent features of material environments in which everyday life unfolds, which can render them as essential to the perpetuation of racism as the painted grid is to the game of hopscotch.

References

Ajzen, I. and Fishbein, M. (1980) *Understanding attitudes and predicting social behavior.* Englewood-Cliffs, NJ: Prentice-Hall.

Allport, G.W. (1935) 'Attitudes', in C. Murchison (ed.) *A handbook of social psychology.* Worcester, MA: Clark University Press.

Augoustinos, M., Tuffin, K. and Sale, L. (1999) 'Race talk', *Australian Journal of Psychology,* 51: 90–7.

Billig, M. (1987) *Arguing and thinking: A rhetorical approach to social psychology.* Cambridge: Cambridge University Press.

Billig, M. (1991*) Ideology and opinions.* London: Sage.

Bobo, L., Kleugel, J.R. and Smith, R.A. (1997) 'Laissez-faire racism: The crystallization of a kinder, gentler, antiblack ideology', in S.A. Tuch and J.K. Martin (eds) *Racial attitudes in the 1990s: Continuity and change* (pp. 15–42). Westport, CT: Praeger Publishers.

Condor, S., Figgou, L., Abell, J., Gibson, S. and Stevenson, C. (2006) '"They're not racist . . ." Prejudice denial, mitigation and suppression in dialogue', *British Journal of Social Psychology,* 45: 441–62.

Dixon, J., Durrheim, K. and Tredoux, C. (2007) 'Intergroup contact and attitudes towards the principle and practice of racial equality', *Psychological Science,* 18: 867–72.

Dixon, J.A., Foster, D.H., Durrheim, K. & Wilbraham, L. (1994). 'Discourse and the politics of space in South Africa: The "squatter crisis"', *Discourse and Society,* 5, 277–296.

Dixon, J.A., Reicher, S. and Foster, D. (1997) 'Ideology, geography and racial exclusion: The squatter camp as "blot on the landscape"', *Text,* 17: 317–48.

Dovidio, J.F. (2001) 'On the nature of contemporary prejudice: The third wave', *Journal of Social Issues,* 57: 829–49.

Dovidio, J.F., & Gaertner, S.L. (1998) 'On the nature of contemporary prejudice: The causes, consequences, and challenges of aversive racism', in J. Eberhardt and S.T. Fiske (Eds.), *Confronting racism: The problem and the response* (pp. 3–32). Newbury Park, CA: Sage.

Durrheim, K. and Dixon, J. (2004) 'Attitudes in the fiber of everyday life: The discourse of racial evaluation and the lived experience of desegregation', *American Psychologist,* 59: 626–36.

Durrheim, K. and Dixon, J. (2005) 'Studying talk and embodied practices: Towards a psychology of the materiality of "race relations"', *Journal of Applied Community and Social Psychology,* 15: 446–60.

Durrheim, K., Foster, D., Tredoux, C. and Dixon, J. (2011) 'Historical trends in South African race attitudes', *South African Journal of Psychology,* 41: 262–78.

Eagly, A. and Chaiken, S. (1995) 'Attitude strength, attitude structure and resistance to change', in R. Petty and J. Kosnik (eds) *Attitude strength* (pp. 413–32). Mahwah, NJ: Erlbaum.

Goodwin, C. (2000) 'Action and embodiment within situated human interaction', *Journal of Pragmatics,* 32: 1489–522.

Greenwald, A. G., and Banaji, M. R. (1995) 'Implicit social cognition: Attitudes, self-esteem, and stereotypes', *Psychological Review,* 102, 4-27.

Greenwald, A.G., McGhee, D.E. and Schwartz, J.L.K. (1988) 'Measuring individual differences in implicit cognition', *Journal of Personality & Social Psychology,* 74: 1464–80.

Kinder, D.R. and Sears, D.O. (1981) 'Prejudice and politics: Symbolic racism versus racial threats to the good life', *Journal of Personality & Social Psychology*, 40: 414–31.
Manstead, A., Proffitt, C. and Smart, J. (1983) 'Predicting and understanding mothers' infant-feeding intentions and behavior: Testing the theory of reasoned action', *Journal of Personality & Social Psychology*, 44: 657–71.
Pettigrew, T.F. and Meertens, R.W. (1995) 'Subtle and blatant prejudice in Western Europe', *European Journal of Social Psychology*, 25: 57–75.
Potter, J. (1996) *Representing reality: Discourse, rhetoric and social construction*. London: Sage.
Potter, J. (2012) 'Re-reading *Discourse and Social Psychology*: Transforming social psychology', *British Journal of Social Psychology*, 51: 436–55.
Potter, J. and Wetherell, M. (1987) *Discourse and social psychology*. London: Sage.
Potter, J. and Wetherell, M. (1988) 'Accomplishing attitudes: Fact and evaluation in racist discourse', *Text*, 8: 51–68.
Puchta, C. and Potter, J. (2002) 'Manufacturing individual opinions: Market research focus groups and the discursive psychology of attitudes', *British Journal of Social Psychology*, 41: 345–63.
Quillian, L. (2006) 'New approaches to understanding prejudice and discrimination', *Annual Review of Sociology*, 32: 299–338.
Rosenberg, M.J. and Hovland, C.I. (1960) 'Cognitive, affective and behavioral components of attitudes', in M.J. Rosenberg and C.I. Hovland (eds) *Attitude organization and change: An analysis of consistency among attitude components*. New Haven, CT: Yale University Press.
Shelton, J.N. and Richeson, J.A. (2006) 'Interracial interactions: A relational approach', in M.P. Zanna (ed.) *Advances in experimental social psychology* (Vol. 38, pp. 121–81). New York: Academic Press.
Taylor, S. (2007) 'Attitudes', in D. Langdridge and S. Taylor (eds) *Critical readings in social psychology*. Maidenhead: Open University Press.
Taylor, S. and Wetherell, M. (1999) 'A suitable time and place: Speakers' use of "time" to do discursive work in narratives of nation and personal life', *Time & Society*, 8: 39–58.
Tuch, S.A. and Hughes, M. (1996) 'Whites' racial policy attitudes', *Social Science Quarterly*, 77: 723–41.
Van Bavel, J.J., Xiao, Y.J., & Cunningham, W.A. (2012) 'Evaluation is a dynamic process: Moving beyond dual system models', *Social and Personality Psychology Compass*, 6, 438-54.
Wetherell, M. (2012) *Affect and emotion: A new social science understanding*. Los Angeles and London: Sage.
Wetherell, M. and Potter, J. (1992) *Mapping the language of racism: Discourse and the legitimation of exploitation*. Hertfordshire: Harvester Wheatsheaf.
Wiggins, S. (2002) 'Talking with your mouth full: Gustatory "mmm"s and the embodiment of pleasure', *Research on Language & Social Interaction*, 35: 311–36.
Wiggins, S. and Potter, J. (2003) 'Attitudes and evaluative practices: Category vs. item and subjective vs. objective constructions in everyday food assessments', *British Journal of Social Psychology*, 42: 513–31.
Wiggins, S. and Potter, J. (2008) 'Discursive psychology', in C. Willig and W. Stainton Rogers (eds) *The Sage handbook of qualitative research in psychology* (pp. 72–89). London: Sage.

Wright, S.C. and Lubensky, M. (2009) 'The struggle for social equality: Collective action vs. prejudice reduction', in S. Demoulin, J.P. Leyens and J.F. Dovidio (eds) *Intergroup misunderstandings: Impact of divergent social realities* (pp. 291–310). New York: Psychology Press.

19 Banal nationalism, postmodernism and capitalism

Revisiting Billig's critique of Rorty

Stephen Gibson

Target article: Billig, M. (1993) 'Nationalism and Richard Rorty: The text as a flag for *Pax Americana*', *New Left Review*, I/202: 69–83.

Introduction

Michael Billig's 'Nationalism and Richard Rorty: The text as a flag for *Pax Americana*', published in *New Left Review* in 1993, will be familiar to most readers as the final substantive chapter in *Banal nationalism* (Billig 1995a), in which it was re-titled, 'Philosophy as a flag for the *Pax Americana*'. Indeed, the arguments presented in the *New Left Review* article are inseparable from the broader banal nationalism thesis, and their influence can only be understood in this context. In the present chapter, my focus will thus be on the version of the critical engagement with Rorty presented in *Banal nationalism*, rather than in *New Left Review*. There is a further advantage to this focus, and one that will become apparent as my argument develops. The modifications that Billig made to the argument presented in *Banal nationalism* included a discussion of a then-recent *New York Times* article by Rorty (1994), published after Billig's (1993) article in *New Left Review*. Rorty's (1994) article is significant in marking a shift on his part towards a more explicit engagement with themes of patriotism and national pride than had previously been the case, and I will suggest that this can be seen as a precursor to his subsequent development of his ideas on these themes in his later volume *Achieving our country* (Rorty 1998).

In what follows, I will begin by outlining the general thesis of *Banal nationalism* and some critical reactions to it, before moving on to spend the majority of the chapter considering Billig's specific critique of Rorty, and Rorty's development of a more explicit set of arguments concerning national pride in *Achieving our country*. It will be shown that Rorty's celebration of national pride is accompanied by an acceptance of capitalism as essentially inevitable, or at least as being something that is beyond 'realistic' challenge. In this respect, Billig's argument concerning the banality of the world of nations can be extended to encompass the banal acceptance of the world of capital. I will subsequently link some of these ideas to Billig's (2012, 2013) more recent writing in which he has addressed what has been termed 'academic capitalism' – the acceptance of market values into the academy. More broadly, I will suggest that engagement with ideological themes such as these constitute an important current in an expanded discursive psychology. Billig's recent work has identified a trend towards a narrowing of focus in academia, and if there is a wider lesson for discursive psychology to be drawn from his critique of Rorty – as from so much of Billig's work – it is that it would benefit from a broadening of purview, rather than an increasing narrowness in its focus.

Banal nationalism

Billig's (1995a) central contention in *Banal nationalism* was that social scientists have concentrated on the periodic outbursts of nationalism ('hot' nationalism), and have neglected the more routine, taken-for-granted nationalism that reproduces extant nation-states and the broader world-of-nations as natural and inevitable ('banal' nationalism). Billig traced the operation of banal nationalism in a number of directions, identifying the way in which a distinction can be drawn between patriotism and nationalism such that 'our' national sentiment can be construed as a healthy patriotic spirit, whereas the national sentiment of others can be treated as dangerous nationalism. Billig notes how national flags hanging limply from public buildings are typically not consciously noticed by people going about their daily business, but that these flags nevertheless work as an implicit reminder of the nation. Billig uses the idea of 'flagging' as a metaphor for other occasions when banal reminders of nationhood are served in the course of everyday life. Because these reminders are not consciously noticed, however, the reminding is not experienced as a reminding. In this respect, banal nationalism involves a complex dynamic of remembering and forgetting. The constant flagging ensures that we remember our status as nationals, and the place of 'our' nation in the world of nations, but this remembering is itself forgotten, leaving the impression that nations are natural and inevitable features of the world. A particularly important form of flagging is in the use of deixical referents – 'little words' such as *we, us, them, our, here* – that can be used to tacitly flag the nation as the relevant frame for discussion of some issue, event or phenomena. Billig demonstrated the presence of such deixical referents across a number of contexts, and notably undertook an exploratory 'day survey' of British 'national' newspapers to highlight the extent to which banal nationalist assumptions were built into their content and structure. For example, Billig noted how references to *the* weather or *the* economy typically assume a national frame without explicitly specifying it as such.

In outlining this thesis, Billig was concerned with the specificities of nationhood. In drawing attention to the shortcomings of general social psychological theories of identity, Billig stressed that 'the historical particularities of nationalism, and its links with the world of nation-states, tend to be overlooked, if national "identity" is considered as functionally equivalent with any other type of "identity"' (1995a: 65; see also Billig 1996). This echoed concerns raised some years previously by Tajfel (1970), who criticised the triviality of theories that seek only generality for its own sake. According to Tajfel, '[i]t is this triviality that presents perhaps the most intractable problem for the "universal" theories: when dealing with concrete cultural or social reality, they explain very little and predict nothing' (1970: 122). Moreover, Tajfel (1960: 846) argued that a social psychology of nationalism needed to be able to account for why '[w]e do not expect a doctor to be ready to die for the British Medical Association; but we are not surprised if someone says: "I am willing to die for my country"'. This concern to account for the extent to which nationalism has constituted the legitimating ideology behind countless deaths is clearly present from the outset of *Banal nationalism*, the opening line of which reads, 'All societies that maintain armies maintain the belief that some things are more valuable than life itself' (1995a: 1). For Billig, then, as for Tajfel before him, nationalism is a topic worthy of social psychological attention in its own right.

Critical reaction to Banal nationalism

Banal nationalism has been hugely influential across the social sciences. As Skey (2009: 333) has noted, it

> led the way in marking something of a shift in focus as research began to move away from the more macro-scale theorising on nationalism to more empirical-based studies, that focused on issues of representation, contestation and localised meaning-making as well as more contextualized case studies.

It is in this respect that *Banal nationalism* can be understood as applying the spirit of the social scientific 'turn to language' to the subject of nationalism.

There is insufficient space in a single chapter to review all the reactions to, and extensions of, Billig's thesis, and as such my focus here will, of necessity, be highly selective. I will focus in particular on two criticisms: first, that Billig underestimated the role of contestation; and second, that Billig overstated the extent to which certain entities might be said to be 'national'.

Contestation

Reicher, Hopkins and Condor (1997) echoed Billig's (1995a) call for a focus on the specificity of national categories, but suggested that taken-for-granted status is not something specific to nations. Other categories, such as 'race', can be understood in similar terms. If banality is therefore not a distinguishing feature of nationalism *per se*, then 'it is necessary to consider when and why our everyday concerns are structured in national rather than other terms' (Reicher et al., 1997: 77). Reicher et al. argued that this poses particular problems for Billig's approach:

> His analysis concerns the way in which people are textually addressed in ways that presuppose a national dimension, but the question of how text relates to understanding and action is not spelt out. Is it that people are simply interpellated in an Althusserian sense? [footnote omitted] This would seem unlikely, since elsewhere (for instance in *Arguing and Thinking*) Billig is concerned to challenge the notion of human beings as automatons and to accord people agency. Nonetheless, in the absence of an explicit position to the contrary, Billig can be seen as eliding media texts with human consciousness.
>
> (Reicher et al., 1997: 77–8)

This anticipates criticisms made elsewhere (e.g., Skey 2009; Reicher and Hopkins, 2001), that Billig underestimated the role of contestation in relation to nationalism. As Reicher et al. note, this is all the more striking given Billig's (1987, 1991; Billig et al. 1988) development of a theoretical perspective that places rhetoric at the heart of social and psychological life. However, in a discussion of the contributions that might be made by rhetorical psychology to the study of social movements, Billig (1995b) did make it clear that the banal acceptance of the world of nations was not something that should be taken to imply that counter-argument was impossible. In drawing attention to the importance of exploring not only that which is the subject for explicit argumentation, he also drew attention to silencing, suggesting that despite nationhood presently being seen 'to be as natural as rivers and mountain ranges', alternatives are possible: 'As sleeping monsters within today's thoughts, they wait to be freshly awakened by a social movement of the future' (Billig 1995b: 80). More recently, Billig (2009) has responded to this criticism by developing more explicitly the extent to which *Banal nationalism* should be understood in conjunction with his earlier work. Moreover, his subsequent work – particularly his re-casting of Freudian repression as a fundamentally rhetorical act (Billig, 1999) – addresses the issue of how, precisely, the same rhetorical perspective can be used to explore that which is left unsaid as much as it can be used to explore that which is the subject of overt argumentation.

The status of the 'national'

Rather than being an end-point of analysis, Billig (1995a: 175) emphasised that 'There is much systematic, empirical work to be done.' Subsequent research has indeed begun to expand on Billig's initial analysis, and in this respect one of the most striking modifications to the banal nationalism thesis concerns the status of those entities presumed to be 'national'.

In a series of papers, Rosie, MacInnes, Petersoo, Condor and Kennedy (2004; MacInnes et al., 2007; Rosie et al., 2006; see also Skey 2009) have argued that Billig's relatively straightforward assertion of the existence of a British 'national' press is problematic in the face of the variety of media within a state such as the United Kingdom. For example, most 'national' newspapers published in London have separate editions for Scotland featuring some modification in content. Similarly, some newspapers aimed at a Scottish readership position themselves specifically as Scottish national newspapers, and even apparently self-evidently regional newspapers can on occasion adopt the language of nationhood, such as the *Yorkshire Post*, which describes itself as 'Yorkshire's national newspaper' (MacInnes et al., 2007). In a slightly different vein, the extent to which *readers* may conceive of their location in the world in purely national terms can be questioned: 'We do not know how far they imagine themselves as members of a community of "English". "Scottish" or "British"readers, nor whether they see the latter as national' (Rosie et al., 2004: 454–5).

In responding to these critiques, Billig (2009) has acknowledged that his initial day survey oversimplified the 'national' dynamics of the UK. But this issue may extend beyond the 'national' press. The work of Condor and her colleagues (e.g., Abell, Condor and Stevenson 2006; Condor 1996, 2000, 2006, 2011; Condor and Abell 2006) on the ways in which ordinary people in England and Scotland understand themselves (or not) in 'national' terms has highlighted the utility of conceiving of both the banality of 'national' referents, and the very status of these referents as 'national', as being social accomplishments, 'the outcome of a socially distributed process of meaning-construction' (Condor, 2000: 199–200). In this respect, Condor points to the importance of contextualising any study of banal nationalism in a close analysis of participant understandings of the entities to which they refer. Thus, analysts are enjoined to be cautious about imposing 'nationalised' readings of deixical referents just because these seem most appropriate *to the analyst*, and to be cautious about attributing 'national' status to an entity, such as 'Britain', when it is not immediately apparent that participants themselves share that understanding.

Condor's work represents the most detailed and systematic attempt to study the 'national' common sense of ordinary social actors, and in this respect the context of the UK has provided a particularly fruitful setting for the expansion of Billig's original thesis. Yet Billig (2009) has recently noted that little further work has scrutinized the nationalism of the USA, which took such a central role in his initial formulation of banal nationalism. Arguably, it is in his critique of Rorty that Billig outlines the particular problems of US nationalism most fully. The next section of the present chapter will thus be concerned with revisiting Billig's critique of Rorty, and extending it in light of Rorty's subsequent volume, *Achieving our country*.

Billig's critique of Rorty

Thus far, I have neglected one important aspect of the banal nationalism thesis. Billig (1995a) was not concerned simply to identify banal nationalism in the everyday lives of ordinary social actors, the speeches of political leaders and the pages of 'national' newspapers; at the heart of Billig's thesis was the banal nationalism of academic theories themselves. *Banal nationalism* appeared at a time when many theorists were suggesting that nationalism was a declining force. Billig challenged such arguments, and showed how they often implicitly took for granted the world of nations. He drew attention to the ways in which banal nationalist assumptions can be identified in the work of several influential scholars, and took particular issue with postmodern approaches that pointed to the emergence of a more fluid 'identity politics' at the expense of national identities. Most notably in this respect, his critique of Rorty challenged one of the doyens of postmodern philosophy. The positioning of this critique as the final chapter of *Banal nationalism* is thus significant. Placing *Pax* in the context of the broader thesis of banal nationalism enables an appreciation of its status as a culmination of the arguments developed in the book.

Billig (1995a: 157) cited Terry Eagleton's damning indictment of Rorty's philosophy as suggesting a world in which 'the intellectuals will be "ironists", practising a suitably cavalier, laid-back attitude to their beliefs, while the masses . . . will continue to salute the flag and take life seriously'. Billig took issue with this description, suggesting that flag-waving can be found in Rorty's work, and indeed he goes on to discuss a then recent article in the *New York Times* in which Rorty (1994) explicitly advocated the need for greater patriotism. Moreover, Billig subsequently traced the links between Rorty's call for (US) patriotism and his formal philosophical writings.

Billig noted that the first person plural (*we, us, our*) takes centre-stage in Rorty's philosophy. Rorty's rejection of universal conceptions of morality leads him to locate the appropriate grounding for moral judgements in the somewhat vague notion of the community: 'the core meaning of "immoral action" is "the sort of thing that *we* don't do"' (Rorty, cited in Billig, 1995a: 162; emphasis in [Rorty's] original).

In outlining Rorty's advocacy of a limited form of ethnocentrism, Billig draws attention to the implicit universality of Rorty's claims – in effect, humans are inevitably ethnocentric, but we have a choice concerning the form that this ethnocentrism takes. Billig shows how Rorty's 'admitted ethnocentrism (which simultaneously is a subtly denied ethnocentrism) enables "us" to praise "ourselves", and to condemn "others". Given that "we" all have to be ethnocentric, then "we" are the best of ethnocentrics' (Billig, 1995a: 164).

As Billig puts it, Rorty's position boils down to the assertion that, '"We" can be proud of "ourselves", because "we" are not the sort of people to be proud of "ourselves"' (p. 165). But precisely who 'we' are in Rorty's texts varies widely, and is sometimes left completely unspecified.

Drawing on ideas discussed in previous chapters of *Banal nationalism*, Billig argues that attention to deixical referents can be particularly illuminating as they are frequently used for 'presenting sectional interests as if they were universal ones' (1995a: 166). Billig refers to this as the syntax of hegemony – the way in which the objectives of the powerful can be elided with those of collectives of which an individual speaker or writer claims membership. Often, Rorty construes the 'we' to whom 'we' should be loyal as 'our' society.

However, Billig notes that – as is the case with many other philosophers and social scientists – Rorty tends to neglect the extent to which 'society' is typically used to mean nation-state. In doing so, Rorty advocates the virtues of a liberal or progressive view of 'society', and indeed in advocating the location of morality in 'our society' Rorty is thereby according the nation-state a particularly central role in his philosophy.

Crucially, however, the story does not end there. The tendency towards universalism in Rorty's writings means that the liberal view of 'society' is not simply conceived as one among many, but as a view that others are exhorted to share. The vaguely bounded 'we' gives way to broader 'we's as Rorty recommends this position to all, seeing 'the history of humanity ... as the gradual spread of certain virtues typical to the democratic West' (Rorty, cited in Billig 1995a: 172).

Achieving our country: From banal nationalism to enthusiastic flag-waving

As Billig observes, 'There is one identity largely absent in Rorty's philosophical "we"s, but hugely foregrounded in his *New York Times* article: a national identity' (Billig 1995a: 167). It thus requires a detailed and scholarly analysis by Billig to draw out the banal assumptions of Rorty's texts. However, it appears that the *New York Times* article was not simply an anomaly, but was something of a foreshadowing of what was to come. Shortly after the publication of *Banal nationalism*, Rorty (1998) expanded on his call for US patriotism in his brief volume *Achieving our country*. Even a cursory examination of *Achieving our country* suggests that, by this point, Rorty had not only begun to notice the unwaved flags, but to wave them fervently himself. In contrast to the texts scrutinized by Billig, references to 'we Americans' (e.g., 1998: 13, 22, 28, 48, 91, 97, 106) are not infrequent, and there is a clear and unambiguous defence of the virtues of national pride from the outset. *Achieving our country* does not, therefore, require the same forensic level of scholarly analysis to unpack the nationalist assumptions at its heart – these are now foregrounded. However, the particular arguments that Rorty advances are worthy of closer scrutiny for they reveal interesting further assumptions about the nature of nations, nationalism and national pride. Moreover, in this extended exposition of his views on national pride, Rorty engages in detailed critique of leftist intellectuals who he holds responsible for a decline in the acceptability of US national pride. When we consider these arguments, the central place of capitalism in Rorty's injunction to national pride is unmistakable. This allows us to draw out one frequently neglected aspect of the banal nationalism thesis: the specifically US form of banal nationalism that so concerned Billig is inextricably bound up with a related set of banal assumptions about the inevitability of capitalism. Such assumptions can be identified in a range of settings, including – as Billig has himself pointed out recently – in academia.

Rorty and capitalism

The anti-Marxist position articulated in the *New York Times* article analysed by Billig is extended in *Achieving our country*. In developing the distinction between the reformist left and the new left, Rorty argues that:

> For us Americans, it is important not to let Marxism influence the story we tell about our own Left. We should repudiate the Marxists' insinuation that only those who are convinced capitalism must be overthrown can count as leftists, and that everybody else is a wimpy liberal, a self-deceiving bourgeois reformer.
>
> (Rorty, 1998: 42)

This is striking insofar as Rorty is not simply arguing against Marxism, or explaining that Marxism was wrong. He is arguing that it is important 'for us Americans' not to be influenced by Marxism. As ever with such formulations, it is possible to ask what this implies for those who are not 'us'. Presumably, it is less important for an unspecified 'them' who are not 'us', not to be influenced by Marxism. Quite simply, this echoes a long-standing political, academic and popular tradition that construes Marxism as 'un-American'.

Rorty's national pride is, in an important sense, tied to his commitment to pragmatism – he acknowledges at the outset of *Achieving our country* that the ultimate goal should indeed be a post-nation-state world, but suggests that such a world is simply not presently feasible. Arguing for the necessity of emotional involvement in one's country, he suggests that:

> The need for this sort of involvement remains even for those who, like myself, hope that the United States of America will someday yield up sovereignty to what Tennyson called 'the Parliament of Man, the Federation of the World.' For such a federation will never come into existence unless the governments of the individual nation-states cooperate in setting it up, and unless the citizens of those nation-states take a certain amount of pride (even rueful and hesitant pride) in their governments' efforts to do so.
>
> (Rorty, 1998: 3)

He nevertheless goes on to criticise those on what he terms 'the cultural Left' who have become deeply suspicious of American national pride, suggesting that 'The current leftist habit of taking the long view and looking beyond nationhood to a global polity is as useless as was faith in Marx's philosophy of history' (Rorty, 1998: 98). Rorty is particularly critical of what he sees as a preoccupation with philosophizing and theorizing, suggesting that much of what passes for the intellectual left consists of debates so abstracted from everyday concerns as to be of no practical use in achieving political change. And yet when Rorty explains why, despite the myriad imperfections of America, the nation-state represents the best available option for political progress, things get even more curious:

> We were supposed to love our country because it showed promise of being kinder and more generous than other countries. As the blacks and gays, among others, were well aware, this was a counsel of perfection rather than description of fact. But you cannot urge national political renewal on the basis of descriptions of fact. You have to describe the country in terms of what you passionately hope it will become, as well as in terms of what you know it to be now. You have to be loyal to a dream country rather than to the one to which you wake up every morning. Unless such loyalty exists, the ideal has no chance of becoming actual.
>
> (Rorty, 1998: 101)

There is thus a distinction between the hopes of those who recognise the problems of America and hope to 'achieve our country', and those who recognise the same problems but hope to achieve a post-national world. The former – including Rorty – are to be commended for sensibly engaging in the realm of practical politics, while the latter are to be castigated for an idealistic refusal to live in the real world. But why? Rorty points to the present inability to imagine alternatives to the world of nation-states, and links this explicitly to an inability to imagine alternatives to capitalism. The cultural Left, according to Rorty (1998: 102), has adopted 'ideals which nobody is yet able to imagine being actualized', not least among which is 'the end of capitalism' (ibid.). Rorty is scathing of the inability of the cultural Left to offer concrete alternatives ('what this new thing will be, nobody knows'; 1998: 103), arguing that the 'insouciant use of terms like "late capitalism" suggests that we can just wait for capitalism to collapse, rather than figuring out what, in the absence of markets, will set prices and regulate distribution' (103–4). In the absence of a proper alternative to capitalism, Rorty's advice is that:

> the Left should get back into the business of piecemeal reform within the framework of a market economy . . . Someday, perhaps, cumulative piecemeal reform will be found to have brought about revolutionary change. Such reforms might someday produce a presently unimaginable nonmarket economy, and much more widely distributed powers of decisionmaking. They might also, given similar reforms in other countries, bring about an international federation, a world government . . . But in the meantime, we should not let the abstractly described best be the enemy of the better. We should not let speculation about a totally changed system, and a totally different way of thinking about human life and human affairs, replace step-by-step reform of the system we presently have.
>
> (Rorty, 1998: 105)

This is a classically pragmatist position, pointing to the dangers of grand theory and abstract philosophy, and arguing that we should work within the here and now. The appeal of such arguments can be understood in part as a function of their status as a rhetorical bottom-line: get real, says the pragmatist, we'd all like a better world, but we have to work with what we've got. In this respect, we have the arch anti-foundationalist resorting to a realist line of argument in order to argue for the Left to work within the status quo – a status quo that takes for granted American national pride and capitalism even as it maintains an abstract commitment to – at some unspecified point in the future – replacing them with something better. But this unspecified commitment – the vague hope that piecemeal reform might lead to a nonmarket economy in a post-national world – is no more clearly articulated than in the doctrines of the cultural Left dismissed by Rorty. And here's the rub: Rorty's pragmatic philosophy is essentially a philosophy of defeat – a philosophy (or perhaps that should be an anti-philosophy) which accepts that the hopes of a genuinely radical alternative to the capitalist doctrine enshrined in the contemporary USA are misplaced.

Such arguments begin to move us some distance from contemporary discursive psychology as typically understood. For many discursive psychologists, engagement with broad ideological themes takes second place to the close analysis of talk and text. Yet it is not to deny the value of the latter to suggest that the former should retain its place at the heart of any discursive psychology. At the present time, the dangers of neglecting ideology are particularly notable for critical scholars, and in this respect it is worth considering the links between banal nationalism, discursive psychology and the bizarre capitalistic logic currently to be found at the heart of academic life.

Academic capitalism and discursive psychology

Rorty's exhortation to leftists to 'get real' and work within capitalism is in itself hardly novel – it is a familiar refrain these days as the business model and its associated creed of managerialism finds its way into more and more corners of social and economic life that might once have been seen as necessitating a quite different form of organization. As has been widely debated in recent times, one such area is academia itself. In some of his recent writings, Billig has drawn attention to the pernicious effects of academic capitalism, and in reflecting on the conditions that gave rise to his seminal *Arguing and thinking*, has discussed the political climate in which it was written:

> *Arguing and thinking* was written when an ideologically driven, right-wing Conservative government was explicitly seeking to control British universities under its free-market economic policies, imposing its philosophy of academic capitalism on higher education. The government's message was that if the universities wished to compete for public funds then they would have to demonstrate their economic usefulness; if not, the weak would fall by the wayside. Learning was not to be valued for its own sake, but if anything had value it should be seen to be useful, especially economically useful. Usefulness could, in their philosophy, be economically computed. To reject computational models of the mind, which viewed humans as machines, and 'to make antiquarian play' was, according to the author,

'to show the old Protagorean "spirit of contradiction"' (Billig, 1987: 8). Thus, in wandering about the library reading all but forgotten texts from the past, the author was deliberately turning his back on the politically driven demands of the present.

(Billig, 2012: 418)

For Rorty, no doubt such an approach would be foolish in the extreme. Rejecting academic convention in order to make a political point would beg the question, 'but what has this rejection achieved?' Despite Billig's own modesty concerning his work, it would not be difficult to point to a number of 'objective' indicators of its success: citation counts, academic awards, keynote presentations, and indeed the selection of Billig's work for comment and discussion in volumes such as the present one and Antaki and Condor's (2014) recent *festschrift*. But to do this unthinkingly, as a matter of course, as the way that one demonstrates academic 'impact' these days, is to accept the rules of the game as defined within precisely those ideologies that we seek to challenge (Billig, 2013). Of course, the vast majority of academics have to play by these rules to a certain extent to remain in gainful employment – and it would be disingenuous of me to suggest that I didn't engage in these language games myself when the occasion demanded[1] – but if we allow ourselves to come to believe that this is anything other than a game designed by those who would re-model academia according to the business approach, we are in danger of forgetting what academia should be. As Reicher (2011: 394) has argued,

> The whole point of Universities is to encourage a long-term perspective. It is to do what private enterprise militates against, which is to look beyond the immediate future (where estimates of gain and loss can be made and reasonable investment risks can be entertained) and start on interesting paths without knowing where they might ultimately lead.

As Billig (2012) notes, the pressures on academics in the present political climate are towards unthinking and uncritical action. In the United Kingdom, the requirement to demonstrate the 'impact' of one's work beyond the academy has recently been elevated to a key position in decision-making processes for the allocation of public funds for academic research. Such an approach encourages short-termism with research increasingly oriented towards producing small-scale 'impact' in the very near future, without challenging broader systems, tending to take priority. This makes the production of genuinely original and path-breaking work much less likely. As Reicher (2011: 394) has argued, 'Such achievements might be rare, but an academic culture that makes them impossible (or even harder) is ultimately self-defeating'. Moreover, 'nationalist'[2] assumptions lie at the heart of this issue. The UK's Economic and Social Research Council (ESRC) – responsible for distributing a large proportion of UK social science research funding – includes as part of its definition of impact the idea of 'fostering global economic performance, and specifically the economic competitiveness of the United Kingdom' (ESRC, 2014). The prioritization of the UK is unmistakable, but so is the foregrounding of 'economic competitiveness' and 'performance'. The world of bounded states is also a world of capitalist economics. This has specific implications for discursive psychology:

> If I look towards the future, I do not dream of an expanded, technically improved discursive psychology, especially one that can prove its usefulness to a right-wing administration that is even more ideologically committed to making higher education entrepreneurial than was the Conservative administration of the late 1980s.
>
> (Billig, 2012: 422-3)

Billig's contention is that some forms of discursive psychology have become conventionalized, and that where once there was radical critique, there is now a risk of political quietude. Rather than set up an academic island, separated from the social scientific mainland as experimental social psychology has done, Billig enjoins us to roam beyond the immediate confines of our increasingly small specialisms. Clearly, the conditions of present-day academia militate against this, and this is why those conditions must themselves be subject to our critical gaze. In engaging critically with major currents in social theory and philosophy, *Banal nationalism* shows not only that it is *possible* to venture outside of the confines of one's own immediate academic specialism, but that it is *vital* to do so. If *Banal nationalism* constitutes one of the most compelling analyses of nationalism in recent times, in the critique of Rorty it also points the way to an analysis of the capitalist assumptions underpinning much of contemporary life. Only a few years after the near collapse of the capitalist system that has formed a central component of 'the gradual spread of certain virtues typical to the democratic West' (Rorty, cited in Billig, 1995a: 172), it may be worth asking the question why the embedding of market values across a wide spectrum of systems and activities continues apace, and how the assumptions underpinning this process have come to be built into the fabric of reality, 'as natural as rivers and mountain ranges' (Billig, 1995b: 80).

Notes

1 To paraphrase Billig (2013: 155-6), we are all knob heads now.
2 The scare quotes here are in acknowledgement of the problematically 'national' status of the UK (see the discussion of Condor's work above).

References

Abell, J. Condor, S. and Stevenson, C. (2006) ' "We are an island": Geographical imagery in accounts of citizenship, civil society, and national identity in Scotland and in England', *Political Psychology*, *27*: 207-26.

Antaki, C. and Condor, S. (eds) (2014) *Rhetoric, ideology and social psychology: Essays in honour of Michael Billig*. Hove: Routledge.

Billig, M. (1987) *Arguing and thinking: A rhetorical approach to social psychology.* Cambridge: Cambridge University Press.

Billig, M. (1991) *Ideology and opinions.* London: Sage.

Billig, M. (1993) 'Nationalism and Richard Rorty: The text as a flag for *Pax Americana*', *New Left Review*, I/202: 69–83.

Billig, M. (1995a) *Banal nationalism.* London: Sage.

Billig, M. (1995b) 'Rhetorical psychology, ideological thinking, and imagining nationhood', in B. Klandermans and H. Johnston (eds) *Social movements and culture.* London: UCL Press.

Billig, M. (1996) 'Remembering the particular background of social identity theory', in W.P. Robinson (ed.) *Social groups and identities: Developing the legacy of Henri Tajfel.* Oxford: Butterworth-Heinemann.

Billig, M. (1999) *Freudian repression: Conversation creating the unconscious.* Cambridge: Cambridge University Press.

Billig, M. (2009) 'Reflecting on a critical engagement with banal nationalism – reply to Skey', *The Sociological Review*, 57: 347–52.

Billig, M. (2012) 'Undisciplined beginnings, academic success, and discursive psychology', *British Journal of Social Psychology*, 51: 413–24.

Billig, M. (2013) *Learn to write badly: How to succeed in the social sciences.* Cambridge: Cambridge University Press.

Billig, M., Condor, S., Edwards, D., Gane, M., Middleton, D. and Radley, A. (1988) *Ideological dilemmas: A social psychology of everyday thinking.* London: Sage.

Condor, S. (1996) 'Unimagined community? Some social psychological issues concerning English national identity', in G. Breakwell and E. Lyons (eds) *Changing European identities.* London: Butterworth Heinemann.

Condor, S. (2000) 'Pride and prejudice: Identity management in English people's talk about "this country"', *Discourse & Society*, 11: 175–205.

Condor, S. (2006) 'Temporality and collectivity: Diversity, history and the rhetorical construction of national entitativity', *British Journal of Social Psychology*, 45: 657–82.

Condor, S. (2011) 'Sense and sensibility: The conversational etiquette of English national self-identification', in A. Aughey and C. Berberich (eds) *These Englands: A conversation on identity.* Manchester: Manchester University Press.

Condor, S. and Abell, J. (2006) 'Vernacular accounts of "national identity" in post-devolution Scotland and England', in J.Wilson and K. Stapleton (eds) *Devolution and identity.* Aldershot: Ashgate.

ESRC (2014) *What is impact?* Available at www.esrc.ac.uk/funding-and-guidance/impact-toolkit/what-how-and-why/what-is-research-impact.aspx (accessed on 5 June, 2014).

MacInnes, J., Rosie, M., Petersoo, P., Condor, S. and Kennedy, J. (2007) 'Where is the British national press?', *The British Journal of Sociology*, 58: 187–206.

Reicher, S. (2011) 'Promoting a culture of innovation: BJSP and the emergence of new paradigms in social psychology', *British Journal of Social Psychology*, 50: 391–98.

Reicher, S. and Hopkins, N. (2001) *Self and nation.* London: Sage.

Reicher, S., Hopkins, N. and Condor, S. (1997) 'The lost nation of psychology', in C.C. Barfoot (ed.) *Beyond Pug's tour: National and ethnic stereotyping in theory and literary practice.* Amsterdam: Rodopi.

Rorty, R. (1994) 'The unpatriotic academy'. *The New York Times*, 13 February. Available at www.nytimes.com/1994/02/13/opinion/the-unpatriotic-academy.html (accessed on 6 June, 2014).

Rorty, R. (1998) *Achieving our country: Leftist thought in twentieth-century America*. Cambridge, MA: Harvard University Press.

Rosie, M., MacInnes, J., Petersoo, P., Condor, S. and Kennedy, J. (2004) 'Nation speaking unto nation? Newspapers and national identity in the devolved UK', *The Sociological Review*, 52: 437–58.

Rosie, M., Petersoo, P., MacInnes, J., Condor, S. and Kennedy, J. (2006) 'Mediating which nation? Citizenship and national identities in the British press', *Social Semiotics*, 16: 327–44.

Skey, M. (2009) 'The national in everyday life: A critical engagement with Michael Billig's thesis of *Banal Nationalism*', *The Sociological Review*, 57: 331–46.

Tajfel, H. (1960) 'Nationalism in the modern world: The nation and the individual', *The Listener*, 63(1624): 846–7.

Tajfel, H. (1970) 'Aspects of national and ethnic loyalty', *Social Science Information*, 9: 119–44.

Index

Italic page numbers indicate tables; bold indicate figures.

Abell, J. 81
Abelson, R. 166–7
abuse, study of 36–7
academic capitalism 290, 298–300
academic impact 299–300
academic theories, banal nationalism 293–5
accountability 94, 226
accuracy, written accounts 225
Achieving our country (Rorty) 247–9
action 19, 94
action-relevance 205
actions, accounts of/for 96
Adorno, T. 249
affection, displaying 154–6
agnostic view, of cognition 90
Allport, F. 103
Allport, G.W. 103, 243–4, 271
analytical perspectives 19–20
analytical promiscuity 189
analytical purpose, and transcription format 77
analytic uncertainty 81
Antaki, C. 44, 50, 147ff, 150, 156, 197, 198
anti-cognitivism 49–51, 53
Arguing and thinking (Billig) 249, 298–9
argumentation 249
argumentative texture 21
Ashmore, M. 29ff, 80, 220
assessments, in interaction 106–10
asylum seekers 62–3
Atkinson, P. 72

attitude: flexibility of concept 105; nature of concept 104; research history 103–4
attitude object constitution 276
attitudes 7, 9; and categorisation 200; challenging dominant attitudes 102–5; changes in research 103–4; changing 272–3; cognitive psychology research 110; context and overview 101–2; embodiment 283–5; espousal of 279; expression/accomplishment 274; and expressions 103, 104; future of research 111; implications of discursive challenge 104; measurement 275–6, *275*; measuring 104; nature and significance 271–4; re-defining 110–11; research history 103–4; rhetorical processes 274; shifting perspectives 274–6; subject-object relations 107–10; subtle variation of assessments in interaction 106–7; theoretical and analytical implications 105–10; traditional vs. discursive approaches *273*; variability 282; variability of accounts 104–5; *see also* racial attitudes
augmentative and alternative communication (AAC) 156
Augoustinos, M. 248
authenticity 72
automaticity literature 244

backdated predictability 92–3
background knowledge 200
Baddeley, A. 216

Bamberg, M. 171
Banaji, M. 215
banal nationalism 9; academic capitalism 290, 298–300; of academic theories 293–5; contestation 291–2; context and overview 289–90; critical reaction 291–3; critique of Rorty 293–5; ethnocentrism 294; and national identity 295–8; outline of thesis 290–1; Rorty and capitalism 296–8; status of the 'national' 292–4
Barnes, R. 50
Barthes, R. 103
Bartlett, F. 220
basic emotions approach 121
behaviour: and cognition 50; understandings of 88–9
Benwell, B. 171
Bergson, H. 218
Bietti, L. 221
Billig, M. 111, 183, 205, 211, 243ff, 245–6, 259, 262, 279, 289ff
blame 237–8
blame-accounts sequences 165
Boden, D. 214
bottom-up approach 44
boundaries, openness 190
breaches 24
Briggs, C. 74, 81
Brown, S.D. 211
Bruner, J. 211, 212
bullying, study of 36
Butler, C. 24, 136–7
Buttny, R. 165

Cartesian dualism 110
categorial practice 204–5
categories: demographic 198; in race talk 247–9
categorisation 8; and attributes 200; category differentiation 259–60; category selection 245–6; conceptualising 182; contemporary influences on MCA 190–1; context and overview 181; as discursive practice 246; fuzzy 183–5; intersubjectivity 186; machine for analysing sense-making 187, 188–9; members and membership 186; Membership Categorisation Analysis (MCA) 173, 181, 185–6, 187–9; natural and contrived data 247; openness 190; and prejudice 243–5; role of talking 186; social categories as social actions 182–5; stereotyping 258; types of 183; *see also* social identity categories
category relevance 198–205
Cazden, C.B. 134
celiac disease 94, 95–6
Chalmers, D. 218
child development 129, 152–4, 156
children: atypical development 156; formulating vs. acting on wants 156–7; interaction and development 152–4, 156; lexical development 211
children's talk: context and overview 129–31; implications of different approaches 142–4; knowledge-in-action 138–42; nature of understanding 131–6; public and accountable 140–1; purpose 135; repair sequences 142; as social action 136–8, 144; social norms 139–40; status of 130.
Childs, C. 123, 126, 156, 157
Chomsky, N. 149
classic studies, selection of 2–3
classroom interaction 131–2
Clinton, Bill 117
co-construction, incident descriptions 154–6
cognition: agnostic view 90; and behaviour 50; and conversation 88; DP view of 90; vs. interaction 88–90; relationship with discourse 162–5; role in and for interaction analysis 91
cognitive approaches, dominance 102
cognitive psychology, critique of 182, 187
cognitive representations 129
cognitivism, interviews 76–7
Colombetti, G. 218
colonization 80
Common Knowledge (Edwards and Mercer) 132
compensatory policies 283
competent membership 48

complementarity, cognition and interaction 89–90
concepts: creation of 105; as practices 133
Condor, S. 197, 257ff, 265, 291–2, 293
consensus formulations 174
consent gaining 61–2
constitutive ethnography 78
constructionism, theoretical development 35
constructionist approach, to language 19
constructionist theories 16
constructivism 48–9, 53, 103
content and context, inseparability 135
contestation 291–2
context of production 81
context, privileging 20–1
contingent problems 71–2, 74
contrived data 58, 61–4
conventionalization 300
conversational normativity 94–5
conversational repair 24
conversation analysis (CA) 6; compared to poststructuralist perspective 22; as distinct from DP 46, 48; DP criticism of 53; emotions 116; gender and language 23–4; influence on DP 44, 52–3, 103, 247; and interpretative repertoires 21–3; methodology 51; and politics 19–21; as tool for DP 53
conversation, and cognition 88
Conversation and cognition (te Molder and Potter) 87, 89
Costall, A. 152
Coulter, J. 121, 147, 152, 211
couples: scripts 165; self-presentation 165–6
critical analysis, legitimacy 20
critical anti-racism 265–7
critical conversation analysis 25
critical discursive psychology, 4; Wetherell's position in 16
critical social psychology, impasse 211
cross-gender identity 24
crying 124–6
cultural identity 247–9
cultural repertoires 22
culture, constructions of 19
culture in action 186

Culture in action (Hester and Eglin) 188–9

Danziger, K. 101, 111
data: context of 67; naturalising 61–4; naturally occurring 45; naturally occurring/contrived 6; *see also* natural and contrived data
data-driven approaches 44, 52, 198
dead social scientist's test 58
Dean, John 214
Death argument 32–3
defensive rhetoric 278
deixical referents 290, 294
demographic categories, use of 198
deracialized discourse 263
descriptions, situating 47
developmental discursive psychology 47–8
developmental psychology 129–31, 137; script formulation 174–5; socio-cultural context 211–12
Devine, P.G. 244–5, 249
Diana, Princess of Wales, reporting of death 224–31, 237–8
discourse: DP understanding of 4; framing 214; as object of inquiry 258–61; relationship with cognition 162–5
Discourse Action Model (DAM) 214, 215
discourse analytic method, applicability 231–6
Discourse and cognition (Edwards) 35, 87, 147
Discourse and social psychology (Potter and Wetherell) 16, 18–19, 104, 182, 246
discourse of hygiene 80
discursive psychology (DP): aims of 3; background 3–5; as challenge 3–4; challenge to convention 7; critical strand 4; definition 1, 5; development 1, 9–10; development trajectories 4–5; as oppositional research 173; situating 5; status 38–9; treatment of language 3–4; understanding of discourse 4
discursive research, development 102
discursive turn 17
discussion, ethical 38

306 *Index*

disposition-warranting 171, 173–5
dissociation model 244–5, 249
division, within DP 217
Dixon, J. 262, 264, 267, 282, 283, 284
domestic violence, script formulation 172
dominant attitudes, challenging 102–5
domination, talk-in-interaction 21
Dovidio, J. 282, 284
Drew, P. 89, 233, 234
dualism 152, 163
Durrheim, K. 262, 264, 265, 266, 267, 282, 283, 284

ecological validity 150
Economic and Social Research Council (ESRC) 299–300
Edley, N. 30, 35
Edwards, D. 1, 3, 5, 17, 29ff, 34, 35, 39, 43ff, 45, 47, 48, 50, 51, 87, 88, 89, 90, 92, 94, 96, 97–8, 99, 114ff, 120, 125, 129ff, 131, 133, 135, 152, 156, 162ff, 181ff, 183–4, 194ff, 198, 210ff, 211, 212, 214, 215–17, 219, 224ff, 233, 234, 246
Eglin, P. 188–9
Ekman, P. 114
embodied cognition 218
embodiment, racial attitudes 284–5
emergency services study 154–6
emic perspective 163
emotional work, interactional implications 155–6
emotion discourse 7, 39, 116–21
emotions: academic context 114–16; assigning causes 119; vs. cognition 118; context and overview 114; contribution of DP 121–2; controllable vs. passive 119–20; cross-cultural perspective 115; disposition vs temporary state 119; event vs disposition 119; feedback 155–6; focus of DP research 121; future research 125–6; grounded vs. consequential 119; hearability 126; historical and cultural differences 115; honest vs. fake 120; individualist approach 115; linguistic philosophy 115–16; natural vs. moral 120; private vs. public 120; rational vs. irrational 118–19; relational perspective 115; respecification and critique 122–3; social constructionist studies 121–2; in social interaction 123–5; understandings of 114–16
emotion terms: competitive anxiety 122–3; flexibility 116; interactive use 116
empathy 125–6
empirical science 215–16
enactive cognition 218
enticing a challengeable 190–1
epistemics, defining 96
epistemics-in-action 87
epistemic stance 98
epistemic status 24, 96–8
epistemological assumptions 274
epistemological positions 53
epistemology, realism/relativism debate 34
Erikson, E. 174
ethical discussion and practice, need for 38
ethics, realism/relativism debate 32–3
ethnocentrism 294
ethnomethodology 103, 116, 164, 187–8, 247
Ethnomethodology (Turner) 190
evaluations 106–10
everyday memory 216–17
everyday racism 265
experiential categorisation 183
explanatory adequacy 20
extended mind hypothesis 218
externalising device 236

fact-interest-accountability triangle 93–4
factuality 91
feedback, emotions 155–6
feminist conversation analysis 25, 26
feminist perspectives 36
Figgou, L. 265
focus: of CA 46; of DP 46, 49–50
focus groups 106
Fonagy, P. 157
food evaluations 107–10
footing, in interviews 75–6
Foucault, M. 103
Francis, D. 188
Furniture argument 31–2

Garfinkel, H. 99, 116
gatekeeping 111
gender: future research 24; and identity 23; language and conversation analysis 23–4; omnirelevance 205–6, 207; relevance 198–205
gender analysis, limitations of 21
gender inequality, in workplace 17–18
gender relevance, establishing 24
Georgaca, E. 152
Gergen, K.J. 35, 115
gestures 285
Gilbert, G.N. 49, 103
Goodman, S. 59–60, 62–3
Goodwin, C. 228, 285
Goodwin, R.Q. 211
Grancea, L. 171
Griffin, C. 61, 80–1
grounded understanding 21
guilt, Death argument 32–3

Hammersley, M. 71
Harré, R. 115, 122
hearability, of emotions 126
Henwood, K.L. 80
Hepburn, A. 36, 39, 45, 46, 49, 59, 60, 61, 67, 70ff, 76, 122, 124–5, 126
Heritage, J. 90, 96, 97, 98, 125–6
Hester, S. 188–9
heterosexuality, as normative 25
Hitchens, P. 60
Hollway, W. 77–8, 81
Hopkins, N. 291–2
Hopper, R. 90, 205, 207
Horowitz, A. 50
hotrodders 184–5, 194
Howard, John 250–1
Hughes, M. 283
hypothetical questions 65–6

idealist philosophers of science 30
Idealized Cognitive Models (ICM) 184
identities 8; approaches to study 16; categorisation 173; cross-gender identity 24; cultural and national 247–9; middle class masculine 22; national 247–9, 295–8; presentation in interviews 71

identity: establishment of 174; and gender 23; legitimacy 63; management 63
ideological analysis 9
Ideological dilemmas (Billig et al) 249
ideology 8–9; racial representations as 261–2
I don't knows 50
ignorance, use in stake management 91–2
impact, academic 299–300
implicit attitudes 272
impression management, script formulation 174
inaction, motives for 33
indexicality 184–5
Indigenous Australians, apology to 250–4
individualism, and careers 18
inequality, principle-implementation gap 281–3
inferences, qualitative interviews 76
information theory 212
inner worlds 164–5
inseparability, content and context 135
intention-promotion 234–5
interaction: analytical starting point 50; child development and ToM 152–4, 156; vs. cognition 88–90; emotions in 123–5; interviews as 59; and reification of responses 260–1; stance and gesture 285; and transcription 79; variation of assessments 106–9
interactional dynamics 79
interactional practices, in qualitative interviews 70–1
interactional relevance 46
interactional remembering 8
interactional-rhetorical model 163
interactional understanding 151
interactions, structured interviews 71
interdependency, of individual and collective 217
interdisciplinary, nature of DP 137
intergroup attitudes 272
interiority 218
internal/external distinction, collapse of 163
Interpretative Phenomenological Analysis 77, 218

interpretative repertoires 16, 18, 19, 21–3
interpretive gap 46
intersubjective knowledge 96
intersubjectivity 186
interviews: as interaction 59; as knowledge producing machine 75; making sense 74; natural and contrived 58; representational practices 72–4; status of 70, 72–4; structured 71; as topic and resource 6–7, 80; *see also* qualitative interviews

Jackson, C. 24
Jeffersonian transcription 72–4, 78
'John Dean's memory' (Neisser) 212–14, 215, 219–20

Kaposi, D. 220–1
Kent, 49
Kidwell, M. 142
Kitzinger, C. 24, 25, 38–9, 172, 173, 207
Klein, N.L. 205
knowledge: joint production 134; locus of 163; sequential accumulation 133–4
knowledge claims, implications 110
knowledge-in-action, children's talk 138–42
knowledge management 94
knowledge states, freezing 98–9
Korobov, N. 171–2, 173
Kuhn, T. 38, 216

Lakoff, G. 181, 182, 183
language: and accountability 226; constructionist approach to 19; as discourse 16; DP understanding of 9–10; expression of attitudes 274; gender and conversation analysis 23–4; performative view 151, 152, 153–4; perpetuating racism 262–3; referential view 115, 123, 148, 150, 152, 156; and reification of race categories 259–60; representational view 151; as social action 148; and social action 182; treatment in discursive psychology (DP) 3–4

Language Acquisition Device (LAD) 149
language-in-use: importance of studying 19; as site for investigating practical ideologies 18
language use, research settings 18
Laplante, J. 173
Latour, B. 30
Lawsongate 214
learning to remember 152
LeBaron, C. 205, 207
LeCouteur, A. 172, 174
Lectures on Conversation (Sacks) 43–53
legitimacy: critical analysis 20; of invoking social categories 16; political issues 21; of social categories 24
Lepper, G. 247
Lerner, G. 134, 206
letting go of mind 217–18
Leudar, I. 152
Levine, M. 197
lexical development 211
Lindström, A. 125
linguistic categorisation 182
linguistic constructionism 49
Lippmann, W. 257
Locke, A. 122–3, 125, 211
Loughborough approach 210–21
Loughborough school 132, 162

machine for analysing sense-making 187, 188–9
MacMillan, K. 224ff
Mapping the language of racism (Wetherell and Potter) 16, 19, 247–8, 249–50, 252
Massey, Sian 231–6
Mayr, A. 238
McCabe, R. 152
McMartin, 36
mealtime talk 94, 107–10, **109**
meaning making, and existence 31
meaning systems 23
media: blame 237–8; DP of 237–8; judging relevance 229; and public understanding 237; reputable vs. disreputable sources 226–8; texts and DP 230–6; third-party representation 231; *see also* recontextualisation

media studies 224
mediated accounts, as vehicles for action 226
mediated communication 8
mediated recontextualisation 238
Mehan, H. 78–9
members and membership 186
membership categorisation 46
Membership Categorisation Analysis (MCA) 173, 181, 185–6, 187–9, 190–1, 202–3, 247
memory: background to study of 211–15; context and overview 210–21; everyday memory 216–17; Lawsongate 212–14; research development 220–1; responses to discursive approach 215–17; scope of research 211–12; as subject of study 216; Watergate hearings 212–14
mentalization 157
mental states 50, 88
Mercer, N. 132
metalevel racism 261, 263, 265, 266
methodological influences, Potter and Wetherell 19
methodological pluralism 220
methodology, CA 51
methods: and context of data 67; questioning 70–1
middle class masculine identities 22
Middleton, D. 152, 211–12, 215–20
mind/behaviour dualism 152
mind, conceptualizing 163
mindlessness 244
mind reading 150–1
mind/world distinction 91, 94
Mishler, E. 77, 78
modal expressions 92–3
modal frameworks 235–6
Molotch, M.L. 214
Mondada, L. 94
monologues, representational practices 74
moral accountability 48, 169–70
moral implications, Theory of Mind (ToM) 157
moral work 234–5
Māori, social status 19
Moss, D. 50

motives 50
motives for inaction 33
motor attitude 103
Mulkay, M. 30, 49, 103
Muntigl, P. 172
Murakami, K. 221
mutual understanding 148

'national' common sense 293
national identity 247–9, 295–8
national pride 295
nation, constructions of 19
natural and contrived data 186, 195; argument for naturally occurring data 58–9; challenging distinction 60–1; context and overview 57; developing Potter's argument 59–60; future of debate 66–7; naturalising contrived data 61–4; procedural consequentiality 64–6; purpose of data 64, 66
natural conversation, focus on 88
naturally occurring data 45, 47, 51, 52, 72, 75, 79, 219
Neisser, U. 212–14, 215, 217, 219–20
neo-positivism 77
new racism 265, 266
new sexism 171–2
newspapers, regional and national 292–3
New Zealand study 249–50, 252
nominals, creation of concepts 105
non-cognitive analysis 8
non-cognitivism 89
non-Jeffersonian transcription 73
non-recognitional person reference 205
non-verbal expression 283–5
normativity 94–5, 184
norms and rules, children's talk 139–40
nostalgia 87

objectiveness 91
objective world 31
occasioned relevance 184
'Oh,' use of 90
omnirelevance 205–6, 207
O'Neill, J. 35
'On the analysability of children's stories' (Sacks) 188
ontological assumptions 274
ontological gerrymandering 98

ontology: move to epistemology 35; realism/relativism debate 34
open-ended interviews, use in research 45
opening questions 72–4
open-mindedness, social identity categories 198
Osvaldsson, K. 154–6

Parker, I. 35, 47
participants' orientations 45–7, 51, 52, 64, 198–200
particularisation, prejudice 245–7
particularism 48
Peräkylä, A. 99
perceptual-realist model 163
performance, as analytical starting point 50
performative view, of language 151, 152, 153–4
personality types 249
personhood 217
person reference forms 24
philosophers of science, idealist 30
Piaget, J. 129, 132, 153
Plejert, C. 156
political impulse 47
political issues, legitimacy and relevance 21
politics of being critical 25–6
Pomerantz, A. 89, 110
positioning 228
post-cognitive interaction research 7
post-cognitive psychology: causative/normative models 96–9; cognition vs. interaction 88–90; context and overview 87–8; conversation and cognition 88; defining 88; knowledge management 94; norms and rules 93–6; radical version 91–3; summary and conclusions 99
post-dualist approaches 218
post-structualist perspective, compared to conversation analysis 22
post-structuralism 103
post-structuralism/conversation analysis debate 6; see also Wetherell-Schegloff debate
Potter, J. 3, 4, 5, 9, 16, 17, 29ff, 44, 45, 46, 48, 49, 51, 57ff, 70ff, 76, 87ff, 88, 89, 90, 91, 92, 94, 101ff, 104–5, 106, 107–8, 111, 122, 124–5, 126, 149, 182, 210ff, 212, 214, 215–18, 246, 247–8, 249–50, 252, 254, 271ff
power, talk-in-interaction 21
practical considerations, and careers 18
practical ideologies 17–18
practice, ethical 38
practices: focus on 88; importance of studying 106
pragmatic pragmatism 33
pragmatism 297–8
preferential policies 283
prejudice 183; categories in race talk 247–9; categorisation 243–5; context and overview 243; flexibility 249; individualisation 254; New Zealand study 247–8, 249–50, 252; particularisation 245–7; personality types 249; rhetorical and discursive approach 249–54; study of 9; summary and conclusions 254
prejudice model of social change 272–3
Princess Diana, reporting of death 224–31, 237–8
principle-implementation gap 282–3
private thoughts (RPTs) 50
problems: contingent 71–2; necessary 71–2, 74, 75, 78–9
procedural consequentiality 24, 64–6, 198
propositional categorisation 183
psychological realism 274
psychological thesaurus 143
psychology, and DP 47–8
psychotherapy 152
public understanding, and media 237
Puchta, C. 106

qualitative interviews: answers and criticisms 77–9; closing questions 81; cognitivism 76–7; commentaries on Potter and Hepburn 77–9; context and overview 70; context of production 81; contexts of recruitment 74; follow-up questions 75–7; footings 75–6; inferences 76; interactional practices 70–1; limitations of 23; opening

questions 72–4; presentation of identities 71; questioning methods 70–1; questions about and for research 71–2; representational practices 72–4, 77–9; research agendas 80; responses to critics 79; return to debate 80–1; sensitive topics 76; social science agendas 75; stakes and interests 76; transcription and interaction 79; *see also* interviews
qualitative research, recognition 102
questions: about and for research 71–2; hypothetical 65–6

race, constructions of 19
race stereotypes 9; context and overview 257–8; critical anti-racism 265–7; reification of race categories 259–60; reification of race thinking 258–9; reification of responses 260–1; social construction of racism 261–7; stereotyping by implication 263–5; summary and conclusions 267–8; *see also* stereotyping
racial attitudes: context and overview 271; embodiment 284–5; future research 281; post-apartheid South Africa 276–9, **282**; principle-implementation gap 282–3; reflections 279–81; *see also* attitudes
racial categories 206–7
racism: as collaborative accomplishment 265; perpetuation through language 262–3; policy responses 284; reification 266; social construction 261–8
racist evaluations 9
Rapley, M. 248
Rapley, T. 72, 81
rationality, and emotion discourse 117
Raymond, G. 98–9
Realist Dilemma 31, 33–4
Reavey, P. 220
recognition, doing 97–8
reconceptualisation 162
recontextualisation 224; categorisation of people 227–8; context and overview 224–5; death of Princess Diana 224–31, 237–8; descriptions as 225–30; discursive psychology of the media 237–8; externalising device 236; intention-promotion 234–5; journalistic gloss 229–30; mediated 238; media texts and DP 230–6; modal frameworks 235–6; third-party 228–9, 237–8; *see also* media
Reed, D. 80
referential judgement 225–6
referential theory of meaning 34
reflexive adequacy 224
reflexivity 30, 33, 38, 39, 59
refugees 62–3
Reicher, S. 291–2, 299
reification: of race categories 259–60; of race thinking 258–9; of racism 266; of responses 260–1
relational perspective 115
relationship counselling 195–6
relativism: as (non)position 34; social science *par excellence* 33–4
Relativist Dilemma 33–4
relativist meta-theory 103
relevance: political issues 21; of social categories 16, 24
remembering 133
repairs 24, 142, 199, 201–2
reportage, control of 229
representational model 98–9
representational practices 72–4, 77–9
representational view, of language 151
researcher-generated interviews, problems of 58–9
researcher influence 58
researcher perspectives 19–20
research, questions about and for 71–2
research questions, formulating 44, 51, 52
respecification 39, 130, 148–9, 150, 162, 174, 186, 187, 218
Reynolds, E. 190–1
rhetoric 184–5, 249, 258–9
rhetorical contrasts 116–20
rhetorical psychology 249–54, 292
rhetorical self-sufficiency 249–53
rhetorical turn 9
Richards, G. 212
Robles, J.S. 106, 107
Roediger, H.L. 215

romantic couples, script formulation 172–3
Rorty, R. 289ff, 297–8
Ross, G. 211
Roulston, K. 79
Rudd, Kevin 252–4
Ryle, G. 152

Sacks, H. 25, 43ff, 57, 88, 99, 103, 116, 121, 153, 164, 181, 184, 187, 194, 198, 247; anti-cognitivism 49–51; early work 45; Edward's reworking 185–7; in ethnomethodology 187–8; formulating research questions 44, 51, 52; influence on DP 51–3; naturally occurring data 45, 51, 52; participants' orientation 45–7, 51, 52; psychology and DP 47–8
salience 98–9
scaffolding 134, 211
Schank, R.166–7
Schegloff, E. 15ff, 19–21, 22–3, 45, 46, 51, 64, 73–4, 76, 164, 188, 189, 197–8, 200
scientific practice, reflexivity 30
script formulation: and accountability 169–70; analysis 169–70; as consensus formulation 174; context and overview 162; developmental psychology 174–5; and dispositions 168; Edward's focus 165; Edward's reworking of script theory 167–9; impact on DP 170–3; impression management 174; influences on 165–7; and norms 168; relationship between discourse and cognition 162–5; summary and conclusions 173–4; theoretical shift 163; uses of 171–2
scripts: and norms 168; ways of understanding 167–9
scripts-d 167–8
scripts-pc 167
scripts-w 167
script theory, Edward's reworking 167–9
second turn proof procedure 186
self-attribution, social identity categories 207
Self-categorization Theory (SCT) 196–7

self-disclosure 81
self-initiated self-repair (SISR) 201
semantic differential 275
semantic schema 183
sense-making 17, 74
sensitive topics 76
sequential accumulation 133–4
sequential analysis 202–3
sequentiality 184
sexism, English Premier League (EPL) study 231–6
Sharrock, W. 152
Shotter, J. 115
Sidnell, J. 226
silencing 292
Silverman, D. 72
similarity-difference 259
"Siren Version" of Death argument 32–3
situatedness 184–5
Skey, M. 291
Smith, J.A. 77–8, 79, 218
Smithson, J. 198–200
Sneijder, P. 92–3
social attitudes 103–4
social categories 16, 24, 182–5, 243–4
Social Categorisation Theory 190–1
social cognition theory 261
social constructionist studies of emotion 121–2
social construction, of racism 261–7
social epistemology 163
social identity categories: ambiguity 207; assumptions 194–5; background to 194; categorial practice 204–5; choice of 197–8; context and overview 194; flexibility of use 197; fuzzy 195; omnipresence 206; omnirelevance 205–6; open-mindedness 198; participants' orientations 198–200; participants' use of 195–8; procedural consequentiality 198; racial categories 206–7; refining analytic approach 201–5; relationship counselling 195–6; relevance of gender 198–205; self-attribution 207; summary and conclusions 207–8
Social Identity Theory (SIT) 205
social inclusion 248

social inequality 266
socialisation 47–8
social knowledge, as knowledge/culture in action 189
socially shared cognitions/understandings 164
social norms, children's talk 139–40
social order, pervasiveness 45
social organization of cognitive displays and embodiments 51
social processes, observing and reporting 76
social psychology: criticism of 17; gatekeeping 111; status of 102
social relations, three orders 99
social rules 95–6
social science: bottom line in debate 30; characteristics 38
social science agendas, qualitative interviews 75
social science *par excellence* 33–4
sociocultural concepts, location and explication 53
socio-cultural context, of developmental psychology 211–12
sociocultural model of autobiographical memory 220
sociocultural psychology 220
sociology of emotion 121–2
sociology of scientific knowledge (SSK) 30, 103, 219
South Africa, post-apartheid racial attitudes 277–9, **282**
speed-dating 172–3
Speer, S.A. 23–4, 25, 59–60, 61–2, 63–4, 65–6, 198
stake management 91–2
stakes and interests, in interviews 76
stance 98, 111, 285
standardized psychological tests 151
static data structures 166
Steensig, J. 94
Stenner, P. 165
stereotyping 183, 243–4; category differentiation 259–60; early research 257; by implication 263–5; moderation 245; research as conversation 260–1; social cognition theory 261; *see also* race stereotypes

stereotyping by omission 263
Sterponi, L. 48
Stivers, T. 94, 96, 226
Stokoe, E. 23–4, 48, 61–2, 172, 174, 198–200, 201–5, 207, 233
structured interviews, interactions 71
subjective stance 39
subjectivity management 92
subject/object distinction 91, 94, 110
subject-object relations 107–10
subject positions 22
Sundqvist, A. 156
Sutton, J. 218
sympathy 125
syntax of hegemony 294
synthetic discourse analytic approach 21–2, 26
system-relevance 205

Tajfel, H. 291
talk: sequential organisation 51; situated nature 45
talk-in-action 135–6
talking, role in categorisation 186
talk-in-interaction: as focus of CA 46; power and domination 21
tape fetishism 220
Taylor, S.E. 259–60
te Molder, H. 87, 89, 92–3
text: and DP 230–6; interpretation of 32; situated nature 45
The authoritarian personality (Adorno) 249
The nature of prejudice (Allport) 243–4
theoretical imperialism 21
theories of meaning, referential 34
theorising, ungrounded 215–16
Theory of Mind (ToM) 7–8, 123; assumptions 150; children's interaction and development 152–4, 156; context and overview 147–8; critique of 147–8, 150–1; definition and description 149–50; displaying understanding and affection 154–6; formulating vs. acting on wants 156–7; mental health 152; Modular Theory 149–50; moral implications 157; summary and conclusions 157; Theory-Theory 149–50; views from

other traditions 151–2; *The social psychology of experience* (Middleton and Brown) 217–20
third-party recontextualisation 228–9, 237–8
third-party representation, in media 231
thought: as central to child development 129; rhetorical and argumentative organization of 133
threats, analysis of 46
Tileagă, C. 220–1
togetherness repertoire 248
topics, range in DP 147–8
traditional cognitive worldview 88
traditional script theory, Edward's critique 166–7
trait attribution 259
transcription: and interaction 79; theoretically embedded 79
transcription format, and purpose of analysis 77
Tredoux, C. 283
truth, critique of 210–21
truthfulness 20
Tuffin, K. 248
Turner, J.C. 196
turn medial tag questions 124–5
turn to language 211
Type 1 knowables 110

uncertainty, analytic 81
understanding, displaying 154–6
universities, role of 299
utterances 182

Veen, M. 94, 95–6
vicarious accounting 48
violence, script formulation 172
Vygotsky, L. 132, 134, 174, 220

Watergate hearings 212–14
Watson, D.R. 78
Weatherall, A. 24, 50, 199, 205
Wells, E. 172
Wetherell, M. 4, 15, 49, 73–4, 104, 182, 246, 247–8, 249–50, 252, 254, 271ff, 285; academic context and concerns 17–19; comparison of conversation analytic and poststructuralist viewpoints 22; conversation analysis and interpretative repertoires 21–3; critical conversation analysis 25; influences on 19, 22; as key figure 16; politics of being critical 25–6; proposed research shift 17–18; research methods 18; Schegloff's reply, 1998 22–3; study of gender inequality in workplace 17–18; synthetic discourse analytic approach 21–2, 26
Wetherell–Schegloff debate 6, 15–16, 23–4, 73–4, 76
Whitehead, K. 206, 264, 267
Whorf, B. 49
'Whose text? Whose context?' (Schegloff) 19–21
Widdicombe, S. 198
Wiggins, S. 46, 47, 94, 107, 108–10, 284
Wittgenstein, L. 115–16, 152, 218
Women, Fire and Dangerous Things (Lakoff) 181, 182
Wood, D. 211
Woolgar, S. 30, 236
Wootton, A.J. 142–3, 153
workplace, gender inequality 17–18
worldviews, traditional cognitive 88
written accounts, accuracy 225

zones of proximal development 134